GAME *of* PRIVILEGE

The JOHN HOPE FRANKLIN SERIES *in*

African American History and Culture

Waldo E. Martin Jr. and Patricia Sullivan, editors

GAME of PRIVILEGE

AN AFRICAN AMERICAN HISTORY OF GOLF

LANE DEMAS

THE UNIVERSITY OF
NORTH CAROLINA PRESS
Chapel Hill

Open access edition funded by the National Endowment for the Humanities.

© 2017 The University of North Carolina Press
The text of this book is licensed under a Creative Commons AttributionNonCommercial-NoDerivatives 4.0 International License: https://creativecommons.org/licenses/by-nc-nd/4.0/

Set in Utopia and Aller types
by Tseng Information Systems, Inc.

Front cover photo of John Shippen, 1913, courtesy USGA Museum

Library of Congress Cataloging-in-Publication Data
Names: Demas, Lane, author.
Title: Game of privilege : an African American history of golf / by Lane Demas.
Other titles: John Hope Franklin series in African American history and culture.
Description: Chapel Hill : University of North Carolina Press, [2017] | Series: The John Hope Franklin series in African American history and culture | Includes bibliographical references and index.
Identifiers: LCCN 2017009057 | ISBN 9781469634227 (cloth : alk. paper) | ISBN 9781469669281 (pbk : alk. paper) | ISBN 9781469634234 (ebook)
Subjects: LCSH: African American golfers—History. | African Americans—Civil rights—History. | Golf—Social aspects—United States. | Golf—United States—History. | Discrimination in sports—United States—History.
Classification: LCC GV981 .D45 2017 | DDC 796.3520973—dc23
LC record available at https://lccn.loc.gov/2017009057

For

Jennifer, Drexler,

Olivia, Mom, Dad,

and Frank

CONTENTS

Preface ix

Abbreviations and Acronyms in the Text xvii

1 **REAL DEMOCRACY IS FOUND ON THE LINKS**
African Americans and the Origins of Golf in the United States 1

2 **ONE HEARS OF NEGRO COUNTRY CLUBS**
Golfing the Great Migration and Harlem Renaissance 40

3 **OUR MASTERS**
The Development of the United Golfers Association 84

4 **I WILL TAKE YOUR OWN GOLF STICK AND WHAM THE WORLD**
Golf and the Postwar Civil Rights Movement 141

5 **GUNS IN THEIR GOLF BAGS**
Black Power on the Links 188

6 **THAI PEOPLE DON'T GET HATE MAIL**
Race and Golf in the Age of Tiger Woods 237

Acknowledgments 271

Notes 273

Bibliography 321

Index 343

TABLES

1. Significant African American–Owned Golf Courses, 1916–1967 47
2. UGA National Championship Results, 1926–1975 89
3. Significant Golf Desegregation Lawsuits, 1941–1970 163
4. African Americans Competing on the PGA and LPGA Tours, 1960–2016 216

PREFACE

December 24, 1955, was "a happy day in town for black folks," recalled Atlanta resident Gary Holmes. Twelve-year-old Gary's father, Alfred Holmes, and his grandfather, local physician Dr. Hamilton M. Holmes, had recently prevailed before the U.S. Supreme Court in *Holmes v. Atlanta*, the first example of court-ordered desegregation in Georgia's modern history. Yet the excitement in the Holmes household and Atlanta's black community "was tempered by a fear of white retaliation" fueled by anonymous threatening calls and "talk . . . of a bloodbath or race war."[1]

That tension centered not on racial segregation in Atlanta's public schools or voting booths but, rather, on its golf courses. *Holmes v. Atlanta* had just forced the city to allow African Americans access to its public links, particularly the historic Bobby Jones Municipal Golf Course, and some residents anticipated violence when blacks headed out on Christmas Eve to test the ruling; rumors swirled that golfers of all races planned to pack guns in their golf bags. "We understand how to play the game of golf and understand the courtesies of the game," seventy-one-year-old Dr. Holmes told *Time* magazine the month before. "You can be sure we will do what is right."[2]

Holmes and Atlanta's black golfers did just that, and their fight against segregation in the seemingly staid world of middle-class leisure was much more than a curious sidelight to the quest for civil rights in schools, churches, and businesses. In fact, it was integrally tied to that narrative; three weeks earlier Rosa Parks and Martin Luther King Jr. had launched the Montgomery Bus Boycott. Six years later Gary's brother, Hamilton E. Holmes, became one of the first two black students to attend the University of Georgia.

This book explores the many black Americans who changed professional golf as well as the countless everyday black players—like those in the Holmes family—who used the game and its symbolism to influence their communities and assert their civil rights. Contrary to popular memory, African Americans played a significant role in shaping modern golf from its origins in the late nineteenth century to today. Surprisingly, that full story has yet to be written.

Thus, this book attempts to narrate a cultural history of race and golf placed within the broader context of the modern civil rights movement and recent American history. It emphasizes golf's emerging popularity in the late nineteenth century; its growth in areas of the Northeast, Midwest, and South before World War II; and the ways in which black people from all walks of life shaped the development of the game's subculture. Arguing that African Americans influenced golf in previously underappreciated ways, the narrative charts how black residents nationwide struggled to play the game and built community institutions in order to confront segregated facilities at the local level. It is a story in which integration was often championed not by national organizations or outside resources but, rather, by citizens who organized campaigns, filed legal suits, and even went to jail in order to desegregate their golf courses—the kind of civil rights leaders historians have dubbed "local people." Their stories enhance our understanding of the postwar civil rights movement and national developments, including NAACP legal campaigns and *Brown v. Board of Education*, the introduction of nonviolent economic boycotts in the 1950s, and the rise of Black Power in the late 1960s.[3]

Furthermore, golf offers a unique lens for examining how race, class, and leisure shaped African American history. Important scholarly histories have touched on these topics and provide a broad methodological and theoretical framework, ranging from Aldon Morris's classic *Origins of the Civil Rights Movement* to more recent work from historians like Glenda Gilmore, Tomiko Brown-Nagin, and Kevin Kruse.[4] (Both Brown-Nagin's *Courage to Dissent* and Kruse's *White Flight* briefly discuss the Holmes family and the fight to desegregate Atlanta's golf courses in the 1950s.) Black golfers are even more intriguing in the context of these histories: they help extend the timeline of the civil rights movement well before World War II, provide a unique exploration of class tension within the black community and national organizations like the NAACP, and illuminate how one sport could both hinder and hasten black equality in contemporary America.

Chapters 1 and 2 chart the earliest examples of African American golf in the nineteenth century and the solidification of neighborhood golf clubs in black communities during the Great Migration, arguing that black people shaped the American game from its very beginning as caddies, players, and even course designers in the South and that middle-class black players were some of the first golf enthusiasts of any race in northern cities like Boston and Chicago. By the 1920s golf had become a frequent pastime in many black communities as well as a symbol of northern possibility and the promise of economic mobility for southern migrants. While some intellectuals associated with the Harlem Renaissance refused to detach the game from its deep ties to white colonialism and racial exclusion, others saw the growth of predominately black golf courses and country clubs as embodying the Jazz Age and a new era of black respectability. These deep contradictions were often—but not always—tied to the basic issue of economic class and the growing wealth discrepancy between more elite, middle-class black neighborhoods and the dominant black experience. Yet golf's unique history complicated such a simple analysis and made deciphering the game's meaning more difficult: migration emphasized industrial opportunity and the promise of burgeoning urban neighborhoods in the North, yet it was often easier for anyone (white or black) to build rudimentary golf facilities or access open space outside America's cities. Thus, by the 1930s it was little surprise that some of the best black golfers in the country hailed from rural areas of the South and Midwest, where many used positions as caddies, groundskeepers, and attendants at segregated golf facilities to access the game and become leading players. Meanwhile, residents of Harlem and South Chicago faced unique challenges accessing regulation golf courses, meaning some black migrants found less access to the game once they left the South. Certain regions and cities—such as Chicago, Cleveland, or New York—did feature black communities where golf's popularity grew because the game was more "open" to black players. But other hot spots for black golf—Atlanta, Jacksonville (Fla.), Baltimore, Washington, and New Orleans—flourished in the heart of segregation. Golf's popularity in a particular black community was dependent on far more than just local segregation laws or the level of "access" whites were willing to grant. It was also tied to the availability of suitable land, public space, adequate weather, black professionals willing to offer golf lessons and equipment, and organized groups and clubs that successfully encouraged their neighborhoods to take up the game.

Chapter 3 moves from charting golf's popular appeal in the black community to a discussion of black professional players and the little-known history of the United Golfers Association (UGA), a black golf organization that was founded in 1925 and served as a parallel institution to the all-white Professional Golfers' Association (PGA) that formed nine years earlier in 1916. Along with many other activities, the UGA operated a national golf tour for professionals and amateurs and continued to host events well after the desegregation of the PGA in 1961.[5] Similar to the story of baseball's Negro Leagues and their central place in American culture, the UGA also featured African Americans who used professional sport to carve out autonomous sites for leisure, business, and fandom. Yet the UGA was unlike any other black professional sporting organization in American history: for one, it emerged and found success at the precise moment when broader public interest in golf—including PGA tournaments—was in decline. Cobbled together from an organized patchwork of local clubs around the country, the UGA also sustained a lasting, national reach that rivaled any single black baseball league and featured a steady stream of players from all regions, hosting national championship tournaments from Los Angeles to Boston and everywhere in between—including Chicago, Cleveland, Pittsburgh, Detroit, Indianapolis, Philadelphia, Washington, Dallas, Kansas City, Memphis, and Miami. The tour and its fans also confronted issues of diversity, economic mobility, and class dynamics within the black community like no other sporting association had to: its players ranged from poor former caddies from the South to middle- and upper-class professionals who held memberships at elite country clubs. Finally, as the UGA was the only national professional golf tour for black players in American history, virtually every black pro before Tiger Woods experienced playing in its events, a long list that includes John Shippen, Robert "Pat" Ball, John Brooks Dendy, Howard Wheeler, Charlie Sifford, Bill Spiller, Ted Rhodes, and Lee Elder. While black women struggled to organize national professional sport leagues under segregation (for example, only three women played baseball in the Negro Leagues), by 1930 the UGA supported a full women's division, which over time featured gifted stars like Marie Thompson, Lucy Williams, Geneva Wilson, Ann Gregory, Thelma Cowans, Ethel (Powers) Funches, Althea Gibson, and Renee Powell. For over thirty-five years the UGA was the only outlet for African Americans who wanted to be professional golfers. Surely no other black sporting organization in American history had such a long-standing monopoly on talent.

While Chapter 3 charts the development of the UGA, Chapter 4 analyzes key legal battles over golf integration after World War II and the role played by the NAACP and other national civil rights organizations in waging that fight, including leading litigators Constance Baker Motley and Thurgood Marshall. It explores the ongoing battles to desegregate America's municipal courses in the 1950s and 1960s—such as the most important legal case, *Holmes v. Atlanta*—and emphasizes how national black organizations debated the game's value and whether to support legal challenges to segregated golf in North Carolina, Georgia, and Alabama. Here the narrative transitions from stories of individuals and local groups who took up the game to one of national organizations and institutions sustaining black players and challenging racial discrimination in golf, including before the U.S. Supreme Court. Yet still there was no consensus on the game's social significance or its value to African Americans. Just as local communities failed to rectify the tension between black golfers as symbolic of integration and economic promise—or symbolic of elitism and racial tokenism—so too did national organizations like the UGA and NAACP fail to reach a consensus on the game's larger meanings.

Chapter 5 discusses golf and black militant movements in the late 1960s and 1970s, exploring how American black nationalist leaders and anticolonial movements in the Caribbean and Africa appropriated the symbolism of black golfers. Popular magazines like *Jet* and *Ebony* celebrated black players, organizations sponsored black golf tours throughout the African Diaspora, and a new generation of professionals—led by Lee Elder—more directly confronted racism in the PGA and sought access to its most exclusive enclaves. Meanwhile, the ongoing internationalization of the civil rights movement placed golf squarely within global debates over race and racial discrimination. The game's popularity in South Africa and Rhodesia made it a target of the antiapartheid movement, especially as more African-born white professionals—like star Gary Player—traveled to play in PGA events. Meanwhile, militant groups in the Caribbean also targeted the game's booming growth in their region, culminating in the 1972 murder of eight white golfers by black nationalists at St. Croix's Fountain Valley Golf Course. While fans have long been interested in Muhammad Ali's popularity in Africa or the black protests surrounding the 1968 Mexico City Olympics, they have overlooked golf as a cite of militancy. Coinciding with Ali's famous 1974 trip to Zaire (where he fought George Foreman in the "Rumble in the Jungle"), Elder's trips to Africa—including his confrontations with apartheid at South African golf tournaments—and his integration of the Masters Golf Tournament in 1975 are just two examples. Radicalism on the golf course meant the rare militant (even violent) episode, yet more important was how the cultural sentiment of Black Power changed the way African American professionals engaged the game and ushered in a growing awareness of golf's relationship to an international struggle against racism. This included the reaction of black and white golfers to the 1968 Olympic boycott, their response to apartheid, and how Elder—the period's top black player—differed from the professionals who came before him.

Finally, Chapter 6 explores the decline of golf in America's inner cities in the 1980s, subsequent efforts to increase minority participation, and the rise of Tiger Woods. Complicating the notion of Woods as a traditional, popular figure in sport desegregation, the narrative instead posits him as a reluctant civil rights hero, contextualizing his popularity and exploring why the media (and many golf fans) struggled to turn back the clock and fit Woods into the mold of historic black athletes like Jackie Robinson, Joe Louis, or even Ali. Although the verdict is still out, it was a process that future historians may consider a failure, not only because the traditional "civil rights era" was over but also because the young Woods himself asked not to be identified as "black" and instead told the world that he was "Cablinasian," a term he coined to describe his multiracial heritage. Nevertheless, Woods was portrayed as an African American breaking down traditional barriers of segregation in advertisements and media events organized by his main sponsor, Nike Inc., revealing a dissonance between his call for multiracialism and the company's insistence that his race be traditionally identified and highlighted as part of its sponsorship. The chapter features an analysis of Woods that draws on a comparison with how the new politicization of race in the "post-civil rights era" influenced the 1980s and 1990s sporting scene as a whole, including the career of basketball great Michael Jordan—another Nike athlete notoriously careful to avoid public statements regarding race or politics.

Ironically, at the turn of the new millennium Nike sought to profit from the celebration of black golf as a crowning civil rights achievement—something many civil rights leaders and organizations had long downplayed. Charting black professional players and the eventual integration of the game's professional organizations is important to a history in need of further development. Yet even more important is challenging the ways in which the black community's popular, day-to-day influence on golf was deliberately removed from popular memory for understandable reasons. At times a curious coalition—ranging from black political leaders and organizations like the NAACP to the most rabid white segregationists—saw the advantage of downplaying the struggle to integrate a game like golf. One side feared criticism of funneling resources toward an "elite" endeavor at the expense of more "popular," "grassroots" struggles like desegregating public schools and transportation, while the other feared the specter of black golf and its implication that the nation's racial hierarchy had indeed been turned on its head in dramatic fashion.

Thus, by the 1970s such pursuits of "elite" desegregation were largely removed from popular memories of the civil rights movement, while the general marginalization of sport by academic historians helped keep them out of most scholarly publications as well.[6] This meant losing the stories of numerous unlikely individuals (including many in the black middle class) who appropriated the movement's shifting rhetoric not only to access schools, jobs, and basic public facilities but also to participate in a game considered the exclusive domain of upper-class whites. In doing so, they faced considerable resistance both within and outside the black community—as well as today's ongoing struggle to include their endeavors as part of the historical civil rights narrative—for even as golf democratized, it continued to symbolize wealth, power, access, land, and privilege. To this day the game's historical whiteness remains a useful trope; nevertheless, the historian's role is to remind us of the difference between those stories that are useful and those that are true.

There were some difficult decisions to make in order to provide a sense of the breadth of African American involvement in golf over the past 130-plus years. Some examples are favored over others, and all of the individual stories, legal cases, and golf courses presented here deserve more attention. Hopefully, *Game of Privilege* will at least start a conversation about changing the way Americans have thought about race and golf for generations. Several colleagues (including some quite knowledgeable of African American history) responded with surprise when I told them I planned to write a book-length history on the subject. A few wondered whether there was enough material—one inquired if it would "basically be a book about Tiger Woods." To me, those reactions signaled I was on the right track.

ABBREVIATIONS AND ACRONYMS IN THE TEXT

AME	African Methodist Episcopal
CCC	Civilian Conservation Corps
CORE	Congress of Racial Equality
FBI	Federal Bureau of Investigation
HBCUS	historically black colleges and universities
IGT	International Golf Tour
LDF	Legal Defense Fund
LPGA	Ladies Professional Golf Association
NAACP	National Association for the Advancement of Colored People
NCAA	National Collegiate Athletic Association
NFL	National Football League
NOI	Nation of Islam
NPS	National Park Service
PGA	Professional Golfers' Association
RAM	Revolutionary Action Movement
SCLC	Southern Christian Leadership Conference
SNCC	Student Nonviolent Coordinating Committee
UGA	United Golfers Association
UN	United Nations
USGA	United States Golf Association
WPA	Works Progress Administration

GAME *of* PRIVILEGE

1

REAL DEMOCRACY IS FOUND ON THE LINKS

African Americans and the Origins of Golf in the United States

MARCH 1922—METAIRIE, LOUISIANA

The wooded land was inaccessible and his design ambitious—some members doubted Joe would ever pull it off. He often worked at night, clearing trees and brush by moonlight to avoid attention from all sides—nosy neighbors, rival groundskeepers, and, most importantly, members of the new Metairie Country Club, the very people who hired him and now doubted his prowess.

In his early forties, former caddie Joseph M. Bartholomew worked tirelessly for three years building one of the first golf courses in Louisiana. When he began, no vehicle could even reach the site, but his vision for the club's layout was bold: the holes would be detailed replicas of celebrated golf holes from around the world, all carved neatly into the Metairie Ridge—a natural levee formed by a branch of the Mississippi River five miles outside New Orleans.

Bartholomew worked secretively to avoid attracting attention from competitors and naysayers. Eventually, his vision became reality with the opening of the Metairie Country Club in 1925. It became one of the most exclusive golf courses in the South, one whose architect was not allowed to play because he was black.[1]

Though most identify fifteenth-century Scotland as the birthplace of golf, there remains some debate over the game's early origins. One popular theory holds that golf evolved from the Dutch *kolven* (or *kolf*), a game played on ice in the Netherlands as early as the 1400s, while another claims that golf derives from the ancient Roman game *paganica*. A search for the sport's origins in the broadest sense—a bat-and-ball game in which participants strike a ball placed on the ground—yields a number of variations in world history, including ancient Africa. The tomb of Kheti, in Beni Hasan, Egypt, dates to approximately 2000 B.C.E. and depicts images of children engaged in such an activity. According to one archaeologist, "In Kheti's tomb young men are shown playing a hockey-like game, controlling what appears to be a small wooden hoop with bent-ended sticks. . . . It is not certain whether this 'hoop' should be interpreted as a hoop, a disk or a solid ball."[2] However, beyond the theory that bat-and-ball games entered the ancient Mediterranean world via North Africa, golf's earliest origins featured little African input.

The game increased in popularity during the eighteenth and nineteenth centuries in Scotland and England, where there is scant evidence of black golfers despite the growth of African and African-Caribbean communities there during the period. Publications and activists (such as Granville Sharpe) estimated England's black population at 20,000 to 30,000 by the late 1700s, contemporary with the 1754 establishment of the Royal and Ancient Golf Club of St. Andrews, the key institution that developed modern golf's rules and regulations.[3] Nevertheless, not until the late nineteenth century did the game's popularity begin to grow substantially outside Scotland.

Golf had been played in North America long before—likely even during the colonial period, with dilettantes occasionally hitting balls in open fields or parks. It enjoyed a brief period of popularity in Charleston, South Carolina, and Savannah, Georgia, in the late eighteenth century. The first golf clubs and balls arrived in America from Scotland in a 1743 shipment to Charleston, where a small group of residents later established the South Carolina Golf Club in 1786, the first documented club outside the United Kingdom. The group met at the city's Harleston Green, a public park. Similarly, locals in Savannah played in a city park and established the Savannah Golf Club in 1796. These pursuits were apparently short lived; there is no reference to the Charleston club after 1799, and the game also seemed to vanish from Savannah by the early nineteenth century. Growing tension with England, culminating in the Embargo Act of 1807 and the War of 1812, may have curtailed golf's development in antebellum America, for there is little further evidence of it in the United States until the 1880s.[4] Because these early golfing pursuits consisted of small groups who used shared park space, they left little in the historical record and few permanent marks on the landscape. There is, however, a 1795 reference to a "Club House" at Harleston Green—likely the first golf-related structure in American history and one that would predate permanent, dedicated golf "links" (or courses) by some ninety years.

The role African Americans might have played in these first clubs is unclear but intriguing, as black slaves likely aided players both in Charleston and Savannah. Henry Purcell, a chaplain at Charleston's St. Michael's Episcopal Church, served as president of the South Carolina Golf Club. Purcell himself may or may not have owned slaves, but other clergy at St. Michael's certainly did, along with many church members. The church's ministers were later involved in visiting and interrogating imprisoned slaves accused of participating in Denmark Vesey's 1822 plot to organize a slave insurrection in Charleston. Vesey's conspiracy, one of the most important in American history, was centered around the city's African Methodist Episcopal (AME) chapel and likely drew particularly harsh reaction from St. Michael's, the city's main Episcopal church.[5] Not only did America's first golfers in Charleston and Savannah likely own slaves, but they also needed substantial assistance to play. Since the clubs used shared park space with no designated greens, holes were dug impromptu and "finders" were employed to locate balls, watch for foot traffic, and carry equipment—thus, the first golf "caddies" in America were probably black slaves in Charleston. Such use of slave labor to assist public leisure would not have been uncommon. Other routine antebellum activities at Harleston Green involved slave assistance, including horse races, cricket matches, and picnicking.[6]

For much of the subsequent nineteenth century, golf disappeared from the historical record and the game struggled to take hold in America. However, by the late 1870s U.S. publications began to recognize the game's reemergence and growth in England. In 1890 the first significant reference to golf appeared in the *New York Times*, which described it as an "ancient game [that] fashionable Englishwomen have developed such a fondness for."[7] The nation's first modern links date to the 1880s, when dedicated courses were constructed in West Virginia, Vermont, Pennsylvania, Iowa, Florida, Nebraska, and New York. In 1884 English and Scottish immigrants completed Oakhurst Links, a rudimentary course near White Sulphur Springs, West Virginia, traditionally considered America's first golf course.[8]

Black participation in the American game was immediate and dramatic, and key black enthusiasts influenced golf's development in the United States during these crucial years. Frances Grant recalled her father, George Franklin Grant, playing in a meadow near the family's

George Franklin Grant in 1870 (Countway Library of Medicine, Harvard University).

home outside Boston as early as the mid-1880s, one of the earliest references to black players—perhaps even before Oakhurst was established in West Virginia. George Grant was born in 1846 in Oswego, New York, the son of Tudor E. Grant, a local barber who opened the family's home to the Underground Railroad before the Civil War.[9] One of seven children, he left home at age fifteen and found work with a local Oswego dentist, where he stayed for five years before venturing to Boston in 1867 to pursue training in dentistry. At age twenty, Grant was accepted to Harvard University's new dental school and in 1870 became the second African American to graduate from the program. More significantly, the school subsequently offered him a position as instructor, and Grant became the first black faculty member in Harvard's history. Serving as Harvard president Charles W. Eliot's personal dentist, he founded the Harvard Odontological Society, and his research included the invention of a prosthetic device for treating patients with misaligned palates. He was also considered a leading national authority on cleft palates.[10]

Grant's interests in innovative devices and invention spilled into his hobbies, of which golf was his favorite. One of the most prominent dentists in Boston, he still faced backlash from white neighbors in nearby Arlington Heights, and by 1890 he had moved to Boston's Beacon Hill district. He held on to the Arlington Heights property—in part because of the space it allowed for golf—and continued to play in the 1890s. He also had friends join him, including some of Boston's leading black residents. One was Archibald Grimké, a former slave and graduate of Harvard Law School who was a nationally recognized civil rights advocate, early opponent of Booker T. Washington, and American consul to the Dominican Republic. Grimké's legal partner, Butler Wilson, was also a black graduate of Harvard Law and regularly joined the golfers. Grimké later served as an early leader in the National Association for the Advancement of Colored People (NAACP) and was president of its Washington, D.C., branch, while Butler was on the NAACP's national board of directors. Howard Lee, a well-known Boston restaurateur, also played with the men.[11] Without a dedicated course, they continued golfing in the meadows surrounding Grant's Arlington Heights home during the summers.

Grant grew tired of continually stooping to create a natural "tee" for his golf balls, which players usually accomplished by pinching mounds of earth together or mixing sand with water to create a substance with sufficient viscosity. He developed a reusable tee, an invention he considered important enough to patent in 1899. Grant's U.S. patent was the first issued for a golf tee, and the contraption was similar to what became the standard wooden tee in the twentieth century (his design featured a wooden base with a removable rubber top).[12] However, Grant faced long odds of profiting from the invention, and how much he even intended to do so is unclear. In some ways he was too far ahead of his time, for few Americans played golf in 1899, and though some players used various strategies for teeing the ball, most continued playing with earth or sand tees.

There was not a lot of money to be made in golf tees, but more interesting was how subsequent golf histories neglected Grant's early contribution to the game and, ironically, credited a white dentist from New Jersey—Dr. William Lowell—with inventing the wooden tee twenty-five years later in 1924. Lowell, too, made little money from his tee, which he painted red and marketed as the "Reddy Tee." He gave $1,500 to U.S. Open champion Walter Hagen and British Open champion Joe Kirkwood to promote them in 1922 and spent most of the Reddy Tee profits suing copycat manufacturers for patent infringement. By the time golf tees became a hot commodity, the market was flooded; in 1940, there were more than 150 registered U.S. patents for tees of every imaginable design and material. Still, George Grant's 1899 patent was the first and bears a striking resemblance to the wooden tees used by golfers around the world since the 1940s. In fact, by 2008 there were an estimated 2.8 *billion* such tees in the United States alone. Yet for decades golf's most prominent publications, including *Golf Digest*, and its official national organization, the United States Golf Association (USGA), continued to credit Lowell with inventing the tee, as do many popular publications today.[13] The fact that Grant, and not Lowell, created the modern golf tee did not fit the traditional narrative of golf's elite, exclusively white origins. Grant's snubbing also testified to how much more powerful the notion of racial exclusion was in the game's popular consciousness, eclipsing class antagonism, for both Grant and Lowell were otherwise affluent, northeastern dentists. "We were not rich, but we lived comfortably," recalled Frances Grant in 1973. "My father had burlap bags of golf tees, but he gave them away instead of selling them. He was an avid golf fan. . . . He loved challenges, but once he overcame them, he lost interest and moved on to something else."[14]

While some elite African Americans joined the early ranks of players in the 1880s, others contributed to the modern game by helping to build some of the nation's first courses and serving as caddies. Joseph Bartholomew did both. Born in New Orleans in 1881, Bartholomew began caddying at age seven for golfers in Audubon Park, where by 1898 the city had opened its first dedicated course. Although it is likely that earlier black caddies or "finders" (perhaps even slaves in Charleston or Savannah) found opportunities to play themselves, Bartholomew was among the first black caddies in the modern era to develop into a skilled player. Copying his clients' swings and then improving on them dramatically, he became a gifted golfer, and many whites considered him the best player in New Orleans. By the 1910s Audubon members were arranging high-profile matches between Bartholomew and the game's leading white professionals, including Walter Hagen, a former caddie himself who made his professional debut in 1912. Bartholomew also competed against Gene Sarazen, who won his first major championships—the U.S. Open and the Professional Golfers' Association (PGA) Championship—in 1922. Bartholomew's course-record 62 at Audubon even surpassed that of Scottish American golfer Fred McLeod, Audubon's head professional and win-

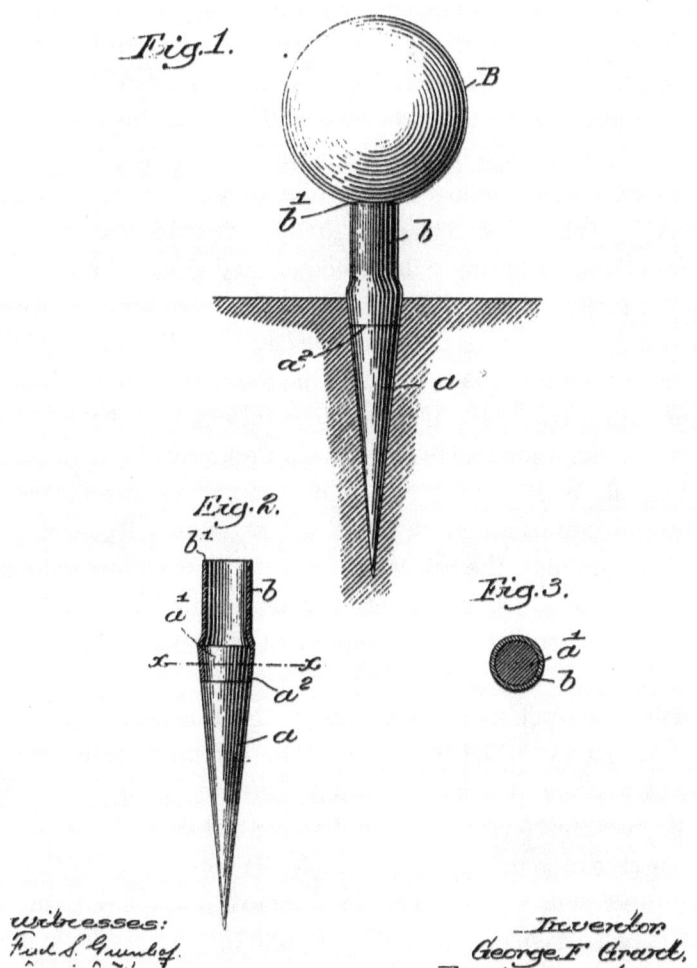

The invention of the modern golf tee: George F. Grant's 1899 U.S. patent (U.S. Patent Office).

ner of the 1908 U.S. Open. McLeod and Bartholomew had many head-to-head matches ("I beat Mr. McLeod and he beat me," Bartholomew later recalled), and McLeod hired Bartholomew to be his assistant.[15]

Along with becoming an excellent player, Bartholomew earned accolades for his skills in grounds maintenance, course design, and golf club repair. His ability to find such opportunities with Audubon's club was significant, considering the increasing racial segregation during the period, especially at the park. Audubon's designer, John Charles Olmsted (the son of famed landscape architect Frederick Law Olmsted), noted in 1899 how New Orleans residents made it clear to him that "negroes . . . were not to be encouraged to come to the park." In 1907 the park's commission explicitly limited membership to whites only and later rebuffed Olmsted's 1915 suggestion that "a place might be assigned for colored people" within Audubon.[16] The young Bartholomew had already been caddying for four years when Homer Plessy and a citizens' committee of black and biracial residents sought to challenge the city's new ban on racially integrated transportation in 1892, culminating four years later with the U.S. Supreme Court's landmark ruling in *Plessy v. Ferguson* (1896), which affirmed the constitutionality of segregation under the doctrine of "separate but equal." In essence, New Orleans's top golfer was a black teenager who watched as a new city with new regimes of legalized racism emerged around him. The era of Jim Crow, with its stifling segregation of schools, public parks, restaurants, restrooms, streetcars, and eventually, golf courses, arrived at the very moment when whites pronounced a black caddie one of the South's best players.

Bartholomew's talents in course design drew as much notice as his high-profile matches with white players. Another, more exclusive private club in nearby Metairie began to court his services. One member in particular, the wealthy New Orleans wholesale merchant H. T. Cottam, persuaded the club to send Bartholomew to New York so he could study with noted course architect Seth Raynor in order to devise a new layout. Raynor had helped design private courses around the country, including the Old White Course at West Virginia's Greenbrier resort, which President Woodrow Wilson was among the first to play when it opened in 1914. Bartholomew stayed in New York as Raynor's apprentice until 1922 and then returned to Louisiana with ambitious plans to build the Metairie Country Club—the course segregation would never allow him to play.

Although Bartholomew's story was extraordinary, numerous African Americans in the late nineteenth century found employment in the booming golf industry at courses around the country. Some of these positions had little to do with golf, especially with the emergence of private clubs featuring a wider range of activities and larger facilities. An 1898 article in the *Journal of the American Medical Association* celebrated the game's health benefits, noting that members of Rhode Island's exclusive Newport Country Club (founded in 1893) were inspired by the "breezy air" to hire a "negro cook" to replace their French chef because the black man's dishes "were considered more wholesome and better suited to a golfer's appetite."[17] Over the next generation, clubs continued to hire African Americans, especially men, as the golf industry expanded. By 1934 black historian Carter G. Woodson estimated that there were 4,049 black males, and only 71 black women, "engaged as attendants in pool rooms, boarding houses and golf clubs."[18]

Woodson's calculation of "attendants" did not include caddies, by far the most common golf-related position for African Americans. Derived from the French *cadet* ("younger boy"), the English "caddie" emerged in the seventeenth century and, by the eighteenth, was used in Scotland to describe an assistant one hired when playing golf. Caddies were common features on America's first golf courses, particularly at the more exclusive clubs and private courses that required players to employ them. Black males served as caddies throughout the country, especially in the South, and most were quite young—ranging from boys aged six or seven, like Joseph Bartholomew, to teenagers. Caddying was not fundamentally racialized; nearly all caddies in Britain were English or Scottish boys, and American clubs employed many white caddies. Yet many of the first U.S. clubs considered it an especially suitable endeavor for black boys, and within twenty years the image of the black child as caddie was firmly entrenched in American popular culture.

It is difficult to estimate just how many African Americans served as caddies before World War I. Although some boys left school in order to do it permanently, caddying was more often seasonal, part-time work scheduled around school, farm work, or other jobs. A 1928 study of child labor in Mississippi noted the prevalence of young black caddies at courses in McComb, Crystal Springs, Hattiesburg, Tupelo, Grenada, Greenwood, and Meridian. Eight black children under age sixteen were listed as permanent "caddies on the golf links," not as many as those working in households (191), laboring as "porters and janitors" (35), or delivering newspapers (29) but roughly the same number as "waiters and waitresses" (10), "clerks in Negro drug or grocery stores" (7), those engaged in "washing and ironing" (13), and cooks (5). The report did note that white children also caddied in Mississippi, yet apparently not as often, for it provided no exact number.[19]

Golf publications in Britain and the United States agreed that black people seemed suited for a range of golf-related jobs around the world. As the game's popularity grew in Brazil, the London-based *Golf* informed readers how West African workers at the port in Bahia were outperforming Afro-Brazilians as carriers in 1896: "Where it takes eight Brazilian negroes to carry a load with difficulty, four African porters carry it cheerfully, singing and chanting as they trudge along."[20] In 1918 Chicago's *Golfers Magazine* featured an essay by one member of the São Paulo Golf Club (established in 1898) who celebrated the group's successful experiment using local caddies. "Our caddies are a varied lot, and their origin would afford study for an ethnologist, for they are descended from Brazilian, Portuguese, Spanish, Italian, the Indian and the Negro," he wrote. "However, they are not the pirate crew we so often find on the links, but are generally well behaved and intelligent, and each year testifies to their improvement in carrying, and also to their proficiency in learning to play the game." American infatuation with golf as a tool of civilization was solidified by the time Henry Ford included an eighteen-hole course at Fordlandia, the industrial town he built in the heart of the Amazon in 1928.[21]

Not only did the first U.S. clubs tolerate African American attendants and caddies; many explicitly desired them, especially in the South. Alongside articles penned by the biggest names in the sport—such as Francis Ouimet, winner of the 1913 U.S. Open, or famed sportswriter Grantland Rice—*Golfers Magazine* ran help-wanted ads from employers specifying a desire for black workers and from potential black employees looking for jobs as country club attendants, stewards, or chefs. Whites in the industry who traveled south (sometimes seasonally) for golf work also had to be ready to serve alongside black laborers. One nine-hole "southern golf club" sought "a professional and wife . . . the former to superintend grounds, the latter to manage house and restaurant. Couple used to negro servants preferred."[22] As black migration to the North increased in the 1910s, the black community even celebrated certain golf-related jobs for the prestige and opportunity they bestowed on southern migrants. Samuel Pierce left his hometown of Portsmouth, Virginia, as a young man, and by 1916 he had become head golf attendant at the prestigious Nassau Country Club outside New York City. Pierce "has won for himself a national reputation," proclaimed the *Norfolk Journal and Guide* to its black readers. "He owns a fine home . . . and takes a keen interest in the affairs of his race, always lending a helping hand to deserving boys from the South." What allowed the young man "to make good in the North" were the intimacy and skill required of caddies and golf attendants, who had the potential to forge stronger bonds with their patrons than did servers in other industries: "A club locker-room man, or valet, comes into such personal touch with the members . . . many men of great means have offered him tempting amounts to give up serving the multitude." Securing a high-level position at an elite, modern golf club offered the same economic potential and social prestige as other celebrated jobs of the Great Migration era, including railway positions. Compared with Pullman porters, however, golf attendants spent considerably more time in intimate contact with their wealthy employers and could forge deeper, more sustained relationships. "In the Nassau Club, competition is keen among the members as to who will have the honor of having Sam's first son named after him," boasted the *Journal and Guide*. "He who succeeds will indeed be honored."[23]

Of course, Samuel Pierce's experience was rather exceptional; most African Americans working in the golf industry did not acquire substantial money or prestige, nor did they name their children after country club members. Many older workers did eventually secure better positions, such as clubhouse attendants, groundskeepers, or instructors. Yet most young black men continued to labor as caddies, and as the sport grew, so too did their numbers. Black caddies soon occupied a remarkable place in the national consciousness, becoming central characters in a myriad of published golf descriptions, short stories, anecdotes, and jokes. The often uneasy intimacy of black domestic service in white homes was common in the South, yet caddies embodied the trope of the black servant exposed to white incompetence, often with embarrassing consequences. It helped that golf was a difficult game that few mastered and most only managed to attempt awkwardly. One author, describing his difficulty trying golf for the first time in 1914, was thankful for his "charitably inscrutable and expressionless negro caddy."[24]

Caddies not only witnessed clients struggles with golf but also participated in the social encounters the game facilitated for its wealthy participants. An 1898 short story reprinted in numerous English and American publications depicted a man and woman engaged in intimate courtship on the golf course under the gaze of a caddie. The piece was probably written by Irish Australian journalist Daisy May O'Dwyer, perhaps a fictionalized account of her 1885 marriage to Jack Bates. In the story, Daisy, grudgingly convinced to play as a means to encourage Jack's proposal, first laments the caddie's intrusion into her privacy: "Why, oh why, was the caddy ever invented? Why, oh why, if it was really necessary to invent him, was he not made deaf, dumb, and blind?" Yet as their round continues, the caddie recognizes the intimacy of the moment and finds ways to leave the couple alone, which Daisy appreciates. "He is always at least ten minutes in finding the ball when it goes over a hill or beyond a fence and, unlike Lot's wife, he is absolutely guiltless of rubber necking. There's a caddie for you!" Having found moments of "caddiless solitude," Jack concludes the round by proposing the two "go around the links of life together."[25]

But unlike other service duties that called for silence and acquiescence, golf usually encouraged caddies to offer their opinions and instruction, sometimes directly challenging their employer's discretion. Like Joseph Bartholomew in New Orleans, some caddies obtained significant respect from whites. G. F. Freeman, a U.S. Navy surgeon stationed at Guantanamo Bay with the Atlantic fleet in 1915, compared his experiences with caddies from around the world. All, he wrote, offered "a great deal of help to the player if the latter would take the caddy's advice." Noting that Chinese caddies kept far quieter "in comparison to some American boys I have met," Freeman praised Jamaican caddies the most: "I shall never forget one little Jamaican negro caddy, at Kingston, who had as a club head a knot from the root of a tree out of the thicket, and a shaft fixed in it also procured from the thicket. . . . The caddy had the swing, however . . . for he could wallop the old gutta ball about one hundred and fifty yards every time, always straight and true, apparently without any effort and with a perfect swing, and I learned about golf from him." Such praise for a caddie's golf abilities could translate into broader gestures of respect. "Caddy boys the world over," wrote Freeman, "have to be studied and treated according to their natures as human beings in order to get the best out of them, and not always blamed for the poor shots of the player."[26]

Eschewing the supposed formality of golf and the stuffiness of its players, black caddies also flirted with social barriers by contributing to course banter and various hijinks. It was, after all, a game meant to be fun, and one's caddie was central to that experience. "Watch papa spank the baby," remarked Englishman Howard Spencer's "little negro caddy"—

to the delight of onlookers—as Spencer prepared to drive at Louisville Country Club during a 1916 tournament.[27] Two black caddies reportedly helped "loosen the tension" at the 1922 PGA Championship at Oakmont (Pa.) Country Club during a match between Gene Sarazen and Bobby Cruikshank, one yelling, "Put her in the hole, man, put her in the hole" as Cruikshank prepared for a key putt.[28] Another anecdote circulated after Scottish professional George Duncan won the 1920 British Open and toured courses in the American South. "Allotted a huge, cheerful Negro" during one round, Duncan selected a spot on the ground and tapped where he wanted his caddie to tee the ball. According to a later version of the story, "Nothing happened, so Duncan tapped again and said: 'I'll have it there, caddie.' Then the Negro looked at Duncan, eyes rolling sympathetically, and asked: 'What's the matter, mistah? You got lumbago?'"[29] And sportswriters insisted that the highlight of Jack Burke's victory at the 1956 Masters was the quip his black caddie made just before a crucial putt to seal the title: "Just cruise it off the rim, boss."[30] In addition to blacks playing and caddying, as bystanders they also witnessed critical events in the sport's early history. When amateur Francis Ouimet and his ten-year-old white caddie upset the field to win the 1913 U.S. Open—the game's most iconic moment before World War I—the press reported that "a negro" held the caddie up to celebrate "in the middle of a group of spectators."[31]

Caddies were expected to provide blunt input, and soon countless anecdotes and jokes featuring subversive, sarcastic, or clever caddies appeared in sporting publications and newspapers around the country, including the black press. "What am I do to with this?" a frustrated player asked his caddie at New Jersey's Cape May Golf Club in 1912 after picking up his own large divot (a duty generally required of caddies). "If I was you," the boy answered, "I'd take it up to the hotel to practice on, sir."[32] A left-handed Chicago lawyer traveled to North Carolina to play at Pinehurst Resort in 1914 and asked his "small negro caddy" for advice on his poor play. "Boss, I ain't discovered nothin'," responded the caddie. "'Cept de fact you have been standin' on de wrong side of de ball."[33] And in 1917 a Philadelphian playing in the South overheard his "old negro caddie" describing another client's poor play: "Dat gemmen jes nachully shoot at nuffin ev'y time, an' ev'y time he hit de bull's-eye plum in de middle."[34] Eventually such real encounters evolved into a genre of clever-caddie jokes. One from 1913 featured an exasperated player yelling at his caddie while digging through the brush: "Thought you'd come out to look after the ball?" "Aye!" responded the caddie, "An' I thought you'd come out to play golf!"[35]

The most popular early anecdotes featured black caddies bantering with the world's richest man, John D. Rockefeller. Rockefeller, history's first billionaire, took up golf in earnest after retiring as head of Standard Oil Company in 1897. By 1910 he was obsessed with it, at one point spending $500,000 in one year on golf, hosting other industrialists on the links (including Harvey Firestone, Henry Ford, and Andrew Carnegie) and constructing courses on the grounds of three of his four estates. Rockefeller also employed a small army of black caddies—one had the sole job of saying, "Mr. Rockefeller, keep your head down," before his every swing—and he was the first to use motion picture film to analyze his own golfing form. According to one biographer, "One of the rules of the game with Rockefeller was, when you showed up for golf, you would be informed by a valet or a manservant that you were not allowed to discuss business on the golf course. This was a highly structured setting, where he could socialize without worrying. He was in a social situation that he could completely control."[36] Many popular anecdotes, however, hinted that no player, including the world's richest man, could ever control his own caddie. In 1910 the *Baltimore Afro-American* described an encounter (perhaps fictional) at Georgia's Augusta Country Club, which Rockefeller and President William Howard Taft frequented: "John D. Rockefeller tried a game of golf on the links near Augusta. On a rather difficult shot Mr. Rockefeller struck too low with his iron, and as the dust flew up he asked his caddy: 'What have I hit?' The boy laughed and answered: 'Jaw-jah, boss.'"[37] Another popular Rockefeller anecdote featured a "negro lad" who wandered across the golf course and was accidentally struck by Rockefeller's ball. According to one variation, "It only stunned the boy a little, and after blinking his eyes for a moment he was himself again. Mr. Rockefeller, who had rushed up fearing that the boy had been badly injured, was relieved to find that he took it so calmly. Pulling a five-dollar bill from his pocket, he gave it to the youngster as a salve for his feelings. The boy looked at the bill and grinned with delight. Then he looked at Mr. Rockefeller and inquired: 'When is yo' goin' t' be playin' agin?'"[38] This particular Rockefeller story probably derived from existing anecdotes that featured African Americans trying to get payouts from wealthy golfers by deliberately getting struck by golf balls. An even more demeaning version appeared in the 1913 book *Golf Yarns*, which described "an old mammy" residing in

The world's richest man on the links: *left*, John D. Rockefeller with a caddie in Augusta, Georgia, 1909; *right*, with caddie Walter Wolfe at Rockefeller's winter estate in Ormond Beach, Florida, 1925 (Courtesy of Rockefeller Archive Center).

"an old negro cabin" who was paid one dollar by a player after she was hit: "The next time around the player sliced his ball again at this same place, and what was his surprise to discover that it had again hit the old mammy in the face. He compared notes with other players in the club house and found out that they, too, had hit the old mammy, and it had always cost a dollar to square matters."[39]

Along with degrading anecdotes about blacks attempting to get struck by golf balls, stories depicting the "loyalty" of black caddies to their employers were also popular by the early twentieth century. Often patronizing (even infantilizing) their subjects, these tales usually overlooked the fact that caddies primarily signed up for the job to get paid. After professionals Louis Tellier and Mike Brady defeated amateurs Francis Ouimet and Jesse Guilford in a 1917 rematch at Boston's Brae Burn Country Club, one magazine announced that the arrival of Brady's "loose-boned, happy go lucky Negro caddy" from Georgia, a man nicknamed "Cube," was the key. Cube set off from Georgia via steamship after the amateurs upset Tellier and Brady in the first match, and he arrived in Boston just in time to help Brady relax; he also reminded the professional to carry his lucky rabbit's foot, horseshoe, and golf bag from their successful outings in Georgia. *American Golfer* reported that the "charms" worked and praised Cube, implying that the caddie's epic journey had more to do with his loyalty to Brady than a potential payday: "[He is] one of those rare characters whose antics help to make people laugh and grow fat."[40]

Such real encounters contributed to the reputation of the philosophical, even "magical" black caddies who soon appeared in fiction. One of the first came in the 1919 short story "The Man Who Quit," in which a disgruntled and frustrated player gives his clubs away and is consoled by a caddie named Jasper. Following a talk about golf and life, the man later has a change of heart and returns to find that all of his clubs, one by one miraculously tracked down by Jasper, are waiting for him in his locker.[41] Subsequently, fictional caddies who used their astute psychological (and spiritual) capabilities to aid white clients appeared often in twentieth-century American literature and cinema, culminating in the 2000 film *The Legend of Bagger Vance*, based on Steven Pressfield's eponymous 1995 novel. *Time* called it "one of the more embarrassing movies in recent history" for its stereotypical depiction of "a magical black caddie who helps Matt Damon win a golf tournament." Director Spike Lee called the caddie character played by Will Smith a "super-duper magical Negro."[42] Black caddie and spectator anecdotes both challenged and reinforced dominant racial stereotypes. Still, examples of caddies outwitting their employers, earning respect from the game's elite, and challenging their wealthy clients tended to appear more frequently in golf literature, as well in as the black press, by World War I.

While it is difficult to separate fact from fiction in the stories of Rockefeller's interactions with black caddies, President Woodrow Wilson's encounters were better documented. Wilson spent three weeks during the winter of 1913–14 in Pass Christian, Mississippi, where he played numerous rounds of golf attended by black caddies. These included the head caddie at the Isles Golf Club, who reportedly approached the president's group during a round and exclaimed, "I'm Ben Williams, Jeff Davis's old body servant, and I wanted to meet Mr. Wilson." The president greeted Williams, and according to other accounts, both Williams and his grandson subsequently caddied for Wilson during his stay in Pass Christian. *American Golfer*, with a sly reference to the Civil War, reported that Williams "has caddied for some of the biggest men in America" and "carried clubs since golf invaded his section of the country." Other black caddies went to great lengths to land Wilson's bag, including one who amused the president's group when he approached Wilson's car and said, "Youse all can't park here. This place am reserved fo the President. You'd better move on." "All right, my boy," responded Wilson. "You ought to be a pretty good caddie. Tell the caddie master I want you to tote my bag."[43]

Wilson even shared his own magical caddie anecdote when the subject of golf came up during a 1915 interview. "When I began to play it was difficult to get caddies," the president said, before joking that the inability of some to hit a golf ball despite proper form was "a commentary on Washington!" Wilson then "laughed," "leaned forward in his chair," and told the following story:

> That reminds me of a man I knew, a relative of Mrs. Wilson's whom we called the Colonel, who wanted to learn golf. He was at one of the clubs in the south; and he went to the grounds keeper and told him he desired the poorest caddie of the lot. "I don't want one of those wise ones," he said, "You give me the worst one you have, and I'll teach him to caddie my way; and he can give me such information as I need." So they gave him a short, squat negro they called Elephant, a big hulk of a boy with not a gleam of sense apparently. The Colonel started off. He made a sort of drive and proceeded to where the ball lay, tagged by Elephant. He found the ball tagged in a depression. Elephant handed him an iron. The Colonel looked at the iron and looked at Elephant. He surveyed the ball. Then he turned to Elephant and shouted: "What'll I do, boy? What'll I do?" "Hit the ball, suh!" said Elephant, "Hit the ball!" That's the philosophy of politics—of everything! . . . Hit the ball; hit it as well as you can—but hit it![44]

Wilson's description of African Americans in *A History of the American People* (1901) and his positive reception of D. W. Griffith's neo-Confederate film *The Birth of a Nation* (1915) may illuminate the president's racial ideology, but perhaps his interaction with black caddies best exemplified his vision of the role of black people in American society. Along with the "Elephant" story, Wilson's appropriation of the Confederate president's former slave as his golf caddie was the ultimate symbol of the new white consensus on race relations in America. The nation's leader turned to a black caddie for his philosophy "of everything," while Ben Williams's transition—from presidential slave to presidential caddie—echoed the nation's path from Reconstruction to Jim Crow segregation.

In addition to caddying, many African Americans influenced the game by helping construct the nation's first courses. Joseph Bartholomew's design of the Metairie Country Club was unique; more common was the untold labor countless black workers provided to build the country's key layouts. This included the South's first major country club, North Carolina's Pinehurst Resort, which developed its first course in 1897–98 and became one of the nation's most exclusive clubs. Historians seeking African American origins at Pinehurst need only look beneath their feet: in 1935 it became one of first courses to feature Bermuda grass (*Cynodon dactylon*). Contrary to its name, the grass was not native to Bermuda but, rather, Africa, where for centuries it was cultivated as pasture grass before African livestock transported it to the Western Hemisphere via the transatlantic slave trade. There is even evidence that slave owners in the New World identified Africans as more experienced in tending African-derived flora and fauna, including Bermuda grass. *Cynodon dactylon* became the most popular turf in the South soon after researchers developed strains best suited for warm-weather golf courses in the early twentieth century. It was used from the beginning at Georgia's famed Augusta National Golf Club (built in 1933). Today a majority of golf fairways in the South—and 40 percent of all courses in America—feature Bermuda grass.[45]

Visitors may not have recognized the African origins of Pinehurst's grass, but they could not ignore the many African Americans who created and sustained the resort with the sweat of their brows. Famed Scottish architect Donald Ross designed the layout at a time when North Carolina was enflamed with violent racial tension; in fact, the same year mobs of white Democrats violently retook control of the state government and killed an unknown number of blacks and white Republicans in Wilmington, a significant incident of mass racial violence at the turn of the century. As white supremacists reclaimed North Carolina's government and incidents of lynching and disenfranchisement escalated around the state, black men reclaimed Pinehurst's wastelands, built its courses, and maintained the grounds, while black women served as laundresses and cooks at its celebrated hotel. From the beginning nearly all of the caddies were young black boys. Despite the proliferation of clever-caddie stories and examples such as Joseph Bartholomew, conditions at Pinehurst revealed the more sobering reality for most black workers in the industry: the work was backbreaking, the treatment was often brutal, and the pay was terrible. Some caddies attempted to organize for better pay but were met with fierce resistance, including from Ross himself. According to one account, Ross once responded to threats of a strike by entering the caddie pen and assaulting a caddie with a five-iron. Pinehurst even denied black women the "privilege" of cleaning its hotel rooms until 1960, and for a majority of the twentieth century the development forbade property owners from selling to Jewish or African American buyers.[46]

Such reliance on black labor to build and maintain golf facilities was common in the South but not exclusive to that region. Moreover, early course developers in the South were more likely to build on open (or relatively open) land, such as Pinehurst in North Carolina or Bartholomew's course in Metairie, Louisiana. Northeast courses often encroached on settlement, prompting developers to eye land once considered unsuitable, including black neighborhoods. In 1901 the family of wealthy silver magnate John W. Mackay sought to construct a private course on their Long Island estate near Roslyn, New York, only to discover a "small negro graveyard." According to the press, "Mr. and Mrs. Mackay . . . were standing near, remarking that it was an ideal spot for a bunker, when to their amazement, a funeral party approached and a coffin was deposited in an open grave, which had escaped attention." It was not unheard of for wealthy owners to overlook the presence of black residents, and even active graveyards, on their land, but what the Mackay family did next for their "ideal" course was truly unique: "As it was absolutely necessary to play over this grave yard, Mrs. Mackay will buy another plot of land, have the bodies removed to it, and to further conciliate the coloured population, she offered to pay the funeral expenses for all negroes who died in the neighborhood within a year, and so all is peace."[47] Despite the gesture, however, such "peace" was predicated on a clear understanding: black neighborhoods, both living and dead, were to make way for the growing number of white public and private golf courses.

While white courses appropriated black labor, and sometimes black land, black courses soon arrived in the Northeast and Midwest as well. Distinguishing the first is difficult; all-black golfing clubs certainly existed before the first dedicated black links. As early as 1898 there was reference to a "new negro golf club" in New York City with a group of "skillful members," composed mainly of caddies at resort courses outside the city who offered lessons to whites and blacks. A 1901 short story described the game's "rampant" appeal on Manhattan's East Side, with young Irish, Italian, and black kids hitting balls up and down Third Avenue. New York City already presented a dual vision of golf: street games and caddie lessons in the park clashed with what one newspaper in 1898 described as the city's "several private golf schools" offering wealthy clients instruction in

Practicing the "royal game" in Detroit, ca. 1905 (Detroit Publishing Company Photograph Collection, Prints & Photographs Division, Library of Congress, det.4a12571).

the "royal game." By 1915 there were already 112 courses within fifty miles of Manhattan.[48]

In urban areas golf quickly developed along socioeconomic and racial lines, with black players carving out autonomous spaces and playing apart from white clubs and courses. Yet the first actual courses independently built or operated by African Americans emerged in the Midwest. Established by the Consolidation Coal Company in 1900, the majority-black town of Buxton, Iowa, had a golf course by 1904. Built with help from the national YMCA, and likely open to the occasional white golfer, it was nevertheless operated by a board of directors "composed of colored men."[49] For the larger black communities in East Coast cities, the first courses were carved from park space in predominately black neighborhoods. Such was the case in 1914 when "beautiful grounds for croquet, golf, fishing, baseball and lawn tennis" were built in Lincoln Park, Maryland, a black community established outside Washington, D.C.[50]

Many entrepreneurs seeking to establish all-black resort towns were the first to introduce more ambitious plans for full-sized courses for black golfers. Idlewild, Michigan—the nation's first African American resort town—was established in 1912 and soon opened a course in 1916 that attracted middle-class black vacationers, most from Chicago, Detroit, and Cleveland.[51] In 1915 two prominent black citizens in Atlantic City announced plans for a "golf links and pleasure resort" in nearby Pleasantville, New Jersey. The planned development, called Douglas Park, already featured a course when the two men, one the pastor of Atlantic City's St. James AME Church and the other a lawyer, sought investors to turn the property into the largest all-black resort on the East Coast. Although the men never achieved that goal, the small development—with street names like Dubois, Howard, Wilburforce, and Freeman—exists to this day just off the Atlantic City Expressway. One former resident recalled how leading black entertainers continued to visit the neighborhood's stately homes as late as the 1940s. Golf featured prominently in the attempts to attract black investment and market Douglas Park. According to one *Philadelphia Tribune* reporter who toured the site in 1915, golf there would present travelers driving into Atlantic City with a new, more respectable vision of the local black community: "Refinement and culture is to reign pre-eminent." The project was also heralded in the *Chicago Defender* and the *Crisis* magazine, W. E. B. Du Bois's flagship publication for the newly formed NAACP.[52]

Two years later, in 1917, another black country club was founded in Cheshire, Connecticut, near Waterbury. There is little information about the Cheshire Country Club's origins, and it does not appear to have lasted long; yet impressive descriptions of the club and its golf course appeared in black newspapers around the country. According to the *Chicago Defender* it had nearly 200 members and was "the only one of its kind in the country owned and managed entirely by and for the Race."[53] In addition to the golf course, the twenty-two-acre site boasted a clubhouse with "a splendid view" and amenities including billiards, a large parlor, a ballroom, and tennis courts.

Interestingly, the Cheshire development was opposed by "ministers of the churches in nearby towns," although it is unclear if resistance came from predominately white or black churches.[54] More likely it was the former, for there is little evidence in this early period of black ministers opposing golf, whereas many white Protestants denounced what was becoming a popular Sabbath-day activity. In New England there were even several examples of players being arrested for Sunday play.

The Club House at Idlewild, Michigan, ca. 1926 (Ben Wilson, Kalamazoo, Michigan).

A 1919 test case of Massachusetts's ban on Sabbath-day sports featured the arrest of two Sunday golfers at Brae Burn Country Club; fortunately for them, the court held that golf was a game, not a sport.[55] Meanwhile, black Protestants were relatively more open to golf, and in black communities preachers were actually early pioneers of the game, for they tended to occupy key positions in the black middle class. In Atlantic City the lead investor in the Douglas Park development was a local AME minister, and members of the first AME church (built in 1915) in Portland, Oregon, joined their pastor for golf outings on the city's municipal links. Black churches and Christian organizations in Chicago called on black youth to take up golf, basketball, and tennis in the city's parks; churches even opened their doors for instructors to provide evening golf lessons. Still, ministers tended to differ over whether the game was appropriate. In 1914 AME bishop and former slave Joseph Simeon Flipper criticized golf while preaching in the South.[56] Playing on the Sabbath certainly drew condemnation in both white and black churches, but black clergy, especially in the Northeast, were more likely than their white counterparts to eschew traditional puritan concerns with sport and instead equate golf with social refinement, economic advancement, and moral uplift.

Aside from these few examples there is scant evidence of all-black private country clubs before 1920; the first definitive one to survive in the historical record was Shady Rest Country Club, established in 1922 in Scotch Plains, New Jersey. Whether or not another preceded Shady Rest, there were certainly groups of black golfers who organized golf gatherings and tournaments within the black community, and some even challenged local governments for greater access to predominately white courses. Here the greatest breakthrough came in Chicago, where before 1920 black residents showed more interest in golf than did any other black community in the United States. This included what the *Chicago Defender* called the "first golf tournament ever pulled off in America by expert race golfers" in 1915, a contest featuring black players from around the country. The winner, Walter Speedy, was a Louisiana native who came to Chicago in 1900 and was among the top players in the city. The tournament was held at Marquette Park on the city's South Side, the same park where violent protesters would later hit Martin Luther King Jr. with a brick during the 1966 Chicago Freedom Movement. The city opened Marquette's golf links in 1913, and the park, surrounded by a growing community of black migrants, appeared to be open to black patrons with few racial restrictions. In addition to having accessible municipal courses, black golfers in Chicago also benefited from several outspoken leaders who championed the game during the 1910s, including Speedy and staff at the *Chicago Defender*. In 1909 Speedy married Nettie George, a style reporter for the *Defender* whose articles championed the game's growth in the city. George was the first black woman to play golf in Chicago (and one of the first to play anywhere in America), and her editorials were among the earliest calls for black women to take up the game.[57]

Despite the tournament at Marquette Park, black golfers in Chicago still faced severe barriers. Four black players, including Speedy, were barred from entering the city's first public links golf tournament, held in 1910 at the Jackson Park Golf Course, located along the lakeshore seven miles from the Marquette links. They sued park officials in response, but the results of the litigation are unclear. By 1915 the four had joined with other black players to form the Alpha Golf Club, one of the nation's first black golfing clubs. The group included Horace McDougal, head caddie at Chicago's swanky Beverly Country Club, a layout Donald Ross was in the process of renovating. After the successful event at Marquette, black players were finally invited to play the city's white champions at Jackson Park later that year.[58] In 1918, however, whites at Jackson Park once again snubbed Chicago's black golfers. After Speedy and another black player, Robert "Pat" Ball, qualified for the city championship, they were mys-

A rare image of Chicago's first champion black golfer, Walter Speedy, in 1915 (*Chicago Defender*).

teriously left off the list of sixty players subsequently published in local newspapers. Nettie Speedy stood up for her husband and the *Chicago Defender* by confronting the tournament organizers and *Chicago Tribune* staff face-to-face in public. "It is not publicity that I seek," she said, "but only fair play, for our newspapers have their own representative here." Nettie even threatened that the *Tribune*'s support for such blatant discrimination in the Chicago golf scene would hurt the Senate campaign of Joseph Medill McCormick, the paper's owner. "It would make quite interesting reading in the political world," she told the writers, "to know that Mr. McCormick was running for U.S. senator and touring the state for votes and one of his writers on his paper would not recognize the athletic prowess of members of our Race." Her warning worked, at least for that year's tournament. The next morning "every daily in Chicago let it be known that men of our Race were dangerous contenders for the golf championship," and Walter Speedy and Ball once again played alongside whites in Jackson Park, where they beat several of the city's best white players and performed admirably while "a large gallery followed them."[59]

The struggle over discrimination in Chicago's city championship was not over, however. The following year organizers once again excluded Ball and Speedy. This time they implemented a regulation that players had to be members of "a regular organized golf club"—and not surprisingly, neither the Alpha club nor the group's subsequent black organization, the Windy City Golf Association, were recognized. The 1919 city championship at Jackson Park was again all white, and that same month Chicago was hit by the worst race riot of Red Summer, with violent mobs of white men (mainly ethnic Irish aided by police) attacking black businesses and residents on the South Side. The riot was precipitated by the murder of a black youth, Eugene Williams, after he drifted into an informally segregated swimming area at a local beach, another incident involving segregated leisure. But it soon highlighted the broader tensions surrounding residential segregation, the emboldening of black veterans returning from service in World War I, increasing black migration to the South Side, and Chicago's worsening racialized labor strife. Within a week there were nearly forty deaths and hundreds of injuries.[60] Yet the report from the Chicago Commission on Race Relations, established by Illinois governor Frank Lowden to investigate the riots, indicated that integrated public swimming was not the only leisure activity that could provoke particularly harsh reaction from whites. In fact, the exclusion of black golfers from the 1919 Jackson Park tournament was the only incident of racial discrimination the city's park commission admitted to supporting in the riot's aftermath—although, the commission wrote, unofficial discrimination "frequently . . . creeps in" at the parks. That the policy of racial exclusion at Jackson Park seemed to apply only to golf and not to other activities hinted at the game's symbolic meaning. Black golfers in Chicago were breaking a more symbolic social barrier than black residents engaged in other park activities.[61]

Despite the snub, Chicago's black golfers continued to insist that they would pursue the game. Even as the South Side burned in August 1919, the *Defender* published the latest scores from Speedy, Ball, and others, proclaiming defiantly, "We, the few golfers of the Race, are hoping to make golfing more popular in the future."[62] And Chicago was not the only city where African Americans launched significant campaigns to access public courses before 1920. In 1917 a group asked the park commissioner in

St. Louis, Missouri, to open the city's Forest Park course to black players one day per week. The commissioner denied the request and instead hinted that St. Louis would consider a "separate links" for the black community. New York City opened the nation's first public course in 1895 at Van Cortlandt Park, which immediately hosted African American players and became the busiest golf course in the country, including a series of interracial matches and tournaments that drew attention in the 1910s. A black man named Jessa Garland even held Van Cortlandt's course record in 1919 and ruffled feathers by bragging about his talents and publicly challenging whites to play against him.[63] In Philadelphia, both municipal courses and African American participation came more slowly. That city's first public course, Cobbs Creek, did not have a black member until 1916, and by 1920 only 6 of its 2,500 members were black. As in Chicago, Philadelphia's black newspaper urged more of its readers to take up the game. "Our people should get in on the ground floor and there will be no color line," proclaimed the *Philadelphia Tribune*, noting specifically that "more young men should play golf" as it "would help them in so many ways."[64] Twenty years later a teenager from North Carolina moved to Philadelphia with few prospects except for one special talent. "I was an 11th-grade dropout who couldn't go back home. I knew only one thing, and that was how to play golf," recalled Charlie Sifford, who was seventeen when he arrived at Cobbs Creek in 1939. "The course was intended for everyone to use, and I was both surprised and delighted to see both blacks and whites playing side by side there. I'd never seen anything like that in North Carolina. . . . Here was a place where I could play without having to worry about some groundskeeper coming by to run me off the course."[65]

Although there were significant examples of caddies-turned-players and urban youth who took up the game, most African Americans who played substantial golf tended to be relatively wealthy, their golfing endeavors celebrated as examples of socioeconomic uplift. In 1911 the *Chicago Defender* noted a black doctor in Asheville, North Carolina, who could "play golf if his name isn't J. D. Rockefeller" and had thereby joined the city's "smart set." That same year a black retiree in St. Louis wrote that he was "hitting the ball hard and playing nine holes of golf every morning before breakfast." Biologist Ernest Everett Just, winner of the NAACP's first Spingarn Medal in 1915, enjoyed playing while working as a professor at Howard University in Washington, D.C. And by age twelve, future journalist George Schuyler had befriended children of Syracuse Univer-

America's first municipal course: Van Cortlandt Park, New York City, ca. 1910 (George Grantham Bain Collection, Prints & Photographs Division, Library of Congress, LC-DIG-ggbain-02914).

sity faculty in upstate New York, where he played on local courses as early as 1907.[66]

Along with black men, a substantial number of black women were also attracted to golf in the early twentieth century and pursued the game with equal passion. When Walter Speedy emerged as Chicago's best black golfer, his wife, Nettie, advocated not only for her husband's access to white city leagues and tournaments but also for more black women and girls to take up the game. Nettie was an accomplished journalist; later in 1926 she traveled to Detroit to cover the landmark Ossian Sweet trial for the *Defender*. Back home she devoted a number of columns particularly to the social scene evolving around women's golf on the South Side. White and black, Chicago's women flocked to the game in large numbers, perhaps rivaled only by women in New York City. Hundreds complained in 1912 when commissioners banned high heels on Chicago's Jackson Park course. Yet Nettie insisted there remained far more black women who could benefit from golf. "I have tried to fathom the reason so few take up the game," she wrote in 1918, eventually blaming the "mistaken idea that golf is a rich man's game." Starting every June she played constantly

ORIGINS OF GOLF IN THE UNITED STATES (27

throughout the warm season: "I change my schedule and each morning at 4 o'clock (weather permitting) I am on my way to the links." She assured females that Chicago's courses were open to black women, even while she fought the overt discrimination her husband encountered nearly every year at the city championship. "There are several public courses in Chicago, two at Jackson Park, one at Marquette, one at Lincoln, one at Garfield, one at Warren's Woods," she told her female readers. "You are fully privileged to play . . . provided, of course, you conform to rules and regulations."[67]

Nettie's call for more black female golfers echoed that of a number of women during the period who equated the game with social prestige and found it perfectly befitting the "New Woman." Descriptions of female golf attire and fashion were common in both the white and black press, along with celebrations of social gatherings associated with the game. Prominent black wives visiting Chicago from as far as Minnesota or Alabama were hosted by Nettie to a round on the city's public links, the encounters dutifully reported on the *Defender*'s society page. The paper also provided summertime recipes for "golf teas" and punches, which offered refreshment from the links and promised to boost postgolf socializing. In August 1918 black women even hosted a "delightful golf party" in Jackson Park the same month Nettie publicly denounced commissioners and the *Chicago Tribune* for locking black men out of the park's city championship. And black religious organizations in the city, such as the Christian People's Athletic Association, provided golf lessons for girls and women.[68] Other black newspapers around the country also called on black women in their communities to embrace the game. As early as 1904 the *Baltimore Afro-American* featured numerous columns describing female fashion on the links and celebrating "modern women" who played.[69] Most of these pieces were reprinted from white media outlets, yet the message was clear: black women could also tap into the social and economic prestige golf symbolized. Interaction with the game meshed with the "politics of respectability" that some historians argue black women drew from to confront both racism and sexism during the period.[70] All of these developments were key for black girls, in particular, for the caddying system that introduced so many young African Americans to the game was an entirely male world.

Not only did women's golf show up frequently in the black press, but by the early twentieth century, black newspapers featured a surprising number of golf-related anecdotes and factoids. Race-related exchanges were popular (such as Rockefeller or clever-caddie jokes), but all of the largest black newspapers in the country—including the *Chicago Defender*, the *Afro-American*, the *Pittsburgh Courier*, and the *Philadelphia Tribune*—also devoted ample coverage to the game in general. Many touted golf's therapeutic and health benefits: "The kind of walking which fulfills every end of exercise," proclaimed the *Afro-American*, "is that which one takes with a golf club in hand." By the 1920s the *Defender* even featured a regular instructional column with golf tips and lessons for players. Golfing advertisements also appeared, particularly for local retailers plugging golf pants for men.[71] Of course, historians must be careful when analyzing the arrival of so much golf material in the black press. As one notes, such advertisements and stories certainly indicate that golf was a "current fad," yet they "fail to provide a mirror because they offer no accurate measure of how many people played . . . or how often they did so."[72] The black press therefore provided both reflections of the black community's actual engagement with golf and more aspirational illustrations that hinted at the game's potential to transform its readers' lives. As the *Defender* proclaimed, golf was the "past time of presidents" that was now "getting a hold on young men." And for southern migrants especially, the coverage of golf in northern black newspapers provided a powerful illustration of middle-class life and symbolized the socioeconomic opportunities available in cities such as Chicago, Pittsburgh, and New York.[73] There were even instances of black celebrities and entertainers participating in golf at the turn of the century, a phenomenon that eventually helped increase the game's popularity after World War I. While on a successful tour of England in 1903, vaudeville star Bert Williams performed for King Edward VII and played golf with Prince Arthur and other elites. Williams, one of the most popular black entertainers before 1920, was perhaps the first African American to play golf in Britain.[74]

Along with helping to popularize golf in the black community, the black press also took the lead in denouncing racial discrimination and segregation associated with the game. In his 1901 essay "The Social Value of Golf," English novelist E. F. Benson insisted the game was suited to "Anglo-Saxon temperament" and "conducive to a higher social excellence." Tongue firmly in cheek, the *Afro-American* responded by playing off the title of Benson's first novel (*Dodo: A Detail of the Day*) and publishing a rebuke of "Dodo Benson."[75] A more common, insidious epithet likely originated in the U.S. Army during World War I, in which shooting dice began to be referred to as "African golf" or "nigger golf"; in 1919 the *El*

Paso Herald reported that gambling over "African golf" had prompted the army to discharge a black private. Labor leader Jere L. Sullivan referred to dice as "Negro golf" in a 1922 national address to the Hotel and Restaurant Employees Union. The term was especially useful in the South, where it juxtaposed a supposedly more refined game with the immorality, gambling, and ill repute associated with dice—while, of course, neglecting the fact that black people actually played real golf.

The popularity of the pejorative term "African golf" was short lived, likely because it was one of the more hypocritical racial slurs in American history: gambling in golf was rampant among white men, and the game challenged horse racing as the most popular activity to bet on. By 1920, referring to golf as "white dice" would have been the more accurate slang. "Daily newspapers must base their jokes on us," denounced an *Afro-American* editorial in 1928, "so they sometimes refer to the game of dice as 'African golf.'" Turning the idea of golf's gentlemanly, Anglo origins on its head, the paper insisted that dice actually had the more refined origins: it was, after all, the game of choice for nobles in ancient Greece and Rome, not golf.[76]

"African golf" was also invoked in one of the first examples of racism leveled at a specific black golf course. Before African Americans in New Jersey could even build the Douglas Park course, *American Golfer* published a racist attack on the group's plans.

> A golf course for the exclusive use of negroes is to be opened at Pleasantville, near Atlantic City.... What could be more delightful than a sea breeze stealing over the course during the course of a dusky ball-some, knee-deep in June or maybe July. In the club-house one might hear: "May I have the extreme pleasuah of a match with yo' fo' two bits a hole this aftahnoon, Mistah Johnsing?"
>
> "I suttinly appreciates yo' proffer, Mistah Hannibal, but I am made up with Miss Eugenia May Briggs fo' a Fo'some with Mr. Reginald Dickus an' Miss Fessenden."
>
> Certainly such an organization would be unique. Some of us have heard of "Nigger Golf" before, but it was played with two cubes.[77]

Along with criticism directed at specific black golfers, racist images and items found demeaning humor in the mere idea of black golf. Edward Kemble, best known for illustrating Mark Twain's 1885 *Adventures of Huckleberry Finn*, featured racist caricatures of blacks playing golf in his cartoons and children's books. In a popular mail-away campaign from the 1920s, James Robertson and Sons, a British manufacturer of jams and preserves, sent U.S. customers a series of racist "golliwog" pins, the first of which was the "Golly Golfer." Yet the most provocative commercial caricature, "Nigger Head" golf tees, helped erase the memory of George F. Grant's invention with a violent image: the tees, also produced in the 1920s, came in a package depicting a black man's head pierced by a golf tee.[78]

Even individuals considered more sympathetic to the black community invoked racism and racial humor through their embrace of golf. Supreme Court Justice John Marshall Harlan wrote several important opinions defending black civil rights and advocating a race-blind constitution, especially in the *Civil Rights Cases* (1883) and his lone dissent in *Plessy v. Ferguson* (1896). Yet the *Afro-American* noticed Harlan's penchant for sharing racial golf jokes. During a Supreme Court session in 1904 he passed a note to former attorney general John Griggs, who was seated in the gallery: "I was out before breakfast this morning and played a white ball against a red one—the red man against the paleface. And the Injun won—two up."[79]

African Americans unanimously denounced racism in golf, yet the game's ultimate symbolism remained open to debate in the black community. Instead of calling for more black participation, some critics were more likely to use golf to stigmatize whites and criticize leadership. No matter its popularity in various black neighborhoods, the game still symbolized elitism, especially when it was played by white leaders who supported increased segregation or stood by apathetically. In Chicago, the black community's success in accessing city courses seemed to contrast with the white violence and rioting directed at blacks in the summer of 1919. In Philadelphia, however, golf continued to stand for white power and apathy; there, black leaders denounced Mayor Thomas Smith for ignoring them after President Woodrow Wilson issued a call for local representatives to address race riots, mob violence, and police brutality—all of which Philadelphia had experienced in several high-profile incidents. Smith's office delayed meeting with black delegates for two weeks because the mayor was playing golf. "Philadelphia . . . has disgraced the United States by openly defying the President's plea," the *Philadelphia Tribune* charged. "Our mayor has had nothing publicly to say and has been too busy playing golf to receive any of our several committees who have called at his office to ask him to . . . make his policemen enforce instead of breaking the law."[80] And even before President Wilson's symbolic 1913 meeting with Ben Williams in Mississippi, black observers used golf

Black golf as caricature: Edward Kemble's 1897 *The Blackberries and Their Adventures* (New York: R. H. Russell, 1897); an 1899 minstrel performance poster (Minstrel poster collection, Prints & Photographs Division, Library of Congress, LC-DIG-var-1822); and the 1928 "Golly Golfer" brooch.

to criticize Republican president William Howard Taft's indifference to the growing racism in southern politics, especially his apathy as black Republicans were thrown out of office. Taft's golf outings during the summer of 1910 drew scorn from the *Afro-American*: "Now playing golf is not by any means a bad way of spending one's time and to it we have not the slightest objection," read one editorial. "But . . . chopping off Negro officeholders' heads seems to be on a par with playing golf, and probably with the President, is mere pastime."[81] This uneasy tension between the celebration or encouragement of black golf and the negative appropriation of golf as ultimate symbol of white privilege would only grow stronger in the South after 1920. The *Afro-American* had one answer for why Maryland officials failed to stop white lynch mobs from attacking local jails in 1931: "Our experience with state attorneys and leading citizens is that when the mob forms, they usually go out to play golf."[82]

Along with black caddies, club attendants, and recreational players, black amateur and professional golfers also influenced the game's early development by participating in America's first nationally organized golf tournaments. By the time Taft became the first president to play golf regularly, such events were held around the country. Black players soon competed in several important amateur contests, including interscholastic tournaments. While in high school, Horace McDougal participated in the 1911 Western Interscholastic Tournament at Chicago's Ravisloe Country Club. He went on to join Northwestern University's golf team in 1923, becoming the first black intercollegiate golfer in history. In 1918 a black student from Atlanta University, Mark Thomas, beat seventy-seven players to win a large amateur tournament in Hartford, Connecticut.[83] Along with interscholastic and club tournaments, golf also had an established national governing body. Formed in 1894, the USGA arranged the first U.S. Amateur and U.S. Open tournaments the following year. Although the amateur tournament drew more attention, individuals who competed in the U.S. Open became the first professional golfers in American history. Initially the vast majority were white men from England and Scotland, such as Englishman Horace Rawlins, winner of the first U.S. Open in 1895. All of those atop the leaderboard (the top ten finishers) in the 1895 Open and all but one in 1896 hailed from Britain or Canada. And yet, in one of the most overlooked moments in the history of African American sports, that lone American on the leaderboard was black.

Considering the attention received by pioneering black professional athletes such as boxer Jack Johnson or baseball star Jackie Robinson—

not to mention the scramble to uncover nonwhite professionals sparked by the rise of Tiger Woods in the 1990s—it is difficult to understand the disregard for golf's first two American-born pros: John Shippen, the son of a former Virginia slave who competed in five U.S. Opens between 1896 and 1913, and Shippen's fellow caddie (and friend) Oscar Bunn, a Native American who competed in the 1896 and 1899 U.S. Opens. In particular, the Shippen family's contributions to professional golf (John's brother, Cyrus, competed in the 1899 U.S. Open) came at a crucial moment in both golf and American history. Before Jim Crow was firmly entrenched in society and before many national organizations or institutions had managed to articulate detailed policies of racial segregation, two black brothers and their supporters saw in professional golf the exact opposite of what it would become: the stereotype of American exclusion. This moment of possibility ended when the PGA opted to ban black members from its inception in 1916, making the achievements of the Shippens all the more fascinating. No other African Americans would compete in the U.S. Open until 1948.

John Shippen was born in 1879 in Washington, D.C., where his father settled after being freed from slavery during the Civil War. The elder Shippen went to Howard University and became an ordained Presbyterian minister, relocating the family to take various church positions around the country. John's engagement with golf began after his father was assigned to a Presbyterian mission on the Shinnecock Indian Reservation in Southampton, New York, in 1888. Four years later, a group of wealthy investors opened Shinnecock Hills Golf Club, the nation's first premier golf course. The course was built by 150 local Native Americans and featured a number of Native American caddies, and the layout designed by Scottish golfers hosted the best players in the country. The use of Shinnecock laborers and caddies at the club was not unique; in other areas of the country in the late nineteenth century, Native Americans appropriated golf via local resort courses. On Michigan's Mackinac Island, the Wawashkamo Golf Club drew prominent vacationers such as Mark Twain and Thomas Edison. Frank Dufina, a native Ojibwe, became the club's professional in 1898 and competed in the 1911 Western Open. Even in the far Southwest, golf made considerable inroads among native groups by the turn of the century. Exhibitors at the 1901 Pan-American Exposition displayed two willow-wood golf clubs and corded balls crafted by Cocopah Indians in Baja California.[84]

In Southampton, John Shippen befriended many of the Native Americans his father worked with, including Oscar Bunn, a young Shinnecock boy who was roughly the same age. Together Shippen and Bunn joined the caddie ranks at Shinnecock Hills and were trained directly by the course's famed Scottish designer, Willie Dunn. Within three years both teens had acquired impressive skills and were regarded as two of the best players in the area. By the time he was sixteen, Shippen had managed to shoot 78 at Shinnecock Hills, just six shots behind Dunn's course-record 72.[85]

The USGA's decision to host both the 1896 U.S. Open and U.S. Amateur at Shinnecock was a logical choice. It was one of five elite clubs whose representatives had formed the national governing body two years earlier in order to organize an annual national championship and administer the rules of golf for the United States. Shinnecock's members encouraged both Shippen and Bunn to enter the 1896 event. By that point Shippen, in particular, had risen above the club's other caddies and was instructing, repairing clubs, and assisting the maintenance staff. His playing abilities and potential to be the first American professional to compete in the U.S. Open drew interest as word spread. "It would not be at all surprising," proclaimed the *Kalamazoo Gazette* two weeks before the tournament, "if before long John Shippen, the negro boy, appeared in the open championship as one of the most threatening candidates for honors. . . . If, when going around the links, he had had clubs carried for him instead of his carrying for somebody else, there is no telling how good his play would be now." Shippen, the sixteen-year-old caddie, had the potential to be "the great American golfer" supporters in the United States had long awaited, "almost as strong as awaiting the great American novelist."[86]

From the perspective of Theodore Havemeyer, co-owner of the American Sugar Refining Company and the USGA's first president, placing Native or African Americans on the list of "professional golfers" was not a tremendously powerful statement. As was the case with many sports during the period, the "professional" moniker meant little and often bestowed less prestige and respect than amateurism. By far the U.S. Amateur was the more important of the two USGA events, and "professional" more often invoked the specter of work performed by "hired help," not riches or fame: each winner of the first five U.S. Opens received $150. In fact, by 1909 the USGA would rule that all caddies, caddiemasters, and greenskeepers over age sixteen were "professional golfers," a policy it did not reverse completely until 1963. Some of the thirty-five entrants at the 1896 U.S. Open, however, were clearly threatened when they discovered they would be competing alongside Shippen and Bunn. While crowds gathered at Shinnecock Hills to watch the U.S. Amateur on July 17, a number of the professionals—how many and who remains unclear, although all would have been Englishmen and Scotsmen—confronted Havemeyer and threatened to boycott the next day's professional tournament unless the USGA removed Shippen and Bunn from the field. Havemeyer flatly refused, all of the players backed down, and the following day the U.S. Open began with few spectators realizing what had occurred behind the scenes. Havemeyer's rebuke of the foreign professionals was a bold stance, yet the philosophy behind it was likely less revolutionary. Not only was it relatively safe to label African or Native Americans in the golf industry "professionals," but according to one account, Havemeyer tried to sympathize with the white players by insisting (incorrectly) that Shippen himself was actually half Native American, hinting perhaps that an exclusion of black players, but not Native Americans, would be an appropriate position for the USGA to take in the future.

Shippen was aware his competitors had tried to remove him from the tournament when he stepped to the first tee at the 1896 U.S. Open, and he was paired with an intimidating opponent: Charles Blair Macdonald, the preeminent American golf course architect of the day, a major figure behind the establishment of the USGA, and winner of the 1895 U.S. Amateur. Yet while Macdonald flopped (he shot 83 and angrily withdrew), Shippen shot 78, putting him in a tie for first place and matching his personal best at Shinnecock Hills when it mattered most. His Native American friend, Oscar Bunn, struggled with an 89. That afternoon, in the tournament's second and final round, Shippen played alone in front of a growing gallery. He was challenging for the lead, but disaster struck when he sliced his drive at the thirteenth hole onto a nearby sanded road, struggled to recover, and rolled in a putt for a dismal 11. As is all too common in golf, one hole kept him from becoming the first American winner of the U.S. Open: he otherwise managed to shoot 81 and finished in a tie for sixth place, seven shots behind the winner, Scotland's James Foulis. "You know, I've wished a hundred times I could have played that little par four again," Shippen recalled shortly before his death in 1968. "It sure would have been something to win that day."[87] His finish nevertheless earned him ten dollars, the first prize money ever awarded to an American-born golf pro.

Shippen's play continued to impress following his professional debut at the 1896 U.S. Open. After he again shot 78 at Shinnecock Hills to win an 1897 match against the club's new professional, R. B. Wilson, *Outing* magazine called it "the best 18 holes yet played in this country by an American

The first American-born professional: John Shippen, 1913 (Courtesy USGA Museum).

born." Supporters urged him to continue challenging the dominance of European professionals and competing in subsequent U.S. Opens, including the 1897 event at the Chicago Golf Club in Wheaton, Illinois. "He was a caddie at Shinnecock Hills, but now ranks as one of the best professionals in this country," proclaimed *Outing*. "It is to be hoped that Shippen will be enabled to play at Chicago, and his club ought to see to it that, despite his color, he is given every opportunity to show what he can do."[88]

While Shippen did not compete again in 1897, he did go on to play in four more U.S. Opens (1899, 1900, 1902, and 1913). Despite worries about playing in a tournament with whites in a southern city, he competed alongside his brother, Cyrus, and Bunn at the 1899 U.S. Open without any incident. The tournament took place at the Baltimore Country Club, where the Shippen brothers were likely the last two African Americans to play the course until well after World War II. John Shippen's best finish, a tie for fifth place, came at the 1902 U.S. Open at New York's Garden City Golf Club. Cyrus Shippen went on to a long career teaching at Dunbar High School in Washington, D.C., where he started a golf team at one of the nation's first black public high schools.[89]

John Shippen continued to play professionally and worked at several premier private courses in the Northeast, including the National Golf Links (Southampton, N.Y.), Spring Lake Golf Club (Spring Lake, N.J.), Bath Beach Club (Brooklyn, N.Y.), and Somerset Hills Country Club (Bernardsville, N.J.). He served three years as club professional at Aronimink Golf Club, outside Philadelphia, and a total of thirteen years as head professional at East Hampton's elite Maidstone Club. From 1913 to 1915 he offered private lessons to a number of prestigious clients, including industrialist Henry Clay Frick and New Jersey senator Joseph S. Frelinghuysen. Of course, Shippen's talents and achievements were limited by the relatively low status of "golf professionals" at the time. He proved that a black pro could be associated with such elite courses—teaching golf, perhaps even hobnobbing with the clientele—but he was by no means a member. White or black, club pros like him were considered part of the servant class who ran such facilities; many were not even allowed to enter the clubhouses at the courses where they worked. After Shippen moved to Washington, D.C., and spent several years away from the game, his subsequent career path exemplified the increasingly segregated world of American golf. He returned briefly to work for a black club, the National Capital Country Club (Laurel, Md.); then in 1931 he began a thirty-five-year tenure as club pro at New Jersey's Shady Rest Country Club, the nation's top all-black private course. Shippen was also likely the first African American player, professional or amateur, to hire a white caddie. Kenneth E. Davis, who caddied for him from 1903 to 1904, went on to manage the Maidstone Club for thirty years.[90]

The participation of black and Native American players in the country's first professional tournaments reverberated across the Atlantic and hinted that the game's growth in America had the potential to democratize golf more than ever before. "We have now playing golf native Indians, Chinese, Cingalese, Negroes, Turks, Hottentots, Siamese, Maoris, dwellers in the Mauritius, and natives from the banks of the Nile," proclaimed Scotland's *Golfer* magazine after news of Shippen's and Bunn's participation in the 1896 U.S. Open reached Europe. "So that in another ten years the Open Championship at St. Andrew's will probably present a thoroughly cosmopolitan aspect." In London, *Golf Illustrated* told readers that "the rage for Golf in America surpasses anything that has ever been seen in this country. . . . At first the votaries . . . were chiefly the wealthy and leisured, but the hard-working business man has now found out its charms and realised its rest and health-giving qualities."[91] Enthusiasts in the United States voiced even more optimism about the game's potential to overcome race and class distinctions. For some it was America, not England or Scotland, that promised to provide its citizens more access to golf. "All classes are taking up the game," Theodore Havemeyer told London's *Golf* magazine in 1897, the year after he rebuked European players for trying to exclude Shippen and Bunn from the U.S. Open.

Ultimately, however, African Americans provided the most inclusive vision of what American golf might become. The *Afro-American* told black readers that even English "paupers" had access to golf links; the implications for municipal courses in Baltimore, Chicago, and around the country were clear. Rather than a symbol of American exclusion, economic stratification, or racial discrimination—a symbol of white privilege—golf in the hands of black Americans promised to be something entirely different. The *Philadelphia Tribune* thus celebrated in 1916 when Clarence Taylor integrated the city's public course with a simple charge: "Real democracy is found on the links."[92] By 1920 it remained to be seen if such a promise would be fulfilled.

2

ONE HEARS OF NEGRO COUNTRY CLUBS
*Golfing the Great Migration
and Harlem Renaissance*

**JUNE 1936—AUGUSTA NATIONAL GOLF CLUB,
AUGUSTA, GEORGIA**

Bruised and bloodied, fifteen-year-old orphan Beau Jack tried to gather himself in the midst of a violent brawl. There were nine other black kids, all bigger than him and all trying to be the last standing. Beau reached within and told himself he wasn't going to go down. For a split second he remembered how his grandmother said that one day he'd either become a preacher or a fighter.

Looked like that day was here.

Sensing the crowd of gathered spectators, Beau listened for supporters. He thought he heard Mr. Jones say something but wasn't sure.

He wised up and drifted quietly to the outskirts of the carnage, while the other boys punched, kicked, and grappled themselves into fatigue. Then Beau pounced. He swung and hit everything near him with an anger and ferocity that stunned the onlookers, even those who saw this type of thing often.

And just like that it was over—or at least that's what he heard someone say. Then he heard the clink-clink of coins hitting the ground. That's when he really knew.

Beau took off his blindfold and picked up his money.

It was a scene that evoked the poverty, violence, and trauma many at the bottom of society faced in the Deep South during the Great Depression. But this was no gang fight on a hardscrabble roadside.

Beau Jack was on duty at the world's most famous golf club. And his boss, Bobby Jones, was the world's most famous golfer.[1]

"There has been a very noticeable increase in golf," reported the Associated Negro Press in its 1927 annual survey of black progress.[2] The brief line—buried in a lengthy, wide-ranging report outlining African American achievements in politics, business, education, and entertainment—was nevertheless important, for golf in America experienced a significant increase in popularity following World War I, the very moment the black community underwent dramatic change. The growth of public golf links and private country clubs in the North and South, as well as the game's expansion in the West, coincided with the initial wave of the Great Migration, in which nearly 2 million African Americans left the South. Both the game and the black community were on the move, and as golf continued to grow in American society, African Americans from all walks of life—from W. E. B. Du Bois and James Weldon Johnson to Miles Davis and James Brown—connected with it in unique ways. In doing so, a new generation helped shape golf's complicated relationship to the black community and American race relations.

After World War I the capital of black golf remained Chicago, the city that attracted the most southern migrants during and after the war. And just as they had earlier in the century, Chicago's black golfers not only continued to play the game but also wrote thoughtfully about its symbolism, introduced southern migrants to the links, and fought hard for greater access to the city's white courses. A group of dedicated writers maintained coverage of the game in the *Chicago Defender*, the city's popular black newspaper with a national circulation that included the South. Both Walter and Nettie Speedy continued writing regular golf columns, Nettie covering female golfers and Chicago's golf-related socials. At Marquette Park's course, black women outnumbered black men on certain days: with "at least a dozen or more foursomes . . . our ladies have gone in for golf in a big way."[3] E. L. Renip, dubbed the *Defender*'s "golf editor," also published a weekly column with lessons and tips for average players. Led by Renip, the publication also began to report regularly on the world of white professional golf, including PGA tournaments. Later in the 1930s sportswriters Eneil Simpson and Jimmie Williams provided the newspaper's weekly golf columns.

Golf in Chicago's growing black neighborhoods, and particularly access to the city's municipal courses, embodied northern opportunity, a higher standard of living, and the optimism of the Great Migration. Walter and Nettie Speedy enjoyed taking migrants and visitors to Jackson Park, where newly arrived southerners had their "first experience watching Race people play golf."[4] Men in the city's black barbershops shared golf anecdotes and playing tips alongside talk of the day's news and other sports. African American women frequenting public courses were particularly powerful images of opportunity, for both black southern migrants and northern white observers, as countless advertisements in white publications during the 1920s presented golf as the ideal leisure activity for the modern woman of means.[5] But Renip reminded readers that the game was not cost or time prohibitive and was well in reach for many black Chicagoans. "For many years the impression has obtained that golf is a rich man's game," he wrote in 1921. "True, practically every wealthy man is a golf devotee, at the same time a vast majority of those who play the game are people who work for moderate salaries."[6] That same year a poem included in William Harrison's book *Colored Girls and Boys Inspiring United States History* celebrated golf as a symbol of black optimism.

> While it is called rich people's game
>   Poor folks should learn it just the same;
> And tramp the meadows and the hill
>   To let fresh air their lungs to fill:
> But if too poor to hire a caddy
>   Then use instead your sweetheart's Daddy.[7]

Chicago featured the most visible black golfing scene during the Great Migration, but the game also grew rapidly in New York City's black neighborhoods, especially Harlem. The most important private black golf club during the 1920s and 1930s—Shady Rest Country Club in Scotch Plains, New Jersey—served Harlem's elite golfers, many of whom were contributors to the period's dynamic cultural movement: the Harlem Renaissance. Established in 1922 by an investment group led by Howard S. Brock, a Philadelphia doctor, Shady Rest was originally Westfield Golf Club, a white country club built in 1897. The purchase of the thirty-one-acre site about fifteen miles from Manhattan drew backlash from some local whites who feared a subsequent decline in property values and generally directed their scorn at Westfield's white members for agreeing to sell the land to African Americans. Yet Shady Rest surprised even the most optimistic investors: by the end of its first year the club had 200 members and a lengthy waiting list, with many members purchasing (or building) cottages near the course in order to spend extended time there during the summer.[8] While the club's popularity and economic success tempered white fears of plummeting land values, they failed to completely eliminate tension surrounding the site. In a passionate defense of Shady Rest, the *New York Tribune* denounced the racism directed at the club and argued that it had much more to do with the specter of black golf, not property values. "This course . . . will cause a million giggles to sizzle across the country. Cartoonists will make funny pictures of it. Vaudeville artists will do sketches about it," lamented the *Tribune*. "Something exquisitely funny seems to excite the white race when it sees the colored race doing things which are ordinary parts of the day's work and play to the white people. . . . Why should not the black man play golf if his economic status gives him leisure for golf?" Black newspapers from as far as Dallas, Texas, reprinted the *Tribune*'s fiery editorial.[9]

The success of Shady Rest was tied to both the economic growth of the region's black neighborhoods and the community's burgeoning spirit of optimism. Members came "from Harlem, the Bronx, Brooklyn, Jersey City, Newark, and countless other New Jersey and New York cities," read one description. "Prosperous Negro doctors, lawyers, merchants, Pullman porters and barbers flock there by automobile and trolley car on Saturdays and Sundays to play golf . . . and enjoy the luxurious ease of country club life."[10] Throughout the 1920s and 1930s the club advertised itself alongside popular Harlem entertainment venues, such as the Apollo Theater and Connie's Inn, as well as New York's Negro League baseball teams. It also advertised nationally in various black publications and solicited members from across the country. The club was popular with both men and women; Shady Rest's female golfers formed a Ladies Auxiliary, and by 1930 the club was hosting regular women's tournaments. Like most private clubs, its caddies were generally young black children, although Shady Rest did employ a few white caddies to carry bags for its black patrons.[11]

In addition to Shady Rest, other private, black-owned courses were established after World War I, including more clubs that sought to meet the demands of New York City's black golfers. In 1924 a Brooklyn manufacturer opened Manaqua Country Club in nearby Amityville, while two other New York–based groups purchased land in attempts to establish black clubs: the first was near West Hampton, Long Island, and another was in Bar Harbor, Maine (apparently both of these developments were never completed).[12] Three African American courses were located directly north of the city in the Hudson Valley; the most successful, Shangri-La Resort, was established when black investors purchased a 775-acre property in Napanoch after World War II. The group included Brooklyn real estate dealer Richard Simon and Harlem café owner Luther "Red" Randolph. At the height of its popularity in the 1950s and early 1960s, Shangri-La appeared regularly in both *Jet* and *Ebony*. The club's social director, Edward Perry, was a former actor who was a close friend (and likely lover) of Harlem Renaissance poet Countee Cullen and who led the USO's touring unit of *Porgy and Bess* during World War II.[13]

If Shangri-La was the most successful black country club in the Hudson Valley, one of the more unique in American history was located nearby: a private, nine-hole layout enjoyed by followers of spiritual leader Father Divine. That course was on a 177-acre commune near Kingston purchased by the group at the height of Divine's popularity and named "the Promised Land" in 1937. (Eventually Divine's organization also purchased the Brigantine Hotel and Golf Course in Atlantic City.)[14] That same year, white residents in Westchester County complained when a group of African Americans bought a course in New Castle, renamed it the Rising Sun Country Club, and announced plans to develop an adjacent 60-acre black resort. According to the *New York Amsterdam News* the move sparked a "furor of protest" from whites; when asked for a list of those who lodged complaints with the town's council, one councilman replied, "If you took the telephone book . . . you'd have the list of those who have objected to the proposal."[15] The bold plan, all the more notable in the midst of the Great Depression, even drew criticism from some African Americans. The previous white club had failed financially, and the economic downturn placed black golfers (and their perceived extravagance) under renewed scrutiny. "I don't doubt that the Rising Sun Golf Club out here in Westchester is a good thing for us to have," wrote one local black dentist. "But . . . I think that with $200,000 Negroes would do much better investing it in small loans and mortgages on property for Negroes: making money, and at the same time aiding some worthy colored people to acquire their homes. I believe that when enough of us have made fortunes large enough to afford that kind of expensive recreation, we ought to have it. Right now we ought to be spending our time and our money strengthening our economic position."[16] Rising Sun opened under black ownership but continued to struggle financially and failed to draw attention away from other black country clubs, including Shady Rest. In addition, the development's broader plans never came to fruition. At some point (it is unclear when) the only African American golf course in Westchester County's history quietly passed back into the hands of white owners. A more successful private venture was the Booker T. Washington Country Club in Buckingham, Pennsylvania, just north of Philadelphia: it was founded in 1924 by 100 black businessmen, most from Philadelphia, Trenton, and Princeton.[17]

Although black country clubs exemplified the opportunity for social and economic advancement in the North, some of the earliest black-owned clubs appeared in the South. Hundreds of black businessmen in Richmond, Virginia, built the region's first, Acorn Country Club, in 1924.[18] The two most important black-owned courses in the South, located in Atlanta, Georgia, and Jacksonville, Florida, were both named Lincoln Country Club. The Jacksonville club was the brainchild of Abraham Lincoln Lewis, Florida's first black millionaire, who in 1935 founded American Beach, a black resort town. Notably, Lewis first established Lincoln Country Club nearby in the 1920s. The course predated the broader development, so the success of his private black golf links likely encouraged him to establish the larger beach community. The Lincoln course hosted its first major tournament in 1928, which sought to crown Florida's best black golfer (the winner, eighteen-year-old high school student Ralph Dawkins, later served as the club's teaching professional in the 1940s). Inaugural tournaments for black women and southern black colleges came two years later, solidifying the club as the center of black golf in Florida, a southern state that would lead the nation in advancing the game. "Golf has become one of the favorite pastimes in Florida," noted the *Chicago Defender* in 1930. "So much so in fact that the citizens of Jacksonville have built one of the finest clubhouses in Dixie, which is equipped with tennis courts, croquet courses, trap shooting, rifle range, boating, and fishing."[19]

Atlanta's first black course was a nine-hole layout at the private Piney Wood Country Club, built sometime before 1928. It was soon supplanted in popularity by a new course established in 1930, eventually named the New Lincoln Country Club, built on land left vacant by the all-black Lincoln Cemetery. Although the Lincoln course was relatively meager, the private club also included a swimming pool, a dancing pavilion, tennis courts, and a clubhouse rebuilt twice after fires destroyed it.[20] In 1951 black journalist Carl Rowan described the neighborhood around Lincoln as the center of Atlanta's black middle class: "Fine homes and fine cars lined the streets. There were sidewalks, and houses painted in pastel colors, with gay green shutters, red-shingled roofs, and attached garages. Stone houses with arched façades had lawns and stone-lined driveways. All this belonged to Negroes. . . . Here were homes with carpets on the floor and running water in the kitchen and Scotch in the den. Here one could find three-speed phonographs and a tuxedo or two. Negroes had a separate country club and a nine-hole golf course all their own."[21] Lincoln became a key oasis for black golfers in the South's largest city, as Atlanta refused to open any municipal courses to African Americans even for segregated use. In the 1930s and 1940s Lincoln also hosted the Southern Open, the South's most important golf tournament for black professionals.

Most private African American golf facilities were owned and operated by relatively wealthy men; however, black women also financed private courses, including New Jersey's Apex Country Club. Established during World War II, Apex was founded by millionaire Sarah Spencer Washington, who made her fortune investing in black hair salons and manufacturing beauty products for black women. The club, later renamed Sandale Golf and Country Club, featured a racially integrated membership.[22]

While many black clubs struggled during the 1930s (Shady Rest, for example, was forced to close in 1938), some managed to survive the Great Depression, including Booker T. Washington in Pennsylvania, Acorn in Virginia, and Lincoln in Atlanta.[23] Following desegregation, by the late 1960s there were few fully private, segregated black clubs remaining in America. Meadowbrook Country Club, founded in 1958 near Raleigh, North Carolina, was a premier private club and important social hub for the local black community. It had nearly 200 members by the 1970s, yet soon it fell into disrepair, membership dropping dramatically after the city's white clubs desegregated. (St. Augustine's University, a nearby black college, purchased Meadowbrook in 2007 and reopened the course).[24]

Along with private and semiprivate courses there were also important black-owned public facilities that helped increase interest in the sport among African Americans. One was Freeway Golf Course in Sicklerville, New Jersey. Established by four African Americans in 1967, Freeway branded itself as catering uniquely to African Americans while it remained public and open to white golfers. In Chicago, African Americans continued to play most often at municipal courses, particularly Jackson Park, Marquette Park, and Palos Park inside the city, as well as nearby Sunset Hills Country Club (Kankakee, Ill.) and Casa Loma Country Club (Powers Lake, Wisc.).

Yet many years of whites and blacks playing alongside one another at Chicago's most popular courses did not necessarily make it easier for the establishment of a black-owned country club. In 1947 a predominately black Methodist church purchased 1,500 acres in Kankakee and established Kankakee Shores Country Club. Some local whites balked at the

Table 1. Significant African American–Owned Golf Courses, 1916–1967

Name	Location	Year of Inception
Idlewild Resort	Idlewild, Mich.	1916
Cheshire Country Club	Cheshire, Conn.	1917
Shady Rest Country Club	Scotch Plains, N.J.	1922
Acorn Country Club	Richmond, Va.	1924
Booker T. Washington Country Club	Buckingham, Pa.	1924
Manaqua Country Club	Amityville, N.Y.	1924
Val Verde Resort	Val Verde, Calif.	1924
National Capital Country Club	Laurel, Md.	1925
Mapledale Country Club	Stow, Mass.	1926
Tuskegee Institute Golf Course	Tuskegee, Ala.	1926
Parkridge Country Club	Corona, Calif.	1927
Groves Center Golf Course	Kansas City, Mo.	1928
Lincoln Country Club	Jacksonville, Fla.	1928
Piney Wood Country Club	Atlanta, Ga.	1928
New Lincoln Country Club	Atlanta, Ga.	1930
Rising Sun Country Club	New Castle, N.Y.	1937
Crescent City Golf Club	Harahan, La.	ca. 1940s
Apex Country Club	Galloway, N.J.	1943
Shalimar Country Club	Omaha, Neb.	1944
Wayside Country Club	Homer Glen, Ill.	1946
Cedar River Golf Club	Indian Lake, N.Y.	1947
Kankakee Shores Country Club	Kankakee, Ill.	1947
Clearview Golf Club	Canton, Ohio	1948
Silver Rest Golf Club	Glen Allen, Va.	ca. 1949
Lee Haven Beach Club	Greenwich, Conn.	1949
Shangri-La Resort	Napanoch, N.Y.	ca. 1954
Meadowbrook Country Club	Garner, N.C.	1958
Freeway Golf Course	Sicklerville, N.J.	1967

majority-black ownership despite the resort serving both white and black patrons. "Six of every eight golfers on weekdays are white people," wrote one black sportswriter, challenging the "disturbing element in Kankakee" that threatened to purchase the land for a segregated, white-only resort development: "If this place is sold and is split up or even run as a country club for whites only it will be a black eye to the Negro race." It is unclear how long the resort remained under black ownership, but it did host black tournaments in the late 1940s and a number of notable black players, including heavyweight boxing champion Joe Louis. Wayside Country Club, another black-owned course that served Chicagoland golfers, was established in 1946 in nearby Homer Glen.[25]

White criticism of black-owned courses was common nationwide; however, the most dramatic example of large-scale resistance to a black country club took place not in the Midwest or even the Deep South but, rather, in Corona, California. One of the country's best resorts, Parkridge Country Club, was opened in 1925 to an exclusively white membership. Perched on a hill with spectacular views, Parkridge boasted a large hotel and clubhouse, indoor spa, shooting range, and private airstrip. Its first member, silent-film star Clara Bow, was awarded her membership after winning a Hollywood dance contest; visitors also included actors Henry Fonda and Burt Lancaster. The golf course at Parkridge was among the best in southern California, yet within two years of its opening the club was struggling financially. In 1927 three black businessmen purchased the resort: one, Journee White, was awarded the Croix de Guerre for service in World War I and made his fortune in Los Angeles real estate. Another, Eugene C. Nelson, was a physician who had just married white actress Helen Lee Worthing.

News of the purchase came right as the Ku Klux Klan experienced the height of its popularity in California (three years earlier the organization had won control over the city council in nearby Anaheim), and the Klan organized an immediate, vitriolic response. Parkridge's white members also sued its white owner in order to stop the sale, attempting "to prevent the club from falling into the hands of the negroes" and leaving "a black spot on Corona's forward progress." The campaign culminated in a dramatic incident of racism directed at black golfers: a burning cross on the club's front lawn. The Klan's threat to wage "race war" against the 663-acre estate ("the best view property in southern California," boasted the *Chicago Defender*) eventually worked: in 1929 the black buyers were forced to withdraw their bid, and Parkridge Country Club soon became a sanitarium.[26]

On the opposite end of the spectrum, some black-owned or black-operated courses evolved over time from sympathetic white-owned courses that welcomed black golfers and specifically targeted the African American community. Such was the case in Boston, where wealthy merchant Charles M. Cox encouraged African Americans to visit his Mapledale Country Club, a 196-acre country estate located twenty-five miles

Parkridge Country Club in Corona, California, ca. 1927 (Used by Permission of the Board of Trustees of the Corona Public Library).

outside the city in Stow, Massachusetts. Cox hired a black man, Robert Hawkins, to operate Mapledale, which featured a large mansion, tennis and equestrian facilities, and a nine-hole golf course. Hawkins had considerable experience in golf management, rising up the caddie ranks at courses in Vermont and Massachusetts. In 1926 he purchased Mapledale, providing a highly visible site for black golf in the 1920s and 1930s. On weekends, white residents noticed caravans of black golfers making their way out from Boston. That same year Mapledale also hosted the first national tournament of the black United Golfers Association (UGA). Like Kankakee Shores and other black-owned facilities, Mapledale continued to be popular with white golfers. By the 1930s it hosted key African American outings and national tournaments even as most of its daily players were white.[27]

In addition to the dramatic growth of black-owned-and-operated golf facilities, golf—as a leisure activity with strong class and racial connotations—emerged in the debates associated with the Harlem Renaissance, a profound cultural movement in the 1920s and 1930s that questioned the fundamental concepts of black identity, art, and culture. The nation's preeminent black intellectual, W. E. B. Du Bois, recognized not only the significance of golf's emergence in black America but also the game's association with white colonialism in Africa and the Caribbean. After attending the 1923 Pan-African Congress in Europe, Du Bois traveled to

Africa for the first time and observed the proliferation of white country clubs. He bemoaned how whites in Sierra Leone contributed to residential and social segregation by carving out "beautiful English suburbs" with "tennis courts and golf links" that insulated them from Africans. "I am morally certain . . . that more is spent by the government on tennis and golf in the colony than on popular education," he wrote. And Du Bois was unaware of what likely would have incensed him even more: the first golf holes built in Africa were constructed in the eighteenth century by Scotsmen manning the British slave castle on Sierra Leone's Bunce Island, with African slaves in kilts serving them as caddies.[28]

Despite his cynicism about the game in Africa, Du Bois still affirmed the symbolism of black Americans taking up golf and moderately praised the proliferation of black golf clubs. Under his editorship the NAACP's *Crisis* magazine celebrated the 1925 opening of the all-black National Capital Country Club outside Washington, D.C.[29] Like nearly all of Harlem's black elite, Du Bois also applauded the establishment of Shady Rest in New Jersey and visited the club. Still, after receiving promotional literature urging him to join in 1923, his response was lukewarm. "In all this development . . . Negroes are evincing tremendous energy and *esprit de corps*," he wrote. "Pictures of new organizations and buildings appear in their pictorials, groups of officers and employees, figures of income. White people, too, express, on seeing and hearing of such enterprises, great gratification, and, upon the slightest pretext, make glowing speeches to prove that this is the way to the millennium." Yet a black country club, no matter how successful or swanky, still represented the advancement of racial segregation.

> In truth, the development is not nearly as satisfactory and inspiring as such persons say or think. It is not a direct advance, it is a great flanking movement . . . the attempt of the Negro to develop as an American citizen, and the attempt, on the part of his white fellow-citizens, to stem that development and hold it within definite and unyielding limits of low wage and semi-peonage; the consequent escape of the ambitious and talented and venturesome, together with a large and larger following of the black masses into a segregated economy. The segregation is developing, and its future development is going to be tremendous.[30]

Over time Du Bois grew increasingly pessimistic whenever he invoked golf, even as he drew closer to country club life, which for him came to represent little more than elite, conspicuous consumption for whites and a false sense of security for blacks. He nevertheless signed up for membership at Atlanta's New Lincoln Country Club soon after he returned to the South in 1933.[31] There is no evidence the game appealed to him, but Du Bois undoubtedly interacted with many players, as Lincoln's golf scene was one of the largest in the South. The fact that he did not take up golf (or address it more often) was telling, considering his long-standing call for African Americans to participate in more sports and recreational activities. In his 1897 essay "The Problem of Amusement," Du Bois argued that "especial attention" be paid to sports in black schools: "Here again athletic sports must in the future play a larger part in the normal and mission schools of the South, and we must rapidly come to the place where the man all brain and no muscle is looked upon as almost as big a fool as the man all muscle and no brain; and when the young woman who cannot walk a couple of good country miles will have few proposals of marriage."[32] However, as Du Bois grew more militant, he saw little value in golf as a recreational or athletic endeavor: its association with middle-class, white elitism was simply too strong. By the 1940s, as black colleges led their white counterparts in establishing intercollegiate golf teams, Du Bois deemed it a frivolous use of alumni donations: "We pay on the nail for . . . golf clubs, but for a college training? I do not know."[33]

In New York City, other leading artists, authors, and intellectuals associated with the Harlem Renaissance noted that golf marked one's status in elite social circles, both white and black. The movement's definitive text, Alain Locke's 1925 anthology *The New Negro*, featured an essay by educator Elise McDougald exploring class divisions among urban black women. In particular, McDougald noted how golf and clubs like Shady Rest offered Harlem's elite women social standing with whites while isolating them from the city's other black women. "Negro wives find Negro maids unwilling generally to work in their own neighborhoods, for various reasons," she wrote. "It is in these homes of comparative ease that we find the polite activities of social exclusiveness. The luxuries of well-appointed homes, modest motors, tennis, golf and country clubs, trips to Europe and California, make for social standing. The problem confronting the refined Negro family is to know others of the same achievement."[34]

As in Chicago, migrants to New York from the South or Midwest, including key contributors to the Harlem Renaissance, encountered golf when they sought to enter the world of Manhattan refinement. Zora

Neale Hurston came to New York City in 1925 to enroll at Barnard College, where she struggled to set aside money for books, academic fees, and other Barnard necessities like a "spring golf outfit."[35] Florida transplant James Weldon Johnson did not play until after he moved to New York. "To get outdoor exercise I took up golf," he wrote in 1933. "For four or five years I was a votary of the game—though remaining a dub." Johnson played regularly during the late 1920s while leading the NAACP and providing a key voice for the Harlem Renaissance. In his memoir he recalled being "on the links of a club over in New Jersey" (likely Shady Rest) in September 1925 when a colleague ran out with news that Detroit police had arrested physician Ossian Sweat for murdering a white man while defending his house from a mob. Johnson rushed to the clubhouse, where he counseled Detroit's NAACP officers via telephone on how to respond to the incident.[36]

Golf was both a backdrop to important events during the period and a subject of debates over racial segregation inspired by the Harlem Renaissance. The movement's most prominent black critic, George Schuyler, rejected the notion of "Negro Art" and debated its proponents in the press. In 1936 he criticized African Americans in the South for their lack of physical fitness. "There ought to be sport clubs, thousands of golf clubs with courts and courses owned, operated, and maintained by colored people in the South, and in the North too, for that matter," wrote Schuyler. To his critics such comments were entirely tone deaf and represented a deep misunderstanding of black life in the South. One of James Weldon Johnson's top literature students, Nashville poet Herman J. D. Carter, responded vehemently in the *Pittsburgh Courier*. "I am disgusted with that man Schuyler," wrote Carter. "I think he should have first attacked those whites who employ the Negroes at such long hours and such low pay, that they don't have time to play golf and tennis, rather than attack the people who couldn't help themselves."[37]

White journalists and intellectuals also commented on the rise of black golf, some echoing Du Bois's cynicism. In a 1929 column popular journalist H. L. Mencken warned that black golf did not represent advancement and opportunity, nor did it offer any solution to the "old divisions" between the ideologies of Du Bois and Booker T. Washington. Instead it typified an increasingly disjointed black community, with out-of-touch black elites who led lives "of easy contentment, of antinomian opportunism, of well-fed complacency, of black Babbitry." Amidst the celebration of black identity and optimism fueled by the Harlem Renaissance, two very different public figures—one a leading champion of black civil rights (Du Bois), the other a white provocateur and racial elitist (Mencken)—nevertheless shared similar concerns over black golfers. "One hears of Negro luncheon clubs, Negro country clubs, Negro golf matches . . . and all the rest of it," Mencken wrote. "A naïve and imbecile class consciousness, grounded upon money, wipes out the old race consciousness, which becomes furtive and discreditable."[38]

This debate over the merits of golf played out within black organizations nationwide. Some black fraternal groups supported the game, including the largest: the Improved Benevolent and Protective Order of Elks of the World (the Black Elks). In Pittsburgh, Black Elks hosted regular golf tournaments at the public South Park Golf Course, while in 1940 the Elks' national convention in St. Louis featured a golf tournament at Forest Park. Golf within the organization was particularly significant because, as historians note, the fraternal order attracted not only "elite professionals" but also "masses of working-class men."[39] Meanwhile, some within the NAACP, such as Ella Baker, echoed the cynicism of Du Bois or Mencken toward the game, while others, like James Weldon Johnson, played regularly and considered golfing part of their civil rights activism. State legislator T. Gillis Nutter, president of the West Virginia NAACP, built a regulation course outside Charleston on which he proudly hosted prominent organization members from around the country.[40] Roy Wilkins, who in 1955 would take command of the NAACP during the critical postwar period, fought to desegregate municipal courses as a young college graduate living in Kansas City in the early 1920s. After he graduated from the University of Minnesota, Wilkins took his first job with the *Kansas City Call* and later remembered how golf exemplified the different reception African Americans received in Kansas City versus Chicago: "In Kansas City, Negroes were not permitted to use the four municipal courses," he wrote. "Because, the head of the park board announced, 'Negroes don't like to play golf'—and that was that." Meanwhile, a young black man who moved North "was still a Negro, but he could fly higher and in wider circles than I could in Kansas City. . . . If he wanted to play golf, he didn't have to go to court to prove he was a citizen and entitled to play on municipal links maintained with the taxes of black people."[41] Denied access, Wilkins and other African Americans in Kansas City still found a unique opportunity to play. In 1928 the wealthy family of Junius Groves, a former slave dubbed the "potato king" after he made millions growing potatoes on his farm outside Kansas City, built a course on the estate and invited blacks from the city. The course at "Groves Center" proved so popular that the family was overwhelmed with visitors and began investing in upgrades. For over a decade Groves Center was the only place where Wilkins and other blacks in Kansas City "went to do our hacking and slicing." By 1940 the Fair Employment Practices Committee reported that African Americans had been granted limited access to municipal golf in Kansas City with "discriminatory privileges," meaning only one of the city's courses was reserved for segregated black use.[42]

Unlike Johnson and Wilkins, others in the NAACP abhorred golf and the elitism of members who played. Once she began working for the organization in 1940, Ella Baker struggled to connect with local branch leaders who frequented country clubs, rejecting what she considered snobbish behavior—especially in the Jim Crow South, where to her nothing signaled barriers to more militant, mass action than blacks who embraced country club society. "I am stopping at the home of three women of leisure whose major past time [sic] is idle chatter . . . [and] who were too busy to attend the meeting last night," she wrote from Georgia in 1942 to Lucille Black, the NAACP's national membership secretary. Baker was again frustrated while organizing in Florida, where she reported how one campaign chairman "is experiencing a slight let down in that I am not a social elite, and cannot join her in a game of bridge or golf at the 'Country Club.'"[43]

Baker was introduced to the game while traveling widely in the South and working with relatively elite NAACP members, whereas many civil rights leaders encountered golf as they migrated to black neighborhoods in the Midwest and Northeast. Still others, however, first experienced golf in poorer, more rural southern locales. In 1927 eight-year-old James Farmer worked briefly as a caddie in Marshall, Texas. Although his family was well off, the childhood experience helped introduce him to racism and relations between poor whites and blacks in East Texas. The future head of the Congress of Racial Equality (CORE), Farmer witnessed racial tension between white and black caddies and was introduced for the first time to Marshall's working-class white children. "There were about equal numbers of white and black boys," he recalled. "There had to be more to the enigmatic white world than the caddy yard. Those ragtag boys didn't live in the fancy houses I'd seen." Farmer's father (a professor at Wiley College) soon forbade his son from working at the course after a racially charged fight broke out between the children.[44]

Black political, social, and cultural leaders thus had dramatically different experiences with golf during the interwar period, and they found no consensus on the game's usefulness or meaning to the black community. But the growing popularity of golf in black urban neighborhoods sent a far clearer message: black golf, like few other leisure activities, embodied the optimism and opportunity of the Great Migration and the Jazz Age. The comparison with jazz was more than conjecture, for golf even contributed directly to the developing jazz scene in northern black neighborhoods. Dashy's Inn Golf Club was a popular early jazz spot in the Bronx, located near Van Cortlandt Park, the municipal course popular with African Americans. New Orleans blues singer Lizzie Miles performed regularly at the club, where she made her New York debut in 1922. One of Baltimore's most celebrated jazz venues was the Coney Island Golf Links and Dancing Pavilion, where patrons could play the city's first miniature course while listening to leading jazz men like Fess Williams and Ike Dixon: "Colored people flock there," wrote one observer in 1930.[45]

Of course, many entertainers also lent their fame to black courses, and some regularly played golf themselves. Pioneering bandleaders Cab Calloway, Duke Ellington, Chick Webb, and Count Basie all performed at New Jersey's Shady Rest, as did singers Sarah Vaughan and Ella Fitzgerald. Calloway and singer Billy Eckstine were also noted as regular players at the predominately black Langston Golf Course in Washington, D.C., after it opened in 1939.[46] After moving to Chicago from Louisiana in 1918, clarinetist Jimmie Noone took up golf and played regularly while headlining at the South Side's Apex Club. And the most influential musician to emerge from St. Louis, Miles Davis, grew up caddying for his father on the city's Forest Park course in the 1930s. Percussionists seemed especially drawn to the game: one of Chicago's popular bandleaders, drummer Floyd Campbell, frequented amateur tournaments, as did Nat King Cole's drummer Lee Young (Cole himself also participated in celebrity tournaments during the 1950s). Legendary trumpeter Louis Armstrong showed little interest in golf, but members of his orchestra were hooked, particularly drummer Fred "Tubby" Hall, who found opportunities to play while touring with Armstrong and competed in amateur tournaments around the country. Female musicians also took up golf, including members of the racially integrated, all-women International Sweethearts of Rhythm. Originally from Piney Woods, Mississippi, the big band toured nationally in the 1940s (including New York's Apollo Theater and Chicago's Regal Theater) and posed for golf-themed promotional photos.[47]

Northern entertainers also played while on tour in the Deep South, both at black private courses and as guests at white clubs. Bandleader Jimmie Lunceford brought members of his orchestra to Atlanta's New Lincoln Country Club between gigs, while Billy Eckstine once performed all night in Charleston, South Carolina, then went straight to the links and finished a round by 7:00 A.M.: "That boy has gone stark, raving crazy about golf," wrote journalist James Hicks. Eckstine is most notable for hiring a twenty-four-year-old Charlie Sifford to be his personal valet and golf instructor in 1946. Golf even showed up in the music itself: pianist and comedian Billy Mitchell's 1936 tune "A Hole in One" features a man who challenges anyone (including Bobby Jones) to a match and tries to seduce a woman with his golf prowess. She rebuffs him, and the two banter back and forth with plenty of sexual double entendre:

> M: Golf course momma, your golf course papa is gonna play on your private course today. . . .
> W: I got several reasons for not playing with you at all. Reason number one, your putter is too small. . . .
> M: My driving shaft is made out of good old flexible timber. . . .
> W: I don't like to play with you because you lose too many strokes. . . .
> M: Well I do lose my temper, at times I have recalled, but I've played with you for several years and I have never lost a ball.
> W: You played with a girlfriend of mine, and this girl claimed you're growing old, and it's likely taken you half a day just to play one hole.
> M: Well I don't see how she could tell you that, because I can truthfully say, that I could have made a hole in one but the flag was in the way.

Recorded in Chicago, the song was a minor party hit.[48]

Even in urban settings, African Americans found opportunities to play regulation golf courses, either at facilities located in their neighborhoods (such as in Chicago) or with day trips to nearby courses inside and outside the city (such as in New York City or Philadelphia). Organizations that served these neighborhoods also provided lessons and outlets to the game; in 1940 Harlem's YMCA branch established a club for young black golfers. Barred from a city course on Staten Island and a semiprivate course in Englewood, New Jersey, the club fought back legally while successfully locating other facilities that were willing to allow black youth on the links.[49] The game also reached the inner city with help from a quirky, little-known phenomenon in American history: a boom in the popularity of miniature golf courses that swept the country in the late 1920s. In North Carolina, Pinehurst Resort's "Thistle Dhu" was the nation's first "mini" golf course, installed in 1919. John Garnet Carter, a white inventor and businessman from Tennessee, took the idea further in 1927 when he patented a "mini golf" game (which he dubbed "Tom Thumb Golf") and installed a course at a hotel he owned on Lookout Mountain. Soon after, a large number of mini-golf courses were built around the nation; a long-forgotten fad (many courses did not survive the Great Depression) but an important one nonetheless, they helped make golf more accessible to black urban neighborhoods during the Jazz Age. Thousands of new "midget golf" facilities had appeared by 1930 when golf club manufacturers announced that sales of putters in America rose by 40 percent in just one year. Moreover, many of these facilities were quite opulent and offered a much more dynamic experience than the standard mini-golf fare that reemerged after World War II. One course in Queens, New York, featured a live caged bear cub that tried to stop patron's golf balls. Another, Whispering Pines Miniature Golf Course in Rochester, New York, was impressive enough that today it is listed in the National Register of Historic Places.[50]

New York City alone had 150 miniature golf courses by 1930, including many in Harlem. One popular black course was built upstairs at the decrepit and ill-used Harlem Opera House, often called the "Old Apollo" theater, four years before the refurbished Apollo opened half a block away. Featuring "winter golf indoors" with "tricky traps and harassing hazards," it was built in the same facility where Joe Louis later put on boxing exhibitions for throngs of fans. The "Savoy Golf Club" was another miniature course built alongside an iconic Jazz Age ballroom. Opened in the Savoy building on Lennox Avenue in 1930, the course dubbed itself the "finest in Harlem." Although it never featured an actual miniature course, Harlem's Golden Gate Ballroom hosted social gatherings and galas put on by the city's various black golfing organizations.[51]

Beyond Harlem, nearly every black enclave in the North experienced the miniature golf fad. African Americans in Philadelphia frequented several locations, including the B.T.W. course (47th Street and Aspen Street), the Cherry Inn Golf Course (55th Street and Cherry Street), and Alabama Golf Club (in the basement of the Olympia Theater). In the 1930s there was even an outdoor course at Mill Creek Park, a site in the heart of Philadelphia's "Black Bottom" neighborhood that gave way to a public housing complex in the 1950s.[52] Pittsburgh boasted three mini-golf courses cater-

Winter GOLF INDOORS

NOW you can play miniature golf all winter long and keep your form good. Full 18 holes with tricky traps and harassing hazards. Well heated, well ventilated.

9 A. M. to 6 P. M., 15c
6 P. M. to Closing, 25c

APOLLO

211 West 125th St.
Upstairs, in Old Apollo Theatre

SHADY REST GOLF CLUB

GOLF, TENNIS, CROQUET, DINING AND DANCING

For Reservations
Phone Westfield 3043
Paved Highways to the Door

Advertisements for mini-golf in Harlem and Shady Rest Country Club, 1930 (*New York Amsterdam News*, November 19, 1930).

ing to black patrons: Egyptian Golf Gardens (next to the Burke Theater), Lincoln Links (on Penn Avenue in the East End neighborhood), and the Dixie Land Golf Course (in nearby Monessen, Pa.). The course names, and the fact that all three advertised heavily in the black community, make it likely they were owned and operated by African Americans. By 1931 the *Pittsburgh Courier* was celebrating "the craze which has swept the city" and calling for black businessmen to open even more facilities: "25,000 of these miniature golf courses have sprung up. . . . Negroes themselves should take advantage of this opportunity . . . before shrewd whites step in."[53] However, just as important jazz venues and black gathering spots were often owned and operated by whites, so too were many of these urban golf facilities. "Why is it that Baltimore Negroes always wait for some white individual or corporation to enter an open field of business among negroes?" complained one *Afro-American* reader about the success of Baltimore's Coney Island Golf Links. "It remained for white people to open the first infant golf course here. Colored people . . . never seem to realize that their money is forever going into the hands of another race, who use the same money to make boots to kick you with."[54]

Nevertheless, because serious golfers frequented these miniature courses seeking lessons from top-notch instructors, the mini-golf boom helped African Americans succeed as professionals in the industry, even at white-owned facilities. Michigan native Jimmie DeVoe taught at a Cleveland miniature course in the late 1920s and early 1930s. Later in the decade he partnered with Shady Rest's John Shippen, and the two organized numerous black golf tournaments. By 1936 DeVoe was spending significant time in Harlem, where he ran his own golf school and shop, operating first out of a local pharmacy before moving into the L. M. Blumstein department store on West 125th Street. He also frequented Los Angeles to offer instruction for a wide range of black athletes, entertainers, and politicians. His golf students included the Mills Brothers, Nat King Cole, Althea Gibson, Jackie Robinson, and future Los Angeles mayor Tom Bradley. DeVoe went on to become the first African American to gain PGA membership in twenty-seven years after the organization desegregated in 1961.[55]

Another black instructor, Dorsey Adams, worked at a unique New York City miniature facility. When promoter Tex Rickard opened the new Madison Square Garden in 1925, the venue included a rooftop minicourse. According to the *Chicago Defender*, two years later Rickard recruited the twenty-five-year-old Adams, a former caddie from Florida, to offer golf lessons on the Garden's roof "teaching the big town folks."[56] Chicago's most talented black professional, Robert "Pat" Ball, also spent time running a mini-golf operation on Wabash Avenue, and two of the city's top black female players—Marie (Jones) Thompson and Geneva Wilson—honed their skills at miniature facilities. Thompson encouraged novices to take up mini-golf because it was cheaper and fun, but she also described its popularity with Chicago's serious players: "One may drop around the peewee course almost any night and there they will find the sharpshooters and near sharpshooters making matches for the next day or week."[57]

African Americans also took up mini-golf in the South, from lavish facilities to more rudimentary courses. Baltimore patrons combined jazz and mini-golf at the Coney Island Golf Links, while in Washington, D.C., the Prince Hall Masonic Lodge built a popular course that stayed open until 2:00 A.M. In addition, a course constructed in D.C.'s East Potomac Park in 1930 was the nation's first public mini-golf links open to black players.[58] The fad also made it easier for individuals to build impromptu courses on their own, carved out of city byways, neighborhood alleys, and abandoned properties. A 1941 Works Progress Administration (WPA) description of the poorest black neighborhood in Little Rock, Arkansas, noted how "neighborhood clubs" supplemented the public school's meager extracurricular offerings with activities such as sandlot baseball games and "persons play[ing] golf with odds and ends of equipment on a crude miniature course on Johnson street."[59] African Americans in Atlanta had no access to that city's municipal links, yet a makeshift, three-hole course still showed up in one of its roughest neighborhoods during the Great Depression. It was not for the faint of heart, either: one player was stabbed to death over a ten-cent bet in 1936, and in 1953 a teen was stabbed ten times during a "tiff over golf balls."[60]

Black secondary schools and colleges also helped popularize mini-golf in the South. Alabama's Tuskegee Institute opened its miniature course in 1930, four years after it became the first black college to build a regulation nine-hole track, and in 1931 Little Rock's Shorter College became the first school in Arkansas (black or white) to construct a mini-course on its campus.[61] Nationally recognized educator Charlotte Hawkins Brown brought mini-golf to her Palmer Memorial Institute in North Carolina; the course was "beautifully located on a wooded part of the campus."[62]

America's infatuation with mini-golf had faded dramatically by the late 1930s; most early courses did not survive past World War II. In Chicago's black neighborhoods the novelty began to wear thin even sooner. "Last year about this time the country was overcrowded with pee wee courses of all descriptions," reported the *Defender* in 1931. "And this season they are forgotten about."[63] Still, the fad's influence on African American golf was tremendous, for mini-golf helped bring the game directly to urban neighborhoods at a crucial, formative time during the Great Migration. It would also return following the war, and eventually courses would again be within reach of America's inner-city neighborhoods. Yet the most interesting black mini-golf course constructed after World War II, and perhaps the most race-conscious of them all, was built not in Philadelphia's Black Bottom neighborhood or inside the Harlem

Opera House but, rather, at a castle deep in the countryside of southern France. There in 1955 Josephine Baker, the iconic entertainer of the Harlem Renaissance, constructed a miniature course at her Château des Milandes castle for her "rainbow tribe" of multiracial adopted children.[64]

As a cheaper option for golfers unable to afford standard courses outside the city, mini-golf reached a different group of black players: dilettantes and working-class patrons who were less likely to encounter full-scale golf. "Millions wanted to play golf but were too poor to belong to golf clubs or to trudge out to them," remarked the *Pittsburgh Courier* about the fad in 1930. "The golf craze had reached the masses of people and they craved to be satisfied. What's more simple than to bring the golf course to them instead of trying to bring them to the golf course?"[65] By the 1950s black neighborhoods in many cities were served by golf shops offering instruction, equipment, and occasionally miniature courses—including Tyler's Golf Shop (Los Angeles), Northrop's Sport Shop (Norfolk, Va.), and Ray Mitchell's Golf School and Sport Shop (Harlem).[66] It thus appears that the golf-related advertisements and images that flooded popular publications in the 1920s were not as aspirational or out-of-touch as once thought. "Advertising men, it seems, didn't notice (or didn't care) that their mania for playing golf, talking about it, and picturing it in their ads was not shared by the majority of Americans at the time," wrote Roland Marchand in his landmark study of American advertising.[67] The popularity of urban golf facilities in black neighborhoods, the growth of high-profile black country clubs, and the constant discussion of the game in the black press all suggest otherwise.

Miniature courses also made golf a quick and attractive date night for young, working-class black couples. Many facilities, including the Apollo course in Harlem, featured weekly "ladies nights" and promotions for youth and students, regularly advertising themselves in black newspapers alongside country clubs like Shady Rest. Charlotte Hawkins Brown specifically cited golf as a quality, wholesome dating activity for young black men and women, perhaps one reason why she installed a course at Palmer Institute.[68] The advertisements and encouragement seemed to work, as young people overwhelmingly fueled the popularity of mini-golf in both black and white neighborhoods. Black personal ads in Baltimore, Philadelphia, and Cleveland routinely mentioned golf as a favorite pastime or potential dating activity.[69]

Black-owned public courses, private country clubs, and miniature facilities helped increase the game's visibility in black neighborhoods and challenged the stereotype that golf was the domain of rich, white men. In addition, civil rights activists and black organizations continued to fight for the desegregation of municipal courses in cities around the country. One important confrontation took place in Washington, D.C., where the black community led a highly visible campaign to integrate golf courses in the nation's capital. Segregation on D.C.'s public links was complicated by the fact that some courses were operated by the local parks department, while others were built and maintained by the federal government. In 1914 a small, three-hole practice course opened in West Potomac Park; it was enlarged to nine holes in 1921. Two additional nine-hole layouts opened in East Potomac Park, the first in 1920 and the second in 1924. Players showed immediate interest; park superintendent Lt. Col. Clarence O. Sherrill, a North Carolina native, reported 155,000 annual rounds between the three courses, and that included strong demand in the black community.[70] In 1920 Sherrill provided African Americans limited, segregated access to East Potomac on Monday afternoons and West Potomac on Wednesday afternoons (when there was less white demand). Nevertheless, white golfers quickly balked at having to give way to blacks at any time in Potomac Park, and two groups of black golfers—the Citizens' Golf Club (later Royal Golf Club), formed in 1922, and the Riverside Golf Club, formed in 1924—pressed Sherrill and the parks department to provide a stand-alone course exclusively for African Americans. The groups succeeded in 1924 when the city constructed Lincoln Memorial Golf Course, a nine-hole "colored" course directly northwest of the new memorial, which itself opened two years earlier in 1922. Subsequent accounts have placed this course southeast of the memorial (in today's West Potomac Park) or east of it (north of the memorial's reflecting pool, currently Constitution Gardens). But in 1927 Howard University sociologist William Henry Jones described the course as "bordered on one side by the monument grounds, on another by the Potomac River and on still a third by the Naval Hospital [23rd and E Streets, NW]."[71] The *Washington Post* also described the location as "between Lincoln memorial and the Naval hospital, west of Twenty-seventh street," which would place it northwest of the memorial, where today Interstate 66 and the John F. Kennedy Center for the Performing Arts are located.[72]

The opening of the Lincoln Memorial Golf Course codified segregation, as African Americans were no longer allowed to use any of the other Potomac Park courses. But the black press still celebrated it as a major accomplishment, in part because the new black course was as good as or

Top, the Citizens' Golf Club at Lincoln Memorial Golf Course in 1924. The memorial is visible in the background (William Henry Jones, *Recreation and Amusement among Negroes in Washington, D.C.* [Washington, D.C.: Howard University Press, 1927]). *Bottom*, East Potomac Park, ca. 1935 (Miscellaneous Items, Prints & Photographs Division, Library of Congress, LC-USZ62-135450).

better than any of D.C.'s white links. Moreover, the significance of an all-black golf course directly adjacent to the memorial was undeniable. "The grounds are in good order and comprise one of the most beautiful spots in Washington," Jones wrote. "The course has its situation in an attractive and unique environment." Noting that the course logged "more than one thousand rounds" in its first three months alone, he even reported that the white starter had to turn away disappointed white golfers who sought to access what they felt was a superior black course.[73]

The clubs that successfully lobbied the city included some of Washington's most successful African Americans. They were led, however, by a young author who had just moved to the capital. Victor Daly was a World

War I veteran who spent time in Harlem after the war (he lived in an apartment adjoining James Weldon Johnson's) and graduated from Cornell University in 1919. By 1924 he had moved to D.C. and was at work writing *Not Only War*, which would become the only World War I novel written by a black veteran. Daly's enthusiasm for golf was matched only by his love of bridge: he was a founding member of the all-black American Bridge Association, which formed in 1932 after the American Contract Bridge League barred African American players. Yet the young Daly was a rather unlikely individual to be founding president of Washington's Riverside Golf Club and leading spokesmen for black golfers in the nation's capital, a group that included the highest-level African Americans in the federal government and some of the wealthiest black people in the country.[74]

Even as they fought for the construction of Lincoln Memorial Golf Course, the golfers also sought to organize an elite private course outside the capital. In 1925 they succeeded with the founding of the National Capital Country Club, a twenty-three-acre parcel in Laurel, Maryland. A group of black investors constructed a nine-hole course, six tennis courts, and an impressive clubhouse at the site. In addition to Victor Daly and other advocates for African American golfers in Washington, National Capital's membership was perhaps the most elite in the history of black country clubs. Its first president was Texas native Emmett J. Scott, the highest-ranking African American in Woodrow Wilson's administration. Scott was chief aid to Booker T. Washington before moving to the capital in 1917 to serve as special advisor of black affairs to the secretary of war. Another club leader was Harry McCard, a cofounder of the all-black American Tennis Association, which had formed in Washington nine years earlier. And the group also included James Cobb, whom President Calvin Coolidge had just appointed as the only African American judge on the District of Columbia Municipal Court. As Jones wrote, National Capital's members were "drawn from the most prominent people in the city."[75]

The successful battle for access to Potomac Park only emboldened Washington's black golfers, many of whom immediately called on the federal government (which operated most of the city's links) to desegregate the courses completely or construct a regulation, eighteen-hole course for African Americans. Government officials grew more open to the idea of satisfying Washington's black golfers by constructing a black course farther from the National Mall. Led by black architect John Lang-

The National Capital Country Club in Laurel, Maryland, ca. 1925 (William Henry Jones, *Recreation and Amusement among Negroes in Washington, D.C.* [Washington, D.C.: Howard University Press, 1927]).

ford, the black community in 1927 began lobbying for a course at the new Anacostia Park. In 1934 the government acquiesced to the idea, and two years later construction began on the west side of the Anacostia River; the bulk of the first nine holes were constructed by the Civilian Conservation Corps (CCC) and the WPA. Opened in 1939, Langston Golf Course was named in honor of John Mercer Langston, founding dean of the Howard University School of Law and Virginia's first African American congressman. Two years later the U.S. Army supplied golf clubs to black soldiers at the adjacent Anacostia Recreation Camp for Negro Soldiers so the men could play at Langston.[76]

Open to both white and black golfers, Langston became one of the most important black golf courses in America, with many African American politicians, celebrities, and leading social figures visiting the course and its clubhouse. As in Chicago, the fight for desegregated public links in Washington also highlighted the interest many black women had in the game. The all-female Wake Robin Golf Club, formed in 1936, was a leading proponent of the Langston project; the group also petitioned Secretary of the Interior Harold Ickes in 1938 for greater access to Potomac Park, as its courses were then managed by the Interior Department's National Park Service (NPS). Langston also became a key stop for African American professional players and the site of several important national black golf tournaments. In 1991 its first nine holes were added to the National Register of Historic Places.

From access to segregated links at Potomac Park in 1920 to the establishment of Langston Golf Course in 1939, black golfers continued to fight for full and equal access to all of Washington's courses. The women of the Wake Robin Golf Club were particularly emboldened after their petition to Ickes helped bring segregated access and the Langston project to fruition. One of the club's leaders, Paris Toomer, was married to Edgar George Brown, the founder of the National Negro Council and a member of President Franklin Roosevelt's "Black Cabinet." Brown served as an administrator with the CCC, where he compiled reports on African Americans in the agency's work camps and advocated against discrimination on their behalf. Brown is well known to historians for confronting CCC leaders on segregation, but his most dramatic, public confrontation actually took place on a golf course in 1941. Joining his wife in protesting discrimination at East Potomac Park, Brown surreptitiously arranged tee times for three black players: Asa Williams (the president of the Royal Golf Club), Cecil Shamwell (a professional golfer), and George Williams (a local schoolteacher). On a hot and humid Sunday in June, Brown and the group attempted to play the course. Paris Brown and two other women from the Wake Robin Golf Club also joined the protest and walked alongside the golfers, as did six officers from the NPS's U.S. Park Police department, which feared the protest could incite violence. According to the *Chicago Defender*, "The men played without interruption until they came to the tenth hole, near the swimming pool. Jeers from the spectators did not stop the game, however."[77] Followed by one of the more unorthodox galleries in American history, including police, reporters, antagonistic whites, and black supporters, the three not only finished their round but managed excellent scores, considering the circumstances (George Williams, the teacher, shot 76). The spectacle marked the first instance of a direct-action protest in the world of golf, the kind of demonstration that would typify the postwar civil rights movement.

From Chicago to Atlanta, Edgar Brown's brazen display made headlines in the black press and drew a response from his top boss, Harold Ickes. It came soon after Ickes had arranged the NPS's most significant contribution to the black civil rights movement: singer Marian Anderson's concert in 1939 before 75,000 white and black listeners at the Lincoln Memorial. Now, two years later, Ickes once again was pressed to address segregation in the heart of the nation's capital. Yet this time the discrimination was not occurring at the privately owned Constitution Hall; it was even more blatant, as Brown and the golfers were challenging racism on the NPS's own golf course, within sight of the very memorial where the Roosevelt administration had registered its strongest opposition to segregation in D.C. Not surprisingly, Ickes reacted fast, indicating that the Interior Department would seek to desegregate all of Washington's park facilities under its jurisdiction, including the East Potomac Park Golf Course. "I can see no reason why Negroes should not be permitted to play on the golf course," he wrote. "They are taxpayers, they are citizens, and they have the right to play on public courses on the same basis as whites. To be sure, we have maintained a golf course for Negroes in Washington, but the cold fact is that we haven't kept it up and it is not surprising that Negroes do not care to play on it."[78]

It was a moment long since overshadowed by the administration's support for Anderson in 1939, as well as A. Philip Randolph's threatened March on Washington in 1941, both of which became defining moments in the history of the civil rights movement in D.C. But for some African Americans at the time, Ickes's call to desegregate Washington's parks in the face of local white resistance, and with it his tacit approval of Brown's direct, brazen protest, was a more dramatic victory. "Too much praise cannot be accorded Secretary Ickes for his laudable order . . . [to] serve all Americans who apply for play on the golf, tennis and other recreation fields of the capital of the nation," wrote one *Afro-American* reader. "This is one of the strongest anti-Hitler strikes of this administration."[79]

Moreover, while the 1939 Anderson concert was a one-time moment when the NPS staged an integrated event to denounce the segregation of a private organization (the Daughters of the American Revolution), permanently desegregating D.C.'s parks proved to be a much longer, drawn-out struggle. Opponents, in both the city's local government and the U.S. Congress, immediately tried to circumvent the move by calling for the NPS to transfer control of the parks to the District of Columbia's Recreation Board. Meanwhile, in 1942 sympathizers in Congress (led by Representative John F. Hunter and Senator Harold Burton, both from Ohio) sought to formalize integration with passage of a recreation bill denouncing segregation in D.C.'s parks. The measure was vigorously opposed by pro-segregationists in Congress, especially Senator Theodore Bilbo (Mississippi) and Representatives F. Edward Hebert (Louisiana) and Aaron L. Ford (Mississippi). Seeking to avoid this very tension, President Franklin Roosevelt himself had proposed transferring some parks to the city as early as 1939, but by 1949 the fight between the NPS and D.C.'s Recreation Board reached a breaking point. That year the Interior Department offered once more to hand over the parks in exchange for a guarantee that the board would eliminate all rules requiring racial segregation at the sites: in a 4-2 vote, the board rejected the offer. In the end, not until 1955 were all of Washington's public golf courses (including East Potomac Park) fully desegregated in the wake of *Bolling v. Sharpe*, the Supreme Court's decision to integrate the city's public schools—thirty-five years after African Americans had first gained access to segregated links in the city, and fourteen years after Edgar Brown's protest at the golf course nearest the U.S. Capitol and the White House.[80]

The NAACP and the Urban League both supported the fight to desegregate Washington's public golf courses, but they played a much larger role in Baltimore, where local branches took the fight for golf into the courtroom. As in D.C., African Americans in Baltimore began calling on the city to provide access to municipal links in the 1920s. Anger escalated after the city raised fares on all streetcar riders in order to pay for the expansion of its white-only parks. "Taking dimes from Negro car riders to purchase golf courses for the rich and well-to-do is worse than robbery," complained the *Baltimore Afro-American*, the city's largest black newspaper.[81] Both Edward S. Lewis, head of the Baltimore Urban League, and Lillie Jackson, president of the Baltimore NAACP, took an active interest in confronting segregation on the city's golf courses (although it is uncertain if either actually played the game). By 1930 Baltimore had acquiesced to an arrangement similar to that of Potomac Park in D.C.: the city opened one of its four public courses to African Americans during certain periods of the week. Clarence M. Mitchell, a nineteen-year-old black journalist, was on hand when the park commissioner confronted angry white residents in the working-class Carroll Park neighborhood and informed them that blacks would have a right to play their neighborhood's golf course (Mitchell went on to be the NAACP's chief lobbyist from 1950 to 1978). "That again is a reflection of the attitude in the city, in those days," he later recalled. "Because that was the section where poor whites lived, whereas in the other areas of the city which had better golf courses, the city did not agree to have them play."[82] Although Carroll Park Golf Course was far worse than Baltimore's three other courses—nine shabby, poorly maintained holes with no sand traps, flagsticks, practice greens, or professional staff—African American players quickly took advantage of the limited access to it. Delegates from the city's black Morgan College frequented the park in subsequent years and hosted school visitors at the course. Another group of black golfers, calling themselves the Monumental Golfers Association, also played regularly and organized men's and women's tournaments at Carroll Park.[83]

Like golfers at Washington's Potomac Park, Baltimore's black players were not satisfied with limited, segregated access to one city course. (Perhaps they were even more dissatisfied, as many in Baltimore criticized D.C.'s black leaders for adopting Jim Crow "willingly" after they participated in dedication ceremonies for the black Lincoln Memorial Golf Course in 1925.)[84] Whereas black golf clubs in D.C. turned to petitioning the federal government, golfers in Baltimore rallied with more help from the local NAACP. The city was already a testing ground for the organization's renewed efforts to confront segregation in the South via a series of coordinated legal challenges. With financial assistance from the Monumental Golfers Association, Lillie Jackson and the NAACP joined a lawsuit filed against the park board in 1934 attempting to eliminate segregation at Baltimore's remaining three public golf courses. After an initial victory, the case dragged on into the 1940s after the city filed a number of appeals. In 1942 a Baltimore jury seemed destined to support the city when jurors polled 9-3 in favor of segregation, only to reverse their sentiment and support the black players after deliberating through the night. For one month the color line fell, and African American players streamed onto the city's other courses for the first time, especially the Mount Pleasant Golf Course. Responding to white protest, however, the parks board soon reversed itself, and the city again appealed the court's ruling. The following year Maryland's Court of Appeals overturned the verdict and affirmed segregation on Baltimore's courses.[85]

By the end of World War II, African American golfers in Baltimore were turning to more direct, confrontational tactics, as was the NAACP. In 1948 a federal court deliberated another case brought by black golfer Charles Law with the organization's help. Law's attorney was Robert McGuinn, who in 1935 had used his lighter skin to pass as white and help Thurgood Marshall investigate racial discrimination in Maryland's public schools. McGuinn was also aided by Charles Hamilton Houston, Marshall's mentor and the architect of the NAACP's legal plan to dismantle school segregation nationwide.[86] As the legal battle escalated, so too did tension on the ground in Baltimore's parks. While the federal court considered Law's case, a group of protesters from the Maryland Progressive Party staged a demonstration at the city's larger, more upscale Druid Hill Park. A group of twenty-one party members (fourteen black and eleven white, most of whom were students) walked into the park, pulled out tennis rackets, and began playing interracial matches. By the time police arrived and began to drag them from the park, a crowd of 500 sympathizers had assembled: "Is this America or Nazi Germany?" one spectator reportedly shouted at police.[87]

The tennis sit-in served its purpose: desegregating Baltimore's parks became a national story right as a federal court deliberated the NAACP's golf lawsuit. Days later the court ruled in favor of the black golfers, and the city was once again told to grant African Americans access to all of its courses. Instead of desegregating, however, the parks board responded with more segregation: opening the courses to black players on certain days of the week (they were actually emboldened by the federal court's decision, which freely admitted that such an arrangement would technically satisfy its ruling.)[88] By this point, after nearly fifteen years of court battles over integrated golf, the board's intransigence was beginning to rankle more whites in Baltimore. Another federal lawsuit was filed challenging segregation in the parks, this time with mostly white plaintiffs that included Martin Dean, a white player who was turned away at Clifton Park's Golf Course on a day when the city had set it aside for black play.[89]

As African Americans confronted Baltimore in more militant ways, whites in favor of segregating the parks responded in kind. Working-class residents in South Baltimore continued to resent the city for opening Carroll Park's shoddy course to black players in 1930, and the park remained a site of considerable racial tension in the ensuing decades. In 1949 a group of fifty white teens chased seven black teens out of the park. When the black youth returned, a vicious brawl ensued, and black teen Linwood Matthews was stabbed to death. Civil rights leaders and black residents blamed the violence directly on the city's park board and its long-standing refusal to integrate the parks fully. To them, the board had Matthews's blood on its hands, especially those members who had voiced the strongest disapproval of integrating Baltimore's recreation space. In D.C. the struggle to integrate public golf courses had elicited strong feelings; in Baltimore it was met with violence. "The killing of a young Negro in a boys' gang fight in Carroll Park . . . has brought to the front again the issue of segregation in the city park system," lamented Baltimore's largest newspaper, the *Sun*. "Segregation on the links has been reduced to an absurdity; and it must be obvious that before long the Park Board will reconsider its position and abandon segregation so far as the ancient Scottish game is concerned."[90] Nevertheless, Baltimore's black golfers (as in D.C.)

had to wait until after the Supreme Court's 1954 ruling in *Brown v. Board of Education* to gain full access to all of the city's courses. In November 1955 the court upheld a lower court's ruling that the legal basis for Baltimore's segregated parks was "swept away by the school decision."[91]

Baltimore was not alone, as violent encounters over integrating municipal golf courses occurred elsewhere in the South. Like segregation itself, the level of tension surrounding race and city parks often depended on the whims of local administrators and political leaders. The South's first private black country club (Acorn Country Club) was built in 1924 and located in Richmond, Virginia, and Richmond's city council was open to developing park land for black residents in the 1930s. Unlike in Baltimore, Richmond's African Americans were encouraged to share requests for park and golf space at council meetings and faced little objection from whites. However, in nearby Norfolk, "we have not been quite so fortunate," exclaimed the black *Journal and Guide*.[92] There the "mere suggestion" that a municipal course be open to black use and potentially developed as black park space was met with "violent protests" from neighboring white property owners. Norfolk's black residents also protested that their tax dollars were paying for the expansion of white courses at a time when there was little public park space for African Americans, let alone golf facilities. Even sympathetic council members hinted that tax funds should be used to meet more fundamental needs, such as repairing decrepit roads and infrastructure in black neighborhoods. Such an argument in an era of extreme austerity held weight with some black residents even as resources seemed readily available for white parks and golf courses. Yet others insisted that the fight for public investment in black recreation was of equal value to fighting for roads, schools, and businesses in black neighborhoods. "How shameful it is . . . that the things which are essential for the health and happiness of one race are not considered equally essential for the other race in the same city," wrote one resident in 1930. Another letter supporting the fight for a black golf course was signed, "A Citizen and Taxpayer."[93] In 1946, Norfolk did start allowing African Americans to play its Memorial Park Golf Course, but only on Wednesdays and Fridays. "Few, if any of the city's colored golf devotees will ever be able to use the golf course," lamented the *Journal and Guide*, "for the simple reason that they must work for a living."[94] Yet once again, anyone who doubted the availability of golfers when presented with the chance to play or the level of demand for golf in the black community was proved wrong. Over the next three years Norfolk's African Americans took immediate advantage of the access, particularly many women who signed up for lessons at Memorial Park seeking to play for the first time. African Americans from Richmond also traveled to play the course, and Memorial Park even hosted the Virginia-Carolina Open Championship, an all-black professional and amateur tournament that drew players from around the country as well as white spectators (including Norfolk's mayor). The explosion of black golf at the park proved that access and opportunity stimulated demand; nevertheless, the course did not last long. In 1952 the city gave up the fifty-acre site so it could be developed into a new campus for the black Norfolk Polytechnic College (Norfolk State University).[95]

In contrast, some African Americans in the South found access to regulation-sized public courses at surprisingly early dates. Golf grew slowly in Texas; by 1900 there were still only five courses in the state, compared with hundreds in New York and Massachusetts. San Antonio's Brackenridge Park Golf Course, the first municipal links in Texas, opened in 1916. Although black players were generally barred from such public courses, some found ways to circumvent segregation, often by serving as caddies, waiters, and attendants at the facilities or by building their own courses. By 1927 a group of black enthusiasts in Dallas had formed the Dixie Golf Club and reported that they played regularly at a nine-hole course "open to the public" (it is unclear if this was a municipal course). In 1931 four of them were even allowed to play Brook Hollow Golf Club, an elite private course designed by A. W. Tillinghast that opened in 1920 and has never had a black member. The *Pittsburgh Courier* was surprised to learn that plans for a black housing development in Dallas included "a golf and country club with a professional Negro instructor. Yes, sir, in Texas!"[96]

Federally funded infrastructure projects in the South, including New Deal programs and World War II developments, also provided some African Americans access to the game for the first time. Black golfers in Houston found a consistent place to play in 1942 after the Federal Housing Administration included a nine-hole course at its Clinton Park housing project, built to house over 500 families of black war workers.[97] President Franklin Roosevelt knew firsthand the problems and possibilities when constructing golf courses in ailing southern districts: he built one himself. Roosevelt played golf voraciously before paralysis disabled him (he was arguably better at the game than any other president in American history). When he purchased a resort in Warm Springs, Georgia, he immediately arranged to construct a course in 1926. The president later noted in a 1937 speech that the golf project opened his eyes to the South's low wages:

> So I began expanding my economic philosophy. I started in the next year ... and let a contract to build a golf course. The contractor, who was an honest efficient contractor, got his labor, partly white and partly colored, around Warm Springs and he paid them seventy cents a day and eighty cents a day—when the weather was good. Figure out the purchasing power of the families of these workers in the course of a year. Could the local stores sell enough to keep the wheels of the factories in the North running?

Nevertheless, Roosevelt conceded that golf course work paid better than growing "five cent cotton."[98]

Whether or not the president himself saw economic uplift in golf course development, New Deal agencies and many African Americans certainly did. Washington's Langston Golf Course was built by workers from the CCC and WPA, while City Park No. 1 in New Orleans—one of the courses former caddie Joe Bartholomew helped construct in 1933—was financed by the Federal Emergency Relief Administration (FERA). Federal projects like these particularly helped the game grow in the South and West, but black neighborhoods in the North also benefited. The most popular municipal course for African Americans in Cleveland was the Highland Park Golf Course, which in 1940 the WPA refurbished using black workers. *Call and Post*, Cleveland's black newspaper, celebrated the WPA's hiring of "many skilled Negro workers" and noted that local white-only unions would not have employed black laborers if the city had managed the project itself.[99]

The South remained the region where African Americans most forcefully called on the federal government to provide recreational space, including golf courses. In 1933, black residents in Norfolk wrote letters petitioning the Civil Works Administration to construct the black park their city leaders had failed to provide.[100] Unlike many southern cities, Atlanta provided black golfers no access to its municipal courses and denied the community's requests for a separate course of their own. Black leaders in turn launched a lengthy campaign aimed at convincing the federal government that Atlanta's African Americans needed a federally built golf facility. The city's Negro Chamber of Commerce petitioned FERA for a course in 1935, while the black *Atlanta Daily World* called on the WPA (which replaced FERA later that year) and continued to press the New Deal agency for black access to municipal links: "If the city is to receive thirty-four parks it is but fair that the colored people get at least six parks and one municipal golf course."[101] Despite the sustained effort, neither the city nor the federal government came through; Atlanta's African Americans would have to wait longer than blacks in any other major city for sustained access to municipal golf. By 1949 Atlanta's five municipal courses remained completely closed to black players. According to the *Atlanta Daily World*, the lack of golf access was the "biggest complaint" among the city's African Americans regarding recreational opportunities and the integration of Atlanta's parks. The city had even allowed black residents access to one of its municipal swimming pools, typically one of the greatest taboos in the Jim Crow South. (Atlanta was perhaps the only large city in America where public pools were integrated before public golf courses.) The city's refusal meant that its courses would eventually be subject to the most important legal challenge to golf segregation in American history, the Supreme Court's 1955 decision in *Holmes v. Atlanta*.[102]

As in Atlanta, black golfers in New Orleans struggled to access municipal courses as segregation hardened after World War I. Joe Bartholomew, the New Orleans professional barred from playing the Metairie Country Club he built in 1925, continued to design courses in Louisiana. He built private tracks in Hammond, Covington, Abita, Algiers Springs, Slidell, and Baton Rouge, along with a course in neighboring Mississippi—all of which, like Metairie, he never played due to segregation. Yet it was in New Orleans where Bartholomew made his largest contributions to the game. He worked briefly as head greenskeeper for the New Orleans Country Club and designed three landmark city courses: City Park No. 1, City Park North, and Pontchartrain Park. Although public, the City Park courses continued to enforce segregation, while Pontchartrain Park was the centerpiece of a privately financed black housing project completed in 1956 (Bartholomew had first designed the layout in 1924). Remarkably, all accounts indicate that Bartholomew received no compensation for building any of his three New Orleans courses. At some point in the 1940s he also constructed Crescent City Golf Club, a seven-hole, all-black course on property he owned in nearby Harahan.

By 1934 Bartholomew had stopped playing golf competitively and founded Bartholomew Construction. Along with building golf courses, the firm contributed to the city's most important construction projects of the 1930s and 1940s, including the campuses of Dillard University and Xavier University, the Parkview Gardens housing project, the repaving of

Tulane Avenue, and the new Charity Hospital (the nation's second-largest hospital when it opened in 1939). In a period when most construction sites were segregated, the company's willingness to employ white and black workers side by side drew attention. Through the success of Bartholomew Construction, real estate investments, and additional companies he purchased, Bartholomew became one of Louisiana's richest African Americans. The former caddie "all but cornered the golf industry in New Orleans," proclaimed *Fortune* magazine in 1949, "perhaps the prize local example of a highly prosperous Negro enterpriser."[103] Although he worked with both whites and blacks ("Joe's got fine equipment—build with him, you save money," remarked New Orleans mayor Chep Morrison), the dark-skinned Bartholomew was never fully accepted by the city's elite mulattos, making his success all the more noteworthy. Amidst the Great Migration and the hardening of Louisiana segregation, the young caddie-turned-businessman stayed in New Orleans, navigated the city's complex racial politics, and used an unlikely resource—golf—to become one of Louisiana's richest men. Shortly after his death in 1971, he became the first black inductee into the Greater New Orleans Sports Hall of Fame. Seven years later the city renamed Pontchartrain Park the Joseph M. Bartholomew Golf Course.[104]

As was the case in Bartholomew's life, caddying remained the most common way African Americans in the South interacted with the game after World War I. Many continued to face harsh treatment and rigid racial discrimination, made worse as the region spiraled further into economic depression and as competition heated up between white and black caddies, attendants, and course maintenance workers. (As President Roosevelt noted, menial golf-course work in the South did not pay well, but it nevertheless became a more attractive opportunity as agricultural jobs worsened.) A series of violent encounters before World War II highlighted the harsh reality many caddies faced and typified how degrading the experience could be. Even worse than the caddie fights in Texas recalled by James Farmer, several disturbing incidents of murder, theft, and racial tension made headlines in the South. In 1927 a black caddie at Highland Park Golf Course in Birmingham, Alabama, was gunned down on the first green by his white caddiemaster. The man supposedly was "caddying out of turn" and threatened his boss with a golf club after he was confronted (the dead caddie's white client came to his defense and denied that the man had wielded a club against his boss).[105] An even more dramatic incident occurred in 1942 at Atlanta's Black Rock Golf Course in Adams

Left, the opening of Pontchartrain Park Golf Course in 1956. Joe Bartholomew is second from left; second from right is New Orleans mayor Chep Morrison. *Below*, inside the clubhouse (Louisiana Division/City Archives, New Orleans Public Library).

Park. John Thomas Russell, a twenty-seven-year-old caddie and talented player, attempted to steal golf clubs from the course at night but was caught by George Thomas, the club's white manager. Panicking, Russell asked Thomas for twenty dollars, then walked him out onto the course at gunpoint. Thomas lunged for the gun, the two tussled, and Russell shot Thomas dead. Over the next year the case quickly made its way through the legal system and exacerbated the racial animosity within Atlanta's already tense world of segregated golf. The city's leading black golfers distanced themselves from Russell and told the white press that he never actually played in any tournaments at the black New Lincoln Country Club. After a highly charged trial in a courtroom "packed with colored and white persons" with "many unable to gain admittance," Russell was found guilty and executed via electric chair in August 1943.[106]

At times even normal encounters between caddies and their handlers devolved into a kind of exploitation where violence was encouraged by wealthy whites and made a part of the caddie's job. During the 1930s it was common at southern country clubs for members to organize fights between caddies for entertainment and gambling. So-called battle royals featured five to ten caddies or clubhouse attendants (usually young men, and almost always black) who brawled for money while white members looked on, the last boy standing declared the "winner." Such displays occurred at the finest clubs in the South, including the most exclusive: Georgia's Augusta National Golf Club.

From its inception in 1932, Augusta National was as open about its policy of only employing black caddies as it was secretive about its membership. "As long as I'm alive," said Clifford Roberts, who founded the club alongside famed amateur Bobby Jones, "all the golfers will be white and all the caddies will be black."[107] One of Augusta's early black caddies was Beau Jack, the orphan who impressed Jones and the other members whenever the club put on battle royals. Working first as a shoe-shiner, Jack was promoted to caddie but told anyone who would listen that he really wanted to be a prizefighter. Soon Jones gathered a group of supporters who arranged for Jack to begin training as a boxer. Within six years the former caddie, who first honed his skills in Augusta's battle royals, had captured the world lightweight boxing title in Madison Square Garden. Jack fought a series of major fights at the Garden during World War II, including one that brought in $35.9 million in war bond purchases, considered by some the largest gate in boxing history.[108]

In 1946, at the height of his fame, Jack made a high-profile return to

Caddie John Thomas Russell with police following his arrest for the murder of George Thomas in Atlanta, Georgia, 1942 (Special Collections and Archives, Georgia State University Library).

his humble roots. He went back to Augusta National during the Masters Golf Tournament, where he was pictured in the press reenacting his role as shoe-shiner and caddie. The *Afro-American* criticized the move: "The last couple of years he has made a million dollars, and last week he was back at the Augusta golf club 'Uncle Tomming,' shining shoes, serving drinks, 'Mistering' everybody in sight. With all the opportunities for ad-

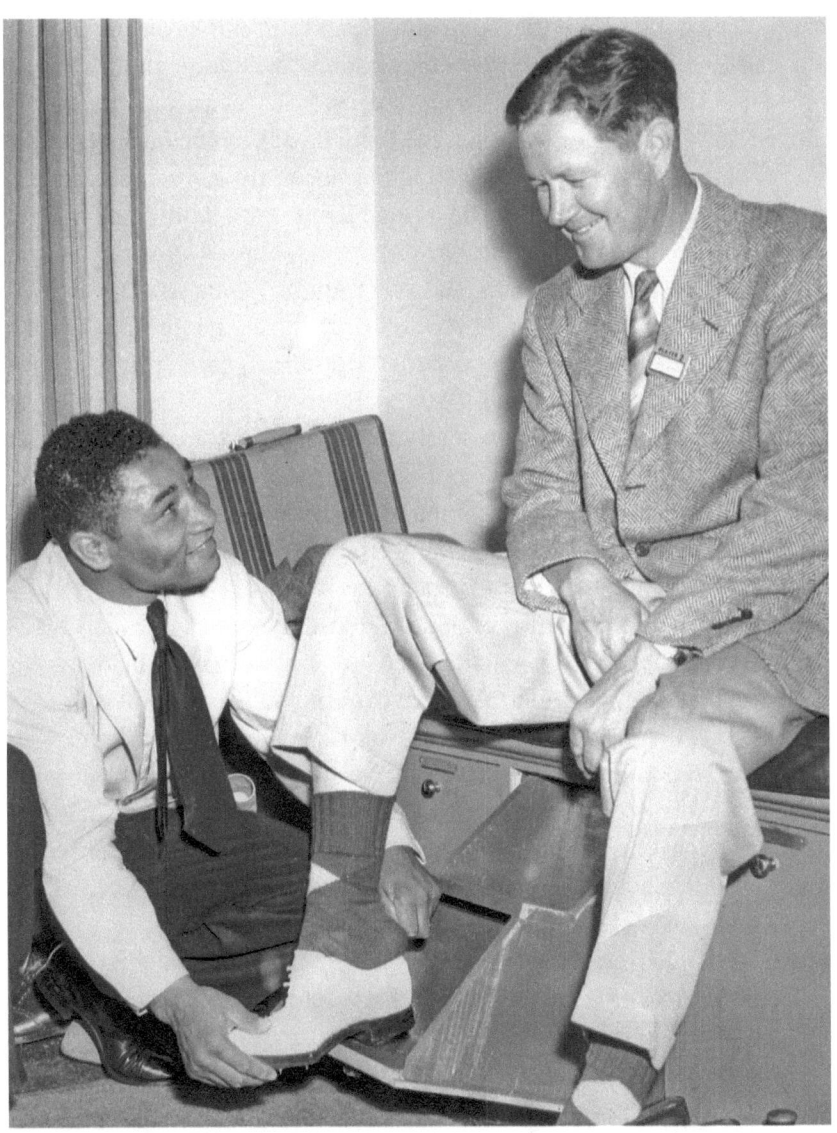

"Mistering everybody in sight": boxing champion Beau Jack and golf professional Byron Nelson at the 1946 Masters, Augusta National Golf Club (Beau Jack folder, New York World-Telegram & Sun Newspaper Photograph Collection, Prints & Photographs Division, Library of Congress).

vancement and culture that has come . . . he still thinks on the level of a shoe shine boy."[109] By 1948 Jack had lost his world title, and his career faded quickly; soon the money was gone just as fast as he had made it. He moved first back to Georgia, then to Miami Beach, where he spent many years shining shoes for unsuspecting patrons at the Fontainebleau and Doral hotels. In his spare time he trained fighters at Miami's famed Fifth Street gymnasium.

Beau Jack's unique story faded into obscurity, along with his experience working at Augusta National Golf Club during its formative years. Yet he likely inspired Ralph Ellison's description of a battle royal in chapter 1 of Ellison's 1952 novel *Invisible Man*. Ellison began writing the iconic scene in the summer of 1945, around the height of Jack's popularity in the press. Jack also influenced up-and-coming boxers and caddies back in his native Georgia. One was a young Augusta teen named James Brown: the future Godfather of Soul also wanted to be a prizefighter, participated in battle royals, and considered Jack his hero.[110]

Along with stories that revealed the tense dynamics between black caddies and their bosses, clients, or white counterparts, incidents off the course also highlighted the harsh lives of southern caddies. In 1939 a caddie at Atlanta's elite East Lake Golf Club was sentenced to life in prison for stabbing another black man in a gang fight. That same decade, millions followed the trial of the "Scottsboro Boys," the sensational legal case in which nine African Americans from Alabama were accused of rape. Americans learned that one defendant, Clarence Norris, was the son of an abusive slave-turned-sharecropper; Norris fled his father at age fifteen and had desperately turned to caddying in rural Alabama.[111]

Unlike Norris, other caddies in the South had exceptional experiences that were quite positive, including some who forged genuine bonds with their employers and club members. In 1928 Frank Ivory was a fifteen-year-old caddie at Edgewater Gulf Resort in Biloxi, Mississippi, when he was assigned to carry the bag of millionaire John J. Raskob. Raskob was vice president of General Motors, chairman of the Democratic National Committee, and principal financier of New York's Empire State Building. He bonded immediately with the "barefoot and ragged caddie"; after Ivory started crying as Raskob prepared to leave, the executive asked the teen to "come along." The two drove off, and Raskob telegrammed his wife back in Delaware: "Am bringing something home."[112] Both the white and black press celebrated the story of the impoverished caddie who "caught a break" and stumbled onto "lady luck," and Ivory appeared to live happily at Raskob's estate for several years. The two exchanged kind notes as the caddie, like Beau Jack, set out to become a professional boxer in 1937 (he found little success). Ivory later served in World War II, then went to tailoring school on the GI Bill before disappearing from the historical record (the last letter from him preserved in Raskob's archive is from 1950).[113]

A golfer adopting his caddie was exceptional, but black caddies often forged respectful, meaningful relationships with white players. In 1930 the members of Atlanta's private Ansley Golf Club honored one beloved caddie who died unexpectedly, arranging for a prominent white minister to perform an integrated funeral service: "Scores of rich white golfers attended the impressive ceremonies," noted the *Pittsburgh Courier*.[114] Caddying continued to serve the needs of racial segregation and discrimination in the South but also provided opportunities for African Americans to shine as players. Earl Hill, a young caddie at Georgia's Jekyll Island Club during the 1920s, recalled having the exclusive resort course all to himself most of the time: "That's where I got my jump in golf, because the millionaires would use the golf course three months out of the year, the other nine months I would use it."[115] In 1914 the exclusive Oakwood Country Club in Lynchburg, Virginia, recruited Morris Alexander, a black player from Philadelphia, to move down and become its new caddiemaster; he went on to set the course record in 1928 and served as a golf pro there until 1967.[116] As the game continued to develop, so too did the complicated racial dynamics between white players and black caddies, especially in the South. The distinction between demeaning abuse, racist patronizing, and genuine friendship was never quite clear: whereas Beau Jack took positive memories from his experience at Augusta National, the *Afro-American* and Ralph Ellison saw little more than exploitation and "Uncle Tomming."

Both golf and African Americans migrated steadily to the western states during the interwar period. In some western cities black golfers found more opportunities to play municipal courses. Such access was spotty, at times curbed arbitrarily by racial restrictions. Denver's first municipal layout, City Park Golf Course, was generally open to black players and home for the black East Denver Golf Club, but the black press still reported instances of African Americans being turned away.[117] The most sustained interest in golf among black westerners came in southern California, where Los Angeles's growing African American population was able to access a number of courses in the 1920s and 1930s, including the municipal courses in Griffith Park. Yet the Western Avenue Golf Course proved more popular with black patrons. Located on the corner of Western Avenue and El Segundo Boulevard in southwest L.A., the course was in a barren field when it was first opened by the city in 1928 but was eventually surrounded by a growing black neighborhood. By the 1940s, Western Avenue had become a key center of black golf in America; Hollywood's black celebrities frequented the course, as did visiting black entertainers, athletes, and stars—including Joe Louis, Jackie Robinson, and Muhammad Ali. In 1982 the city renamed the course Chester L. Washington Golf Course in honor of the longtime editor of the *Los Angeles Sentinel*, L.A.'s largest black newspaper. While Western Avenue became a de facto black municipal course, African Americans also frequented other public golf facilities in southern California. L.A.'s first organized group of black golfers, the West Coast Golf Club, hosted their tournaments at a municipal course in Santa Monica during the early 1930s. The group was also among the largest of the many black golf clubs in America: a 1934 gala in Pasadena had more than 700 participants. One of the best black players in L.A. during this early period was amateur Oscar Clisby, who in 1931 won a Los Angeles public links tournament, becoming the first African American to win a major golf event in California.[118]

As in a number of cities, notably Chicago and Washington, black women in Los Angeles played an important role in increasing the game's popularity. Male or female, perhaps the greatest advocate for L.A.'s black golfers was Maggie Mae Hathaway, an actress and singer who migrated to California from Louisiana in the 1940s. (She was Lena Horne's stand-in for the 1943 film *Stormy Weather*.) In 1955 Hathaway took up golf after winning a bet with Joe Louis, and she never looked back. She was a talented player who immediately resented the many courses in Los Angeles that restricted African Americans, and she organized several rallies in response. Most importantly, Hathaway's direct action in the world of golf spread to broader issues, and she became a leader in the national civil rights movement. In the 1960s she served as president of the NAACP's Hollywood chapter and, along with Sammy Davis Jr., organized the first NAACP Image Awards in 1967. Still, Hathaway maintained a strong presence in the game that helped launch her activism. In 1963 she founded Minority Associated Golfers, one of the first organizations to identify and support young black golfers interested in becoming professional players. A longtime fixture at L.A.'s Chester L. Washington Golf Course, she also taught the game at Jack Thompson Golf Course, another municipal course two miles away (among her white students was future Los Angeles mayor James Hahn). In 1997 the city renamed the course Maggie Hathaway Golf Course in her honor, making Los Angeles the only city with two municipal courses named for African Americans. For thirty years Hathaway penned a regular golf column for the *Los Angeles Sentinel*, giving her a sustained, national voice in the game that few other black women ever had (save perhaps Chicago's Nettie Speedy earlier in the century).[119]

As its golf scene quickly expanded, Los Angeles became a key destination for black golf professionals. Jimmie DeVoe, who in 1962 became the first African American to reintegrate the PGA, was drawn increasingly to L.A. in the 1940s, where he developed his reputation not only as a player but also as an instructor to Hollywood's African American stars. DeVoe helped organize L.A.'s black Cosmopolitan Golf Club in 1944, which hosted monthly tournaments at the private Brentwood Country Club. Three years later the Vernondale Golf Club was formed, California's first black women's club.[120]

All across the country, by World War II golf to many black Americans was no longer a distant concept or foreign activity. The game was everywhere—from urban street corners in black working-class neighborhoods and the fields of rural black farmers to the more elite, private black country clubs. In every instance a common sentiment emerged, fueled by the period's broader social and political contexts: it was one of urgency, not privilege. The opportunity was at hand for African Americans to truly influence the game's national development and, at the same time, make the sport uniquely their own. One *Afro-American* reader put it succinctly in 1936: "Golf is a game that we must get into."[121]

In many ways the black community had already done just that. What remained was a sustained fight to break down the game's most formidable barriers. The first step would be the creation of a remarkable organization long since forgotten by most Americans: a national, professional African American golf tour.

3

OUR MASTERS

The Development of the United Golfers Association

AUGUST 1955—WESTON GOLF AND COUNTRY CLUB, TORONTO, ONTARIO

Arnold Palmer stared at the leaderboard, shocked his name was not on top. The twenty-five-year-old rookie was playing one of his first PGA tournaments and had just shot 64 in the opening round of the 1955 Canadian Open, a fabulous score equaling the course record. The event brought the world's leading players to Toronto, where for the first time in Canada's history a golf tournament was being televised nationally.

Palmer was sure he had bested the field, but above his name read one other.

"Charlie Sifford?" he said to no one in particular. "How on earth did Charlie Sifford shoot a 63?"

"Same way you shot a 64, chief. Except I did you one better."

Palmer turned and saw the thirty-three-year-old Sifford standing behind him. There the two men met for the first time—the most popular white and black golfers of their generation. For the next fifty years elite golf would periodically bring them together, always with mutual respect and friendship.

But it was no coincidence they'd met in a foreign country. Days later Palmer posted 64-67-64-70 for a total of 265 (-23), overtaking Sifford with the lowest score he'd ever post in his career and winning the tournament. He returned to his country with the first of sixty-two career victories on the PGA Tour, well on his way to becoming "The King" and revolutionizing the game for American TV audiences and a legion of fans dubbed "Arnie's Army."

Sifford returned to a country where he was excluded from

most tournaments because a clause in the PGA constitution limited membership to "professional golfers of the Caucasian race." Armed with the knowledge that he could compete with any golfer in the world, he returned to play most of his tournaments on a different tour, one organized by the UGA.

That summer Palmer went to Detroit to compete for the PGA Championship at Meadowbrook Country Club. Sifford went for the UGA Championship at Rackham Golf Course, which he won for the fourth straight time. Black and white, UGA and PGA, this was the world of segregated professional golf, one in which paths constantly crossed all over the country even as discrimination enforced separation. It was a world that put racism on tour.[1]

Beginning in 1926 and lasting into the 1980s an important entity—long overlooked by fans and historians—organized a national golf tour open to all players regardless of their race. The organization, called the United Golfers Association for most of its life, provided thousands of African American players—men and women, amateurs and professionals—access to competitive golf tournaments around the country. Under the loose umbrella of this national entity, UGA tournaments were planned and hosted by local groups of black golfers, some of whom had established their own organizations years before (like Chicago's Alpha Golf Club and Windy City Golf Club) and others that formed in the 1930s and 1940s. There were initially twenty-six member clubs under the UGA's auspices, but the number grew steadily, reaching an estimated ninety by the 1960s. It is difficult to ascertain how many members each individual club boasted, and certainly some participants were more active golfers than others; but many of these groups, particularly the largest in cities like Chicago, Cleveland, and Washington, D.C., served thousands of golf enthusiasts.[2] These clubs were the key to maintaining black support for golf in cities around the country, and they maintained their organizational independence even as the national UGA grew in stature. Examples included the St. Nicholas Golf Club (New York City), the Sixth City Golf Club and the Forest City Golf Association (Cleveland), the Vernondale Golf Club and the Cosmopolitan Golf Club (Los Angeles), the Paramount Golf Club (St. Louis), the East Denver Golf Club (Denver), the Riverside Golf Club and the Wake Robin Golf Club (Washington, D.C.), the Twentieth-Century Golf Club (Evanston, Ill.), and the Fairview Golf Club

(Philadelphia). Three of the most prominent in the South were the Crescent City Club (New Orleans), the Hillard Golf Association (Dallas), and the Lone Star Golf Association (Houston).

City clubs also banded together to form black regional golf associations, such as clubs from Philadelphia and New York City that formed the Eastern Golf Association in 1932 and whose annual tournament, the Eastern Open, became a regular UGA event. In 1954 eight groups from San Francisco, San Diego, Phoenix, Seattle, Portland (Ore.), and Los Angeles (including Cosmopolitan and Vernondale) formed the Western States Golf Association.[3]

The first attempts at organizing a "national" golf championship for African Americans came soon after the establishment of these city clubs. In 1922 the Windy City Golf Club, with help from the *Chicago Defender* and Walter and Nettie Speedy, hosted a small national open golf tournament in Chicago. Three years later, Shady Rest Country Club in New Jersey hosted a larger, two-day tournament it dubbed the "National Colored Open Golf Championship." That event drew thirty-five players from ten different states, most from New York, Philadelphia, and Chicago. Competitors included Chicago's top player, Robert "Pat" Ball, as well as John Shippen, who twelve years after competing in his last U.S. Open was teaching and coaching in Washington, D.C., and soon became Shady Rest's club professional. Neither man managed to best the winner, Harry Jackson, who also hailed from Washington. Although relatively small, the event managed to attract two cameramen from "Fox News," the silent newsreel established by producer William Fox in 1919. Fox's men shot footage of the players, the Shady Rest facilities, and the small gallery of onlookers; this was the first black golf tournament ever filmed and perhaps even the earliest surviving footage of African Americans playing golf.[4] The following year Mapledale Country Club in Stowe, Massachusetts, hosted another national tournament. Robert Hawkins, the former caddie and course manager who purchased Mapledale, brought a larger group of players; nine came from Chicago alone, including Robert "Pat" Ball, Walter Speedy, and Horace McDougal. Hawkins and the participants formed the United States Colored Golfers Association, with players pledging to send the best members of their respective city clubs each year to determine a national champion (two participants from Washington, Beltram Barker and George Adams, were particularly helpful in organizing the group). In 1929 the association changed its name to the United Golfers Association. Shady Rest and Mapledale continued to schedule

Competitors tee off in the 1925 National Colored Open at New Jersey's Shady Rest Country Club (Fox Movietone News outtake A7928 A7932. [35mm Black and White Film]. Moving Image Research Collections. University of South Carolina.).

tournaments, often on subsequent weekends so the same players traveling to compete in New Jersey then participated in the UGA Championship the following week in Massachusetts. The winner of the inaugural 1926 UGA National was Harry Jackson, the same man who had won the previous year at Shady Rest. Thus, between Shady Rest and Mapledale the UGA forged the nation's first black professional golf tour.[5] Within five years it had added its name to several more tournaments hosted by black clubs around the country.

For the next thirty years this tour was the primary outlet for black professional players. Even as USGA and PGA tournaments began to allow a trickle of African American competitors after World War II, the UGA continued to play a critical role in fostering black professional golf well into the 1960s. Its tournaments featured hundreds of black men and women professional players as well as amateurs. In the 1920s and 1930s this included the same individuals who pioneered professional golf at the turn of the century, helping to organize local clubs in their cities and fighting segregation at municipal courses. John Shippen was forty-six when he took part in Shady Rest's inaugural national championship; his best playing days were behind him, yet he continued to compete in UGA events and even won the 1926 and 1932 Shady Rest tournaments. A gallery of 500 spectators watched the veteran capture his 1926 title in a match-play duel against George Aaron, a member of Harlem's St. Nicholas Golf Club and runner-up in the New York City public links championship.[6]

The UGA's top player during its first decade was Chicago transplant Robert "Pat" Ball, a southern native who caddied for famed white amateur Bobby Jones in Atlanta before heading north. Ball won many UGA tournaments, including the national championship four times (1927, 1929, 1934, and 1941). When he returned to Chicago after his first victory in 1927, he was celebrated by Walter Speedy and the city's black golfers, who threw a banquet in his honor and crowned him the "Golf King"; two years later he set the course record at Shady Rest en route to winning the 1929 UGA National. Pat Ball's wife, Cleo, was also an exceptional player, and the duo swept the 1941 UGA National in Boston, Cleo taking the women's crown the same year Pat claimed his last men's championship.[7] Pat Ball briefly ran a miniature golf facility in Chicago before the city recognized his accomplishments in 1939, naming him the head professional at Palos Park; he was the first African American pro at a municipal course in U.S. history. His position was all the more significant because half of Palos Park's golf patrons were white. Transitioning from competitive golf (he was forty-two by the time he won his last UGA championship in 1941), Ball became a leading golf instructor and focused on cultivating the game among Chicago's black youth after World War II.[8]

Chicago produced other successful UGA players, including Porter Washington. Washington moved to Massachusetts to become head professional at Hawkins's Mapledale Country Club, where he defeated Ball in the finals of the 1928 UGA National with a record-low round. He also won that year's Philadelphia UGA tournament at Cobbs Creek and continued playing UGA events into the 1940s.[9] Horace McDougal was another early UGA standout from Chicago. After joining Northwestern University's golf team in 1923 to become the first African American to compete in intercollegiate golf, McDougal served as club professional at Wisconsin's Casa Loma Country Club, host of the 1930 UGA National. Like Walter Speedy before him, he wrote regular golf pieces for the *Chicago Defender* and was named the newspaper's "golf editor."[10]

UGA tournaments initially drew golfers from the Northeast and Midwest, but by 1930 players from the South and West regularly participated, especially in the national championship. This included Californians like

Table 2. UGA National Championship Results, 1926–1975

Year	Location	Men's Champion	Women's Champion
1926	Mapledale Country Club, Stow, Mass.	Harry Jackson, Washington, D.C.	
1927	Mapledale Country Club, Stow, Mass.	Robert Ball, Chicago, Ill.	
1928	Mapledale Country Club, Stow, Mass.	Porter Washington, Chicago, Ill.	
1929	Shady Rest Country Club, Scotch Plains, N.J.	Robert Ball, Chicago, Ill.	
1930	Casa Loma Country Club, Powers Lake, Wisc.	Edison Marshall, New Orleans, La.	Marie Thompson, Chicago, Ill.
1931	Sunset Hills Country Club, Kankakee, Ill.	Edison Marshall, New Orleans, La.	Marie Thompson, Chicago, Ill.
1932	Douglass Park Golf Course, Indianapolis, Ind.	John Brooks Dendy, Asheville, N.C.	Lucy Williams, Indianapolis, Ind.
1933	Sunset Hills Country Club, Kankakee, Ill.	Howard Wheeler, Atlanta, Ga.	Julia Siler, St. Louis, Mo.
1934	Rackham Golf Course, Detroit, Mich.	Robert Ball, Chicago, Ill.	Ella Able, Indianapolis, Ind.
1935	Mohansic Golf Course, Yorktown Heights, N.Y.	Solomon Hughes, Gadsden, Ala.	Ella Able, Indianapolis, Ind.
1936	Cobbs Creek Golf Course, Philadelphia, Pa.	John Brooks Dendy, Asheville, N.C.	Lucy Williams, Indianapolis, Ind.
1937	Highland Park Golf Course, Cleveland, Ohio	John Brooks Dendy, Asheville, N.C.	Lucy Williams, Indianapolis, Ind.
1938	Palos Park Golf Course, Chicago, Ill.	Howard Wheeler, Atlanta, Ga.	Melanie Moye, Atlanta, Ga.
1939	Griffith Park Golf Course, Los Angeles, Calif.	Cliff Strickland, Riverside, Calif.	Geneva Wilson, Chicago, Ill.
1940	Palos Park Golf Course, Chicago, Ill.	Hugh Smith, Thomasville, Ga.	Geneva Wilson, Chicago, Ill.
1941	Ponkapoag Golf Club, Canton, Mass.	Robert Ball, Chicago, Ill.	Cleo Ball, Chicago, Ill.
1942	No Tournament [World War II]		
1943	No Tournament [World War II]		
1944	No Tournament [World War II]		
1945	No Tournament [World War II]		

Table 2. Continued

Year	Location	Men's Champion	Women's Champion
1946	North Park Golf Course, Pittsburgh, Pa.	Howard Wheeler, Atlanta, Ga.	Lucy Williams, Indianapolis, Ind.
1947	Cobbs Creek Golf Course, Philadelphia, Pa.	Howard Wheeler, Atlanta, Ga.	Thelma Cowans, Detroit, Mich.
1948	Coffin Golf Course, Indianapolis, Ind.	Howard Wheeler, Atlanta, Ga.	Mary Brown, Erie, Pa.
1949	Rouge Park Golf Course, Detroit, Mich.	Ted Rhodes, Nashville, Tenn.	Thelma Cowans, Detroit, Mich.
1950	Anacostia Golf Course, Washington, D.C.	Ted Rhodes, Nashville, Tenn.	Ann Gregory, Indianapolis, Ind.
1951	Seneca Golf Course, Cleveland, Ohio	Ted Rhodes, Nashville, Tenn.	Eoline Thornton, Los Angeles, Calif.
1952	North Park Golf Course, Pittsburgh, Pa.	Charlie Sifford, Charlotte, N.C.	Alice Stewart, Detroit, Mich.
1953	Swope Park Golf Course, Kansas City, Mo.	Charlie Sifford, Charlotte, N.C.	Ann Gregory, Indianapolis, Ind.
1954	Cedar Crest Golf Course, Dallas, Tex.	Charlie Sifford, Charlotte, N.C.	Thelma Cowans, Detroit, Mich.
1955	Rackham Golf Course, Detroit, Mich.	Charlie Sifford, Charlotte, N.C.	Thelma Cowans, Detroit, Mich.
1956	Cobbs Creek Golf Course, Philadelphia, Pa.	Charlie Sifford, Charlotte, N.C.	Thelma Cowans, Detroit, Mich.
1957	East Potomac Park Golf Course, Washington, D.C.	Ted Rhodes, Nashville, Tenn.	Ann Gregory, Indianapolis, Ind.
1958	North Park Golf Course, Pittsburgh, Pa.	Howard Wheeler, Atlanta, Ga.	Vernice Turner, Ocean City, N.J.
1959	Langston Golf Course, Washington, D.C.	Richard Thomas, Annapolis, Md.	Ethel Funches, Washington, D.C.
1960	?, Chicago, Ill.	Charlie Sifford, Charlotte, N.C.	Ethel Funches, Washington, D.C.
1961	Ponkapoag Golf Club, Canton, Mass.	Pete Brown, Jackson, Miss.	Vernice Turner, Ocean City, N.J.
1962	Fuller Park Golf Course, Memphis, Tenn.	Pete Brown, Jackson, Miss.	Carrie Jones, Jackson, Miss.
1963	Langston Golf Course, Washington, D.C.	Lee Elder, Dallas, Tex.	Ethel Funches, Washington, D.C.

Table 2. Continued

Year	Location	Men's Champion	Women's Champion
1964	Douglass Park Golf Course, Indianapolis, Ind.	Lee Elder, Dallas, Tex.	Renee Powell, East Canton, Ohio
1965	Rackham Golf Course, Detroit, Mich.	Cliff Brown, Cleveland, Ohio	Ann Gregory, Indianapolis, Ind.
1966	?, Chicago, Ill.	Lee Elder, Dallas, Tex.	Ann Gregory, Indianapolis, Ind.
1967	Miami Springs Golf Course, Miami Springs, Fla.	Lee Elder, Dallas, Tex.	Ethel Funches, Washington, D.C.
1968	?, Washington, D.C.	James Black, Charlotte, N.C.	Ethel Funches, Washington, D.C.
1969	Freeway Golf Course, Sicklerville, N.J.	Jim Dent, Augusta, Ga.	Ethel Funches, Washington, D.C.
1970	Alling Memorial Golf Club, New Haven, Conn.	James Walker, Rocky Mount, N.C.	Exie O'Chier, Detroit, Mich.
1971	North Park Golf Course, Pittsburgh, Pa.	Jack Price, Pittsburgh, Pa.	Exie O'Chier, Detroit, Mich.
1972	Chevy Chase Country Club, Chevy Chase, Md.	James Black, Charleston, S.C.	Mary Truitt, Chicago, Ill.
1973	Freeway Golf Course, Sicklerville, N.J.	?	Ethel Funches, Washington, D.C.
1974	Braintree Municipal Golf Club, Braintree, Mass.	Charlie Owens, Tampa, Fla.	Clara Kellnudi, Mashpie, Mass.
1975	Pine Ridge Golf Course, Baltimore, Md.	Charlie Owens, Tampa, Fla.	Laurie Stokien, Washington, D.C.
1976	Torrey Pines Golf Course, San Diego, Calif.	Lou Harve, ?	Debra Bennett, Los Angeles, Calif.

amateur Oscar Clisby, winner of a 1931 Los Angeles public links tournament, as well as Cliff Strickland, a caddiemaster from the Victoria Club in Riverside, California, who won the 1939 UGA National in Los Angeles when the event was held in the West for the first time.[11] Yet the largest surprise in the UGA's early years was the flood of talented black players from the South who began to dominate the circuit in the 1930s and continued to outperform northern golfers after World War II. Starting with New Orleans resident Edison Marshall's victory at the 1930 UGA National, southern players won eight out of ten national championships. Following

Horace McDougal (*far left*) and the 1925 Northwestern University men's golf team (*Syllabus Yearbook*, Northwestern University).

the war, a new generation of players who developed their games in the South—such as Ted Rhodes (Nashville, Tenn.), Charlie Sifford (Charlotte, N.C.), and Lee Elder (Dallas, Tex.)—would continue to lead the tour.

No one should have been surprised at this ascendance of southern players. Although the UGA was established in the golfing communities of the Midwest and Northeast, where most of its tournaments took place and where African Americans had successfully fought for access to municipal courses, golf thrived in the heart of the segregated South. There far more African Americans encountered the game as caddies and groundskeepers while finding more opportunities (and space) to establish their own segregated links. Nevertheless, black observers were shocked when southerners started outperforming the most talented players from Chicago, Cleveland, and New York City. "This national golf tournament is taking on a North vs. South row," proclaimed the *Chicago Defender* in 1938. "Unless the North wants to be humiliated, the golfers in this section had better get busy. Those southern boys can sure shoot." Sportswriters scrambled to explain how the nation's best black golfers could reside in the South; some speculated that the region's warmer weather ("they play the year around") helped overcome the barriers to golf erected by racism and segregation.[12] This surprise was another indication of how the reality of race and golf differed from public perception. Southerners dominating the UGA seemed to belie the notions of northern opportunity and refinement symbolized by golf and entrenched in the minds of many African Americans. The active golf scene that existed in southern black communities did not fit the popular narrative that helped fuel the Great Migration.

Edison Marshall was the first of many UGA southern champions. A fixture at New Orleans's Audubon Park, where Joe Bartholomew had developed his game, Marshall joined a contingent of southern players from Tennessee, Georgia, Alabama, and Louisiana who made their way to the 1930 UGA National at Wisconsin's Casa Loma Country Club for the first time. After taking the title, Marshall followed up by winning again the following year at Sunset Hills, another Chicago-area course. Beating Chicago stalwarts (including Pat Ball) on their home turf, he and other talented southerners (another from New Orleans was his friend John Roux, who finished third in 1931) sparked a rivalry that helped the UGA become a truly national golf tour. Players now competed not only for themselves but also for regional pride. The rivalry was cemented by Marshall's personality, which the northern press compared to that of white baseball star Art Shires, infamous for his hubris. Marshall's victory speech in 1930 was short and sweet: "Well, I'll be back next year to take the cup again, and I am sorry there will be no trophy for the rest of you players." On hand was sportswriter Al Monroe: "If there was an accompanying smile," he wrote, "we were not among those seeing it."[13]

Solomon Hughes was another of the southern contingent that dominated UGA competition before World War II. Born and raised in Gadsden, Alabama, Hughes caddied for whites at the Gadsden Country Club and won a number of UGA events, including the 1936 UGA National at Lake Mohansic Golf Course in New York's Westchester County. Hughes was so popular among black golfers that the world's most famous athlete tracked him down in rural Alabama. During World War II, Joe Louis (nicknamed the "Brown Bomber") was stationed in nearby Fort McClellan. Louis, whose celebrity status allowed him to leave his base frequently, spent many evenings befriending Hughes and his wife and taking lessons from the pro. The men were often joined by fellow serviceman Sugar Ray Robinson, the future welterweight and middleweight boxing champion who was also a golf fan. The men remained friends for many years, with

Hughes winning the 1945 Joe Louis Open—the UGA event in Detroit sponsored by the Brown Bomber—and Louis asking Hughes to be his personal golf instructor. (Hughes politely declined, having moved his family north to Minneapolis during the war.)[14]

Atlanta's black golf scene, centered at New Lincoln Country Club, produced a number of the UGA's southern stars. Three-time national champion John Brooks Dendy (1932, 1936, and 1937) grew up caddying at the white country club in Asheville, North Carolina, where at age twelve he fashioned his first set of clubs by attaching broken club heads to broom handles; six years later he won his first UGA National. Enrolling at Atlanta's Morehouse College, Dendy went on to win the nearby Southern Open in 1932, 1934, and 1936. During a 1933 exhibition at the South's second-most-important black links, the Lincoln Golf Course in Jacksonville, Florida, Dendy wowed the gallery with a hole-in-one at the 342-yard, par-four first hole, followed by three consecutive birdies; the 1-2-3-4, six-under-par start was later recognized in *Ripley's Believe It or Not*.[15] Most of Atlanta's standout golfers were multiple-time winners of the Southern Open, the top black tournament in the South. Along with Dendy, other winners included Zeke Hartsfield, Howard Wheeler, Hugh Smith, Sanders Mason, and Ralph Alexander. Atlanta's talented players also interacted with the city's burgeoning white golf scene: like Pat Ball, Hartsfield and Wheeler also caddied for Bobby Jones at the all-white East Lake Golf Club. Hartsfield later became head professional at Lincoln.[16]

The most accomplished of these Atlanta players, and perhaps the most eccentric in UGA history, was Howard Wheeler. Wheeler was born in Atlanta and grew up on its golf courses, caddying at Brookhaven Country Club and eventually becoming caddiemaster at East Lake. The tall, long-hitting player wowed onlookers with his powerful drives and unorthodox style, which featured a unique and awkward grip. "Wheeler was a cross-handed player, which means that he gripped a golf club opposite the way nearly everybody else does it," recalled rival Charlie Sifford, who first met Wheeler in 1939 when Sifford was seventeen years old. "It looks awkward as hell. . . . I was so busy telling myself that Wheeler couldn't possibly hit the ball right that I didn't pay attention to the shots he was making with his short, quick swing."[17] When he was twenty-one, Wheeler won his first Southern Open, and he went on to win six UGA championships (1933, 1938, 1946, 1947, 1948, and 1958), a record matched only later by Sifford. Peaking in the late 1940s, when he rivaled Ted Rhodes as the top black player in the country, Wheeler played at a high level for a long time and

Howard Wheeler performing trick shots in 1954 (*Jet*, July 29, 1954).

managed to recapture his form following an extended break for service during World War II, a rarity for professional athletes in any sport. The twenty-five-year gap between his first UGA championship (1933 at Chicago's Sunset Hills) and his last (1958 at Pittsburgh's North Park) was also a record. Like many southern-born players, Wheeler moved north during his career. In 1938 he resettled in Philadelphia and became a fixture at Cobbs Creek, where he dueled with the young Sifford after the cocky teen called him out one day. "I'm Charlie Sifford, and I'm gonna whip your ass on that golf course," Sifford said when they first met. "Wheeler asked me how much money I had in my pocket [$20].... Fine, he said, we'll play for ten dollars a nine, match play. He stepped up to the tee, and backhanded a ball a good 270 yards. He proceeded to systematically take me apart."[18] Eventually the two partnered and became an unbeatable team playing cash games in Philadelphia.

Wheeler matched his unorthodox style with an eccentric personality and ability to perform crowd-pleasing trick shots. At first he received a chilly reception from northern golf fans. When Wheeler came to Chicago and defeated hometown hero Pat Ball at the 1933 UGA National, the *Chicago Defender* announced that the "long, lanky lad" was "not popular with the gallery because of his high pitched temperament." He also sported "trousers any tailor would shudder to accept" and "a shirt that was soiled from both use and exposure."[19] Yet Wheeler eventually won over fans and was dubbed the UGA's "Clown Prince of Golf." He could tee a ball on top of random objects, like a box of matches or a soda bottle, and hit booming drives. "Before anyone knew what a trick-shot artist was, [he] was hitting 300-yard drives with balls that were teed up on top of Coke bottles," recalled Sifford. "Wouldn't scratch the bottle, but the ball would take off like it was shot from a cannon.... It was the damndest thing you ever saw. If he'd been alive 40 years later than he was, Wheeler could have made a fortune giving trick-shot exhibitions."[20]

In addition to southern players helping the UGA develop a national footprint in the 1930s, the tour even took on an international dimension. Bermuda's thriving black golf scene prompted several residents to travel and compete in UGA events. The biggest international splash came from one of the tour's lesser-known players: vaudeville star Frank Radcliffe. Radcliffe was an accomplished amateur golfer who won the amateur title at the 1935 UGA National.[21] Joining entertainer George Sorlie's traveling stage show in 1939, Radcliffe performed on tours across Australia and Europe. His golfing prowess drew considerable attention, especially a series of exhibitions in Australia that made headlines when he broke scoring records on four prominent courses. At Bathurst Golf Club he bested a record held by renowned white golfer Norman Von Nida, one of Australia's top professionals. He did the same at Brisbane's Gailes Golf Club, this time beating American Gene Sarazen's record. "In a practice round, with borrowed clubs, at Victoria Park, he proved himself one of the longest hitters to be seen in Brisbane for many a long day," proclaimed the *Sydney Referee*.[22] Radcliffe also played exhibition matches against the top two English golfers of the era, British Open champions Alf Padgham and Henry Cotton.

Australian fans were enthralled with the "colored U.S. champion," while curious black sportswriters back in the United States noted that Radcliffe was not the UGA's best golfer by far, nor was he even a professional. "We have any number of golfers who turned in better scores as a pro than Mr. Radcliffe who is a whale of a golfer as an amateur," wrote one.[23] Nevertheless, Radcliffe's amazing run marked the first time a UGA player (or any African American) received overseas attention in competitive golf. "Travelling extensively he has played on most of the courses of international fame in the British Isles," exclaimed the *Queensland Times*. "As far north as the Balgownie course, in Scotland, also at the Braid Hills (Edinburgh), Hoylake, Lythan, St. Anne's, and Westward Ho [Royal North Devon]."[24] A UGA player would not attract such attention playing abroad until Lee Elder toured Africa and won the 1971 Nigerian Open, over thirty years later.

The UGA drew talented men, but in 1930 it developed a notable feature that distinguished it from other black sporting organizations: a full women's division. Female competition came only after dedicated women struggled to convince the tour to include them at its events. The first four national championships featured no women despite some expressing interest. Organizers bluntly insisted that the quality of play among black women would not attract fans. In 1930, however, they agreed to include a women's tournament as part of the UGA National at Wisconsin's Casa Loma, in part to prove that interest among black women and the level of competition were both inadequate. To the UGA's surprise, sixteen women signed up and paid to compete, almost as many as the male competitors (twenty-two). Moreover, they exhibited impressive skills, none more than Marie Thompson. A member of Chicago's Pioneer Club (the group founded by Walter Speedy), Thompson was an early promoter of the game among the city's black women, joining others like Nettie Speedy and Cleo Ball.

Well aware that the male players, the gallery, and the black press were curious to gauge the level of competition among black women, Thompson arrived at Casa Loma on a mission and did not disappoint. She destroyed the competition (beating her nearest competitor by sixteen shots) and impressed onlookers with her play. Her performance helped guarantee that all future UGA championships, and most UGA events, would include a women's division. The following year she won the championship again at Sunset Hills in Kankakee, Illinois.[25] Not only was she the first black woman to win a "major" golf tournament (women always competed as "amateurs" in the UGA, whereas most tournaments had separate "amateur" and "professional" divisions for men), but she was also the first to achieve some celebrity attention for her skills. Her contentious divorce in 1935 became a minor scandal in the black press, as Thompson charged her husband with cruelty, married another man the following year, and moved to Detroit. There she was instrumental in the development of the Detroit Amateur Golf Association and continued to perform well at UGA events; she finished in the top ten at each UGA National from 1933 to 1941. Thompson's fearless play under scrutiny inspired a growing number of women to sign up for competition. While sixteen women were in the field for the first UGA National in 1930, forty-five competed at the 1941 championship in Canton, Massachusetts.[26]

Southern men excelled in UGA events during the 1930s and 1940s, but female players from the Midwest stood atop the women's division. In fact, only two women residing in the Deep South ever won the UGA championship: Melanie Moye (Atlanta) in 1938 and Carrie Jones (Jackson, Miss.) in 1962. In addition, some of the best women on the early UGA tour hailed from two cities not particularly known for producing top male players: St. Louis, Missouri, and Indianapolis, Indiana. A thriving club of black women played regularly at the Douglass Park Golf Course in Indianapolis, including Lucy Williams and Ella Able. Williams won the UGA National four times (1932, 1936, 1937, and 1946) as well as the inaugural Joe Louis Open in 1946, while Able won the UGA championship in 1934 and 1935. The 1933 national champion, Julia (Towns) Siler, hailed from St. Louis and enjoyed a long career: she recorded more than 100 victories at the local, regional, and UGA levels, including the senior women's title at the 1959 UGA National.[27] Williams, Able, and Siler all reportedly drew sizable galleries in the 1930s: large crowds at Douglass Park followed Able and Williams whenever they squared off against each other, while matches between Siler and Able were the highlight of intercity contests between St. Louis and Indianapolis black golf clubs, occasionally drawing more attention than the men's matches.[28]

Meanwhile, Chicago continued to produce both male and female UGA standouts, including Pat and Cleo Ball, husband-and-wife national champions in 1941, and Geneva Wilson, women's national champion in 1939 and 1940. Wilson joined the ongoing fight against segregation in Chicago golf, suing a white-owned miniature course on the South Side in 1939 after the facility turned her away.[29] The following year she won her second consecutive UGA National in Chicago, notable because it was organized by the Chicago Women's Golf Club, the first time a female club hosted the championship. The other top women's organization, Wake Robin Golf Club in Washington, D.C., also provided leadership to the tour. In 1941 Wake Robin's president, Paris Brown, was elected vice president of the UGA.[30] By World War II, black women had gone from being totally excluded by the UGA to organizing and participating in its most important tournaments. Yet the world of competitive golf remained far from equal, as women bemoaned the relative lack of attention female players received in the press and the little prize money available. The year after Lucy Williams won the 1946 Joe Louis Open, the tournament barred women from competing after some complained about the large discrepancy between male and female prize money.[31]

Louis was the world's most popular athlete and provided key support to help increase the UGA's visibility. World heavyweight boxing champion from 1937 to 1949, he achieved more fame than any American athlete before him, and his passion for golf was legendary. Louis first played soon after he became a professional boxer in 1934, and by 1939 he had started to "take my golf game very seriously." He often played between fights, insisting reporters join him on the course if they wanted an interview and seeking out black professionals to help improve his skills.[32] That year he hired his first golf instructor, Louis Rafael Corbin, a black professional from Bermuda who frequently traveled to the United States and challenged racial discrimination in white tournaments. Corbin was barred from playing in New York's 1936 Metropolitan Open but in 1939 became the first black player to compete in the Michigan Open.[33] Louis also played with Clyde Martin, the first head professional at Langston Golf Course in Washington, D.C. (a large oak on Langston's fifth hole was dubbed the "Joe Louis Tree" because the champ hooked so many drives into it). Martin was born in Maryland and caddied for white professional Tommy Armour at Bethesda's Congressional Country Club. Louis and Martin played together consistently from 1939 until Louis joined the army in 1942, most often on Rackham Municipal Golf Course, Louis's home course in Detroit.[34]

The Brown Bomber was bitten hard by the golfing bug. He was on Rackham's fifteenth hole when he was notified in 1941 that his wife was filing for divorce, resentful at becoming "a golf widow." He also gambled lavishly on the game: black professional Bill Spiller once won $14,000 from him in a single weekend and bought a house. In 1946 Louis threatened to sue *Ebony* after an expose claimed he owed $60,000 in golf debts and played high-stakes matches with entertainers Bing Crosby and Bob

Hope for $1,000 per hole.[35] By 1939 he was organizing his own golf tournament at Rackham, and in 1941 he started attending the UGA's annual national championship. That year his Detroit tournament became an official UGA event: the Joe Louis Open. "This tournament will prove to the whites that we have some Hagans and Sarazens too," he told the press. Early winners included his first two instructors, Corbin (1939) and Martin (1941).[36] While African Americans frequented all six of Detroit's municipal courses, the Joe Louis Open helped Rackham—which hosted the UGA National in 1934, 1955, and 1965—become a key gathering spot for black golfers and events. Forty percent of its players were African American by 1951 when the city appointed a black pro, Willie Mosely, to serve as its head professional.[37]

World War II put the UGA (and the Joe Louis Open) on hold but failed to dampen Louis's enthusiasm for golf. He joined the army's Special Services Division and staged ninety-three boxing exhibitions for over 2 million soldiers, performing with other celebrity golf aficionados like boxer Sugar Ray Robinson. Louis's celebrity status allowed him to pursue golf while enlisted, even at segregated military bases in the South. This included his lessons with UGA pro Solomon Hughes outside Fort McClellan, Alabama, as well as golf with white GIs at Fort Riley, Kansas. He also played with Allied troops on courses in England.[38]

A fairly accomplished player, Louis entered his first serious amateur tournament at Langston Golf Course in 1940, where an estimated gallery of 3,000 watched him play with UGA president George Adams and shoot a terrible 97-95-90. Yet he improved dramatically during and after the war, eventually scoring in the high 70s and low 80s on difficult courses (he once shot 69 at Rackham). He won amateur titles at the UGA's Eastern Open in 1947 and his own Joe Louis Open in 1948. In 1950 the *Pittsburgh Courier* even ranked him the top black amateur golfer in the country, although his fame certainly helped boost such perceptions. By that point Louis had begun to hint that he would quit boxing permanently for golf.[39] For the UGA, the success of Louis's tournament was more important than his skills as a player. From its inception the Joe Louis Open was "the richest golf tournament in the world for Negro players," its prize money and the Brown Bomber's celebrity connections drawing more fans and press coverage than any other event.[40] In 1947 the men's winner received $1,000 out of a total purse of $2,500, more than the $1,500 purse up for grabs at the UGA National. By 1950 Louis had upped the purse to $4,000.[41]

In addition to funding the UGA's most successful tournament, Louis also provided critical financial support to black players as they pursued professional golf. Along with Louis Rafael Corbin and Clyde Martin, several other UGA pros joined Louis's golfing entourage, traveling with him around the country, offering him golf lessons, and attempting to integrate white tournaments under his sponsorship; most notable were Solomon Hughes, Bill Spiller, and Ted Rhodes. In addition, it was Louis who convinced his friend entertainer Billy Eckstine to hire twenty-four-year-old Charlie Sifford in 1946 to be Eckstine's personal valet and golf instructor, a partnership that lasted ten years and helped Sifford become one of the most important golfers in history. "Joe Louis was the most big-hearted man I have ever met in my life," Sifford wrote in his memoir. "He just loved the competition, and he loved to help people out. He didn't care about the money. . . . He was the most generous man I've ever seen, as well as one of the few black men committed to making things better for his people. In his day he was a towering symbol of strength and pride for the black man. He was a true hero."[42] Without Louis's support the UGA tour would not have thrived the way it did in the late 1940s and 1950s, nor would it have received as much notice and press attention, especially from white fans. Louis was thus an ideal ambassador for black golf who helped black professionals appeal to whites and, eventually, integrate the PGA. UGA organizers and fans certainly agreed and never forgot; in 1975 the tour dedicated its fiftieth anniversary UGA National to Louis, fans besieging the champ at San Diego's Torrey Pines Golf Course six years before his death.[43]

The UGA offered black professionals a space to pursue competitive golf in a segregated society and a platform to challenge discrimination in the world of white golf, especially tournaments sanctioned by the PGA and USGA. Unlike in other sports, white players did not even have to show up: access to certain facilities allowed UGA standouts to compare their talents with white pros simply by posting comparable tournament scores on the same courses. When Ted Rhodes won the UGA's 1948 Houston Open on Memorial Park Golf Course, local fans noted that his score flirted with acclaimed white pro Jimmy Demaret's course record.[44] Head-to-head contests also took place before World War II, as leading UGA players entered the occasional white tournament and arranged exhibition contests against white pros. Pat Ball, first snubbed by white golfers in 1918 after he and Walter Speedy were barred from the Chicago city championship, continued to challenge discrimination at white tournaments more than any black golfer since John Shippen. By the 1920s he was winning local tournaments against white players, including the Cook County Open in 1927, 1929, and 1934. In 1928 he and Porter Washington staged an exhibition match against two white PGA pros at Shady Rest.[45]

Even Howard Wheeler, whom many contemporaries considered less willing to confront discrimination in golf, played high-profile exhibitions against whites, including a 1938 match that featured Wheeler and Frank Radcliffe defeating white pros Charles Halarack and Gene Battistoni (Battistoni qualified for the U.S. Open in 1938 and 1941). The interracial contest drew a large gallery to Chicago's Palos Park.[46] However, Wheeler made fewer inroads into white professional golf compared with other black pros, especially those who peaked later in the 1950s and 1960s. He took occasional jobs that provided financial security and allowed him the freedom to play (for a time he was a chauffeur for entertainer Ethel Waters), all the while earning more money from unsuspecting players in cash games than he ever would at professional tournaments. As a result, his legacy and contribution were particularly forgotten, much like the legendary black players who dominated Negro League baseball yet were unknown to whites. "As good as Howard Wheeler was," recalled Sifford, "he never talked to me about wanting to play professional golf on the white tour. . . . Howard just didn't have that kind of personality or persistence to push his way into pro golf. He was content to be the local favorite and to take on anyone who wanted to challenge him on his home course."[47]

The most significant prewar challenge at a national tournament took place in 1928 when Pat Ball and another black golfer, Elmer Stout of Newark, New Jersey, qualified for the USGA's Public Links National Championship and traveled to Cobbs Creek in Philadelphia to compete. It was a course familiar to Ball, who had won a UGA tournament there the previous year. Ball and Stout participated in the opening rounds (Ball was tied for sixth place after the first round), and both men qualified for the tournament's final. Although some white participants had objected, everything appeared fine until USGA officials abruptly informed the men that they were disqualified from the tournament for a scoring error. Ball and Stout immediately went to a Philadelphia court and sought an injunction to halt the event and allow them to continue playing. What followed was an emergency, four-hour court hearing in which the players squared off against lawyers representing Ganson Depew, head of the USGA's Public Links division and nephew of former New York senator Chauncey Depew. The details revealed in the hearing proved embarrassing to Depew and the USGA. Disgruntled players and USGA officials had indeed discussed whether or not to even allow Ball and Stout in the tournament before it began. Worse, although players were responsible for policing themselves (the honor system), Ball and Stout had been followed by men posing as reporters who were charged with looking for infractions in order to remove them from the tournament. At the end of the hearing, the court ruled in favor of the two black players despite the USGA's plea that the tournament was nearly over, many participants had already left town, and an injunction would ultimately lead to its cancellation. The judge suggested Ball and Stout play against the white tournament "winner" in order to determine the actual winner, an idea the USGA rejected. Unperturbed, the judge responded, "If you don't want this match stopped, you must make some arrangements to put these men back in the game."[48]

Vindicated from charges of cheating, Ball and Stout then approached USGA representatives outside the courtroom with a significant gesture: in order to save the tournament, they would voluntarily withdraw "for the good of the game." It was, the judge announced, an example of "exceptionally good sportsmanship." The USGA also applauded the men and offered to pay their expenses, while reaction in the black community was mixed. Ball and Stout were cheered for exposing racism in the rarefied world of a national golf tournament: "Very unceremoniously the blue-blooded scions of golfdom were hauled into a court of civil action to answer charges of discrimination . . . by shady-skinned sons of Africa," proclaimed the black *Philadelphia Tribune*.[49] But other black observers soured at the men's decision to bow out of the tournament, especially after a court had ruled in their favor. "It was a mistake, a great, big mistake, in not stopping the Golf Tournament if they refused to begin the tournament over again and give the barred men a chance to compete against the other players," wrote one upset fan. "For be it remembered, the barred men were accused of cheating, for this, if for no other reason, they should have put the 'iron' to the souls of the cowards who would dare to besmirch the characters of men who are honest sports."[50] One black sportswriter echoed that criticism: "It is okay to show high-class sportsmanship . . . providing that you are dealing with high-class sportsmen," he wrote. "We have got to fight fire with fire and quit compromising."[51] The players' lawyer, Raymond Alexander, was a young black graduate of Harvard Law School who took the case for free. Alexander defended Ball and Stout in court and subsequently in the black press, where he praised their sportsmanship and argued that the judge's decision would help future legal challenges to segregated schools in Philadelphia (Alexander would later become the city's first African American judge in 1959).⁵²

Unfortunately, the sportsmanship that saved the 1928 USGA Public Links Championship was not returned. When Ball attempted to enter the 1933 U.S. Open at Chicago's Medinah Country Club, he received a letter from the competition committee indicating he was banned from all future USGA national tournaments owing to his "conduct" in Philadelphia five years earlier. The note was signed by Prescott Bush, who later became head of the USGA in 1935 and a U.S. senator (as well as father and grandfather to future U.S. presidents George H. W. Bush and George W. Bush, respectively).⁵³ Along with Ball and Stout, other UGA players, including Louis Rafael Corbin and Howard Wheeler, made numerous attempts to follow John Shippen's legacy and reintegrate USGA national tournaments, especially the U.S. Open.

Ball was briefly successful, entering tournaments hosted by the Western Golf Association (WGA), an organization founded to promote golf in the Midwest and counter the USGA's "eastern establishment." He played in the WGA's signature Western Open twice, in Detroit (1930) and Dayton, Ohio (1931), where he was the only black competitor in a field of leading white pros like Gene Sarazen and Walter Hagen. The WGA responded in 1932 by prominently including the phrase "caucasians only, except by invitation" on its entry blanks and barring UGA players for the next twenty-four years. A group from Tampa, Florida, including Southern Open champion Sanders Mason, was rejected from the 1938 Western Open in St. Louis.⁵⁴

Struggling to access PGA-, USGA-, and WGA-sanctioned events, UGA pros in 1942 were offered a unique opportunity to play against elite white professionals at an unsanctioned tournament: the "All-American Open." Noted businessman and golf promoter George S. May organized the event at his Chicago-area course, Tam O'Shanter Country Club. With PGA and USGA events facing wartime cancellation, May's vision was simple and bold: with a shrewd marketing plan and the largest cash prizes in history, he would attract the world's top players and turn golf into a national spectator sport. More important for UGA players, and cheered by African Americans, was May's ardent support for integration, and in 1942 he insisted that his event would be opened to all qualified golfers. "The words 'national' and 'All-American' in the names of these tournaments mean exactly what they say," he responded after a black Chicago alderman asked if African Americans were permitted to participate. "I am fully aware that Negroes are being called upon . . . to do their full share in the national war effort and I know that many thousands of your people are presently serving. . . . Their participation will not only be permitted at the Tam O'Shanter tournaments, it will be welcomed."[55]

Along with black amateurs, ten professionals were invited to the 1942 All-American Open (also called the "Tam O'Shanter Open"): Pat Ball, Howard Wheeler, Edison Marshall, John Brooks Dendy, Zeke Hartsfield, Frank Radcliffe, Clyde Martin, Calvin Searles, Hoxie Hazzard, and Eddie Jackson. Although none finished in the top thirty, a large gallery followed the players, especially the popular Wheeler, who finished top among the black participants (T-64) and received a $200 prize for "most colorful golfer."[56] Wheeler's trick shots particularly wowed the crowds.

The Tam O'Shanter Open made history again the following year after May convinced a reluctant PGA to make it a sponsored PGA event, the first in history to feature black professionals. This time thirteen teed up, including Wheeler and Calvin Searles, a caddie at the New Orleans Country Club who finished first among the black players. The largest gallery flocked to watch a popular black amateur compete: Joe Louis. Among the spectators was sixty-five-year-old Walter Speedy, the grandfather of Chicago's black golf scene in one of his final public appearances before he died that December.[57]

While black women struggled to make inroads into white tournaments and women in general had far fewer outlets in the world of competitive golf, the Tam O'Shanter Open welcomed them as well. At the 1944 Tam O'Shanter, Geneva Wilson became the first black woman to compete against white women in a major tournament. In subsequent years she was joined by Thelma Cowans, Ann Gregory, and Mary Brown. Male or female, black entrants also improved their performances over time and competed gamely against the world's best. Gregory finished eighth among the women at the 1951 Tam O'Shanter, while Calvin Searles in 1944 was challenging the world's best white player, Byron Nelson, for the lead in the final round before a late quadruple bogey left him in twenty-second place.[58] Searles's fine play in a tournament dedicated to servicemen was quite poignant: within months he was killed in action in France, a promising golf career cut short by both racial segregation and war.[59]

With African Americans forging a national tour and competing alongside white professionals in the nation's richest tournament, a curious sentiment emerged in the early 1940s: the idea that professional golf was actually more racially tolerant than other sports, especially baseball.

After all, at Tam O'Shanter dozens of black golfers competed against the world's best white players, including southerners like Byron Nelson, Ben Hogan, Sam Snead, and Babe Didrikson Zaharias, five years before a lone Jackie Robinson stepped onto a Major League Baseball field. The notion of golf as the last bastion of white privilege, so powerful in American history, was challenged yet again. Fans took notice, some even finding in golf the motivation to challenge segregation elsewhere. "Negro stars are competing . . . in golf tournaments," hailed the *New Journal and Guide* in 1939. "Baseball seems to be the most stubborn of all, but, it too, can be cracked, and it will be."[60] Such calls escalated dramatically after the integration of the Tam O'Shanter in 1942: "Last summer the biggest professional golf tournament was open to Negroes," remarked the *Cleveland Call and Post*. "Baseball is the only major sport that draws a color line." In Baltimore, the *Afro-American* fumed at segregation in Major League Baseball by telling its readers that golf was "open to all."[61] In the game's popular memory this burst of optimism surrounding race and professional golf was short lived and soon forgotten. Along with the desegregation of Major League Baseball, the end of World War II would present fans with a new set of high-profile examples reiterating the unwillingness of the PGA and USGA to pursue integration, especially in the all-important events hosted by private golf courses.

Meanwhile, after suspending its tour during World War II, the UGA returned to action stronger than ever, nurturing a new crop of elite players in the late 1940s and 1950s. Foremost among them was Theodore "Ted" Rhodes. A native of Nashville, Tennessee, Rhodes grew up in the 1920s caddying for white players at the Belle Meade and Richland country clubs, occasionally finding opportunities to practice with a discarded 2-iron. His pursuit of golf was remarkable considering how inaccessible the game was in the black neighborhoods of Nashville: all of its municipal courses were closed to African Americans, and unlike many cities in the South it had no segregated black course. The young Rhodes practiced in local parks, building his own play areas by sticking tree branches in the ground and fashioning rudimentary "greens" around them.[62] He then served in the CCC and joined the navy during World War II. In 1943 the thirty-year-old Rhodes overheard golfers discussing a new tournament in Detroit. "I heard one of the Nashville pros talking about his score in the [Joe] Louis Open," he recalled. "And I said to myself, 'I can beat that.'"[63] And he did; he failed to win on his first try but then captured Louis's UGA crown four straight years from 1946 to 1949.

Ted Rhodes at Chicago's Tam O'Shanter Golf Course in 1952 (Courtesy USGA Archives).

More important than Rhodes's success in Detroit was that he endeared himself to Joe Louis and Billy Eckstine, the entertainer who became Charlie Sifford's patron. Louis, ever searching for talented golfers to patronize, offered to sponsor Rhodes and fund his pursuit of professional golf, just as he had Solomon Hughes. Unlike Hughes, Rhodes took the offer and used the opportunity to become the best black golfer in America, traveling alongside Louis (often serving as his valet) and playing as much golf as he could. Louis's money, fame, and connections to the white golfing world immediately helped. He paid for Rhodes to spend significant time in southern California and take lessons from Ray Mangrum, a notable white instructor from Texas. (Mangrum was a five-time winner on the PGA circuit, and his brother, Lloyd Mangrum, won thirty-six times, good for thirteenth on the all-time list for most career PGA victories.) Mentored by one of the period's top white pros, Rhodes matched his success in the Joe Louis Open with stellar performances in the UGA National, which he won three consecutive times from 1949 to 1951 immediately after Howard Wheeler's three-peat from 1946 to 1948.

Wheeler and Rhodes forged a celebrated rivalry at a time when black interest in competitive golf surged with postwar optimism. Like Wheeler, fans were enthralled with Rhodes and liked his eccentricities: nicknamed "Rags" because of his meticulous style and dress (he was known for wearing distinctive, multicolored Tam O'Shanter caps), Rhodes won awards for being the best-dressed golfer on tour. His easygoing demeanor also earned accolades, although neither his laid-back attitude nor Wheeler's trick-shot antics got in the way of serious golf.[64] When it came time to compete, the men were true professionals, and the UGA competition could be fierce. "For the first time in my life, I found myself surrounded by a whole bunch of black guys who could really play," wrote Charlie Sifford of his first UGA tournament. "The National Negro Open was our Masters."[65] During a tense final round at the 1949 Sugar Ray Robinson Open (like Louis, Robinson also sponsored his own UGA tournament), Rhodes got mad when he heard a noisy fan in the gallery and insisted that the man leave the course. He did not care when the offender turned out to be Robinson, the event's celebrity host. Rhodes went on to shoot a record 62 on Staten Island's South Shore Golf Club to win the tournament, which he also won in 1947 and 1948.

Rhodes solidified his ascendancy over Wheeler in 1949 when the UGA's two biggest tournaments, the Joe Louis Open and the UGA National, took place in the same city (Detroit) one week apart and Rhodes won them both.[66] When the *Pittsburgh Courier* published a ranking of black golfers in 1952, he was the runaway leader, and in 1954 he became the first black professional to land an endorsement, signing a three-year deal with Ohio's Burke Golf Company.[67] By 1960, however, his health had begun to falter, reportedly due to a kidney ailment. Having won an estimated 150 UGA tournaments, including the national championship four times (1949, 1950, 1951, and 1957), Rhodes moved back to Nashville and devoted himself to teaching and mentoring younger players; his list of talented pupils included Sifford, Lee Elder, Althea Gibson, and Jim Dent. In 1969 he died at age fifty-five. "Ted Rhodes was like a father to me," Elder said the next day. "He took me under his wing when I was 16 years old and completely rebuilt my golf game and my life." One month later Nashville renamed its Cumberland Municipal Golf Course the Ted Rhodes Golf Course.[68]

Charlie Sifford recalled how the same humbleness that endeared Rhodes to his black fans and fellow competitors also helped history overlook his accomplishments. "Teddy Rhodes was the black Jack Nicklaus," he wrote. "His only fault was that he was far too soft-spoken a person, too much a gentleman, to make waves and try to force his way onto the white tour."[69] Sifford drew mentorship from Rhodes and the tour's other top player of the 1940s, Howard Wheeler, to help him dominate the UGA during the 1950s and become its all-time greatest player. Sifford was born in Charlotte, North Carolina, in 1922 and raised in a strict Baptist family. His father worked at a local fertilizer plant. At age ten he began caddying at the Carolina Country Club, and by thirteen he was earning as much in tips from the white club members as his father made at his job. He was also the best golfer on the course, caddie or member, shooting in the 60s. While much of Sifford's earnings went to his mother, he kept some to nurture his favorite hobby: cigars. He began smoking them at age twelve and never quit despite repeated school suspensions. For the rest of his life he was rarely seen on a golf course without one.[70]

In the South, white country club members often turned a blind eye, or even openly approved, when young black caddies, but not black men, occasionally played the course. When Sifford turned seventeen, some members started to complain about seeing him on the links too often. "I was made to understand that I might be in physical danger out there on the golf course," he recalled. "It was okay for me to whack balls around the course when I was a black caddy playing with the other black caddies, or when I was carrying a member's bag. But now I was becoming serious about my game and I didn't want to live with playing only when somebody threw me a handout." The club's owner, sympathetic and insistent that Sifford had a potential future in golf, convinced him (and his parents) that he should drop out of school and live with his uncle in Philadelphia: "He told me that there were good golf courses up there that wouldn't have any trouble allowing me to play."[71]

Arriving in Philadelphia in 1939, Sifford met accomplished black players like Howard Wheeler and became a fixture at Cobbs Creek. During the war he served in the army (and saw action at the Battle of Okinawa) and soon after began serving as Billy Eckstine's personal valet/golf

Charlie Sifford with his wife and son in 1961 (Look Magazine Photograph Collection, Prints & Photographs Division, Library of Congress, LC-L9-61-4520).

instructor and entering as many professional tournaments as he could. He played a UGA event for the first time in 1946 (the UGA National in Pittsburgh) and took over the tour in 1951, winning four of the six tournaments he entered, including his first UGA victory in Atlanta's Southern Open.[72] He went on to match Howard Wheeler's record by winning the national championship six times (1952, 1953, 1954, 1955, 1956, and 1960), including a record five-straight UGA Nationals. Like Ted Rhodes, Sifford signed an endorsement deal with Burke Golf and in 1956 began performing exhibitions around the country marketing his own signature line of Burke golf clubs to African Americans.[73] He was not as eccentric as Wheeler but more extroverted than Rhodes. "Sifford wears conservative sports clothes, scorns neckties and likes informality," wrote one sportswriter. Nothing embodied that informality more than his cigars, which became his signature with fans in the late 1940s. Sports pages and UGA publications were filled with references to the "cigar-smoking stylist" who was "seldom seen either on or off the course without a cigar firmly clenched in his teeth."[74]

The UGA provided Sifford some national recognition and helped certify him as the top black golfer in the country; however, his success in the 1950s also exposed the tour's limitations. In terms of the golf courses themselves, the discrepancy between white and black professional golf was often a chasm that exceeded that of other sports. Sifford and his fellow competitors usually honed their skills on the nation's public links, including popular municipal courses in poor shape. Trying to break into white tournaments at nicer courses meant tackling more than just racial discrimination; it also meant altering one's game dramatically for faster greens that still "held better," well-watered fairways, and different sand textures. By 1950, supporters of Ted Rhodes were adamant that he and other black pros would be even more competitive with whites were they allowed to practice on and get better acquainted with the type of courses that hosted PGA events. Sifford and other African Americans who later managed to cross over to the PGA in the 1960s and 1970s would fondly remember the UGA but always bemoaned the "lousy" course conditions they had to contend with.[75]

There was also the problem of money, for UGA success failed to pay the bills. By 1956 Sifford still struggled to make ends meet and relied on occasional gambling, hustling, and generous support from patrons just to keep playing. He recalled that Billy Eckstine, who no longer needed a valet or golf instructor, kept him on his payroll anyway "to help me out." Fans themselves also donated. In Los Angeles, members of the Cosmopolitan Golf Club and Western States Golf Association established the "Charles Sifford Trust Fund" to help him (and other black pros) keep playing and gain admission to white tournaments. The most Sifford ever earned winning one of his six UGA championships was $800, and he only totaled an estimated $17,000 in tournament earnings before 1961. UGA domination did not provide a living: "I really needed to make some money in golf," he later wrote.[76]

If a top player like Sifford struggled to make a living on the UGA tour, those with less success had even greater obstacles to overcome. Few were able to devote themselves full time to golf. Some worked in the industry—from caddies to course professionals and instructors—but others did not. Porter Washington, 1928 national champion, played for years on the tour while working as a chef in Boston, while 1940 champion Hugh Smith worked at an industrial plant in Georgia. John Brooks Dendy, 1932, 1936, and 1937 champion, was so financially strapped that he went back to serving as a locker-room attendant at the same Asheville, North Carolina, country club where he grew up caddying.[77] By the late 1940s, Bill Spiller, the most outspoken professional on the UGA, loudly protested the lack of resources available to black players and the economic implications of a segregated PGA. Among the most talented black golfers (and despite the $14,000 he won from Joe Louis), Spiller could barely afford to travel to UGA events. He was furious when Sugar Ray Robinson abruptly canceled his 1951 tournament in New York after many players had already arrived. "I'm not certain I'll be back East next year," he told the press. "There's no chance to make enough money to support one's self during the tournament season."[78]

Unlike most UGA players, Spiller was a college-educated man who had tried (and failed) to make a living as a teacher, then worked as a railroad porter before dedicating himself full time to professional golf. This made his dejection over the lack of money in black tournaments, and his rage at the PGA, all the more palpable. Born in rural Tishomingo, Oklahoma, he moved to live with his father in Tulsa when he was nine. Spiller attended all-black Wiley College in Marshall, Texas, and sought work as a teacher after graduation. But he soured on a $60-per-month position at a black high school and soon headed to Los Angeles in search of better opportunities. In 1942 he was twenty-nine years old when a friend convinced him to try golf for the first time, perhaps the latest start for a professional player in the game's history. Within four years Spiller had won several black tournaments in southern California and joined the small cadre of players, instructors, and celebrities in Los Angeles who supported black golfers, including Ted Rhodes and his white teacher, Ray Mangrum, as well as Jimmie DeVoe and Joe Louis. Through Louis, Spiller abruptly found himself playing alongside Hollywood's white elite far from the segregated world of small-town Oklahoma. Yet he had a history of fierce resistance to discrimination (he carried a gun for much of his life after a white shopkeeper in Tulsa slapped him when he was a boy—"and he pulled it a time or two," his son recalled).[79] With a fierce temper and a willingness to debate anyone on issues of race and segregation, Spiller was a dangerous black golfer, well educated and unintimidated by the pageantry of white country clubs. He once confronted Fred Astaire when the entertainer snubbed him at L.A.'s Bel Air Club. "I'm in the locker

Bill Spiller at the 1948 Los Angeles Open (AP Photo/Ed Widdis).

room putting on my shoes and Fred Astaire walks in and gives me a stare as if to say, 'What the hell are you doing here?'" Spiller remembered years later. "If eyes could kill, I would have died right there. But I looked right back at him, didn't bat an eye. He finally said, 'Well, I guess maybe you're supposed to be here.'"[80]

Even with help from Joe Louis, Spiller struggled to make ends meet, taking a series of jobs in Los Angeles (including at a post office) that took time away from practicing and traveling to tournaments. Although he was not as successful on the UGA tour, his headstrong temperament made him a key figure in attempts to integrate white tournaments during the late 1940s and 1950s, especially in California. While some players, such as Howard Wheeler and Ted Rhodes, were more hesitant to challenge segregation, Spiller became the UGA's most vocal advocate demanding immediate desegregation in competitive golf. "Spiller was much more of an activist than Teddy or the other blacks," wrote Charlie Sifford. "He complained loud and long to anyone who would listen about his rights to play the game, and he was known for picketing professional golf tournaments. ... Spiller was always the most militant of the black golfers."[81]

After World War II a new generation of players also appeared in the UGA women's division. Among them was Thelma (McTyre) Cowans, winner of five UGA Nationals (1947, 1949, 1954, 1955, and 1956). Cowans came from an athletic family and was one of the few UGA standouts who got their start playing golf in school. She excelled in a number of sports while at Atlanta's Morris Brown College in the late 1930s and pressed the institution to form a women's golf team after a doctor recommended she take up the game; the students played at New Lincoln Country Club. After relocating with her family to Detroit, Thelma and her sisters, Theresa and Dorcas, continued to play and joined the Detroit Amateur Golf Association, the organization UGA pioneer Marie Thompson had helped form a decade earlier. In 1946 she married Russ Cowans, the editor of the black *Michigan Chronicle* and a regular contributor of golf columns to the *Chicago Defender*.[82] Her competitive golf career peaked as she moved to Los Angeles in 1949, joining the Vernondale Golf Club (which became Vernoncrest Golf Club in 1955) and playing alongside her sisters and entertainer Maggie Hathaway, L.A.'s biggest advocate for black golfers.

One of the UGA's smallest players, Cowans was nevertheless a fierce competitor who ruffled the feathers of fellow golfers. She was unafraid to beat her own sisters, who also competed in UGA events with less success, and was known for a having a Napoleonic streak on the links. She had an icy relationship with Eoline (Jackson) Thornton, the 1951 UGA women's champion who also lived in Los Angeles and played out of the Vernoncrest Club. The two women were not on speaking terms, even during the finals of the 1954 UGA National in Dallas, where they squared off in a tense match without saying a word to each other.[83] The 1956 women's championship was even worse, as Cowans sparked the largest controversy in the UGA's competitive history. Paired against Baltimore's Alma Arvin in the women's final, Cowans arrived late to the course after Arvin had already completed nine holes. Citing USGA rules (which all UGA events were played under), the UGA initially declared Arvin the winner, but organizers reconvened and decided to restart the match. Cowans proceeded to win her sixth and final championship, but the victory came at a cost, with most of the other female players denouncing the decision and threatening to boycott future tournaments. Afterward she slowly distanced herself from competitive golf; however, no one could deny her talent. When Charlie Sifford won the 1957 Long Beach Open the following year, becoming the first African American to win a major integrated tournament, he credited the victory to a last-minute putting lesson from Cowans.[84]

Yet the most talented black woman on the UGA tour in the 1950s was Ann Moore Gregory, who won five UGA Nationals (1950, 1953, 1957, 1965, and 1966) and in 1956 became the first black woman to play in a USGA national championship. Born in Aberdeen, Mississippi, she worked as a maid for a white family while in high school and then left the South to live with her sister in Gary, Indiana. She was an accomplished tennis player, winning the 1937 Gary City Tennis Championship, who married LeRoy Percy Gregory in 1938 and initially balked at the amount of golf her new husband played. However, after he was drafted into the navy during World War II, she found solace on the links and joined the Chicago Women's Golf Club. Her first UGA victory came in 1948, and in 1950 she won six of the seven tournaments she entered, including the UGA National.[85] Just six years after barely breaking 100 on the golf course, Gregory was shooting in the 70s and setting course records at UGA events in Michigan, Illinois, Ohio, and Indiana. She was particularly liked by fans who marveled at her relatively late start in golf and dramatic improvement.

The attention Gregory drew also highlighted how a shift in postwar gender ideals prompted female athletes to pursue their sports in a new social context. The black press celebrated how the humble housewife managed to juggle a full-time job in Gary, a family, and a burgeoning national golf career. As they did with the era's most celebrated white female golfer, Babe Didrikson Zaharias, sportswriters and fans emphasized Gregory's femininity in a way that echoed the new expectations levied on female athletes (and women in general) during the 1950s. Notably, these expectations were not trumped by her race. "Anyone looking for an example of what Negro womanhood can achieve in sports can turn to Mrs. Gregory," exclaimed the *Cleveland Call and Post*.[86] Fans were delighted when Gregory indicated she had no problem with her daughter shunning sports and instead learning piano at home: "My main thought . . . is my little girl," she told the *Chicago Defender*. "I will not let golf get between me and my family, although I love the game."[87]

Led by players like Gregory, Cowans, Wheeler, Rhodes, and Sifford, the UGA expanded its talent pool and fan base in the late 1940s and early 1950s, while attempts by its players to challenge white competitors also increased. In Chicago a dispute with the PGA led George May to end his annual Tam O'Shanter Open in 1958 but not before the event showcased black and white golfers squaring off in front of a national audience for most of the decade. Rhodes was tied for fourteenth in 1949, the best finish by a black man in the event's history. White fans cheered the players, and children flocked to get Joe Louis's autograph as he roamed the fairways.[88] Even Bill Spiller, who shared few positive stories of the PGA or its events, fondly remembered the appreciation of white fans at Tam O'Shanter. "While we're having lunch a kid tapped me on my shoulder and asked for an autograph," he recalled. "I said, 'Mine?' and he said, 'You played in the tournament, didn't you? Well, I want your autograph.' Then I noticed there were about twenty kids lined up. Shows you the difference in how generations react. Kids have no prejudice. That was a good lesson for me." The 1953 Tam O'Shanter Open broke barriers again when it aired on ABC, the first nationally televised golf tournament in American history. The black press even likened George May to Branch Rickey, the Major League Baseball executive credited for championing integration after he signed Jackie Robinson.[89]

Yet the battle was far from over. Unlike in most professional sports leagues, in golf, tournaments drifted in and out of the purview of the game's main governing bodies—the USGA and PGA—with distinctions between "officially sanctioned," "co-sanctioned," or "independent" events often blurred for both fans and players. When Robinson stepped onto the field for the Brooklyn Dodgers, no one questioned the extent to which it was a *true* Major League Baseball contest. Such was not the case in the world of professional golf. Reluctantly lending its name to the Tam O'Shanter Open, the PGA was nevertheless governed by an organization that had reaffirmed its commitment to segregation even as white fans cheered Howard Wheeler and Joe Louis in Chicago at an event it co-sponsored. The PGA's informal ban on African American membership, which began with the organization's inception in 1916, was codified in 1934 when it amended its constitution to limit membership explicitly to "professional golfers of the Caucasian race . . . residing in North or South America."[90] More tournaments appeared willing to drop barriers to black participants, but the PGA had doubled down on segregation well before the war and was now more explicitly racist than it had ever been.

Moreover, the PGA constitution made it clear that the organization was not interested in pursuing any sort of "gentlemen's agreement" on segregation, restricting black players for tournaments in the South but welcoming them at northern events. Such an approach was popular in the sporting world during the 1930s and 1940s, including intercollegiate athletics. All of the black players (including the militant Bill Spiller) had not even hinted at trying to enter PGA tournaments in the South. "You fella's aren't going to Mississippi or Alabama anyway," Texas pro Jimmy Demaret told Spiller when he supported Spiller's attempt to integrate a PGA event in California. "I said he was right," Spiller recalled. "I always appreciated Jimmy's attitude." However, with its Caucasian clause, the PGA was intent on banning black golfers at tournaments anywhere in the country.[91]

The curious case of one professional, Dewey Brown, exemplified the extent to which the PGA went to exclude African Americans from its membership in the 1930s and 1940s. Born on a North Carolina farm in 1898, Brown moved with his family to New Jersey and started caddying at age eight. He worked his way up through the ranks at Madison Golf Club (Madison, N.J.), Morris County Country Club (Morristown, N.J.), Shawnee Golf Resort (Shawnee-on-Delaware, Pa.), and the famed Baltusrol Golf Club (Springfield, N.J.). Brown became a respected golf course superintendent and skilled club-maker and was considered one of the finest in the nation: he built clubs for 1916 U.S. Amateur champion Chick Evans as well as President Warren G. Harding and Vice President Charles Dawes. His skills as a player and instructor were well known, and working at the leading private clubs in New Jersey and eastern Pennsylvania brought him close to elite golfers and entertainers: he caddied for John D. Rockefeller and the Vanderbilt family and later played with Al Jolson, Bing Crosby, Bob Hope, Fred Astaire, Walter Hagen, and bandleader Fred Waring.

In 1928 Brown quietly sent an application, which did not mention his race, to join the PGA and was accepted, becoming the first African American in history to be admitted to the organization. His light skin reportedly helped him fly under the radar, and he may have passed for white with some golf acquaintances. Yet six years later, in 1934, the PGA added the Caucasian clause to its constitution and abruptly rescinded his membership: although the specifics remained a mystery (as they do today),

Brown was convinced someone brought his African ancestry to the organization's attention. Unwavering, he continued working at the finest courses in the area, including Rockaway River Country Club (Denville, N.J.) and Knoll Golf Club (Boonton, N.J.). In 1947 he purchased the Cedar River Golf Club in Indian Lake, New York, which he ran until his death in 1973.[92]

The blatant exclusion of Dewey Brown and the addition of the Caucasian clause in 1934 signaled how far the PGA would go to prohibit black participation. Nevertheless, local organizers and hosts held considerable power over their own tournaments, including events cosanctioned by the PGA. Joining George May's Tam O'Shanter Open, two other events were quietly allowing black players to qualify by the mid-1940s: the Los Angeles Open at Riviera Country Club and the Canadian Open, held at various courses in Canada. In 1944 Jimmie DeVoe became the first African American to play in the L.A. Open, followed by Bill Spiller in 1945. Both were hardly noted in the press at the time, their participation overshadowed by Babe Didrikson Zaharias making the 1945 field, the only woman to ever qualify her way into a PGA event.[93] Spiller was joined by Ted Rhodes in 1946, and for the next several years a number of black players, including Howard Wheeler and Joe Louis, participated in the tournament at Riviera, where they competed alongside white professionals with even greater success than at Tam O'Shanter. Spiller was tied with Ben Hogan one stroke off the lead after the opening round of the 1948 L.A. Open. Rhodes finished the tournament in twentieth place, and Spiller was thirty-first; in 1950 Rhodes finished twelfth. Yet even when welcomed to play a PGA tournament regularly in Los Angeles, the men continued to face discrimination and awkward encounters. One year the three black players in the field were all paired together. "When I came out on the first tee I told the starter, 'You know, something puzzles me. How come we all three got paired together, all the blacks?'" Spiller recalled. "He said, 'You know how it is, we got some Texas guys to deal with.' I said, 'I thought this was the L.A. Open, not the Texas Open. If they don't want to play with us, tell 'em to go the hell back to Texas.' Well, the starter's microphone was on all the time and, boy, the crowd heard all that, went wild, clapping and whistling. We could hardly get off the tee."[94]

By finishing in the top sixty at the 1948 L.A. Open, Rhodes and Spiller automatically qualified for the following week's PGA event in Richmond, California, outside Oakland. They were joined by a third black player, local qualifier Madison Gunter. However, after a practice round, they were informed by an official that only PGA members could compete in the Richmond Open. Led by Spiller, the three players responded with a $250,000 lawsuit. For many fans it was the first time the Caucasian clause, now fourteen years old, became publicly known—more importantly, the PGA settled in court with what appeared to be a groundbreaking promise that it would no longer bar black players from tournament play.[95]

Unfortunately, it proved to be an empty gesture. Instead of opening doors for African Americans to access PGA events, the organization drew from the segregationist playbook and began employing semantics: "open" tournaments became "open invitationals" overnight. That summer Ted Rhodes and Solomon Hughes, with urging from Joe Louis, attempted to sign up for the PGA's St. Paul Open in Minnesota only to be told the tournament was now an "invitational." Black leaders in the city, including Whitney Young, future director of the National Urban League, protested and pointed out that tickets printed earlier for the event clearly indicated an "open" tournament.[96]

Access to the L.A. Open and the lawsuit over the exclusion of Spiller, Rhodes, and Gunter from the Richmond Open made California a battleground over race and the PGA, drawing the state's high-profile tournaments and golf celebrities into a national debate over segregation far from the Deep South. In 1949 Joe Louis penned an angry letter to Bing Crosby after Spiller and Rhodes were barred from Crosby's popular PGA tournament at Pebble Beach. The black press criticized the singer for standing by silently, "without even lifting his famous voice in protest."[97] In the wake of the Richmond Open decision, George May traveled from Tam O'Shanter in Chicago to California and lashed out at the PGA, the USGA, and white golfers, whom he claimed were not comfortable playing alongside black competitors: "those narrow-minded hot-shots from the South, refusing to play with the Negroes." He even called one out by name (Ben Hogan) and confronted PGA president Ed Dudley in person to protest the Caucasian clause. "They don't want the fellow from the wrong side of the tracks to get into golf, they want to restrict the game and keep it for the rich men," said May. "Y'know what those groups are afraid of? They fear a Negro will come along and win one of the tournaments."[98]

Tensions boiled over again in 1952 after Spiller, Louis, and California amateur Eural Clarke were banned from the PGA's San Diego Open. Spiller qualified for the tournament while its sponsors, San Diego's Chevrolet dealerships, invited the boxing champ to compete as a celebrity amateur. Spiller, sensing a controversy with the PGA and knowing that

Louis's involvement would draw more attention, encouraged the Brown Bomber to accept. Sure enough, shortly before the event the three were approached at the San Diego Country Club and told they were not allowed to play per PGA membership rules. Now assured that the PGA had lied in its settlement over the Richmond Open four years earlier, Louis this time responded with his harshest public comments yet. Encouraging the sponsors to cancel the tournament (and offering them double the charity money if they complied), he formally announced his retirement from boxing and declared a "war on Jim Crow in golf."[99] Louis indicated that the PGA's new president, Horton Smith, had personally called to inform him of "the ban on nonwhites" as PGA players and officials made their way to San Diego from the previous week's event (the Bing Crosby Pro-Am at Pebble Beach). Smith, a Missouri native, was an accomplished professional player in his own right: he won the first-ever Masters in 1934 and again in 1936.

But Louis was "the champ"—a black boxer immensely popular with white fans—and this time the gloves were off. Calling Smith "another Hitler," the Brown Bomber went after the PGA leader. "Smith believes in the white race like Hitler believed in the super race," he railed. "It's about time this ban is brought into the open."[100] Louis contacted his friend, the white radio host Walter Winchell, who broadcast the story on his national radio program; support for Louis's stand poured in from around the country. It was clear the symbolism of professional golf had shifted dramatically from the optimism of the late 1930s and early 1940s. Golf now appeared to be one of the lone holdouts over racial inclusion: "This is the last major sport in America in which Negroes are barred," said Louis, who called the snub the first time he had ever experienced racial discrimination in sports.[101] The *Atlanta Daily World* agreed that the PGA had made golf "one of the last frontiers of athletic discrimination in the United States," as did the *Pittsburgh Courier*: "If negro and white Americans can play baseball, football, basketball, and other games together, what can there be against them playing golf together?"[102]

Lost in the public feud between Louis and Smith was the fact that the real instigator was the most militant black pro golfer in history, Bill Spiller. Amidst the tension he managed to shoot 77-75 and qualify outright for the San Diego Open. Yet when Smith arrived at the club and arranged a private meeting with Louis and tournament officials, Spiller was not invited: everyone (including Louis) feared how he would react. "I was the guy doing all the rebelling and I think they didn't know how to talk to me because I wasn't a yes man," Spiller later said.[103] White pro Jimmy Demaret spotted him on the grounds of the San Diego Country Club and told him about the meeting. Spiller walked in, and the tension immediately escalated. "You're Bill Spiller aren't you? Is there something you want to say?" Smith exclaimed. Spiller unleashed years of frustration that prevented him from ever having a real golf career: "I know and you know that we're going to play in the tournaments. We all know it's coming," he said. "So if you like golf the way you say you do, and I do, I think we should make an agreement so we can play without all this adverse publicity. And take that Caucasians-only clause out of your constitution so we can have opportunities to get jobs as pros at clubs." Smith responded that golf was a social game and the PGA had to be "careful who we put" on club jobs. The confrontation threatened to devolve into a fight. "Mr. Smith," said Spiller. "I heard a rumor that you said if you were as big as Joe Louis, you would knock me down. Well, if I hated someone that much, I wouldn't let size bother me." He was offended by the way Smith and the PGA condescended to black professionals. "I said he should talk to me like a man," Spiller later remembered of the encounter. "Not a kid who doesn't know what he's talking about."[104]

The PGA responded with a predictable solution: the beloved amateur Louis would play the San Diego Open on a sponsor's exemption (alongside Smith himself), while the professional Spiller was out. It was a clear public relations maneuver. Fans and the press would see the Masters winner and PGA president play a friendly round of golf with a beloved black athlete, overshadowing the blatant segregation of black professional golfers from a tournament in southern California. On the event's opening morning Spiller did his best to publicize the injustice, staging the first (and only) sit-in in the history of professional golf. He sat on the first tee with his clubs and prevented the tournament from starting until he was dragged away by Louis and friends. Louis then proceeded to play one of the more awkward rounds in golf history with Smith (the man he had called "another Hitler" days before) as Spiller fumed, feeling betrayed by Louis for agreeing to play the tournament without him.[105]

The shunning of Spiller was quickly forgotten, but the PGA still took a major blow in the press. Fan support for Louis marked the first time the PGA was hit hard by a public relations backlash over segregation. Jackie Robinson and other celebrities voiced their support, while telegrams from sympathetic fans and labor organizations (including the Congress of Industrial Organizations) poured in. Louis was "Still the champ!" proclaimed one black newspaper, which praised the boxer for not forgetting "his beginnings in prejudiced-ridden Alabama" and trying "to slug away at one of the last bulwarks of prejudice in sports—that which exists in golf."[106] Smith and the PGA began to relent under the pressure. After playing alongside Louis, the president announced that the PGA's tournament committee had unanimously voted to remove its tournament barrier to black pros. Local hosts and sponsors would still be allowed to ban players, but the PGA itself would not step in. It was a promise similar to the one made in 1948, but this time it would hold until the removal of the Caucasian clause in 1961.[107]

Over the next few weeks black players were invited to the 1952 Phoenix Open and Tucson Open. At the Phoenix Country Club Louis and Spiller were joined by Rhodes, two other black amateurs, and Charlie Sifford. The black players were all paired together and told to tee off first, early in the morning before many of the white professionals and fans had even arrived. Sifford removed the flagstick from the first hole and discovered that "somebody had been there before us. The cup was full of human shit, and from the looks and smell of it, it hadn't been too long before we got there that the cup had been filled."[108] Informed by club officials that the black players would not be allowed to use the locker rooms, Spiller insisted, "I am going into that locker room and I am going to take a shower." Rhodes and the others—arguing, as Sifford recalled, that the players "had to move slowly and not make waves if we were going to play any more white tournaments"—tried to talk him out of it to no avail. Ten minutes later Louis had to physically drag Spiller out of the shower after a club official insisted he was in danger: "He suggested that somebody might try to drown Bill."[109]

Gaining admission into a pro golf tournament thus proved to be the first of many barriers, and the racism players faced at sites around the country—on both white and black golf tours—turned the standard geography of segregation on its head. The players faced blatant abuse at PGA stops in California and Arizona in the 1950s, while the UGA's Cleveland Open ran into problems after players charged the city with closing Highland Park's locker rooms to prevent African Americans from using them. Meanwhile, the UGA happily announced in 1954 that Dallas's Cedar Crest Golf Course provided a warm welcome for its first UGA National in the Deep South, opening its facilities completely for black players and fans.[110]

Black competitors also received better treatment from country club facilities, clubhouses, and surrounding communities at events in Canada, and several times in the 1950s Rhodes, Spiller, and Sifford played three PGA cosponsored tournaments north of the border: the Montreal Open, the Labatt Open, and the Canadian Open. Spiller once finished fourteenth in the Labatt Open, his best-ever performance at a PGA event.[111] Tournaments in Canada not only drew top PGA golfers and welcomed black players but also took place in cities where African Americans could easily arrange transportation and lodging. Unique to other sports, professional touring golfers faced the difficult challenge of making (and funding) their own travel plans in order to get to tournaments. Black players faced the added uncertainty racial segregation provided; gaining admission to a golf tournament was fruitless if they failed to find local drivers, hotels, and restaurants near the course willing to serve them. Sifford ate and slept in his car many times while playing white events: "I don't know how many times I heard: 'Nigger, if you don't get away from here I'm going to call the police,'" he told *Ebony*.[112] As Canada's most prestigious event, the Canadian Open was thus worth the expense for black golfers to get there. Rhodes and Sifford played several times starting in 1953; Rhodes even drove all the way from Los Angeles to Vancouver for the 1954 Canadian Open. Yet it was Sifford's record-setting performance in 1955 (where he first met Arnold Palmer) that eclipsed these other Canadian appearances, allowing a more racially inclusive nation to help black golfers make headlines in their own country and infiltrate the PGA.[113]

Back in the United States, most PGA events did not invite African Americans until after the organization desegregated in 1961; however, black players continued to find sporadic opportunities in the 1950s. Rhodes was denied access to the 1952 Western Open in St. Louis; but in 1956 he joined Sifford in reintegrating the tournament, and they became the first black players in the event since Pat Ball in 1931. The barrier likely fell because the 1956 Western Open took place at San Francisco's Presidio Golf Course, a facility owned by the U.S. Army.[114] Rhodes finished twenty-fourth in the 1954 Insurance City Open in Connecticut, a precursor to the Sammy Davis Jr.-Greater Hartford Open. After Solomon Hughes was again denied entry to the St. Paul Open in 1951, he and Rhodes were finally allowed to compete in 1952, and in 1953 Rhodes was even tied for the lead after the first round. By 1955 Sifford and Rhodes were playing up to ten white events a year, including a series of PGA stops in the Midwest: the Miller High Life Open in Milwaukee and the Fort Wayne Open in Indiana (where they were joined by Spiller), along with the St. Paul Open and the Rubber City Open in Akron, Ohio, the PGA's first event at famed Firestone Country Club.[115]

Although the UGA supported these attempts to desegregate white events and established a "Discriminatory Practice Committee" to advise its players and publicize instances of discrimination, white tournaments were not always the most attractive option for black golfers.[116] During his spectacular 1949 season Rhodes received an invitation to the PGA's $5,000 Cedar Rapids Open in Iowa, scheduled for the same weekend as the UGA's $4,000 Joe Louis Open. Louis himself applauded the invitation and encouraged Rhodes to play the white event that week, yet Rhodes turned down the PGA and instead showed up in Detroit, where he won for the second straight year. Black players appreciated the social significance of access to white tournaments, but they were also professionals seeking events they believed gave them the greatest chance at winning the most money.[117] Moreover, some black tournaments were organized as celebrations following integration, symbolic events that continued to draw black professionals for many years. In 1964 a federal court ordered Georgia to integrate the Jekyll Island Club, a state-owned resort on the Atlantic coast. Earl Hill, who had caddied for whites at the club in the 1920s, immediately organized a tournament for black golfers at the site. From 1964 until the early 1980s, the Southeastern Golf Tournament (nicknamed "The Classic") drew top black golfers such as Rhodes, Jimmie DeVoe, Zeke Hartsfield, Charlie Sifford, and Lee Elder. The tournament also included performances from a number of entertainers; singer Otis Redding helped raise funds for the inaugural event, and in subsequent years Jerry Butler, Wilson Pickett, and Percy Sledge all performed. The Classic's late arrival and persistent success proved that desegregation would not necessarily mean the end of important black golf tournaments. On Jekyll Island the opposite was true: integration provided a new opportunity for black professional golfers to gather in the South at their own event.[118]

Along with successfully integrating some PGA events, UGA players also continued to enter USGA tournaments after World War II, especially the U.S. Open. In 1948 Rhodes qualified for the event at L.A.'s Riviera Country Club and finished fifty-first, becoming the first African American to play in a U.S. Open since John Shippen in 1913. The following year he played again at Chicago's Medinah Country Club.[119] Compared with the PGA, with its explicitly racist constitution, the USGA was more accommodating on paper; however, clear barriers remained for black players. Push-

Participants in the 1965 Southeastern Golf Tournament at Georgia's Jekyll Island Club. Included are Charlie Sifford (*far left*), Ted Rhodes (*far right*), Joe Louis (*third from right*), and former Major League Baseball pitcher Joe Black (*second from left*) (Courtesy USGA Museum).

ing forty years old, Howard Wheeler continued to try to qualify for the U.S. Open, finally making it in 1950 at Philadelphia's Merion Golf Club. Yet playing in one of the world's top golf tournaments turned out to be a lonely experience for him: Wheeler was virtually shunned, playing practice rounds alone after he could not find a partner. When he qualified again the following year, Wheeler traveled to Detroit's Oakland Hills Country Club and had difficulty finding any help from officials. He could not even figure out when he was supposed to tee off: one representative told him to check the newspapers, but his name never appeared in the published list of players. Wheeler, knowing he had qualified, showed up at the course anyway and was finally given a late tee time, but he missed the cut by one stroke.[120]

UGA women also entered white events more frequently after the war, although not until Althea Gibson in 1963 would a black woman play in a Ladies Professional Golf Association (LPGA) event. Along with participating in the Tam O'Shanter Open, UGA women put on exhibitions against white players, mostly in California. Thelma Cowans moved to Los Angeles in 1949 and played public matches against her new friend Betty Hicks. Hicks was a talented white player who won the 1941 U.S. Women's Amateur and was named the Associated Press female athlete of the year.[121] Women also led the way in integrating important local events in the region, such as city tournaments in Pasadena and Long Beach. In 1952 Eoline Thornton made headlines when she upset white golfer Allene Gates, actor Johnny Weissmuller's wife, at the Pasadena City Championship.[122] That same year the UGA's top female, Ann Gregory, asked the Chicago Women's Golf Club to apply for membership in the USGA in order to make her eligible for the U.S. Amateur and the U.S. Open. The group was accepted, and Gregory played the 1956 U.S. Women's Amateur at Meridian Hills Country Club in Indianapolis, Indiana, becoming the first black woman to play a USGA-sponsored event. Her first-round opponent, Carolyn Cudone, was a dynamic player who went on to win five straight U.S. Women's Senior Amateurs. "There was a mob at the first tee," Cudone later recalled of her match with Gregory. "A lot of them were reporters. I was shocked by the crowd's size because in those days, first-round matches didn't often draw so many people." But on that occasion tension percolated around Meridian Hills. A white worker at the course warned Cudone's father that his daughter "better win today" or the two would not be welcomed back. "I teed off first and got off a good shot that got a big cheer from the crowd," she said. "Ann's shot went at least 20 yards longer than mine but got only a tiny cheer." The two battled back and forth (Gregory was 2-up on the back nine) before Cudone narrowly prevailed 2 and 1. "My husband said I didn't have a snowball's chance in hell," Gregory quipped as she shook Cudone's hand. "I guess I fooled him."[123] Gregory went on to play in several more U.S. Amateurs and U.S. Opens.

For both men and women who pursued professional careers, playing in PGA or USGA tournaments only worsened the degradation they subsequently faced when restricted from minor, local events. No matter how elite the player, the level of discrimination did not always correlate with a golf tournament's stature or preeminence, a unique aspect of competitive golf. One assumes that Jackie Robinson, having played in Major League Baseball, would have been welcomed back to the minor leagues or a local park game. And yet in 1959 Howard Wheeler—by then a veteran of two U.S. Opens who played with top white players at private courses around the country—was banned from Philadelphia's minor Italian American Open at Roosevelt Municipal Golf Course, right in his hometown. In fact, organizers canceled the event after the city warned that Wheeler and a

Jesse Owens (*left*) with an unidentified group of golfers, ca. 1965 (The Ohio State University).

fellow black golfer were legally entitled to play.[124] Slights like these could be worse (and more disrespectful) for a black professional than trying to get into the nation's elite events. The fight for UGA players to integrate the PGA and USGA had come a long way, yet the pace of change was not keeping up with the rest of the country. By the time Jackie Robinson announced his retirement from baseball in 1957, he was urging fans to turn their attention to a new game. "Golf is the only sport in which a Negro does not have an equal chance today," he told a national television audience on NBC's *Meet the Press*. "There are cases where Negroes are allowed to participate in golf tournaments but in the great majority of tournaments they are not allowed in them."[125] Robinson was one of many high-profile black athletes, from Jesse Owens and Joe Louis to Michael Jordan and Charles Barkley, who would turn their attention (and public comments) to golf as they aged. "Golf had come to mean to me what running had in my youth," wrote Owens of his devotion to the game in the 1950s and 1960s.[126]

All of these instances in which black players entered white tournaments helped draw more attention and respectability to the UGA. From its origins in the 1920s, the organization attracted steadily more press coverage and a broader fan base, including whites. Echoing the recording of the 1925 tournament at Shady Rest by Fox News, Paramount Pictures filmed coverage of the 1935 Southern Open in Atlanta, including an entire exhibition match between John Brooks Dendy, Zeke Hartsfield, and Howard Wheeler. The company intended to screen the footage in its theaters around the country, although it is unclear if that happened (and none of the footage survived). By the late 1940s, results from UGA tournaments were widely broadcast. Final-round coverage of the 1949 Joe Louis Open aired on network television in Detroit; the black press hailed it as "the first time in sports history a negro-sponsored event" was televised. Coast-to-coast coverage of the 1955 UGA National in Detroit was provided by WJR radio, the city's CBS affiliate and one of the largest stations in the country. The struggle to get white golf on radio and television by no means outpaced the UGA. The first nationally televised golf tournament was the 1953 Tam O'Shanter Open, an event ABC reluctantly broadcast only after George May paid the network to do so. Regular PGA coverage did not come until later in the 1960s; in 1956, for example, the national television networks carried only five and a half hours of golf coverage during the entire year. Broadcasters balked not only at the slow pace but also at the expense (televising a golf match cost more than twice as much as a National Football League [NFL] game).[127]

In addition to media coverage, the UGA attracted support from prominent celebrities, entertainers, and politicians. Leaders in Chicago and Detroit were particularly involved. When Chicago hosted the UGA National for the first time in 1930, festivities included a speech by Albert B. George, one of first black judges elected to a municipal bench. Three years later Oscar De Priest, the first African American elected to Congress from outside the South, and the first in the twentieth century, presented the winner's trophy to champions Howard Wheeler and Julia Siler.[128] Support from white political leaders came quickly as well. In 1932 former Illinois governor Len Small praised attempts to host more black golf tournaments in his state. Michigan governor G. Mennen Williams was on hand at the 1949 UGA National in Detroit, while Detroit mayor Albert Cobo honored the city's 1955 UGA National by declaring "National Golf Week." Chicago mayor Edward Joseph Kelly also welcomed UGA golfers, and when Cleveland hosted its second UGA National in 1951, Mayor Thomas Burke attended the festivities.[129]

The UGA even called on and received the support of the federal government when the organization attempted to bring the 1942 UGA National to Washington, D.C. Three years after the black women of the Wake Robin Golf Club successfully petitioned U.S. Secretary of the Interior Harold Ickes for access to Potomac Park, they sought to host the championship in Washington for the first time at Anacostia Park. Ickes not only approved the plan but offered to present the winner's trophy himself. Unfortunately, the event was canceled due to World War II (no UGA National took place from 1942 to 1945).[130]

Appearances by politicians and welcoming governments helped legitimize the UGA and link the symbolism of African American competitive golf to the advancement of black political clout. But celebrities in sports, music, and entertainment really helped draw more fans to the world of black golf. The earliest celebrity UGA supporters were popular athletes from other sports who took an interest in golf, including a number of black boxers. Harry Wills, not Joe Louis, was the first famous boxer to support the tournaments. The top black boxer of the 1920s, Wills attended the 1926 Shady Rest event at the height of his popularity, the same year he struggled with boxing's color line to arrange a fight against white champion Jack Dempsey. Two other black boxers eventually lent their names to UGA events: the Joe Louis Open in Detroit and the Sugar Ray Robinson Open in New York City. Predominately black golf clubs were also useful locations for boxers in training; Chicago's heavyweight champion Ezzard Charles set up his camp at Sunset Hills in the late 1940s.[131]

Athletes in football, baseball, and track lent their support to the UGA as well, including University of California standouts Kenny Washington and Jackie Robinson, both of whom enjoyed golf and attended tournaments. After he graduated and before he integrated the modern NFL in 1946, Washington joined Joe Louis at L.A.'s Griffith Park for tournaments hosted by the city's black golf clubs (the same golfers hosted the UGA National at Griffith Park in 1939).[132] Jackie Robinson developed an even stronger passion for the game. As a youngster he sneaked onto Pasadena's private courses to steal golf balls and sell them back to players. By the time he arrived at the University of California, he had borrowed a friend's set of clubs and played for the first time, shooting 99: "If I had a set of my own, there's a game I'd really like to take up," he told reporters on the day he enrolled. By the end of his college tenure, he had won the Pacific Coast Intercollegiate Golf Championship and was shooting in the mid-80s. When he integrated Major League Baseball in 1947, he reported

Sammy Davis Jr. (*right*) with amateur golfer Harvey L. Boykins at the 1954 UGA National in Dallas (From the collections of the Texas/Dallas History and Archives Division, Dallas Public Library).

that golf was his "favorite hobby," which helped endear him to his white teammates. His fellow Brooklyn Dodgers signaled their acceptance of Robinson by inviting him to join them on the links.[133]

Musicians and entertainers echoed prominent athletes in supporting UGA events. Many of the same Jazz Age celebrities who first took up the game continued to play alongside a new generation of black music and film stars. Sammy Davis Jr. loved golf and played with Hollywood's white elite as his popularity rose in the 1950s. Once while on the course, comedian Jack Benny asked Davis what his handicap was: "I'm a one-eyed Negro who's Jewish," he deadpanned. Davis attended UGA events (including the 1954 championship in Dallas) and in 1970 lent his name to a tournament hosted by New Jersey's black-owned Freeway Golf Course. That tournament was so successful it was moved to Hartford, Connecticut, and eventually became the Sammy Davis Jr. Greater Hartford Open, a PGA Tour event from 1973 to 1988.[134] The list of white entertainers who sponsored UGA events was equally impressive. That support escalated when the UGA National came to Los Angeles in 1939, where various competitors were awarded trophies donated by a bevy of Hollywood stars. The list included African Americans such as actress Louise Beavers but also many white celebrities, including Al Jolson, Johnny Weissmuller, Frank Capra, Alan Mowbray, Preston Foster, Frank Borzage, and Edgar Allan Woolf.[135] Another sponsor, Bing Crosby, was notable because he was later embroiled in the controversy over integrating PGA tournaments after the war. Crosby and Bob Hope played a large role in advancing the visibility of professional golf in the West and increasing television coverage of the tour; Crosby had just hosted his first Bing Crosby Pro-Am two years prior in 1937, a tournament that was soon held annually at Pebble Beach and became one the most successful for the PGA. In 1939 the UGA received an overwhelmingly positive response in California, foreshadowing how tournaments in the state—including the L.A. Open, the San Diego Open, and the Bing Crosby Pro-Am—became postwar battlegrounds over the PGA's exclusion of black professionals.

The UGA worked to secure corporate sponsors along with the support it received from prominent white and black community leaders, politicians, and entertainers. For most of their history, UGA events received local support from relatively small, black-owned businesses. But by the 1950s, tournaments secured sponsorship from larger corporations, an indication not only of the UGA's growing visibility but also of the gradual integration of corporate America and postwar attempts to solicit black consumers. Moss Kendrix, a Morehouse graduate who established a public relations firm, was hired by Coca-Cola in 1948 to establish an advertising campaign targeting the "Negro market"; he was the first African American to secure a major corporate marketing account in U.S. history. An avid golfer, Kendrix saw opportunity in UGA sponsorship. He and white representatives from Coke attended the UGA National from 1953 to 1955 in Kansas City, Dallas, and Detroit, the company providing trophies at all three tournaments. It was the beginning of a long-standing relationship between the entities, and Coke continued its sponsorship well into the 1960s. Not surprisingly, when the company's first "Negro market" ads debuted in 1955, they featured images of young black men wielding golf clubs (Kendrix had personally recruited the students from Morehouse and Clark colleges).[136]

Not to be outdone was Coke's major Canadian rival, the Seagram Company, which sent a representative to award Charlie Sifford the 1955 championship trophy in Detroit right when it, too, began running golf-themed advertisements in black newspapers. Marketers certainly used golf in black advertisements to invoke middle-class aspiration, just as they did

1954 Seagram's advertisement (*Chicago Defender*, June 26, 1954).

in white advertisements. Yet the growing popularity of UGA tournaments and golf in the black community was quite real, challenging historians to rethink the 1950s "Negro market" campaigns as purely aspirational. "Part of the enjoyment of golfing is getting together with friends at the Clubhouse, famous as the 19th hole," read one 1954 Seagram's whiskey ad in the *Chicago Defender*. Considering that Chicago had already hosted the

UGA National a record five times (and would go on to host three more before 1975), surely Seagram's and Coke were not so much peddling fantasies but, rather, targeting actual black golfers. This was certainly the case by 1976, when Anheuser-Busch and American Airlines sponsored the fiftieth UGA National at San Diego's Torrey Pines Golf Course.[137]

Corporate sponsorship and the attendance of prominent individuals helped expand UGA tournaments into larger, multiday events. By including a "full social program" for participants and fans—banquets, dances, musicians, and speeches—Chicago's three UGA Nationals in the 1930s set a precedent for future gatherings to combine the golf tournament with a wide range of other events for the black community.[138] While the UGA never recorded attendance, it is clear that more fans showed up as the tour grew in stature. As early as 1936 the UGA National at Philadelphia's Cobbs Creek drew so many observers that the city's mounted police were called in to hold the gallery back. The 1951 championship drew a record 400 golfers (prompting the UGA to close the tournament to more entrants) and an estimated 5,000 fans to Cleveland's Seneca Golf Course. Earlier that year the UGA's Southern Open in Atlanta was held on the same weekend as the NAACP national convention, which arranged to bus delegates from the conference to the New Lincoln Country Club. There fans enjoyed a barbeque, shook hands with Joe Louis, and watched Charlie Sifford win his first professional tournament.[139] UGA events also attracted white fans to the links, especially after celebrities like Louis began to compete. One quarter of the gallery at the 1941 UGA National was white after Louis announced that Massachusetts governor Leverett Saltonstall agreed to let the event take place at Boston's Ponkapoag Golf Course, an exclusively white club.[140] As the number of fans increased, so too did the number of players who signed up to compete in events, prompting some tournaments to limit entries and enforce stricter qualifying standards. The record for participation was the 1959 UGA National, which featured over 500 golfers competing on three different courses in Washington: East Potomac Park, Langston, and Dupont.[141] Although most UGA tournaments took place in the Midwest and Northeast, tour stops in other regions pointed to growing interest from players and fans nationwide. In the 1930s a strong contingent of western clubs, particularly in California, led to the 1939 UGA National taking place in Los Angeles. The Moulin Rouge resort in Las Vegas, the first integrated hotel-casino in U.S. history, was scheduled to host the 1956 UGA National before the venue abruptly closed.[142] And although holding tournaments in the South was a major struggle, the tour nevertheless managed to do so—most notably with Atlanta's annual Southern Open; UGA Nationals in Dallas (1954), Memphis (1962), and Miami (1967); and tournaments in Louisville, Dallas, Houston, and Jacksonville, Florida. The significance of holding UGA events in the heart of the segregated South was clear. Organizers of the Houston Open successfully petitioned the city to let them host the three-day event at white-only Memorial Park Golf Course, ending the tournament on June 19: "the traditional Emancipation Day celebration for the negroes of Texas."[143]

In addition to newspaper coverage and fan attendance, the UGA successfully increased its visibility via specialty publications like the *United Golfer*, its own organ. Established in 1930, the monthly newsletter reported organizational news, provided updates on tournament results, and kept readers informed about legal challenges to segregation on municipal courses around the country. Another important publication was *Tee-Cup*, a magazine established in Los Angeles by the Western States Golf Association after its founding in 1954. Produced by J. Cullen Fentress, sports editor for the black newspaper *California Eagle* and president of L.A.'s Cosmopolitan Golf Club, *Tee-Cup* reported widely on the world of black golf, particularly western tournaments and challenges to discrimination on California courses. It included a regular column on golf rules from Jimmie DeVoe, the Harlem professional who by then had permanently moved to Los Angeles and finished fifth at the 1953 UGA National, as well as comprehensive coverage of UGA tournaments and profiles of its stars. The magazine was a second, de facto UGA organ highlighting developments on the West Coast in the late 1950s.[144] Fans also learned about the tour's importance in numerous other sporting publications. This included a prominent 1953 essay by Joe Louis in *Our Sports*, a magazine devoted to African Americans and sports. That year Jackie Robinson served as a guest editor and solicited Louis to write an article on golf. The result was a piece in which Louis revealed his love of the game, called efforts to integrate professional golf "my toughest fight," and recognized the power of the UGA to help push the PGA toward accepting integration.[145]

The UGA's visibility among black and white fans nurtured the careers of black golf professionals and ultimately prompted the PGA's acceptance of African Americans. However, the tour's significance went further: it also changed the game and its meaning in American culture, presenting a fundamentally different vision of professional golf. Unlike most sporting institutions formed under segregation, the UGA remained committed to its vision of a truly race-blind golf tour, a sentiment echoed by pioneering black competitors. As early as 1922 the *Chicago Defender* indicated that all amateurs were invited to its national tournament, including whites: "Owing to the fact that many players of color were denied the right, illegally, to play in the so-called 'city' tournament, the bars are down and any person can play in the first national amateur golf championships regardless of race, creed or color."[146] Although there is no evidence that white players competed in 1922, the statement foreshadowed a hallmark of black professional golf and subsequent UGA tournaments. Unlike baseball's Negro Leagues, which did not experiment with the occasional white player until the 1950s (facing decline after Robinson's integration of Major League Baseball), the UGA was never an "all-black" golf tour, and its events were always open to everyone. Charles Halarack, a white man, took fourth place at the 1938 UGA National in Chicago.

Michigan's UGA tour stops were particularly race blind: in 1954 the winner of Flint's Vehicle City Amateur was Don Jarrard, a white professor at Flint Community College and former captain of Michigan State University's golf team. The popularity of Joe Louis (and his willingness to fund a large prize purse) drew many white golfers to the Joe Louis Open. When Ted Rhodes won the event in 1949, he beat a field that included five white PGA players. Walter Speedy fought racism at Chicago's municipal courses and exclusion from the city's golf tournaments in the 1910s, so it was poignant in 1954 when the female winner of the Walter Speedy Memorial Tournament was Lois Drafke, a sixteen-year-old white amateur from suburban La Grange High School.[147] The eventual integration of the PGA and the USGA only accelerated this long-standing inclusion: by 1967, 75 percent of the 300 youth enrolled in the UGA's junior division were white, as were 10 percent of its players by 1974. Perhaps the most symbolic moment of integration—and one that signaled the end of the UGA as a "black" professional golf tour—came in 1971 when a white man, Jack Price, won the UGA National.[148]

Another notable UGA gesture to integration was its name, which did not include "colored" or "negro" but instead invoked the race-blind notion of "united." Its founders chose to adopt such a stance from the beginning, at a time when many black organizations (including the NAACP) specifically invoked race in their titles. By the 1950s some African American sportswriters were calling on black sporting leagues, like baseball's Negro American League and Negro National League, to drop "negro" and "colored" from their names. In 1950 Fay Young of the *Chicago*

A 1956 cover and advertisement from *Tee-Cup* magazine promoting programs for junior black golfers in southern California (*Tee-Cup*).

Defender pressed black leagues to welcome white players by noting the number of whites competing in the Joe Louis Open.[149] In 1953 three UGA clubs in Portland, Oregon, and Seattle, Washington, directly asked the NAACP's national office for advice on whether to continue calling their events "negro" tournaments.[150] On the other hand, some observers saw the irony of organizations branding themselves race neutral amidst the ongoing segregation and discrimination that warranted their creation in the first place. In 1957 Langston Hughes poked fun at the issue via his fictional character Jesse B. Semple, the working-class Harlemite popular with Hughes's readers: "'It is time to encourage integration,' Joyce come telling me. Well, them women have got a integrated name for that club, but nary a white member as yet. Just like the Colored Golfing Association changed its name to the Associated Golfing Association—but I don't hear tell of no white players associated with them up to now. Them same Negroes are still playing golf with the same other Negroes as before. . . . Who is fooling who with all this name changing lately, I want to know?"[151]

The UGA was different not only in terms of its name or the racial makeup of its players and fans but also in the way its golfers played the game. Competitors like Wheeler, Sifford, and Rhodes introduced a unique aesthetic to professional golf—styles, practices, words, and gamesmanship that fans had not yet seen in the world of white competitive golf. Scholars recognize how Negro League baseball players brought a different look to the national pastime. Barnstorming teams entertained fans with comedic tricks like "shadowball," and players employed tactics rarely seen in white baseball. Some argue that black players like Jackie Robinson employed bold, improvisational base-running that echoed jazz music, "jazzing the basepaths" in a way white fans had never seen.[152] From Howard Wheeler's cross-handed grip and trick-shot performances to Ted Rhodes's colorful wardrobe and Charlie Sifford's iconic cigar-chomping, UGA players likewise injected professional golf with a unique aesthetic. Handing out awards for the best-dressed golfer at its events, the tour emphasized that the way its players looked mattered, including the way they differed from white professionals on the course.

In addition, while male-centered bantering, gambling, and hustling were long associated with golf (including common interactions between white players and black caddies going back to the nineteenth century), UGA players combined these antics with professional golf in a way that white professionals rarely had to. Nearly all of the top UGA players—Hartsfield, Wheeler, Spiller, Sifford, Elder, and Rhodes—brought with them a long tradition of hustling and gambling, often forged as caddies and young players trying to scrape together a living in a game that offered them little potential to earn "respectable" money. Lesser-known competitors took it further, like George Wallace Jr., known as "Tater Pie" or "Potato Pie." Originally from Atlanta, the illiterate Wallace was a legendary golf hustler who traveled around the country in search of high-stakes cash games: he once spent a week in Oklahoma winning $60,000 from a wealthy oilman. "Tater Pie was a professional gambler," said Rafe "Ray" Botts, a fellow UGA player who went on to participate on the PGA Tour after integration. "He was a country boy and talked funny. He always had a pocketful of money. He wouldn't expose his game until it was too late for his opponent. He was like a ghost. It was like, who is this guy?"[153]

At times UGA organizers (and the black press) attempted to combat the perception that black players were rampant hustlers. The tour banned gambling at the UGA National after one sportswriter criticized it for allowing "wide open" gambling at the 1956 event in Philadelphia. "This has become a nation-wide disgrace," he charged, "and unless something is done about it, the players will be witness to a murder on the links someday."[154] The press also urged black players (professionals and amateurs) to abide by course rules and follow proper etiquette, especially when sharing public courses with whites. "Let's leave the vile and obscene language at home, golf is a gentlemen's game," one reporter implored.[155] Black sportswriters in Pittsburgh publicly denounced "foul-mouthed" players on municipal courses. "Some Negroes, sporting golf clubs, are taking the basement language of Fullerton Street to district golf links," charged the *Pittsburgh Courier* in 1956. "This Negro, whose language is a constant mixture of profanity, vulgarity and obscenity, is obnoxious wherever he is found, but he is particularly harmful when, taking advantage of openings that have been made for respectable Negroes, he carries his gutter language to places and among people where such language is offensive and stigmatizes the entire group."[156]

Yet critics faced an uphill battle on the issue of gambling, especially among UGA golfers. In an era with few lucrative prizes or endorsements available to even the most talented black players—in an expensive sport that required them to shell out thousands of their own dollars in travel and lodging expenses to participate on tour—gambling was a way of life, and most UGA pros made more money on the side than they ever did in golf tournaments. "While guys like Ben Hogan and Sam Snead and Lew Worsham were getting headlines every week for dueling at PGA tourna-

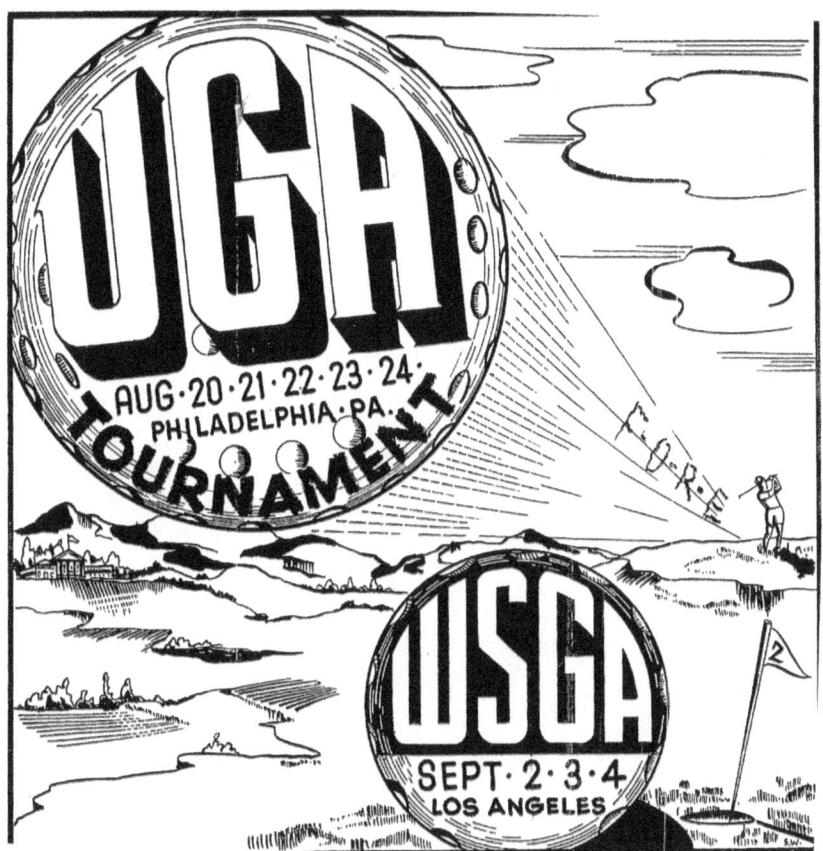

Advertisement for the 1956 UGA National and the Western States Golf Association Open (*Tee-Cup*).

ments on the best courses in the country, Spiller and Rhodes and Wheeler were playing for bets on public courses, shooting their 63s and 64s for the benefit of some poor sucker whose money they were taking," recalled Charlie Sifford. "It was hustle or be hustled."[157] Of the UGA champions, Zeke Hartsfield was particularly known for tricking unsuspecting bettors out of their money. "Zeke had his own unique way of getting back at the golf world for not being allowed to play in the pro tournaments: he was perhaps the world's greatest hustler," wrote Sifford. "Hell, even if they'd let Zeke play on the PGA Tour, he probably couldn't have afforded it, because he made so much money by hustling."[158]

Stories of players like Hartsfield, Wheeler, Sifford, Spiller, and Rhodes became legendary partly because their accomplishments were hidden from white fans for so many years. But they were the players who made the largest impression on the professional game and drew attention. For every Charlie Sifford there were hundreds of truly unknown African Americans who invested significant time and money, talented players who joined the UGA tour and attempted to be professional golfers in a society that denied them basic civil rights. For most, even their names are now lost.

Then there were UGA players like Alfred "Tup" Holmes, amateurs who never became professionals but still used the game to change America. In 1938 the Tuskegee University student won his first UGA amateur event, the Southern Open. In 1955 he won something bigger: the most important golf-related Supreme Court case in U.S. history.

4

I WILL TAKE YOUR OWN GOLF STICK AND WHAM THE WORLD

Golf and the Postwar Civil Rights Movement

DECEMBER 11, 1960—AUGUSTA NATIONAL GOLF CLUB, AUGUSTA, GEORGIA

"Wrong Will Fail, Right Will Prevail," read one sign.

"Lincoln . . . Emancipation!!! Ike . . . Civil Rights????" proclaimed another.

Over sixty students from the local black college had demanded to meet President Dwight D. Eisenhower. Turned away, they were now starting to picket. Secret service kept the crowd as far away as possible, hopefully out of hearing range for Ike and his fellow golfers. His press secretary insisted the president "was unaware of their presence."

Eisenhower golfed quietly as the demonstration continued outside. It was the last of the president's twenty-nine visits to Augusta National during his eight years in office (1953–61), yet this trip was different. This time he was confronted with the largest golf protest he ever faced, the first of many demonstrations at the iconic course.

This time the movement had finally reached the gates of Augusta National.[1]

World War II was a watershed for the twentieth-century civil rights movement. The war disrupted American society, emboldened many of the 1.2 million black Americans who served around the world, and prompted all citizens to redefine the nature of their democracy. For the same reasons, the war played a major role in expanding the black community's interest in golf. The segregated U.S. Army provided occasional opportunities for black soldiers to play, and some of them encountered the game for the first time during the conflict. Arizona's Fort Huachuca housed the largest number of black soldiers in the country and offered golf lessons to its 14,000 black troops. In Washington, D.C., the army also made clubs available for the 500 black men at its Anacostia Recreation Camp for Negro Soldiers, located adjacent to Langston Golf Course.[2] Even black soldiers stationed at installations farther south found opportunities to play. At North Carolina's Fort Bragg, the army appointed a local black golf pro, Pfc. Eugene Levette, to organize summer athletic events for the black troops: not surprisingly they included a popular golf tournament. When African Americans campaigned in 1951 to end segregation at the base, they specifically highlighted local golf facilities. Texas native Martin Guillory caddied for white professionals, including Jimmy Demaret, before he enlisted in 1940. While stationed at Virginia's Fort Lee, Guillory practiced on the base's course and was granted leave to compete in UGA events; he eventually won the amateur title at the 1950 UGA National.[3] Golf was also an important part of Joe Louis's many visits with troops around the world, just as it was when white stars like Byron Nelson, Bob Hope, and Bing Crosby staged exhibitions for soldiers. When the War Department solicited black leaders for athletes to include on its troop tours, the most-wanted list included big names like Jesse Owens, Jackie Robinson, and Satchel Paige, but also the crowd-pleasing Howard Wheeler.[4]

Golf was also a part of the wartime "Double V" campaign supported by the black press, one that linked fascism abroad with discrimination at home and called on black Americans to confront both. The UGA canceled many events during the war but staged an "All Out for Victory" tournament in 1942 (which Wheeler won) at Washington's Anacostia Park. Shady Rest Country Club continued to stage its annual tournament on the Fourth of July, an event that took on even more patriotic overtones during the conflict.[5] The war interrupted many PGA and USGA events, allowing new tournaments, like the Tam O'Shanter Open, to step in with more liberal policies on black participants. It also emboldened black players as they attempted to integrate white events. In 1942 former Northwestern University golfer Horace McDougal and other UGA players, including Pat Ball, Clyde Martin, and Joe Louis, tried to qualify for the Hale America National Open at Chicago's Ridgemoor Country Club. The event was organized by the USGA, the PGA, and the Chicago District Golf Association as a replacement for the canceled 1942 U.S. Open. When club officials informed the players of its white-only policy, they appealed to the USGA, which indicated it was unwilling to overrule a private club's policies. The organization had "Hitlerized" the players, lamented the *Chicago*

Defender. McDougal, himself a World War I veteran, penned a series of patriotic letters protesting the USGA that appeared in black newspapers nationwide. "While we are at war with an enemy who overlooks nothing that will reduce the morale of our men and their loved ones," he wrote, "is it patriotic and American-like to give that enemy additional material for his fiendish work? . . . In spite of such treatment in many lines of endeavor, this noble race of people remain steadfast in their loyal support of the stars and stripes which we all love."[6] Meanwhile, a group of black ministers in Cleveland denounced what they called the "fascist action" of Ridgewood Country Club after it refused to host them.[7]

Charges that the USGA "Hitlerized" black players or Joe Louis calling PGA president Horton Smith "another Hitler" were controversial but not entirely off target. Just as the Germans slandered African Americans (the Nazis banned jazz music in 1935), fascist propaganda in Italy used golf to demean black GIs. One poster featured a racist image of a black American soldier wielding a golf club, echoing Edward Kemble's nineteenth-century golf drawings that lampooned social advancement and refinement in the black community. Black sportswriters noted that America's enemies (fascists and, eventually, communists) saw no place for black golfers and yet were welcome themselves to compete in PGA events if they qualified. As one complained, the PGA "slammed the door in the faces" of African Americans like Bill Spiller and Ted Rhodes, while "most foreigners are allowed to compete, including any of Uncle Joe Stalin's followers."[8]

Nevertheless, the war provided some black Americans access to golf they otherwise would not have had. An increasing number of educational institutions also established golf teams and clubs, another current that helped the game grow in postwar black communities. Early examples signaled that the advent of golf programs in schools would influence African Americans. In 1929 a black high school student nearly won the Oregon state golf championship at Portland's white Multnomah Country Club. At the collegiate level a few black golfers competed for predominately white universities, including Horace McDougal at Northwestern University (1923) and George Roddy at Iowa University (1930). Roddy was Iowa's top player and one of the best in the Big Ten Conference, although he did not compete in the 1930 conference championship under mysterious circumstances (rumors swirled it was because the event took place at Chicago's Westmoreland Country Club, where African Americans were not welcomed). Roddy went on to win several amateur titles on the UGA tour

"As they would like us": this 1944 poster invoked the specter of African American golf in fascist Italy (Published with the permission of The Wolfsonian—Florida International University [Miami, Florida]).

and became a professor and golf instructor at North Carolina A&T College.[9] Elsewhere in the Big Ten, in 1930 two black undergraduates vied in the finals for the University of Michigan student golf title. The winner, A. D. V. Crosby, was club champion at Atlanta's black Piney Wood Country Club and later served as president of the UGA from 1946 to 1952. After World War II the number of black golfers at predominately white universities remained low, but the growing visibility of collegiate golf made their participation important. Forrest Jones Jr., a black standout at Douglass Park in Indianapolis, joined Indiana University's golf team in 1956 and became its number one player. That put him in matches against top college golfers like Jack Nicklaus and Tom Weiskopf at Ohio State University.[10]

Some black schools even predated their white counterparts in establishing golf clubs and building courses. In the early 1950s a few black secondary schools in the South, like Atlanta's Booker T. Washington High School, had already established golf teams before nearby white schools.[11] Alabama's Tuskegee Institute was the first black college to build a course, which it opened in 1926. Two other black colleges, Lincoln University in Pennsylvania and Lincoln University in Missouri, also had on-campus links by 1932; the students in Pennsylvania laid out their own rudimentary course surrounding the football stadium.[12] Intercollegiate contests took place as well; the black Lincoln Golf Club in Florida hosted one of the first in 1930. Beginning in 1938 Tuskegee also hosted a golf championship for the Southern Intercollegiate Athletic Conference, drawing teams from Morehouse College, Fisk College, Clark College, Morris Brown College, Florida A&M College, Alabama State College, and Xavier University (Louisiana). Tuskegee's course even hosted a UGA professional event the following year, yet another tournament won by Howard Wheeler.[13]

In Ohio, black Wilberforce University formed a golf team (one of the school's football coaches, Ed Ritchie, was a big fan of the game) and in 1937 played a series of matches against predominately white Ohio Northern University. These were the first integrated golf competitions in intercollegiate history and perhaps even the first intercollegiate athletic contests between historically black and white schools. The first match was hosted by Wilberforce at Dayton's Fairmont Golf Course, followed by Ohio Northern hosting the black collegians at Lima's Lost Creek Country Club.[14] Golf continued to grow at black colleges after World War II, with student demand increasing even where there were limited opportunities to play. "The interest level was there," recalled Wendell Davis, who coached golf at rural Prairie View A&M in Texas. "We didn't have a golf course. But out there . . . was prairie and we'd go out there and drive."[15] Black fraternities and sororities, including the women of Alpha Kappa Alpha, also propagated the game among collegians by organizing tournaments and social outings. The majority of black college golfers drew little attention except for the few who competed for predominately white universities or who went on to win UGA tournaments. Yet these forgotten collegians all had unique stories of how and why they embraced the game in the crucible of the postwar civil rights movement. One was Joseph "Singlewing" Williams, who joined Florida A&M's golf team in the early 1950s. For a small-college golfer, his 220-yard drives and scores in the 70s were typical for the period: the fact that he played with one arm was not (his left arm was severed in a gun accident when he was eight years old.)[16]

College golf and military service were thus important developments that helped advance the game in the black community. Both helped William Powell develop his unique passion for golf. The grandson of slaves, Powell was born in Alabama and moved with his family to Minerva, Ohio, near Canton. He started caddying at age nine, became an accomplished player in high school, and joined the golf team at Wilberforce University with his brother Barry; they both participated in the unprecedented 1937 matches against Ohio Northern. During the war Powell served with the U.S. Army Air Force in Europe and returned in 1946 with a renewed disdain for American segregation. "A sick feeling came over me," he later wrote, recalling how he and fellow returning soldiers stepped off a train in Louisville and were forced to divide themselves by race on the platform. "After all we'd been through, after all we'd seen, and after all we'd done for our country it was worse than a slap in the face."[17] The disrespect continued when he returned to Ohio. Working first as a janitor and then as a security guard, Powell could not find a public golf course in the Canton area that allowed him to play, despite his collegiate accomplishments and his experience golfing with whites while stationed in England during the war. Undaunted, he refused to give up on the game: "I was ready to move on with my life and golf was going to be a part of it."[18]

So Powell came up with an ambitious plan: "I'd had enough," he remembered. "I decided, 'I'll just build my own.'"[19] Denied a bank loan and turned down for a GI loan as well, he went forward anyway with help from two black physicians, a loan from his brother, and a second mortgage on his house. Working eighteen-hour days, Powell purchased

The Powell family in 1960: (*left to right*) Bill Jr., Marcella, Larry, William, and Renee (Courtesy USGA Museum).

a 78-acre dairy farm in East Canton, cleared the land, and by 1948 had opened a nine-hole track: Clearview Golf Club. Despite some initial episodes of vandalism and hostility, the layout welcomed golfers of all races and flourished. In 1978 Powell expanded the course to eighteen holes on 170 acres. Clearview was a testament to the singular effort of the Powell family; William's wife, Marcella, helped build and operate the facility and his son, Larry, became the course superintendent. William and Marcella's daughter, Renee, grew up on Clearview (she first played at age three) and later served as the club's professional. In 1967 she would also become the second black woman to compete on the LPGA Tour. Dubbed "America's Course," Clearview was significant beyond the fact that Powell was the only African American in history to design, build, and operate his own golf course. It was a truly integrated facility, drawing a substantial number of white golfers from the moment it opened: in 2001 it was added to the National Register of Historic Places.

While Clearview was unique, William Powell's willingness to challenge golf segregation after the war echoed the broader context of his times, as many African Americans launched more direct, emboldened attacks on racism during the late 1940s and 1950s. For most black golfers this meant increasing demands for access to public facilities. Thousands around the country petitioned local governments to either build black courses or let blacks use white courses. The largest appeal was in Miami, where 3,000 African Americans signed a petition calling for access to the city's lone municipal course in 1948. Similar petitions were submitted in Charlottesville, Virginia (1949), Shreveport, Louisiana (1950), Atlanta (1951), Jackson, Mississippi (1952), Columbus, Georgia (1954), and Macon, Georgia (1960). In a few cases these requests were enough to gain segregated access to facilities and eventually even full integration: a petition from black residents prompted Macon to integrate its public course "without incident" in 1961.[20] Yet in most places they sparked bitter conflicts, with integration taking place only after a few dedicated individuals filed lawsuits and engaged in years of legal wrangling. Sometimes locals initiated these petitions on their own with little organization, while in other cases civil rights organizations were involved. A 1964 petition to integrate courses in Alexandria, Louisiana, was put together by the Southern Christian Leadership Conference (SCLC), the organization founded by Martin Luther King Jr.[21]

While petitioning for access to public courses at home, postwar African Americans also showed more interest in playing the game on the road. As more Americans hit the highways in the 1950s, black travelers sought facilities that welcomed those who wanted to incorporate golf into their travels. Postwar guide books and pamphlets for black readers—such as *Grayson's Travel and Business Guide*, *The Negro Motorist Green Book*, and *Travelguide*—featured listings of golf courses nationwide that welcomed black patrons. (The cover of the 1952 *Travelguide* featured a smartly dressed black woman loading a set of golf clubs into a convertible.)[22] These were especially helpful in the West, a popular destination for road trips where it was hard to predict how course owners would respond to black patrons. The 1949 *Travelguide*, under the tagline "Vacation and Recreation without Humiliation," reminded readers that two of Denver's municipal courses allowed black golfers. (Meanwhile, another Denver public course, Park Hill Golf Club, excluded them until a lawsuit from four players forced its integration in 1962.)[23] In postwar California, African Americans could access many courses, especially in the Los Angeles area, but there remained public facilities that discriminated. In 1957 San Francisco's famed Harding Park Golf Club refused membership to a black patron, reversing its decision only after it faced heavy criticism.[24]

Notably, coverage of golf in black guidebooks indicated that the game's appeal was rising in black communities even as its popularity waned among whites. More accessible than ever to new segments of black America, golf was growing not only in Chicago and Philadelphia but also in newer black neighborhoods and unlikely locations. A 1951 study in Omaha, Nebraska, surprisingly found that a larger share of black union workers (20 percent) frequented the public golf course than their white counterparts (15 percent).[25] Some golfers applauded the diversity they witnessed developing on local links. Unlike many forms of public recreation, municipal golf was a potentially intimate social experience; if the course was busy enough, players were asked to spend the entire day paired with others they had never met. "I enjoy teaming up and playing golf with total strangers. Talk about a study in human nature!" wrote one white man to the *Pittsburgh Courier* in 1946 after he was placed in a foursome with three black golfers. "I never saw such good sportsmanship," he exclaimed. "I learned a lot about golf . . . but more about real companionship on a golf course that day."[26] Contrary to the popular notion of golf elitism, persons who utilized public parks, beaches, tennis courts, and swimming pools could expect at least a modicum of privacy—but not golfers on a busy municipal course. The political implications were significant, especially in smaller towns with only one or two public courses. Instead of enforcing separation and exclusion, municipal golf was actually poised to mix the races better than other forms of public amusement and recreation. The mayor of Gary, Indiana, recognized this in 1947 when he called for more golf tournaments and outings between the city's two public courses, one that generally served black golfers and the other whites.[27]

Alfred "Tup" Holmes also recognized the social implications of integrated public golf. Although there is no evidence they met, Holmes shared a lot in common with William Powell: both came from golfing families known for their love of the game, both played golf for black college teams in the late 1930s, and both confronted segregation on courses in ways that shaped the broader civil rights movement in their communities. The son of Hamilton M. Holmes, an Atlanta physician and golf aficionado, Tup Holmes was a standout golfer at Tuskegee, where he won the school's first intercollegiate tournament in 1938 and again in 1939. (The two-time Southern Intercollegiate Athletic Conference champion was nevertheless turned away from the inaugural National Collegiate Athletic Association [NCAA] national golf championship in Des Moines, Iowa.)[28] Having reached the highest level of college golf available to a black student, Holmes returned to Atlanta after graduating and became a top UGA

Cover of 1952 *Travelguide* (Chicago History Museum, ICHi-74347; Travelguide, Inc.).

amateur while pursuing work, first as a funeral director and eventually as a union steward at Lockheed Aircraft. He won several amateur titles on the circuit, including events at Tuskegee in 1938, 1939, and 1940; the 1939 Forest City Open in Cleveland; and the Southern Open in Atlanta, where he was amateur champion three consecutive years from 1938 to

1940. "'Tup' is now without a doubt the most outstanding amateur in the South," proclaimed the *Atlanta Daily World*.[29]

After the war Holmes's golf career peaked. He won amateur titles twice at the UGA National (1947 and 1958) and sparked a fierce rivalry with golf's most popular black player, Joe Louis. Holmes was unfazed by Louis's fame whenever he faced off against him, eliminating the heavyweight champion directly in a head-to-head match en route to the 1947 title at Philadelphia's Cobbs Creek. He and his family were among the 150 members at Atlanta's New Lincoln Country Club, and all of them were fierce competitors, especially Tup; his father, Hamilton; and his brother, a local minister named Oliver Holmes. Once while driving home after a bad round, the seventy-year-old Hamilton stopped his car in heavy traffic so he could swing his clubs beside an Atlanta highway. "Some folks are getting old and no good," he told his sons. "I'm getting old and good."[30]

Despite the family's golfing prowess and prominence—"Everybody in Atlanta, from top to bottom, knew my husband," Tup's wife, Isabella, recalled—they had no access to courses other than Lincoln. Atlanta barred African Americans from its five municipal links and provided no segregated facilities for black players. A leading family in one of the region's largest cities, the Holmes clan nevertheless joined black Atlantans in traveling elsewhere to play on public courses and participate in the broader, regional black golf scene. "We went almost every weekend to some facility out of the city—Nashville, Columbus, Birmingham," remembered family friend Charles T. Bell. "There were a number of cow pasture courses that blacks maintained. We had this camaraderie. They'd come visit us; we'd go visit them. We'd leave Sunday morning, drive 200 miles, play golf and then drive back that night."[31]

Throughout the 1940s blacks in Atlanta had demanded that the city either integrate its courses or build a black municipal facility. In July 1951 the Holmes family went a step further and directly petitioned the parks department to play Bobby Jones Municipal Golf Course. Named for the famed Augusta National founder (and Beau Jack patron), Bobby Jones was Atlanta's best public course and the one whites favored most. Denied access, the family and Charles Bell then sued the city on behalf of 300 black golfers dubbed "the Atlanta Golf Committee," double the membership of the New Lincoln Country Club. With help from Atlanta's NAACP chapter and a local black attorney, Roscoe Thomas, the lawsuit would make its way through the legal system over the next four years, a critical period in the national legal battle over civil rights.[32]

Not only did the case, *Holmes v. Atlanta*, eventually reach the U.S. Supreme Court; it also helped reveal the limits of *Brown v. Board of Education*, the landmark civil rights decision handed down in May 1954. Two months later, Atlanta's public schools were as segregated as ever and its federal district court behaved as if *Brown* had never happened: the court ruled in favor of the Holmes clan but only because the city did not have a separate, equal facility for black golfers. It instructed Atlanta either to build one or to provide black residents segregated access to existing municipal courses. Atlanta's white city council had already debated proposals for a $75,000, tax-funded black course supported by Mayor William Hartsfield. "Let the boys in the high income bracket go out to Lincoln Golf Course," urged one councilman in 1953. Responded another, "They've got as much right to a golf course as white people, and they're going to get it, too."[33] Atlanta eventually set aside two days per week (Mondays and Tuesdays) for black residents to play its municipal courses. Georgia's attorney general praised the federal court's decision for "reaffirming the separate but equal doctrine" and "properly snubbing the psychological theory followed by the U.S. Supreme Court in the school segregation cases."[34]

Presented with the option of accepting limited, segregated access to white courses, the Holmes clan was pressured to give in and drop the case. The moderate *Atlanta Daily World* saw little significance in the *Brown* decision and urged the family not to appeal the case to the Supreme Court. Some family members also worried about the implications of continuing the legal battle. "I took calls from a lot of black people who thought this was folly," remembered Tup's sister, Alice Holmes Washington. "They kept saying, 'Why are ya'll doing this? Don't rock the boat. Try to talk Tup out of this; he's the hothead.'" Isabella Holmes also urged her husband not to continue: "My reaction as wife and mother was don't do it. We did go through those days with a lot of harassment. Telephone calls, things so ugly that I wouldn't dare repeat it. It was a pitiful thing for the family. It was something I lived with, but something that was very hurtful."[35] Already the case had forced the city to respond to a civil rights lawsuit in a way no other decision had, including *Brown*. For some blacks in Atlanta, that was enough.

The case was also becoming divisive within the NAACP. A federal decision affirming segregation was not sufficient; however, to continue devoting resources to an appeal—potentially taking it all the way to the Supreme Court—once again raised the specter of golf elitism within the organization. Constance Baker Motley, a key member of the NAACP's

Legal Defense Fund (LDF), recalled that by the 1950s the LDF had decided "to bring cases that would benefit blacks as a whole"—one rationale behind the strategy of attacking segregation in public education. Motley noted that her boss, LDF director Thurgood Marshall, expressed skepticism over *Holmes v. Atlanta*. "Thurgood's response was loud and clear: 'No, we are not going to spend any money on a golf course case because we could not justify spending money for a few doctors in Atlanta to play golf. We are going to use the money to get the black kids admitted to white schools.'"[36] Marshall's hesitancy was echoed by many elite white liberals who supported the NAACP, such as University of North Carolina sociologist Thomas J. Woofter. Woofter, who led the Commission on Interracial Cooperation, also belittled the idea of national organizations helping fight golf discrimination. "It is more important that the masses of underprivileged children have decent recreation facilities than that a few who want to keep up with the Joneses be allowed to play golf with the white people," he wrote.[37]

Yet the response from the Holmes clan was clear: "I want to play golf anytime I want to, on any city course I want to," Tup told reporters as NBC's *Today* show filmed Oliver being turned away again from Bobby Jones Municipal.[38] They promptly filed an appeal. From that point on, although the national NAACP remained an important party to the case, *Holmes v. Atlanta* reached the Supreme Court in November 1955 largely through the generosity of a few black lawyers in Atlanta, funding from the Holmes family themselves, and $1,800 from the NAACP's Atlanta chapter. Meanwhile, the family was well known and respected in black Atlanta, but there were still concerns over its ability to handle the scrutiny of national media, especially the elder Hamilton Holmes, who was unafraid to speak his mind despite admonishments from NAACP leaders. "Due to Dr. Holmes's inexperience in handling newsmen, he was inveigled into talking, after having been warned repeatedly," wrote Atlanta chapter president John Calhoun to the NAACP national office.[39] Benjamin Mays, the president of Morehouse College and a member of the NAACP National Board of Directors, was on hand when the chapter agreed to continue supporting the appeal, but at the national level the organization moved on to other cases.[40]

As the suit headed to the Supreme Court, it became clear that Thurgood Marshall was wrong: vigorous reaction from both whites and blacks made *Holmes v. Atlanta* far more than just a case about "a few doctors." Instead, it was one of the first instances in which all Atlanta citizens confronted segregation in post-*Brown* America. To Marshall, the perception of elitism attached to golf devalued its importance to the civil rights movement. But the opposition felt otherwise: "To what extremes will they go next?" asked Georgia governor Herman Talmadge in his 1955 book *You and Segregation*. The answer was not suing to desegregate schools, water fountains, or bus terminals but, rather, Bobby Jones Municipal. "The first such suit involved the use of public golf courses," Talmadge continued. "The NAACP and its Negro members were not satisfied with the decision [segregated access two days a week]. They appealed to the United States Supreme Court. They do not want to play on golf courses where only Negroes are playing that day. They want to play with White men and women and they are determined to force themselves on the white players."[41] Roy Harris, another key segregationist who served on Georgia's Board of Regents and fought to block integration at its universities, agreed that yielding to black golfers was a threat to white schools. "Negroes are determined to break down segregation through the invasion of the fields of entertainment and sports first," he warned the board.[42]

The fears of Talmadge and Harris were realized in November 1955. Citing both *Brown* and a case that integrated public parks in Baltimore earlier that year, the Supreme Court ruled in favor of the Holmes family and ordered Atlanta to open its municipal courses to black patrons immediately. It was the first time in Georgia's modern history a court had ordered desegregation, and the decision reshaped one of the city's most visible arenas of racial separation. As historian Kevin Kruse notes, Atlanta's golf courses offered "the most glaring discrepancy" between white and black public space in the city. The significance of the ruling was therefore dramatic: in Atlanta the movement of "massive resistance" among pro-segregationists would be an ideological reaction to *Brown* fueled by the practical, visible implications of *Holmes*.[43]

The fallout over the ruling also revealed the booming popularity of golf in postwar Atlanta. Mayor Hartsfield rejected calls to close the courses rather than desegregate them, noting that 70,000 white players would be denied golf with such a move. Over 200,000 rounds were played on the courses in 1953, more than one round for every white person in the city (Atlanta's total population in 1950 was 331,000, of which 41 percent were black).[44] Completely shuttering public courses was a more likely response in smaller towns and rural locations, such as tiny Danville, Virginia, which simply closed its course immediately after four black residents first played it in 1956.[45]

For Hartsfield, public golf was far too popular with white Atlantans to close the courses, and the only other option was full integration. As the holidays approached, he attempted to ready the public and assuage anxieties. The mayor assured whites that his office had contacted other southern cities, like Dallas, Louisville, and Houston, and was told that courses in these locales were integrated without any "untoward incidents" between the races. He also insisted that blacks in Atlanta had no interest in golf, arguing that "only a few dozen Negro players" would be seen. And like observers on all sides of the conflict—from Thurgood Marshall to Herman Talmadge—Hartsfield invoked golf elitism to support his most unique argument: that the game itself would allay white anxieties. "Golf by its very nature is a segregated game," he told the press, "and neither necessary nor compulsory."[46]

In the end, Hartsfield's decision to integrate the courses as quietly as possible, on Christmas Eve 1955, belied his optimistic statements. And fears of "untoward incidents" on Atlanta courses were entirely justified. In Montgomery, Alabama, a local black boycott of public buses, prompted by the arrest of Rosa Parks on December 1, was in its third week and starting to receive attention outside the region. Less than a month later, the home of Martin Luther King Jr. in Montgomery would be bombed, the first instance of violence directed at the budding civil rights leader. In that city the lack of black faces on the buses was the flash point of the controversy. In Atlanta it was the arrival of black faces on the links. National media outlets clamored to document the story, including some that had yet to send representatives to cover the Montgomery boycott. CBS, NBC, and the Associated Press all contacted the Holmes family and asked when the players would head to Bobby Jones Municipal on Christmas Eve. Media and family members fielded violent threats from anonymous callers as rumors swirled that white and black players would pack "guns inside their golf bags."[47] The most outspoken of the plaintiffs, Dr. Hamilton Holmes, decided to avoid the media attention and not play. "I certainly don't fear them," he told the press when asked about the anonymous threats. "It's a bunch of the rabble who don't play golf causing all the trouble. They wouldn't know a golf club if they saw one."[48] Tup, Oliver, and Charles Bell also shunned the limelight. Instead of showing up at Bobby Jones, they quietly went to another course, North Fulton Municipal, where they played a historic round of golf. Their attorney, Roscoe Thomas, walked alongside them. "Naturally, there was a lot of tension that first day," recalled Bell. "We teed off just like anybody else. The fun

Alfred "Tup" Holmes, Oliver Holmes, and Charles Bell become the first African Americans to play municipal golf in Atlanta, North Fulton Golf Course, December 24, 1955 (Associated Press).

came on the fourth or fifth hole. That's when the news media came running at us . . . but we didn't panic. There were catcalls and the 'N' word spread around the course, but it died down after a little bit."[49] Tup noted that the 150 whites on the course were cordial: "The white golfers in front of us stopped, asked how we were doing and compared scores with us."[50]

Integration of the public courses immediately highlighted the pent-up demand for golf among Atlanta's 135,000 black residents. On that Christmas Eve another group of blacks also played the North Fulton course, a third brave group showed up at Bobby Jones, and several more called another course, James L. Key Municipal, for Monday tee times. "By the third or fourth week, everyone was grabbing a set of clubs and going to play," recalled Bell.[51] Four years later Tup would again threaten to sue the city (and Mayor Hartsfield) after the Black Rock Golf Course in Adams Park forced the cancellation of a black tournament out of concerns over

156) THE POSTWAR CIVIL RIGHTS MOVEMENT

large galleries of black spectators and players. In 1960 black golfers were on the sixth hole at Black Rock when a group of white men drove a car up the fairway firing gunshots into the air: "Negro get off our golf course," one yelled.[52] By that point it was clear that both Thurgood Marshall and Mayor Hartsfield were wrong: the appeal of golf to Atlanta's black community and the passion stirred in whites by the specter of integrated courses made *Holmes* far more than an inconsequential, elite lawsuit. Moreover, such violent displays of white supremacy on public golf courses were occurring elsewhere in the country, not only in the South. In 1953 two white men in a car fired a shot at a black foursome while the men were on the ninth tee at Chicago's Pipe O' Peace golf course.[53]

Georgia's leading white politicians also recognized the threat of golf integration and denounced Hartsfield for complying with the Supreme Court's order. To them *Holmes* was the opening battle over *Brown*, and whites had lost in dramatic fashion. "If the city has chosen to throw in the towel there is nothing I can do about it," lamented Marvin Griffin, the state's new governor. "This is but a foretaste of what the people can expect in those communities where the white people are divided at the ballot box and where the NAACP element holds the balance of power on election day."[54] Ardent segregationists, like Governor Griffin and Georgia attorney general Eugene Cook, told their constituents to fear the potential legal ramifications of golf integration in no uncertain terms. "It seems the NAACP is able to get most anything it wants from the Supreme Court ... that is designed to further its program to force inter-marriage of the races," said Cook.[55] The LDF's lukewarm support for the case and doubts about it being a significant attack on Georgia segregation made little difference. Opponents identified *Holmes* as a substantial victory for the NAACP because it struck down an important symbol of social segregation: white-only golf. As word spread and images of black golfers stepping onto Atlanta courses circulated nationwide, reaction heralded the significance and encouraged the NAACP to emphasize the case. "As you may know this is NAACP's first decision in Georgia.... It will certainly help with decisions to come in other areas," wrote John Calhoun, Atlanta's chapter president, to the national office.[56] Three months after he attended the Emmett Till murder trial in Mississippi, U.S. Congressman Charles Diggs praised the ruling in an Atlanta speech and joined Calhoun in calling *Holmes* the chapter's biggest accomplishment of 1955, celebrating the black golfers two weeks after the courses were integrated.[57]

More moderate African Americans also praised the ruling but saw it as a victory of conservatism, not a launching pad for increasingly militant campaigns. The black *Atlanta Daily World*, which had earlier criticized the Holmes clan for appealing the case and rejecting the city's offer of limited, segregated access, now celebrated the ruling: "This decision to permit Negroes to play on their city-owned golf courses may open the way for the development of future golf champions."[58] Yet by the summer of 1960 the paper was using *Holmes* to rebuke NAACP leader Roy Wilkins for supporting plans for mass sit-ins at public beaches and parks. Calling public recreation "one of the more sensitive aspects of the segregation question," it argued instead for more "simple, well-planned, test cases" like *Holmes*: "Why endanger the lives of innocent women and children by urging them to go out in great numbers to test the laws that obviously are illegal?"[59]

The fallout reverberated nationwide, as some celebrated *Holmes* while others agreed with Georgia's governor that the decision, unlike *Brown*, would be difficult to circumvent and force the integration of public parks and recreational facilities as a prelude to integrating schools. "The Supreme Court's decision probably will end all segregation cases in Kentucky," Louisville's city attorney ominously announced. Florida's attorney general concurred: "It will add to the problems of Florida and its communities." Elsewhere in the South official reaction was even more abrupt. "There will be no mixing of the races in our state parks," said South Carolina governor George Timmerman. In Alabama, Birmingham mayor James Morgan joined many in vowing to close down public courses rather than integrate them: "We must either bow in meek obedience to this decision or we must take steps to prevent the cramming of this policy—so alien to our way of life in the South—down our throats."[60] When Georgia state legislators convened in Atlanta after the holidays, they immediately tried to circumvent Mayor Hartsfield, introducing a series of bills to force the segregation of all public recreation, revoke municipal charters for towns that integrated their parks, and grant cities the right to privatize facilities.[61]

Thus from NAACP leaders to rabid segregationists, everyone debated what, if any, link existed between *Holmes* and the broader struggle to integrate schools and voting booths. Meanwhile, the answer was clear to the Holmes family. Emboldened by their success in the golf suit, they set out to integrate another public entity: the University of Georgia. Tup's son, Hamilton Holmes Jr., was fourteen years old when his grandfather, father, and uncle won their case before the Supreme Court. Five years later, he successfully sued the University of Georgia with help from Constance Baker Motley and the NAACP, becoming one of the first two black students to integrate the university in 1961. Concerns about the Holmes family's suitability with the press were now long gone: "The plaintiffs ... were among the best we had in any case," Motley wrote in her memoir.[62] Significantly, she failed to note that Hamilton came from the same family that had brought the earlier golf suit.

The Holmes clan had nevertheless linked the integration of golf and education in Georgia's history. Hamilton Holmes Sr. lived long enough to watch his grandson graduate from the University of Georgia and become the first African American admitted to the medical school at Emory University. One day in 1965 the eighty-one-year-old patriarch went out to the golf course, shot his age, and then returned home and died peacefully; two years later Tup died of cancer. Fittingly, both men are now buried in Lincoln Cemetery, the same ground where Atlanta's most important black golf course emerged in the 1930s. With New Lincoln Country Club long gone, Mayor Andrew Young went to Adams Park in 1983 and participated in ceremonies to rename Black Rock Country Club the Alfred "Tup" Holmes Memorial Golf Course. In ten years the course where African Americans were threatened with gunshots was transformed into the most popular links for black Atlantans from all walks of life. "Tup Holmes played a significant role in the birth of the civil rights movement," said Young at the dedication, "and in doing so contributed to the growth, vitality and spirit of this city."[63]

Holmes was the most visible golf desegregation suit but many were filed during the modern civil rights movement, at least twenty-eight significant cases from 1941 to 1969 alone. They came from all over the nation (including the North) and featured lawsuits from top NAACP leaders and former caddies alike. One of the first was filed by Roy Wilkins in New York. By 1940 Wilkins had relocated from Kansas City to Harlem and was the NAACP's second in command under Walter White. He continued to fight golf segregation in New York the same way he had in Kansas City, this time suing Orange County's Central Valley Golf Club for excluding him and his associates (including New York City commissioner Hubert Delaney, a close friend of Mayor Fiorello La Guardia). The prominent positions of the black men and their powerful white friends meant little to Central Valley; the small, privately owned course was open to the public but argued in court that it was "not a place of public accommodation, resort, or amusement" and therefore was exempt from state antidiscrimination laws. Numerous signs along the highway advertising the course as "open to the public" were not enough to sway the judge: Wilkins and Delaney lost the case.[64] However, the embarrassing slight prompted sympathetic lawmakers to clarify that golf courses open to the public were indeed "public amusements," and in 1942 New York governor Herbert Lehman signed the "Falk Bill," specifically adding golf courses to the list of public spaces where discrimination by "race" and "creed" were outlawed (the bill was championed by a prominent Jewish attorney in Manhattan, Alexander Falk, and also helped Jewish golfers access courses).[65] Three years later the state passed its comprehensive "Law against Discrimination," considered the first human rights law in American history. Although they lost their case, Wilkins and Delaney had used golf to help New York close gaping loopholes in its antidiscrimination laws and adopt the most comprehensive legislation of its kind.

Moreover, New Yorkers also saw the implications of these stronger antidiscrimination bills through the lens of golf. Courses that openly advertised to the public increasingly asserted that they were actually private clubs. In 1947 a group of black players sued the Westchester Hills Golf Club in White Plains, just outside New York City. A ritzier, "semi-private" course than Central Valley, Westchester Hills was nevertheless available for public use; its lawyers even argued that the club was fully private despite having a hotel on site. Unlike in the suit filed by Wilkins and Delaney seven years earlier, the course lost this time, and the plaintiffs were awarded $1,000 in damages, at that point the largest judgment for an antidiscrimination violation in state history.[66]

African Americans nationwide applauded New York's progressive legislation and the victory over Westchester Hills, noting that courses there were not alone in trying to subvert state antidiscrimination ordinances. Yet attempts to desegregate courses elsewhere did not fare as well. Black leaders in Illinois and California unsuccessfully lobbied for similar legislation in their states. The same year as the Westchester Hills decision, a black accountant from Chicago, Theodore Jones, lost his case in Massachusetts when he sued Martha's Vineyard Country Club for turning him away during a vacation. His attorney failed to convince the court that the course was a "public amusement" despite numerous advertisements stating the club offered "a cordial welcome to all Vineyard visitors."[67] Two other cases in Illinois and Michigan also failed in the late 1940s; both targeted courses run by the Methodist Church that claimed to be private yet were open to the white public.[68]

(*Chicago Defender*, June 30, 1951)

"The Best Way I Know To Stop Your Husband From Playing Golf, Is To Play With Him."

Northern courses, such as Central Valley and Westchester Hills, thus manipulated distinctions between "public," "private," and "semiprivate" long before southern leaders responded to *Brown* and *Holmes* by privatizing municipal links. Before 1950 there were numerous instances of deceptive privatization on northern courses, as well as city courses leased to private entities to avoid integration; examples included prominent courses in Massachusetts, New York, New Jersey, and Ohio.[69] Two men who had served as president of Cleveland's NAACP branch, Clayborne George (1923–28) and Chester Gillespie (1936–38), filed a lawsuit against suburban Lake Shore Country Club in 1942. The case was significant because most people (including blacks in Cleveland) assumed the course was fully private: it was a well-known property that had just been sold by the city's most exclusive country club. The new manager, a white professional who regularly played with Joe Louis, argued in court that Lake

Shore remained a private course.[70] Initially the judge ruled in favor of the club, yet eventually the plaintiffs won on appeal after a long legal battle exposed how the course used membership merely as a "ruse" to exclude black patrons. Foreshadowing the civil rights movement's open housing campaigns of the 1960s, Gillespie and George recruited white sympathizers to approach the club. All of them testified that they were welcome to play after paying a simple fee in line with any public course: "membership" at Lake Shore simply meant being white and asking to play. The court reversed its decision and ruled in favor of Cleveland's black golfers in 1950. Even Thurgood Marshall, cynical as he was about the broader influence of golf cases, congratulated Gillespie and George for sticking with the case and exposing the club's blatant racism: "I have been watching for the opinion since you talked to me about the case and it is a real victory," he wrote Gillespie.[71] Gillespie soon expanded his legal assault, targeting golf facilities throughout the region that operated as public while using private membership to exclude black patrons. This included Epworth Heights Golf Club in Ludington, Michigan, which turned him away in 1947 even though it advertised itself as a public links.[72]

Holmes was therefore not the first NAACP golf lawsuit, nor was it the first case to emerge in the postwar South. In New Orleans, Mandeville Detiege, a black soldier who had just returned home after the war, was still in his winter uniform when he decided to seek shade under an oak tree while waiting for a bus. He was arrested for being in white-only City Park. In 1949 Detiege sued in federal court for full access to the park's "golf links, picnic grounds, tennis courts, and other recreational facilities."[73] The case proceeded for a decade before the U.S. Supreme Court affirmed a lower court's decision to integrate City Park in *New Orleans City Park Improvement Association v. Detiege* (1958). Ironically, there is no evidence that Joe Bartholomew's name was brought up in court. Nevertheless, the decision meant that African Americans for the first time were allowed to play the park's four public golf courses, twenty-five years after Bartholomew designed City Park No. 1.[74] In nearby Baton Rouge it was six more years before blacks were allowed to play municipal golf, after a federal court ordered the capital to integrate its parks in 1964.[75]

Unlike *Detiege*, two other early lawsuits in the South—in Portsmouth, Virginia, and Houston, Texas—centered specifically on golf. The growing black population in Portsmouth (and adjacent Norfolk) supported a thriving golf scene for many years, gaining access to Memorial Park's municipal course in Norfolk two days a week and organizing tournaments

Table 3. Significant Golf Desegregation Lawsuits, 1941–1970

Year(s)	Location	Lawsuits
1941	Orange County, N.Y.	Delaney v. Central Valley Golf Club
1947	Oak Bluffs, Mass.	Jones v. Attridge and Martha's Vineyard Country Club
1942, 1948	Baltimore, Md.	Durkee v. Murphy, Law v. Mayor and City Council of Baltimore
1950	Cleveland, Ohio	Gillespie v. Lake Shore Golf Club
1950, 1957	Miami, Fla.	Rice v. Arnold, Ward v. City of Miami
1951	Houston, Tex.	Beal v. Holcombe
1951	Louisville, Ky.	Sweeney v. City of Louisville
1955	Atlanta, Ga.	Holmes v. City of Atlanta
1955	Beaumont, Tex.	Fayson v. Beard
1956	Charlotte, N.C.	Leeper v. Charlotte Park and Recreation Commission
1956	Nashville, Tenn.	Hayes v. Crutcher
1956	Pensacola, Fla.	Augustus v. City of Pensacola
1957	Portsmouth, Va.	Holley v. City of Portsmouth
1957, 1960	Greensboro, N.C.	Simkins v. City of Greensboro, Wolfe v. North Carolina
1958	New Orleans, La.	New Orleans City Park Improvement Association v. Detiege
1957, 1958	Fort Lauderdale, Fla.	Moorhead v. City of Fort Lauderdale, Griffis v. City of Fort Lauderdale
1961	Charleston, S.C.	Cummings v. City of Charleston
1961	Birmingham, Ala.	Shuttlesworth v. Gaylord
1961	Mobile, Ala.	Sawyer v. City of Mobile
1962	Jacksonville, Fla.	Hampton v. City of Jacksonville, Florida
1962	Denver, Colo.	Clark v. Sherman
1963	Little Rock, Ark.	Freeman v. Little Rock
1965	St. Petersburg, Fla.	Wimbish v. Pinellas County, Florida
1969	Savannah, Ga.	Wesley v. City of Savannah
1970	Durham, N.C.	U.S. v. Central Carolina Bank and Trust

that attracted blacks from around the region. Black golfers in Portsmouth sued in 1951 and were allowed to use that city's two municipal courses one day per week.[76] But soon a new generation of players demanded an end to segregated golf in the region. They were led by twenty-nine-year-old James Holley, a 1955 graduate of Howard University who sued Portsmouth the following year after course managers told him he could only play golf on Fridays. He won the case in April 1957, prompting full integration not only of the courses but also of Portsmouth's parks and swimming pools. Moreover, the legal victory emboldened Holley and put him squarely on a path to leadership in his community. In 1968 he desegregated the city council, and in 1984 Portsmouth's majority-white population elected him mayor, the first African American to hold that office in the region. "He was an icon," recalled Portsmouth state senator Louise Lucas. "He thought there was nothing that this city couldn't accomplish, his Portsmouth Family, as he used to call us."[77]

In Houston, the legal battle began when four former caddies returned from military service in 1945 and established the Lone Star Golf Club, an organization to advocate on behalf of the city's black golfers. Three years later the group held a large protest at a municipal course that drew crowds of onlookers and the police.[78] Eventually, five other black players, including a jeweler, a funeral director, and a doctor, sued the city in 1950. They were represented by two white attorneys in Houston, Herman Wright and Arthur Mandell, as well as black attorney William Durham, in whose home Thurgood Marshall and LDF leaders had spent many hours working on *Sweatt v. Painter* (1950), a landmark Supreme Court case that struck down segregation at the University of Texas Law School. (*Sweatt* also prompted Austin to integrate its Lions Municipal Golf Course later that year, making it likely the first municipal course in the South to desegregate.)[79] Meanwhile, Houston's golf case (*Beal v. Holcombe*) received little national attention but was still a significant victory for black Texans. One reason was because Houston, like Atlanta, used golf to signal its immediate response to *Brown v. Board of Education*. In 1951 a federal judge reversed a lower court ruling and ordered Mayor Oscar Holcombe to come up with a plan to desegregate Houston's municipal courses.[80] The city at first appealed to the U.S. Supreme Court, but in 1954—just days after *Brown*—the new mayor, Roy Hofheinz, abruptly ordered the case dropped and opened Houston's golf courses to all. It provided the first indication of how city leaders would respond to the landmark ruling on public schools. Black observers were encouraged, as that same week

Baltimore announced it was desegregating its public schools: "Two of the South's biggest cities have joined the march of progress," proclaimed the *Pittsburgh Courier*.[81] In the eyes of the press the integration of Houston golf courses and Baltimore schools went hand in hand.

Within weeks a number of Texas cities followed Houston's lead and voluntarily integrated their courses, including Dallas and Corpus Christi (San Antonio, Fort Worth, and Galveston all followed by 1956). One popular Dallas municipal course, Cedar Crest Golf Course, even hosted the 1954 UGA National in September, drawing top black professionals (and stars like Sammy Davis Jr.) to a facility that four months earlier had completely excluded African Americans. Within a few years 70 percent of Cedar Crest's golfers were black, as are half its patrons today.[82] In Fort Worth eight black players showed up to golf on the first day after integration, while post-*Brown* changes on the links reverberated in smaller towns as well: "I had never seen a Negro playing on the municipal golf courses," remarked the school superintendent in rural San Angelo. "Until after we integrated, and I had a foursome in front and one behind me one day right after that."[83] Still, *Beal* and *Brown* were not enough in Beaumont, Texas. There, six black golfers had to win their own federal lawsuit to open the municipal course in September 1955.[84]

While some golf-related suits emerged from a small cadre of enthusiasts or a single individual (like Mandeville Detiege in New Orleans), an important case in Miami began with the golf petition signed by 3,000 black residents in 1948. The city responded by allowing them to play Miami Springs Golf Course one day a week (Mondays), making it the first municipal course in Florida open to black players. Yet the fight for integration in this important golf mecca was far from over. Segregated access to Miami Springs and the city's plans to build a separate black links were not enough for most in the community, who noted that popular municipal courses in nearby Coral Gables and Miami Beach also continued to ban black patrons.[85] With help from the NAACP, a group sued the city, and in 1950 the case (*Rice v. Arnold*) became yet another that went all the way to the U.S. Supreme Court, five years before *Holmes*. Victory seemed assured at first; the court ordered Florida's top court to review its support for segregation at Miami Springs in light of two important school integration decisions from earlier that year: *Sweatt v. Painter* and *McLaurin v. Oklahoma State Regents*. Harry Moore, head of the NAACP in Florida, boasted that the decision would ultimately "permit Negroes to play on the Miami municipal golf course any day in the week."[86] Hopes were dashed, however, after Florida's supreme court ruled in favor of the city. A second appeal to the U.S. Supreme Court was denied in 1952.[87]

Rejected even after legal help from the national NAACP and a hearing with the Supreme Court, Miami's black golfers pressed on. In January 1956 retired pharmacist Elmer Ward and another group of players sued in federal court after they were once again turned away from Miami Springs. This time the case featured one unique fact: Ward had never played golf in his life and showed up at the course without golf clubs. "Clubs are of no use when you don't know how to play the game," he told the press. "My purpose was, and is, to establish my rights as a citizen." Ward's stand emphasized the importance of municipal access to cultivating the game in the black community. "I am interested in learning to play," he said, "and I know that would be next to impossible under the limitations imposed by the city."[88] Miami fought the case vigorously—even countersuing Ward and four other black players—before finally bowing in April 1958 and integrating Miami Springs, a full decade after the 3,000 petitioners first demanded access and three years after public courses in nearby Miami Beach had already integrated. Immediately, Palm Beach opened its public course to African Americans as well, while Coral Gables came last in 1959.[89] Residents in southern Florida soon discovered that the largest black petition for public golf in U.S. history was more than a coordinated civil rights campaign: it represented real interest in the game. Managers at Bayshore Golf Course in Miami Beach immediately reported seeing as many as thirty-two black players on the course at any given time.[90]

Elsewhere in Florida, Constance Baker Motley and the NAACP offered more support as local activists fought valiantly to open public courses. In Jacksonville, the *Holmes* decision and a long history of black golf at Lincoln Golf Club did little to sway city officials. One golfer, Frank Hampton, emerged as a local civil rights leader during the 1950s. After a long fight he was named the city's first black policeman in 1955; however, three years later he left the force in order to wage a new legal battle: suing the city after he and fellow black golfers were banned from a tournament at one of Jacksonville's two municipal links. As in Miami, victory seemed straightforward in the wake of *Brown* and *Holmes*, especially after a district court ruled in his favor and a timeline for desegregation was set. Yet shortly before integration, the city made a surprising announcement: it was closing the courses and putting them up for sale—"to prevent disturbances and problems," according to the mayor. (Jacksonville's parks commissioner put it more bluntly: "If we integrate these courses there will be trouble ... there will be bloodshed.")[91] With help from Motley and NAACP attorneys, Hampton fought vainly in federal court to prevent the sale. Fortunately, the judge found that a reverter clause indicating that the land would return to the city if its private owners failed to use it for golf was enough to deem it public space. Integration was ordered and achieved in 1963.[92]

Motley also worked closely on a golf suit with St. Petersburg's NAACP president, Ralph Wimbish, who joined black residents in petitioning to play the city's municipal course, the most popular links in East Florida. As in Houston and Atlanta, St. Petersburg also used golf to signal its initial reaction to *Brown v. Board of Education*, only this time the city closed the course within days of the ruling. Two years later the county quietly leased a large tract of land by the airport to a private corporation to build another course. Yet the attempted "white flight" of public golf fooled no one, as the course was quickly overwhelmed when black golfers from around the state began to show up. "We have taken the 'public' off our sign and have made it a private golf club," the manager complained to the press. "The first day we were open we had four Negroes drive up in a Miami-licensed car and play. They insisted on using a restroom which hadn't even been hooked up for plumbing."[93] By 1965 those very words helped incriminate the county in federal court (the ruling specifically cited the manager's interview) after Motley and Wimbish sued. Ten years after *Holmes*, the NAACP was still winning important golf suits in the South despite ever-more-complicated attempts by local authorities to hide public courses.

Despite his criticism of golf lawsuits, Thurgood Marshall found himself getting more involved in some of them. Most notable was the case to integrate courses in Nashville, Tennessee, significant because it was home to Ted Rhodes, the period's most popular black pro golfer. Rhodes had taught himself to play swinging clubs in Nashville's black public parks, constructing his own makeshift golf holes. As in Atlanta, the case also exposed how the postwar civil rights movement divided local black leaders and pitted moderates against progressives. In Nashville that tension first emerged over golf after a Baptist minister and a student were both turned away from two municipal courses, Shelby Golf Course and McCabe Golf Course, and sued the city in 1951. Nashville's two black councilmen, Z. Alexander Looby and Robert Lillard, were both attorneys but diverged over how the city should respond to black demands for public golf. With the support of white leaders, Lillard advocated that Nashville build a segregated black links, while the Caribbean-born Looby was more militant and opposed appeasing whites on the issue. He had just served on two important NAACP cases: defending twenty-five black men charged with starting a 1946 race riot in Columbia, Tennessee, and helping Marshall with a U.S. Supreme Court case in 1951 defending four black men accused of raping a white woman in Groveland, Florida. Looby eventually was a leading advocate for integrating Nashville's schools later in the 1950s.[94]

Yet in 1952 Looby's biggest fight was over golf, and it was not going well: the case, *Hayes v. Crutcher*, seemed doomed after a federal judge ruled against the golfers with a shocking opinion that wholly supported Lillard's call for segregated golf. "Nature has produced white birds, black birds, blue birds, red birds and they do not roost on the same limb or use the same nest," read the opinion issued by Nashville's federal district court. "Such recognition and preference for their own kind prevails among all other animals."[95] It was one of the starker defenses of segregation to come from a federal court in the 1950s. Looby and Nashville's NAACP chapter organized the black community in response, and an overflow crowd arrived at the next city council meeting and denounced Lillard and plans for the black links. Meanwhile, Looby asked NAACP executive secretary Walter White directly for help on the issue. Lillard and the city's white leaders had conspired to block the case and stifle the majority of blacks in Nashville who denounced segregated golf: "That is the type of opposition that I have been having every [sic] since I took office," he wrote to White, sending information and press releases to the national office.[96] The unrest, and Looby's direct help in other LDF cases, was enough to draw support from New York City, including from Thurgood Marshall. Looby and Marshall appealed the case and in 1954 won an injunction to open Nashville's municipal courses to black players on certain days of the week. On the first day, seventy-five black golfers showed up to play at Shelby Park, where they found a six-foot-high wooden cross planted in the ninth hole, where it had burned the night before.

Two years later, following *Brown* and *Holmes*, a federal court ordered the full integration of Nashville's public courses. Considering the fierce opposition from whites (and moderate blacks), the subsequent change was dramatic. Within fifteen years of Nashville having no separate golf facility for African Americans, let alone an integrated links, black players were frequenting its municipal courses by 1969, and that year the city renamed one in honor of Ted Rhodes.[97] While extreme, the cross at Shelby Park was not unique. Massive resistance to black golf in Nashville was echoed in Memphis, only there it erupted in response not to a legal deci-

P. O. Sweeney and his wife in Louisville, Kentucky (*Ebony*, June 1969).

sion but, rather, to a UGA tournament. In 1956 local members of the White Citizens' Council and other pro-segregation groups flooded a Memphis city council meeting and "created a furor" after officials announced plans to allow the black tournament to take place on the city's Audubon Park course. Fierce resistance in Memphis continued into the late 1950s and delayed integration for longer than other cities in the region. Four of the city's seven municipal courses were still segregated when the UGA returned in 1962 to hold its national championship at Fuller Park Golf Course.[98]

Through Constance Baker Motley and, more reluctantly, Thurgood Marshall, the LDF thus found itself supporting a number of golf suits around the country. The man who replaced Marshall as the NAACP's chief counsel in 1956, Robert L. Carter, worked closely on a case in Louisville, Kentucky. In 1949 a local black dentist, P. O. Sweeney, organized black residents to file a lawsuit after he was denied access to one of the city's municipal courses. *Sweeney v. City of Louisville* soon became a broader case as the group sued for the complete integration of all "recreational, athletic, swimming, golf, park, and entertainment facilities."[99] When Carter began arguing *Sweeney* in 1951, he had just served as the NAACP's lead counsel in *Sweatt v. Painter*, and four years later he would present

THE POSTWAR CIVIL RIGHTS MOVEMENT (169

part of the NAACP's oral arguments in *Brown*. In Louisville, however, his golf case struggled. Even as African Americans protested at town hall meetings and the mayor's office, the city argued forcefully in court that there was not enough black demand for golf to justify a "negro course," an argument that prevailed in the Kentucky Court of Appeals. Yet in federal court the group achieved partial victory, as the court saw few options for providing separate-but-equal golf facilities other than allowing blacks to use the existing links. "How this shall be done presents a problem for the Director of Parks and Recreation," read the opinion in *Sweeney v. City of Louisville*, "to determine what shall be done to afford substantially equal facilities to Negro golfers, necessarily having consideration for the number of Negro golfers."[100]

Notably, the plaintiffs failed in their bid to desegregate Louisville's other public amusements, including the amphitheater. Instead of the last bastion of white privilege, golf in Louisville was thus among the first public facilities to integrate and led the way for subsequent challenges in other arenas. Moreover, the court recognized that this was due in part to the uniqueness of the game: for residents, white or black, it required substantial space and investment no matter the level of interest. Louisville desegregated its courses in February 1952, and demand from black golfers immediately increased: within three years the city had a UGA-affiliated club. Other Kentucky municipal courses desegregated later, including in Paducah (1956) and Frankfort (1961).[101]

Just as a golf lawsuit emboldened the Holmes family to fight for integration at the University of Georgia, in Florida yet another resident used golf to become a local civil rights leader and integrate public schools. Charles Augustus and two other black players sued Pensacola in 1955 for access to the municipal Osceola Golf Course, a case they won the following year. *Augustus v. City of Pensacola* received some national attention (including in the *Chicago Tribune*); but it did not involve Motley or the national NAACP, and the course integrated quietly.[102] However, the victory was an important experience for Augustus and his family, one that encouraged him to fight a larger legal battle on behalf of his ten-year-old daughter, Karen. With help from Motley and the LDF, Augustus sued again in 1958 to desegregate the schools, and he won in 1962. *Augustus v. Board of Public Instruction of Escambia County Florida* allowed Karen to attend O. J. Simms Elementary School (she was the first African American to integrate the region's schools) and was an important victory for the LDF. "The *Augustus* case was the first in which we sought, under *Brown*, the reassignment of teachers on a nonracial basis," wrote Motley in her memoir. "Up to this point, all school desegregation cases had focused on pupil assignments."[103] Once again, Motley overlooked her plaintiff's earlier successful golf suit (it is not clear if she even knew about it). Nevertheless, Pensacola joined the list of cities where golf played a key role in advancing the black community's local fight to integrate schools.

Largely through her connection to some (but not all) of these Florida cases, Motley seemed to be the LDF insider most sympathetic to golf lawsuits, some of which did receive considerable help from the national office. Yet other important suits remained in the hands of local plaintiffs and lawyers, including the case of six black golfers in Greensboro, North Carolina, who went all the way to the Supreme Court in 1960 with little support. Greensboro's segregated municipal course was built in Gillespie Park by the WPA in 1940. By 1949, black residents were regularly showing up at Gillespie with golf clubs and forcing the course to turn them away. Reluctantly, the city council built a separate black links but only after some council members demanded to know exactly how many of Greensboro's African Americans were interested in playing. Black leaders, arguing that interest would expand once access was provided, chafed at the question and noted the irony of the city trying to calculate black people's interest in a game it systematically denied them.[104] The new arrangement—a municipal course for whites at Gillespie Park and another for blacks at Nocho Park—did not satisfy George Simkins, a Greensboro native who left town for college and returned in 1949 to set up his own dental practice. What he found was a city bending over backward to separate its golfers by race. "The city had two golf courses," he recalled. "We tried to get them to fix up Nocho, and they never would do it, yet they were slipping out and fixing up Gillespie."[105]

On December 7, 1955—in the same week the Montgomery Bus Boycott began and two weeks before Atlanta desegregated its municipal courses—Simkins and five other black golfers attempted to play Gillespie Park. After the course manager rebuffed them, the players left their greens fees on the counter, walked out of the clubhouse, and started golfing anyway. By the third hole, police had arrived and arrested them for trespassing, sparking another case that eventually reached the U.S. Supreme Court. As Greensboro moved to sell both its white and black courses in response to the protest, Simkins contacted his local NAACP chapter after the men were convicted in February 1956.[106] Unlike the Holmes clan in Atlanta, he found little support at first; the chapter declined to take the case and offered only $100 in support. Simkins sent a five-page, handwritten letter pleading for help from the national office. "I have just about [be]come convinced that the local officers of the Greensboro chapter of the N.A.A.C.P. are either afraid to tackle this golf course case or are unwilling for personal reasons to do so," he wrote. "If my request is not possible, my group intends to struggle on by ourselves as we have done in the past."[107] Yet NAACP state leaders in North Carolina, citing rumors that some Greensboro golfers believed the organization's involvement would "prejudice the case in court," successfully urged officials in New York to hold off. "There is little else the National Office can do about the local situation," read the response to Simkins's appeal. "It remains for you and the members of the Branch to work out something."[108] Without help, the resources required would be significant (for instance, the lawsuit to integrate municipal courses in Baltimore had taken ten years and cost $10,000).[109]

True to his word, Simkins carried on the fight, and the men, dubbed the "Greensboro Six" by the press, successfully funded their own defense on appeal to the North Carolina Supreme Court. However, threatening the sanctity of white golf with a bold display of trespassing was not easily forgotten in Greensboro; prosecutors immediately retried them on slightly different charges, and they were convicted again, this time sentenced to thirty days in jail. In 1957 Simkins sought an injunction against the course in federal court and prevailed in *Simkins v. City of Greensboro*. The decision, which forced Gillespie Park to open its course to black people, is long forgotten to most Americans but made legal history regardless: it was the first time a federal court clearly indicated that *Plessy v. Ferguson* was overturned. "[*Brown v. Board of Education*] merely rejects *Plessy*'s reasoning as applied to public education," wrote legal scholar Jack Balkin. "Most people believe that *Brown* did overrule *Plessy*, and certainly the Justices understood in 1954 that this was the consequence of their decision. Nevertheless, it was not until 1957 that a federal court held that *Plessy* was overruled [*Simkins v. City of Greensboro*]."[110]

The players had prevailed in forcing the course to open, but they still had to fight to overturn their convictions and avoid jail. That battle, *Wolfe v. North Carolina* (Leon Wolfe was another of the Greensboro Six), reached the U.S. Supreme Court in 1960. Once again Simkins sought help from the NAACP's national office to no avail, but for a different reason: Thurgood Marshall insisted Simkins's local lawyers had bungled the case by not including the *Simkins v. City of Greensboro* federal trial and injunc-

The Greensboro Six in 1957: (*left to right*) Phillip Cooke, Samuel Murray, Elijah Herring, Joseph Sturdivant, George Simkins, and Leon Wolfe (© *Greensboro News & Record*, All Rights Reserved).

tion in the record. "The lawyers had made a mistake," Simkins recalled. "I went up to Thurgood, that's how I met Thurgood Marshall and Jack Greenberg. I went up to New York and asked Thurgood, 'We need you, because I can't fight these lawyers, and the city and everybody by myself. I need the NAACP to help us.' He looked at the record, and told me, 'Your lawyers ought to be the ones to go to jail. . . . They have screwed this case up. I'm not going to mess my record up by taking a case like this, because you cannot win. You're going to lose it by one vote.'"[111]

This time Marshall was correct: in 1960—six years after *Brown* and five years after *Holmes*—the U.S. Supreme Court upheld jail sentences for the Greensboro Six in a 5-4 ruling. The players had hired a respected black attorney in North Carolina, Jasper A. Atkins, to argue the case; but it was not enough, and Chief Justice Earl Warren's impassioned dissent did not help either. The men were saved from jail only after North Carolina governor Luther Hodges commuted their sentences and ordered them to pay a fine.[112] A five-year legal saga that began with three holes of golf at Gillespie Park was finally over, but not before it had rekindled racial tension in the city and laid the groundwork for more militant civil rights agitation. Press reports noted that one of the Greensboro Six, Elijah Herring, was the victim of "telephone threats, dynamiting attempts, and hurled missiles," while an arsonist burned down the golf course's clubhouse one week after *Simkins v. City of Greensboro* ordered it to integrate. "Everything was dangerous back then," Simkins later said. "Anything you tried to integrate was."[113]

While the Greensboro Six awaited the Supreme Court's ruling in *Wolfe v. North Carolina*, four black college students walked into Greensboro's Woolworth's Five-and-Dime department store on February 1, 1960, and launched the most famous sit-in movement in American history. The Greensboro sit-ins soon overshadowed golf at Gillespie Park and became a symbolic turning point in the history of the civil rights movement. For most historians they mark the arrival of more militant, confrontational black protest in postwar Greensboro, but not all residents forgot the significance of the golf agitation that came before. George Roach, Greensboro's mayor from 1957 to 1961, reminded an interviewer in 1978 that white leaders had already dealt with "a test of segregation" years before the sit-ins. "It had started with . . . the Gillespie Golf Course," he said. A *Greensboro Record* reporter, credited in 1960 with breaking the story of the Woolworth's sit-in, agreed: "My first detailed association with any of the civil rights movement was in 1955 when six black men . . . played nine holes of golf at Gillespie Park Golf Course," she remembered.[114]

George Simkins's subsequent life and career also highlighted the significance of the golf protest. He embraced the newfound access to Greensboro's parks and recreation facilities with glee. Ironically, in 1961 he made the finals of the city's tennis championship and won what was surely an awkward match: his opponent was the white city attorney who had prosecuted him six years earlier for trespassing at Gillespie Park. The man who insisted on playing golf and tennis with whites used those victories to continue fighting segregation in a variety of public facilities, schools, and housing, including an important victory in federal court over Greensboro's public hospital that helped integrate medical facilities nationwide.[115] Initially rebuffed by local NAACP leaders over his golf case, Simkins became president of the Greensboro chapter in the late 1950s and led it until 1985, never forgetting how the moment he refused to leave the first tee at Gillespie Park started it all. That was the day "I had gotten involved in civil rights," he said four years before his death in 2001.[116]

Compared with the rest of North Carolina, the battle to integrate Greensboro's links showed how support from the NAACP and the lengths whites would go to in preserving segregated golf were both uncertain. In nearby Charlotte the LDF supported sixteen golfers who sued to integrate the municipal Bonnie Brae Golf Course in 1951. They quietly won the case in 1956 when the state's only female judge ordered the city to integrate all of its courses. The black press celebrated how "feminine wisdom" had prevailed in Charlotte while golf in Greensboro descended into chaos. Six years later golf at Bonnie Brae was a fixture in Charlotte's black community, and the judge, Susie Sharpe, was the first woman elected to a state supreme court in U.S. history. In 2011 the course was renamed Dr. Charles L. Sifford Golf Course to honor the city's famed black player (the University of St Andrews awarded Sifford an honorary doctorate in 2006).[117] Moreover, the integration of Bonnie Brae came before most other facilities were desegregated in Charlotte, including public buses. Both North Carolina's NAACP chairman and Charlotte's lone black city councilman agreed the case was "a forerunner that broke the back of hardcore resistance to the use of public run facilities."[118] Just outside Charlotte, the integration of golf in Gastonia went even more smoothly, as black players reversed stereotype and invited whites to play the course with them. Beginning in 1950 Gastonia set aside Mondays for African Americans to play its municipal course. When whites showed up anyway, the black golfers welcomed them, and the players quietly integrated themselves. "We just worked it out," the course's white pro explained to the press: national civil rights organizations trumpeted the example of interracial cooperation.[119]

By 1957 integrated public golf had spread to much of North Carolina, including Asheville, Asheboro, High Point, Thomasville, Wilmington, and Winston Salem (twenty whites in Asheboro resigned their membership at the municipal course rather than play alongside black citizens).[120] Meanwhile, most black golfers in neighboring South Carolina were still banned from public courses. In 1958 a group of fourteen petitioned Charleston for access to its municipal course, noting they had to drive to Wilmington to play (a round-trip of nearly 400 miles).[121] After the players went to the course directly and were turned away, they filed a lawsuit. In 1961 they won the case, *Cummings v. City of Charleston*, and that June the course was integrated without fanfare, at the very moment Charleston's citizens awaited a similar ruling on integrating public schools. Applauding the peaceful transition, African Americans urged the city to use *Cummings* as a model for school desegregation. "It can be done!" exclaimed the *Afro-*

James Otis Williams integrating Charlotte's Bonnie Brae Golf Course in 1957 (*Charlotte Observer*).

American. "Charleston's Municipal Golf Course was integrated quietly Friday without fuss or fanfare—the first such step in South Carolina. . . . A similar suit is pending seeking the abolition of segregation in Charleston's public schools."[122]

From Atlanta to Greensboro, blacks throughout the South were using golf cases to help them become leaders of the civil rights movement in their communities. Like George Simkins, Thomas Brewer was another local NAACP head who made golf integration a central component of his chapter's activism. Unlike Simkins, it cost him his life. Brewer was a black physician who moved to Columbus, Georgia, in the 1920s and established the city's NAACP chapter in 1939. By the 1950s he was already a well-known activist in the region; he had worked to provide more opportunities for black soldiers at nearby Fort Benning, organized publicly for black voting rights and school integration, and helped Columbus integrate its police force. Yet none of these accomplishments drew as much press as his January 1956 attempt to integrate Columbus's municipal golf course. Brewer and four other players (including a local gas station owner and lumber dealer) threatened to file a lawsuit after the city turned them away. Unlike some golf agitators (like Elmer Ward in Miami), these men were accomplished golfers who played regularly at Fort Benning. All five shot in the high 70s and low 80s, including Eddie Walker, a black employee at the base who had one arm. With help from the black press, Brewer's campaign was Columbus's headline civil rights issue in early 1956. "The whites are closed mouth. The colored people are enthused," he told national reporters when asked to describe how the golf fight was affecting the city.[123] One month later a white department store owner shot him seven times during an argument. Brewer died instantly, and his death was reported around the country. Local residents insisted he was targeted because of his civil rights work, while the black press reported that another NAACP leader in the South had been assassinated for his militancy, this time leaving his battle to integrate the golf course unfinished. "I prevailed on him last Saturday morning to stop his campaigning," Brewer's wife told reporters through tears. "He gave his life for his people."[124]

While nearly thirty golf-related lawsuits influenced the legal battle for integration, the game also seeped into the national civil rights narrative outside the courtroom. The movement exploded during the administration of Dwight D. Eisenhower, a man who loved golf more than any U.S. president in history and who traveled to Georgia's Augusta National Golf Club twenty-nine times while in office.[125] By far it was golf, not civil rights or any other domestic issue, that most often prompted him to visit the South. The two courses Eisenhower commonly played—Augusta National and Burning Tree Club in Bethesda, Maryland—had no black (or female) members, and there is no evidence he ever played alongside black golfers anywhere. The president did play public courses while in office, including one of his favorites: Atlanta's Bobby Jones Municipal, which he visited with friends after the *Holmes* decision and afterward embarrassed his private secretary by sharing "the latest nigger jokes" he heard while on the course.[126] E. Frederic Morrow, one of the few African Americans in Eisenhower's administration, served as an advisor to the president and loved golf. He played with prominent golfers like George S. May (who welcomed him to Tam O'Shanter in 1957) and his friend Jackie Robinson. Yet in 1955 Vice President Richard Nixon seemed surprised when Morrow told him that he was unable to golf at private courses in the Washington, D.C., area. Nixon, who frequently joined Eisenhower at Burning Tree, assured Morrow that they would hit the links: "Well, as soon as this pressure permits, I'll get two or three of our gang together and we'll play at one of the local clubs."[127] In the end, apparently neither Eisenhower nor Nixon ever invited Morrow to play.

Golf was also major fodder for Eisenhower's opponents: "Ben Hogan for President. If We're Going to Have a Golfer, Let's Have a Good One," read one critical bumper sticker.[128] In 1957 his Georgia golf trips rankled critics after the Little Rick Nine incident forced him to wade directly into the civil rights crisis. Telegrams to the president poured in from both opponents and supporters of integration, many needling him over golf. "I think this is more important than a game of golf," wrote one woman from Birmingham, Alabama, reminding him that "the white people of Birmingham Ala and of the south disapprove of your decision in sending troops to Little Rock." Meanwhile, a pro-integration telegram urged the president to "throw away golf clubs" and go to Little Rock to "lead negro children into school yourself."[129] Letters to the black press agreed: "It would be much healthier for the President's conscience if he does something about this rather than play golf," wrote one reader.[130] Eisenhower eventually dispatched federal troops in September and forced Arkansas governor Orval Faubus to integrate Central High School (six years before a federal court integrated Little Rock's municipal golf courses in 1963).[131]

The president's next trip to the South came two months later, in November 1957, when he again traveled to Augusta National. This time tension swirled before the visit. The radical pro-segregation *Augusta Courier* denounced "the butcher of Little Rock" for sending the troops to Arkansas: "He didn't like it when they interrupted his golf game long enough to sign the order."[132] Yet Eisenhower still received a warm welcome from most whites, dodging reporters' questions as he stepped off the plane to cheering crowds at Augusta's Bush Field and hurrying off to the golf course: "Let's get going," he said. "I've got to get in nine holes."[133] Even the moderate black *Atlanta Daily World*, which supported *Holmes* earlier in 1955, celebrated Eisenhower's many trips to the course, including another the following year: "Welcome again, Mr. President. Let golf continue to make Augusta famous."[134]

Yet the November 1957 visit was the president's fifteenth in five years, and for many civil rights advocates his golfing escapades and friendly dealings with the elite course exemplified his apathy toward a growing movement. "The world has noted your eloquent pleas for freedom in Europe, South America and Asia," read one civil rights petition. "Yet your only southern trip has been to play golf on the segregated Augusta Golf Course." Others put it more bluntly: "You are little more than the highest salaried golf pro in the country," wrote a Pennsylvania college student. Another from Ohio's Oberlin College demanded that Eisenhower answer for segregation at both Augusta National and Burning Tree.[135] Several times Langston Hughes used his bombastic character "Jesse Semple" to assail both the president and Augusta National. "I wish Eisenhower would not go golfing in Georgia.... He is about the most golfingest, goofingest President I ever seen," Semple remarked in one column. In another he mockingly described plans for celebrations of a "White History Week," culminating with Eisenhower "teeing off at Augusta, down in Georgia. Every TV screen in the country would show our great President knocking a golf ball all the way from Georgia to Alabama—Go, Jim Daddy!—right into Reverend King's Montgomery backyard." And in a third column Semple imagined himself delivering a rousing speech to the United Nations, imploring the world "to contend with what Harlem thinks." He ended with the poetic jab, "I will take your own golf stick and wham the world so far up into orbit until you will be shaken off the surface of the earth and everybody will wonder where have all the white folks gone."[136]

The movement's frustration with Eisenhower escalated after he declined a series of meetings with prominent African Americans and worsened the snubs by heading to the links instead. In February 1957, months before the crisis in Little Rock, Martin Luther King Jr. and the SCLC asked for a meeting with the president in Montgomery, where the victorious bus boycott had just ended but supporters still faced violent backlash from whites. King urged Eisenhower to deliver a speech on civil rights in the South and denounce the violence. When the president declined and instead traveled to Augusta National, African Americans penned angry letters in response. "If anyone doubts the second class citizenship status of the American Negro, let him consider the following: President Eisenhower could not leave the golf course in Georgia to visit Montgomery, Alabama," wrote one man from Harlem. Another in Philadelphia was less surprised: "He didn't give up his golf for the other countries. Why would he for the Negro?"[137] Even back in Washington, D.C., Eisenhower continued to play segregated golf rather than meet with civil rights advocates. In November 1958, 10,000 people descended on the capital for a civil rights march led by Coretta Scott King, actor Harry Belafonte, A. Philip Randolph, and Jackie Robinson. Eisenhower declined to meet with any of the delegates and instead spent the day at Burning Tree, as Belafonte and a group of students picketed the White House. Three weeks later he again chose golf at Burning Tree over a meeting with Dorothy Height and representatives from the National Council of Negro Women.[138]

Notably, one black organization did have better luck getting a response from President Eisenhower: the United Golfers Association. During the

1959 UGA National in Washington, the White House allowed delegates to visit while the president was away. In a small ceremony one of Eisenhower's aides accepted gifts on his behalf, including an honorary UGA membership and a citation signed by Charlie Sifford wishing Ike "might someday enjoy the thrill of a hole-in-one." The president responded with a letter indicating he was "truly grateful" for the membership and wished for UGA members "many hours of the sport we love so much."[139]

By the time students from nearby Paine College picketed Eisenhower's final trip to Augusta National in December 1960, it was clear that increased civil rights agitation was prompting more direct, militant challenges to golf segregation outside the courtroom. This included the student sit-in movement, which at times targeted public golf facilities. "Like the sit-in demonstrations, desegregation of public owned golf courses is showing signs of spreading in Southern states," exclaimed the *Atlanta Daily World* in 1961.[140] After the Eisenhower protest, students in Georgia employed more pickets and sit-ins at Augusta National, as well as in local campaigns elsewhere in the state. Savannah's sit-in movement, which began in March 1960, successfully targeted the municipal golf course, prompting the city to integrate the facility in 1961 and appoint a black representative to the parks board.[141]

Tactics also escalated in adjacent Mississippi, especially its capital, Jackson. There black residents were angered after the city proposed a segregated, black municipal course in 1955 (many white golfers voiced opposition as well, upset that their city planned to use public dollars for black golf).[142] Jackson's African Americans had long found sporadic opportunities to play golf on private courses, including while working as caddies and support staff at Colonial Country Club and Millsaps College. Colonial was a well-known club that hosted an LPGA event in 1957 and 1958, while the course at Millsaps, opened in 1901, was the oldest in Mississippi. "Growing up around Millsaps College, I grew up on the golf course," recalled Fred Clark, who was born in 1943 and caddied at both Colonial and Millsaps during the 1950s. "And they wouldn't allow black students to play on the golf course. Although I played out there."[143] In 1968 Jackson's other private club, the Country Club of Jackson, was the first to formally invite an African American after Mississippi NAACP chairman Aaron Henry, a pharmacist, was welcomed to a meeting of the Mississippi Pharmaceutical Association. "So I went down to the meeting and went down to the country club—ain't never played golf in my life," Henry recalled. "I swung my stick—ain't no black guy here ever been out there either." Henry was not intimidated and ruffled feathers by bringing as his guest Myrlie Evers, the widow of slain activist Medgar Evers: "And out of about 400 persons present there were only two black people present and that was me and Myrlie."[144]

As for public golf, Jackson's NAACP Youth Council took on the issue with more assertiveness in the late 1950s, demanding access to the city's municipal courses. The persistent youth were turned away for a myriad of reasons (including not having golf shoes), but in 1963 two black students were finally allowed to play under police surveillance. The city faced white backlash after the news broke and immediately attempted to re-segregate the links.[145] Black golfers in the North showed their solidarity for such bold tactics. In July 1961 the Philadelphia NAACP hosted a golf tournament at Cobbs Creek to raise funds for the hundreds of Freedom Riders jailed in Mississippi that summer; the UGA's Fairview Golf Club helped organize the event.[146]

In the South golf also intersected directly with the local movements led by King and the SCLC. Just as the game received a mixed reception from top NAACP leaders, from Ella Baker and Roy Wilkins to Constance Baker Motley and Thurgood Marshall, so too did its symbolism differ among SCLC leaders. The SCLC was an organization led primarily by southern black ministers, who at times embraced golf but also signaled that recreation was less important in the crusade for divine justice and equal rights. The stereotype of golfers as church escapees was strong: during a Thanksgiving Day sermon at King's Ebenezer Church in Atlanta, Rev. Ralph Abernathy bemoaned those who golfed on Sunday "instead of worshipping and praising God."[147] Yet SCLC ministers understood that the movement was about equality in secular life, and in many southern towns municipal golf courses remained the largest swath of white-only space; that alone made them visible, symbolic battlegrounds even without golf. When the sit-in movement reached Sewanee, Tennessee, in 1962, the Ku Klux Klan burned a large cross on the golf course in response.[148] SCLC ministers likewise recognized the need to take the fight to the links. "We must find ways to carry our objectives and the nonviolent movement to the people not only in the churches," remarked Rev. Joseph Lowery in his keynote address at the SCLC's 1964 convention, "but in the pool halls . . . golf courses, barber shops, checker games, tennis set and domino set—the middle class, lower class and those with hardly any class."[149]

The organization's leadership featured one prolific golfer: Rev. Wyatt Tee Walker, King's chief of staff and SCLC executive director from 1960 to

1964. As a young, flamboyant pastor in 1950s Virginia, Wyatt had a fondness for yachting, golf, and Bermuda shorts, which set him apart from most southern preachers. Once he became executive director, he continued to play with supporters, including Jackie Robinson.[150] However, when a local municipal course in Virginia was leased to avoid integration, Walker chose to downplay his interest in the game for fear of being branded an elitist, a decision he came to regret. "I'm an avid golfer," he told an interviewer in 1967. "I always felt that we should have made an attack on that, but I didn't want to lead it because everybody knew I like golfing; that would be selfish. So I always worked on the schools or something other than the golf course. To this day, I understand it hasn't been worked out."[151]

The SCLC started dealing more directly with golf after turning its attention to Georgia in 1962. That April King made his first visit to Augusta, strategically scheduled to take place one week before Augusta National hosted the most important golf tournament in the world, the Masters. King spoke at Tabernacle Baptist Church, where he called for "a second emancipation proclamation" in the South. He was joined by Rev. C. S. Hamilton, leader of Augusta's NAACP chapter, who encouraged the congregation "to integrate and attend" the Masters "on Sunday."[152] (This was a significant statement coming from a minister.) The audience cheered, and Atlanta's WSBTV aired footage of Hamilton's call and King's speech, interspersed with clips of white patrons at Augusta National. Although local groups had already picketed the course for two years, King's visit helped legitimize Augusta National (and golf in general) as a worthy target of the civil rights movement. "King 'Masters' Augusta," headlined the SCLC's press release. "King was accorded an unprecedented response in this western Georgia resort city prior to the internationally famed Masters Golf Tournament."[153]

In 1962 the SCLC focused most of its attention on Albany, four hours south of Augusta. Don White was eleven years old when the movement came to his county. He lived on a cotton plantation twenty-five miles outside Albany when King arrived to conduct one of the more iconic civil rights campaigns in history. That year King, the SCLC, and the Student Nonviolent Coordinating Committee (SNCC) spent significant time in the city, facing off against local police chief Laurie Pritchett. Ultimately, the Albany Movement achieved little success (some even called it King's biggest failure), but for White it helped produce important opportunities.

The campaign targeted Albany's segregated municipal course, but rural black kids like White tended to have less knowledge of the game: "I'd seen a putter, I think, and a driver, too," he recalled. "But I had no idea what they were used for."[154] Yet Albany was headquarters for MacGregor Golf, one of the world's largest manufacturers of golf equipment. MacGregor was a major contributor to the local economy and growing rapidly; in 1961, just months before the movement started, it opened a massive, 175,000-square-foot production facility in Albany. The company also signed an endorsement deal with Jack Nicklaus, then a promising, twenty-one-year-old player who had just turned professional that November.[155] Meanwhile, White had no experience with golf but did have a special gift for craftsmanship, spending countless hours working on projects with his grandfather in the family's shed. After high school he got a job grinding iron heads at the plant. "When I started at MacGregor, I had never picked up a golf club in my life."[156]

By 1972 Nicklaus was the world's top player, and his clubs were handcrafted by Don White; by 1980 many considered White the best clubmaker in the industry. "Using only a lathe, White is able to transform nine chunks of steel into the best-looking, softest-feeling, most evenly balanced set of forged irons money can buy," proclaimed *Sports Illustrated*. For twenty-five years he made clubs for dozens of top professionals, from Arnold Palmer and Nancy Lopez to Greg Norman and Ben Crenshaw. "Don has a gift from God," said pro Chi Chi Rodriguez. "It's what the greats like Ruth, Picasso and Mozart all had—genius."[157] Nicklaus visited the Albany plant the week before he won his first Masters in 1963, presenting Georgia governor Carl Sanders with a set of his signature irons produced at the facility. "Thanks, Jack, for a real fine Georgia product," the governor quipped.[158] In 1978 Nicklaus met with White personally before he decided to purchase MacGregor Golf.

It was a remarkable journey for White, one that began with an opportunity at the Albany plant and was helped by the movement. However, it ultimately provided few economic benefits. His clubs were used to win twelve major championships and tens of millions of dollars, but until 1988 he made $10 an hour; in 1996 his salary was only $35,000. "Maybe it hasn't been fair," said one MacGregor representative. "But we've sort of kept Donny under wraps so nobody steals him."[159]

Sites like Augusta National, Bobby Jones Municipal, and MacGregor's Albany plant made Georgia an important meeting ground for race and golf, but the game did not go away when the movement turned its attention back to Alabama. In 1963 the SCLC launched a campaign in Bir-

Discrimination? I Don't See Any Discrimination!

(*Baltimore Afro-American*, March 2, 1963)

mingham that became the largest, most visible in its history. Wyatt Walker spent a week in California before heading to Alabama: "playing a little golf, relaxing, and getting myself strong for Birmingham."[160] Meanwhile, King had a good friend in the city, John Drew, in whose home he usually stayed whenever he visited. Drew was a black real estate executive and neighbors with Arthur Shores, Birmingham's NAACP attorney. Both Drew and Shores were crucial to the 1963 campaign and hosted King throughout that year, and they were also close friends who loved golf. Their infatuation prompted regular golfing vacations to Jamaica, excursions that were well known in Birmingham and drew adverse attention. (Ralph Abernathy wrote that the duo's golfing drove "whites wild with envy.")[161] Yet as in Atlanta, Greensboro, and elsewhere, golf also divided Birmingham's NAACP chapter, well before the SCLC arrived. Some moderate members emphasized the issue in the late 1940s and privately encouraged the city to build a black golf course. They included the branch's president, W. C. Patton, as well as its former president, E. W. Taggart. Others in the leader-

184) THE POSTWAR CIVIL RIGHTS MOVEMENT

ship were appalled: resigning in 1952, branch secretary Emory Jackson denounced the "elitist" move as "a shocking and disgraceful departure from NAACP principles."[162] In 1953 Patton, Taggart, and the moderates prevailed, and the city opened its black-only golf course, which it named for a white man: Birmingham mayor Cooper Green.[163]

The move came just in time to help Birmingham's white officials justify segregated golf in the wake of the Supreme Court's landmark rulings. In 1954 voters passed a referendum banning whites and blacks from participating together in "games of cards, dice, dominoes, checkers, softball, basketball, baseball, football, golf and track." While cities like Houston responded to *Brown* and *Holmes* by integrating municipal links, the black press noted that Birmingham was doing the opposite: emboldened by its black course, it was redoubling efforts to segregate public recreation. Enforcement of the ban was up to Birmingham's outspoken, pro-segregation police commissioner, Eugene "Bull" Connor. The city was later joined by Selma (1956) and Montgomery (1958), which also specifically listed golf in their ordinances barring integrated recreation.[164]

Meanwhile, as Birmingham drew a harder line on segregated golf, its more militant black activists began to exert more influence. Local minister Fred Shuttlesworth, an SCLC cofounder who later encouraged King to launch the 1963 campaign, laid the groundwork in 1959 by organizing a lawsuit of fifteen black residents who sued for access to Birmingham's recreation facilities. In 1961 they prevailed in *Shuttlesworth v. Gaylord*. Notably, it was a federal ruling that drew primarily from previous cases specifically focused on golf, including *Holmes v. Atlanta, Holley v. City of Portsmouth, Fayson v. Beard, Ward v. Miami, Moorhead v. City of Fort Lauderdale,* and *Simkins v. City of Greensboro*. Birmingham's white leaders responded within hours of the ruling: "So far as I am concerned, all white and colored parks, swimming pools and golf links will be closed," Bull Connor announced.[165]

Birmingham thus closed its four municipal courses before King and the SCLC launched their movement in April 1963, making it the largest city in the country to shutter its public golf facilities in response to the civil rights movement. *Shuttlesworth* and the local NAACP debate over the black golf course quickly faded into the background as the world watched Connor battle with hundreds of student protesters in the city. Yet many whites, including Mayor Arthur Hanes, vividly remembered the golf issue and yearned for the moderate NAACP that had supported segregating public courses ten years earlier. "You talk about economics for

Negroes, their standard of living in Birmingham is higher than that of 100 per cent of the black people throughout the world outside the United States," an exasperated Hanes pleaded as the city descended into chaos. "Have a golf course for 'em. Cost the taxpayers $22,000 a year to subsidize it, for the Negroes to play golf. Now what is so wrong to ask them to play golf on their own golf course, which is the same as the ones the white people have?" That night a bomb went off at Birmingham's Gaston Motel, where King had been staying hours before. Another damaged the house of his younger brother, A. D. King. Birmingham's 1952 municipal course for black golfers was now fueling white resentment of the movement, helping turn Birmingham into Bombingham.[166] And it remained a particular sore spot with city leaders: integrating courses was one of the movement's demands during the demonstrations but was not a part of the unofficial agreement that ended the unrest in May. Not until June 27 did the city finally reopen and integrate three of its four municipal courses, more than seventeen months after they were closed.[167]

Events in Montgomery and Birmingham overshadowed those in other black communities in Alabama that fought to integrate their public links. In *Shuttlesworth* the coalition had sued to integrate all public facilities, while that same year blacks in Mobile won a similar lawsuit that specifically targeted the municipal golf course. Unlike Birmingham, Mobile did not build a separate black links and instead argued in court as late as 1958 that it wanted to do so but lacked the money. In 1961 a federal judge ordered the integration of the course in *Sawyer v. City of Mobile*, handing victory to the players but denying them the $5,000 in damages they sought as compensation for years of driving to Pensacola and New Orleans to play.[168] The case made few headlines but was noteworthy for a different reason: it was the first time golf desegregation drew the attention of the Federal Bureau of Investigation (FBI). An FBI field report from Mobile noted the ruling and mentioned that integration was subsequently "confined to the Golf Course and no mention was made of its facilities, such as the Club House and rest room." The report also indicated that Mobile's African Americans immediately took advantage of the court-ordered access, even though the city was intent on continuing segregation of the nongolf amenities: "Negroes are using the Municipal Golf Course in segregated groups," it read. "It was reported that the golf pro . . . said that a separate apartment in the Club House will be set aside for the use of Negro players."[169]

The FBI's interest in everyday life on an Alabama municipal course signaled what was to come. By the late 1960s the civil rights movement—which for some was a unified, simple call for dignity in the South—grew more complex and contentious, as battles over race, identity, and integration raged nationwide. An increase in more militant, violent confrontations threatened to fracture the movement (and America) beyond repair. For most historians it is the point in the story where recreation and amusement truly take a back seat: surely nothing is more incompatible with golf than groups like the Black Panthers and the Revolutionary Action Movement. Yet by the 1970s a new generation of African Americans were as interested in the game as ever; many of them had no problem reconciling golf with the times and bringing Black Power to the links.

5

GUNS IN THEIR GOLF BAGS
Black Power on the Links

SUMMER 1960—COBBS CREEK, PHILADELPHIA, PENNSYLVANIA
Standing face-to-face in the street, Max Stanford and the white police officer were about to come to blows. Driving to Cobbs Creek for a round of golf, the head of Philadelphia's Fairview Golf Club had nearly collided with the patrolman's car after the officer cut him off at an intersection. Cursing at Stanford, the angry officer jumped out of his vehicle and approached. Stanford, too, emerged to defend himself.

He was arrested and brought to the local station. His son, Max Jr., ran two and a half miles from the family's home and arrived just as his father was being arraigned. It was not the first time Max Jr., a freshman in college, had seen his father militantly stand up to whites, and he was not afraid to, either.

"When the cops told me to leave, I said that I wasn't going anywhere, that this isn't Mississippi," he remembered fourteen years later. "Anticipating the attack of the pigs, my father and I paired off back to back, preparing to do battle; because he wasn't going to let anything happen to me and I wasn't going to let anything happen to him."

Soon Max and his father were redeemed. The magistrate rebuked the white officer, apologized to the elder Stanford, and—in the words of Max Jr.—asked "if he wanted to press charges against the pig that arrested him." Stanford declined and walked out of the precinct with his son.

Five years later Max Sr. would become head of the UGA. His wife, Winnie, was president of Green's Ladies Golf Club, Philadelphia's top organization for black female players. Together they were national leaders in the world of black golf who saw no disconnect between racial militancy and their love of the game. It was also a seminal moment in the life of young

Max Jr. Two years later he established the Revolutionary Action Movement, one of the most militant Black Power organizations in American history. For the Stanford family and Philadelphia's black golf scene, a new phase of militancy went hand in hand with the game of privilege.[1]

On September 6, 1972, five men arrived at St. Croix's Fountain Valley Golf Club armed with an array of pistols, shotguns, and machine guns. Rounding up white golfers and black workers, they robbed the pro shop, hurled racial insults at the whites, and started shooting, murdering eight on the spot and wounding four others. It was a massacre that shocked the U.S. territory and significantly influenced the island for years to come. "This is absolutely the worst thing ever to happen in the Virgin Islands," St. Croix's lieutenant governor said as he organized one of the largest manhunts in Caribbean history.[2] Twenty-five years later, scholar G. Elmer Griffin, a native islander, concurred: "We have never stopped recounting these events here in St. Croix, despite considerable pressure to forget. The massacre exists like a grim and poignant fable, a lament and a warning about biting the tourist hand that feeds you."[3]

What at first seemed a horrific robbery turned out to be much more: a bloodbath over race, tourism, and black militancy played out on what famed architect Robert Trent Jones Sr. described as "the loveliest golf course I ever designed."[4] Dressed in army fatigues, the perpetrators were Afro-Caribbean, and six of the dead were white tourists. Considered a top golf facility in the region, Fountain Valley was a brand-new course owned by Laurance Rockefeller, grandson of golf devotee John D. Rockefeller. Laurance commissioned Jones to carve the 330-acre course out of 4,000 lush acres (nearly 8 percent of St. Croix's total area) he purchased in 1966. Under the management of his company, RockResorts, the course was adjacent to the island's lush rainforest. For some islanders it symbolized misguided golf development catering to the luxurious whims of white tourists. St. Croix's government was predominately black, and most of its land remained black owned as well. Yet Fountain Valley embodied a growing disparity in wealth that ran along racial lines: most of the island's businesses were owned by a small group of whites who controlled much of its capital. "Fountain Valley Golf Course was the symbol of racial and economic inequality on St. Croix," Griffin wrote. "The territorialization, elitism, and culture of service that characterize resort golf made it an ample target for resentment killing."[5]

The FBI certainly feared as much. Most Americans were transfixed by terrorism elsewhere in the world (the Fountain Valley killings occurred one day after the Munich massacre, in which terrorists abducted and killed eleven Israeli athletes at the 1972 Summer Olympic Games), but the incident on St. Croix elicited an intense response from the U.S. government. Attorney General Richard Kleindienst ordered the FBI and the U.S. Marshals Service to take over the case, and the Pentagon dispatched 150 soldiers to help coordinate the manhunt and enforce an islandwide curfew. "We became an occupied territory," Griffin recalled.[6] Local whites petitioned for the outside help, claiming the island's black leaders were incompetent and corrupt. As rumors spread that the killings were meant to spark a race war, two dozen FBI agents set up a command post at the course and began to broaden their investigation amid reports of "planned arson against [the] property of white residents."[7]

Within a week all five men were captured, and ten months later they stood trial. The suspects also sent detailed statements to the Black Panther Party in Oakland, California, in which they pronounced themselves political prisoners, proclaimed their innocence, and insisted authorities had tortured them in captivity. Soon the case of the "Virgin Island 5" was a cause célèbre for radical, black nationalist organizations. The Panthers set up a defense fund and denounced "plans to use these five young men as scapegoats to appease White anger at the slayings."[8] Two prominent civil rights attorneys traveled to St. Croix to represent the men. One, William Kunstler, had defended the Chicago Seven, Malcolm X, and Martin Luther King Jr. Kunstler offered to defend the five pro bono and eventually represented one at trial. The other attorney, Chauncey Eskridge, had just defended Muhammad Ali before the Supreme Court in *Clay v. U.S.* (1971) and was the SCLC's chief legal counsel in the late 1960s.[9]

Unlike the Panthers, other radical groups did not dispute the men's guilt and instead celebrated the violence. Trinidad's black nationalist movement, the National Joint Action Committee, called them "Black Freedom Fighters" who were "struggling to secure the Liberation of their people from Euro-american control, by any means necessary." The committee also recognized the broader, symbolic link between golf and racism as well as the more specific context surrounding the incident: "It was no accident that the Fountain Valley Golf Course became a target for our brothers fighting for their freedom in St. Croix. This Golf Course is only a small part of a large complex that is owned by the infamous Rockefeller family.... Black people are conscious that TOURISM IS WHORISM and are prepared to prevent it.... So the blow that was dealt at the Fountain Valley Golf Course was a blow for all Black people. It was an act to free us."[10]

In the end, most sympathizers stateside did not condone the violence and insisted the Virgin Island 5 were innocent. Backed by their high-profile lawyers, the men testified that FBI agents had detained them on a Fountain Valley putting green and subjected them to a range of torture, including electrical shocks, chokings, beatings, and pistol whippings. One defendant, Meral Smith, testified that a noose was placed around his neck and he was hanged from a tree on the course, where FBI agents jerked him from the ground dozens of times to elicit a confession. These claims further enraged the Panthers, who denounced the "extreme torture" used against the men: "A recent... hearing in the case of five Black Virgin Islanders disclosed new and condemning evidence of the corruption and brutality of the U.S. colonial police," announced the *Black Panther* newspaper.[11] By November 1972, agents with the U.S. Naval Criminal Investigative Service were warned that "natives" in the Virgin Islands planned to "terrorize" the territory in response to the incident. And rumors swirled that stateside groups like the Panthers would join in, traveling to the islands to "shoot Whites and burn their properties and businesses."[12]

The federal government dispatched a team of U.S. marshals to provide security for the tense proceedings (led by the same man who directed security for the Chicago Seven trial in 1969). While Kunstler continued to portray the men as "Robin Hood revolutionaries," the trial descended into what one local paper called "a civil rights circus," as the group's ringleader, Vietnam veteran Ishmael LaBeet, declared his guilt in a series of courtroom outbursts.[13] After lengthy deliberation the jury convicted all five in August 1973, and they were sentenced to life in prison. In 1984 LaBeet was on American Airlines flight 626 en route to a federal prison in Pennsylvania when he emerged from the lavatory with a gun, overpowered four armed guards, and ordered the pilots to fly the plane and its 198 passengers to Cuba, where he received asylum.[14] Two years later Rock-Resorts reopened Fountain Valley and renamed it the Carambola Beach Resort and Golf Club, making it, as Griffin notes, "the only course in the history of golf to begin as a resort, become a massacre scene, then become headquarters for an FBI manhunt, only to return unchanged to the business of golf."[15] Yet it was never the same place; when President Bill Clinton visited St. Croix for golf in the 1990s, he avoided the island's top course because of its violent past.

The Fountain Valley massacre was the most striking incident of racial violence in the history of golf. Beginning in the late 1960s, however, black militancy intersected with the game on numerous occasions. As organizations like the SCLC, SNCC, and CORE staged protests to integrate golf courses, more radical groups, such as the Black Panthers, tended to cast the game aside as permanently racist. The Panthers' support for the Virgin Island 5 had nothing to do with making golf more inclusive; to the Panthers, golf was forever, hopelessly white. When Bobby Seale ran for mayor of Oakland in 1973, he promised to increase municipal golf fees by 50 percent to help pay for expanded social programs because it seemed an easy way to redistribute capital along racial lines.[16] Some black nationalist groups went much further in their critiques, particularly those that emphasized Marxism and rebuked the black middle class. Leaders of the Congress of African People denounced the NAACP for supporting the "few Negro elite" and "the integration of country clubs, tennis clubs, golf clubs, etc."[17] Hekima Ana, vice president of the nationalist group Republic of New Africa, recalled growing up in a poor neighborhood of Charlotte and reselling golf balls he stole from whites on the nearby course, a key childhood experience that shaped his understanding of wealth discrepancy and poverty in the city. The popularity of golf in Charlotte's black community and the integration of its courses meant little to the young radical: "We were always looking down, hoping to find a penny or maybe a nickel."[18] In New Jersey supporters of activist Amiri Baraka and the Black Arts Movement also had little patience for the game, especially when they discovered that the white leader of the state's Democratic Party, Salvatore Bontempo, operated a white-only country club near Newark. "Despite the countless number of Black people who worked very hard in supporting this so-called liberal white politician, Salvatore is really an arch enemy of Black people," announced Baraka's newspaper *Black New Ark*, railing against segregation at Braidburn Country Club. "It is a pathetic situation! A demented cracker like Salvatore can manage to flock to the black community during election time as a liberal white boy; then at night, he's back in the suburbs having 'Klan' cocktails inside a luxurious wall-to-wall carpet country club."[19]

There was thus little room for black golf in organizations like the Republic of New Africa, the Congress of African People, or the Black Panthers, yet still a surprising number of militants had no problem embracing the game. Robert F. Williams was a civil rights leader in Monroe, North Carolina, who sought exile in Cuba and was expelled by the NAACP after he embraced black nationalism and armed resistance; his 1962 book *Negroes with Guns* was a major influence on the Panthers. But Williams also recognized the popularity of golf among African Americans in Monroe, Charlotte, and Gastonia, and issued militant calls for greater black access to the links. Three times during the summer of 1960 he also led groups of black youth to the public swimming pool at the Monroe Country Club, a campaign he had first launched in 1957 (they were turned away by crowds of whites hurling racial slurs and threatening violence). Two months before he fled the country in August 1961, his radical newsletter denounced the continued discrimination blacks faced at Monroe's supposedly integrated public golf course: "Although local whites (out of the goodness of their hearts) have opened the Jim Crow walls at the city-owned golf course a 'little' guests of Afro-Americans are continuously being insulted, cursed and turned away by the operator. This proves that such give-ins on their terms cannot and should not be acceptable by the Afro-American masses.... A hand-out is always on the terms of the giver while a demand must be met according to terms agreeable to all."[20]

The greatest link between black nationalism and golf was forged in Philadelphia, where radicals met at the city's black Fairview Golf Club and where UGA president Max Stanford's son, Max Stanford Jr., founded the Revolutionary Action Movement (RAM) in 1962. The elder Stanford's rise to become head of the UGA epitomized how working-class African Americans found access to the links. Born in 1918 in rural Maryland, he joined the CCC in the 1930s, was a photographer with the Signal Corp during World War II, and afterward worked as an exterminator in Philadelphia. Although Max Jr. became a leading figure in the Black Power movement, Max Sr. was a fierce militant in his own right. "Dad often told me that he did not like the honky and had fought the honky for many years," the younger Stanford wrote of his father in 1969. "He was not an integrationist.... He took great pride in blackness though he did not express it in the jargon of today's militants who are revolutionaries. He could have been considered a bourgeois black nationalist."[21] In the 1950s the elder Stanford became a leading figure in the world of black golf, serving as head of the Fairview club (founded in 1927, it was one the UGA's original affiliates) and later as UGA president from 1965 until his death in 1969. He also encouraged his wife to take up the game, and during the 1960s

Black women playing at Cobbs Creek Golf Club in Philadelphia, Pennsylvania, ca. 1960s. Included are seven-time UGA women's champion Ethel Funches, two-time champion Vernice Turner, and runner-up Alma Arvin (Courtesy USGA Museum).

Winifred "Winnie" Stanford served as president of the city's largest organization for black female golfers, Green's Ladies Golf Club. Under their leadership Philadelphia's black golf scene continued to thrive, and Fairview established a meeting space at 5725 Vine Street. Less than a mile from Cobbs Creek, it was a de facto private clubhouse for the municipal course's black golfers—from everyday, working-class players like Max Sr. to Philly golf stars like Howard Wheeler and Charlie Sifford. Led by Max Sr., Fairview hosted the 1956 UGA National at Cobbs Creek (which Sifford and Thelma Cowans won). In 1968, the legendary Wheeler collapsed and died during a meeting at the clubhouse.[22] Shortly before his own death in 1969, Max Sr. was also one of the founders of Freeway Golf Course, located fifteen miles outside Philadelphia in Sicklerville, New Jersey. That year it became the first black-owned-and-operated course to host the UGA National.[23]

The Fairview clubhouse at 5725 Vine was thus a key meeting space for black golfers in America, and by the late 1960s it was also under sustained FBI surveillance. Like many African Americans in West Philadelphia, the Stanford family engaged in increasingly heated confrontations with whites, especially law enforcement officers. In 1957 the community accused police of robbing the body of a dead black golfer on Cobbs Creek after he was killed by a lightning strike. Three years later Max Sr. and his son had their memorable encounter with police following a traffic incident.[24] Moreover, followers of the Nation of Islam (NOI) had also started meeting at the clubhouse. Malcolm X lived briefly in Philadelphia and regularly visited its NOI contingent thereafter. In 1957 an FBI informant reported him mocking Eisenhower ("the great white father") for his golf vacations in Georgia during a speech at the Philadelphia temple.[25] By 1964 a dissident group—led by Wallace Muhammad, son of NOI founder Elijah Muhammad—was questioning the elder Muhammad's leadership and began meeting on their own at 5725 Vine. The clubhouse established by UGA president Max Stanford Sr. for black golfers at Cobbs Creek now rivaled the local NOI temple as a gathering place for black radicals in Philadelphia, which drew FBI surveillance. Agents noted that twenty-five prominent "dissident NOI members" attended the first meeting; most were followers of Wallace Muhammad or Malcolm X who had been "expelled from the NOI."[26] As well as attracting FBI attention, the clubhouse also developed a seedy reputation among some moderate African Americans. In a letter to the *Philadelphia Tribune* one black couple encouraged the community to "fight the Fairview Golf Club, which would be destruction to our youth and neighborhood.... We do not need the Fairview Golf Club with its bar [and] dancehall."[27]

As the NOI met at Fairview's clubhouse, Max Stanford Jr. was busy taking his father's militancy to new extremes. He helped establish RAM in 1962 and quickly convinced Malcolm X to join the group at a meeting in Harlem (RAM would be the only secular political organization Malcolm ever joined before his 1964 pilgrimage to Mecca). Stanford also clashed with police again during a 1963 protest that turned violent, and by 1967 Philadelphia's police commissioner and future mayor, Frank Rizzo, considered him the city's most dangerous militant. FBI director J. Edgar Hoover agreed, publicly calling RAM "a highly secret all-Negro, Marxist-Leninist, Chinese Communist–oriented organization which advocates guerrilla warfare to obtain its goals."[28] In 1966 Stanford and a group of RAM members were arrested for planning to assassinate NAACP executive director Roy Wilkins and Whitney Young, head of the Urban League. By the time Stanford was exonerated, he was under permanent FBI surveillance, including investigations into his family's background and his father's involvement in the black golf scene. The fact that both men shared the same name, Maxwell Stanford, raised further red flags. Agents were wary when they discovered the elder Stanford was helping organize international golf tours for African Americans. The outings began in 1967, and Stanford helped lead one of the first that summer: a two-week golf trip to Spain. Agents followed the lead-up to the trip, concerned over either of the Stanford men leaving the country, especially the potential for Max Jr. to travel surreptitiously on his father's passport.[29] In 1964 the younger Stanford had already visited Cuba, where he met with the radical leader who most inspired him: Robert F. Williams. Williams served as a mentor and sent letters from Cuba. In turn, RAM called Williams its "president-in-exile," and Stanford helped distribute Williams's newsletter (the *Crusader*) around the country.[30] On the subject of golf, however, the two appeared to feel differently. A generation of militants, from more mild agitators like Max Stanford Sr. to radicals like Williams, had no problem embracing golf or fighting for black access to the game. But RAM's publications eventually echoed younger groups like the Black Panthers, the Congress of African People, and the Republic of New Africa, criticizing black golfers as elitist and out of touch with the movement. RAM followers traveled to Jamaica and published a scathing description of "a vacationing Afro-american dentist from Washington, D.C." When asked, the man indicated he did notice "some poverty on his way to the golf course" but claimed "it couldn't be too bad" because of the island's warm climate. "Then he gathered up his golf clubs and moved on," concluded the bitter report.[31]

The Stanford men thus represented opposites when it came to golf and black militancy. Golf had uniquely merged with black radicalism in Philadelphia, especially in the Stanford family, which Max Jr. acknowledged when he praised his working-class father for embracing Black Power while leading the nation's largest organization of black golfers. Yet there were limits to the extent to which young revolutionaries were willing to overlook the game's historical connection to whiteness, imperialism, and capitalism.

However, some black nationalists embraced golf for a completely different reason: because they championed black capitalism, not Marxism. This included many organizations that placed themselves in the tradition of radical leader Marcus Garvey. For these, the key to black militancy was the establishment of a separate, self-sufficient capitalist economy that served African Americans. Football star Jim Brown founded one of the more popular "black capitalist" groups in 1969: the Black Economic Union. While embracing Black Power, and even the culture of black nationalism, the union nevertheless rejected militancy and instead called for more black-owned businesses in America's urban areas and a flourishing of black capitalism. A prolific golfer, Brown helped organize a series of Black Economic Union golf tournaments to raise funds for his organization.[32] One supporter was Maggie Hathaway, the crusader for black golf in Los Angeles who also linked black capitalism, golf, and Black Power. In 1969 entertainer James Brown lent his likeness to "Black and Brown trade stamps," intended for black businesses to distribute to their customers as a loyalty program. Hathaway urged golfers to use them at Los Angeles courses and golf shops, an economic protest at the lack of black ownership in the city's golf industry. She joined others in noting that few manufacturers had ever supplied golf equipment to the black community, and when they did, their efforts had not met with success. After his deal with Burke Golf in the early 1950s, Charlie Sifford inked a more substantial deal with Kroydon Golf for his own signature line of golf clubs. Advertised in black newspapers around the country, the clubs were introduced in 1960 but flopped. In a series of controversial remarks, Sifford publicly blamed black people for not buying his clubs. Yet just seven years later, times had changed dramatically, and to Hathaway, Sifford's Kroydon deal failed simply because it was too far ahead of its time. She and other golfers, such as Jim Brown, renewed calls for black players to use their golfing dollars in support of black capitalism. "Our purchasing power has contributed a large percentage of the equipment makers gross," UGA president Porter Pernell told *Black Sports* in 1973, noting that black golfers on average outspent whites by 50 percent on golf equipment. "The market is quite large not to have Blacks in from the business end."[33]

While some radical organizations reconciled their militancy with golf, more significant was how the generalized, popular sentiment of Black Power and its cultural ethos infiltrated the links. This included older organizations like the SCLC, the NAACP, and CORE calling for bolder changes to the game, as well as a new generation of cultural figures who managed to embody Black Power as they played. At Western Avenue Golf Course, the center of L.A.'s black golf scene, players were delighted to spot Muhammad Ali jogging the course in 1969: the champ told Maggie Hathaway he loved to run on golf courses more than anywhere else.[34] A maestro of Black Power, soul singer Marvin Gaye caddied as a youth in Washington, D.C., and took up the game himself in 1967 to alleviate nerves. Gaye frequented Griffith Park in Los Angeles and Detroit's Rouge Park Golf Course, "but golf has made me a nervous wreck," he quipped in 1971. His friend football star Mel Farr even claimed that Gaye came up with the title of his seminal anthem "What's Going On?" while on a golf outing in Detroit.[35]

The sentiment of Black Power meant moving beyond earlier calls to integrate municipal courses and demanding access to golf's most privileged spaces: private country clubs. Those confrontations allowed the game to remain on the radar when groups like the SCLC, CORE, and SNCC turned their attention to northern cities. In 1963 CORE staged what it called a "picnic-in" at New Jersey's East Orange Golf Club. Thirty protesters refused to leave the first green because the private, white-only club leased the land from the city for $1 per year.[36] By 1960 the Ohio Civil Rights Commission reported that many public courses in the state were attempting to privatize; Cleveland's Manakiki Golf Course and Sleepy Hollow Golf Course drew the most attention after they were leased to private clubs that barred black members. Only after an NAACP lawsuit were both courses fully opened to the public, a battle that made golf particularly contentious as activism escalated in Cleveland. In 1964 a white policeman complained of being harassed "in derogatory fashion" by his fellow officers when they discovered he regularly played golf with blacks at the public course.[37] Meanwhile, Detroit's black golfers, including Joe Louis, were celebrated fixtures at public courses like Rackham but roundly rejected at local private links, including Glen Oaks Country Club and Hillcrest Country Club. Louis's manager, Julian Black, even sued Hillcrest for discrimination after the club barred him and his wife.[38]

Some African Americans sought to bypass desegregating these elite courses by establishing new, integrated country clubs. Jackie Robinson led a high-profile, failed attempt to build one such course in New York. Although he was a megastar celebrated for breaking down racial barriers in sports, Robinson struggled to join country clubs after retiring and spent the 1960s vying for tee times on an overcrowded municipal course near his home in Stamford, Connecticut, sometimes waking up at 4:30 A.M. to play. He was embarrassed by a series of encounters at nearby High Ridge Country Club, which was three-quarters Jewish and supposedly the area's first nondenominational, nonracial club. One member rebuked Robinson's sponsor for inviting the baseball star too often, noting that "he's colored, and it looks kind of strange for him to come here every week."[39] Robinson and Joe Louis were both welcomed by most club members, including sportscaster Howard Cosell and bandleader Benny Goodman, but a group of female members threatened to leave if Robinson was offered membership. "It became a divisive issue," recalled one former member. "And when Jackie got wind of the opposition, he backed off and stopped playing at High Ridge."[40] At least one member, music producer John Hammond, resigned in protest over Robinson's shunning.

Frustrated by the existing private clubs, Robinson helped form an interracial group (including actor George C. Scott) that attempted to build their own in 1966. Calling themselves the Pheasant Valley Country Club, the group twice sought to purchase properties—first the Putnam Country Club in Mahopac, followed by a 216-acre parcel in Lewisboro—but local residents blocked both attempts. Each time Robinson and his peers petitioned the NAACP for help and filed complaints with the State Commission on Human Rights, to no avail. In the end, the hero who integrated Major League Baseball lost his fight to build a truly race-blind country club. As the project crumbled and black investors pulled out, Robinson resented how African Americans had boldly stood by him when he joined the Major Leagues but were too afraid to upset the staid world of private golf: "They told me in effect, 'we're not ready for this,'" he wrote in a bitter editorial.[41] Although the story ultimately passed from the headlines, at the time it was a serious blow to his public standing as a champion of racial integration. In 1968 he criticized another black baseballer, San Francisco Giants star Willie Mays, for being a "do-nothing negro" and not fighting hard enough for civil rights. Mays responded by throwing the golf failure back in Robinson's face: "I think that I have the respect of the people of San Francisco," he said in a press conference. "I play all the golf courses. I'm the first Negro to be a member of the Concordia Club. I also belong to the Press Club. Now you know that wasn't possible ten years ago. And I haven't done these things and gotten these things by 'doing nothing.'"[42] It was a high-profile spat between two of the most popular black athletes in the world, one that took place during the tumultuous spring of 1968 (King was assassinated one month later). Yet Mays and Robinson bickered over their efforts to advance integration by comparing how well each had overcome racial barriers in golf, not the national pastime.

By the late 1960s African Americans were pushing to join country clubs more than ever, and many clubs responded by continuing to hide their public components in order to skirt legal and popular challenges to all-white membership. The strategy, so key to massive resistance on southern golf courses, now spread throughout the country. One of the most consistent campaigns against such privatization was launched by the NAACP in Los Angeles and led by Maggie Hathaway. By 1969 L.A.'s golfers were rooting out several "public-private" courses that continued to discriminate even though they benefited from municipal leases, including Downey's Rio Hondo Golf Club and Lawndale's Alondra Golf Course. "Alondra Park is a disgrace to intelligent black golfing tax-payers," wrote Hathaway. "I am convinced that once you get a lease on a golf course, you are the owner, while the taxpayers are helpless."[43] Hathaway also claimed that a large police presence at Riviera Country Club for the PGA's L.A. Open intimidated black patrons, and she bemoaned the lack of minority workers at public courses in Orange County. The movement also targeted more elite, fully private facilities in southern California—like Riverside's Soboba Springs Country Club, which kicked a black player off the course in 1969 even though he was a sponsored guest of white members.[44]

While blurred lines between public and private courses existed nationwide, southern cities continued to take privatization to the extreme. One of the most successful attempts occurred in Knoxville, Tennessee, where for over seven years the city council avoided the mayor's overtures to integrate the municipal Whittle Springs Golf Course by leasing it to a private club.[45] Usually that was the form privatization took: public courses were loaned to a private group formed directly in response to the threat of integration. Greensboro, North Carolina, tried the same tactic with Gillespie Park after the protest led by the Greensboro Six, as did Norfolk, Virginia, after black citizens demanded access to Memorial Park. When Thomas Brewer and his friends tried to integrate the municipal course in Columbus, Georgia, the city argued it was private because day-to-day operations had been handed over to the local Lions Club.[46] Of course, other towns went even further, including voter-approved elimination of all public recreation to avoid integration. Whites in Huntsville, Alabama, passed an amendment allowing their city "to give away" its public golf courses, parks, playgrounds, and swimming pools in order "to keep whites and Negroes from using them together."[47] Rather than lease its course to a private group of whites, Fort Lauderdale, Florida, actually sold it to them outright for half of market value; the move was upheld by the Florida Supreme Court. After court-ordered integration, Jacksonville tried to keep African Americans off its links by hiking municipal golf fees from $18 to $150.[48]

Most of these blatant attempts to privatize municipal golf were uncovered by the 1970s, but sometimes a city course was hidden from the public for an entire generation. Such was the case with Bide-A-Wee Golf Course in Portsmouth, Virginia. James Holley led the charge to integrate Portsmouth's municipal courses, culminating in his 1957 victory in *Holley v. City of Portsmouth*, and he used that success to integrate the city council in 1968 and become Portsmouth's mayor in 1984. Yet during his first year as a councilman Holley learned of a shocking rumor: Bide-A-Wee, the city's elite, private country club, actually stood on municipal land. Built near a predominately black neighborhood by PGA Champion Chandler Harper in 1956, the facility was nationally respected: it hosted several Virginia State Opens and World's Senior Championships. Charlie Sifford was the only African American to play the course when he competed in the 1975 Senior Championship. By then Holley had helped convince the federal government to investigate whether Bide-A-Wee was actually a public course operating in violation of the Civil Rights Act (he recalled getting "no help at all from any of the civil rights groups like the NAACP").[49] A subsequent FBI investigation revealed what Holley and black citizens suspected: the private club was operating what should have been a city municipal course, but the battle was far from over. In 1976 the Justice Department sued the course, and the case dragged on for over a decade. Not until 1988 was the general public given access to Bide-A-Wee, and further litigation was necessary to open club membership to the public as well, a controversy that lasted into the 1990s. In the end, a public municipal course was able to hide itself as a private country club for over thirty years. It was a story that shocked locals and complicated race relations in Portsmouth for decades. "I am embarrassed by the events that have transpired here," wrote one white resident in 1988. "But shame is the only way to describe my emotions dealing with Bide-A-Wee golf course."[50]

Thus the new era of militancy on the links meant aggressively following the money and using federal civil rights legislation to identify all-white courses with connections to public finances. In 1965 King and the SCLC began polling black farmers to investigate whether federal agricultural programs were discriminating in the South. The questionnaire briefly mentioned a little-known fact: subsidized loans from the Farmers Home Administration were offered not only for purchasing or operating farms but also "to individuals for building recreational facilities such as golf courses." The SCLC thus asked respondents to report any segregated courses that received Home Administration support.[51] Surprising results poured in: hundreds of private, white golf clubs had received such loans throughout the country. By August 1969 the issue reached the U.S. Congress, where a group of black congressmen led by Michigan representatives John Conyers and Charles Diggs blocked a $265,000 loan to the segregated Natchez-Trace Golf Club in Tupelo, Mississippi, and called for a federal investigation. Natchez-Trace responded by advertising for black members in area newspapers and then announcing it had welcomed three: a local mechanic, a TV repairman, and a milkman. Conyers and Diggs hinted that the men had been paid by the club.[52] Natchez-Trace won the battle and got its money, but the Agriculture Department lost the war. In October Walter Cronkite broke the story nationally on the CBS *Evening News*, telling viewers about the Farmers Home Administration's "golf and butler policy" and noting that all-white courses had received the loans nationwide, including in New York, Delaware, Iowa, and California.[53] The congressional investigation revealed a total of 664 "white and exclusive" golf clubs assisted by the program: "Now, we shall call on the Farmers Home Administration to open these facilities to the public," announced black congressman William L. Clay (D-Mo.).[54] While that never happened, the investigation did help end discrimination in federal mortgage programs and came at a key moment, inflaming more militant calls for economic justice as the civil rights movement embraced the Poor People's Campaign. On the CBS *Evening News*, Representative Conyers noted the irony of government subsidies going to white country clubs while congressmen threatened to curb federal food stamps. Amidst a Nixon-era backlash to welfare, some put it far more bluntly. "Whose hand is out?" asked the *Chicago Defender*. "These arrogant rich racists would chisel a black mother with a house full of children out of her last welfare dollar. They want that tax dollar to help plant golf course grass."[55]

Along with pressuring country clubs to include black members or forgo public assistance, tearing down the remaining racial barriers in golf also meant demanding equality in all of the game's social dimensions. Calls for integrating the "nineteenth hole"—golf course clubhouses, bars, restaurants, locker rooms, and spas—thus played a major role in escalating the battle and forced some private clubs to solicit black members for the first time. In 1957 Michigan's attorney general announced that no country club in the state was private if its clubhouse operated with a liquor license, meaning those that served alcohol were subject to antidiscrimination laws.[56] In the South there were many white golfers who were open to mixing the races on the course but feared it would lead to unacceptable social interaction between whites and blacks off it, and they drew the line at integrating dining and bar facilities at public links. In Miami, the NAACP and the black community won the desegregation of municipal courses in 1958 but still had to fight vigorously to integrate the clubhouse at Miami Springs Golf Course, which the city tried to keep private. Four years later even white patrons were complaining after they were barred from the building while the course hosted a black tournament.[57] Similarly, the NAACP in Corpus Christi, Texas, demanded the integration of the clubhouse at Oso Beach Municipal Golf Course after the city opened the links to the black community but kept the building segregated.[58] Yet perhaps the most dramatic instance of "nineteenth-hole" segregation came in Jackson, Mississippi, where NAACP Youth Council members were allowed to play the municipal course under police surveillance in 1963; but when the teens entered the clubhouse, they found that city officials had completely emptied it, even removing the furniture.[59]

By the late 1960s such auxiliary facilities and activities were the primary battleground over integrating golf, providing new ways to challenge claims of privacy. Advocates of federal civil rights legislation rightly feared the limitations of the landmark 1964 Civil Rights Act. A Tennessee commission charged with interpreting the law insisted it only applied to discrimination in "passive" forms of recreation—such as movie theaters or sports stadiums—not "active" forms like golf or bowling. Yet eventually the courts gave the Civil Rights Act quite expansive powers in the world of golf beyond what many imagined. One of the most important victories came in Durham, North Carolina, after a federal judge insisted the private Hillandale Golf Course was subject to the act and ordered it to integrate in 1970 because the course had a pro shop that sold items to the public. In Savannah, Georgia, a federal court also ruled in 1969 that the Civil Rights Act forbade private groups from renting municipal courses to conduct white-only tournaments.[60] Such decisions meant that by the 1970s all-white, private clubs were feeling the heat more than ever, and many dove even further into isolation to avoid the law, eliminating all nonmember access to the course or closing down pro shops and restaurants that served the public.

The new civil rights legislation not only targeted semiprivate facilities but helped pressure public figures to avoid segregated, fully private clubs as well. No one was immune to the potential backlash of joining an all-white club. President Eisenhower and Vice President Nixon had drawn criticism from progressives in the 1950s over golfing at Augusta National and Burning Tree, and soon even conservatives were on the attack when it suited their political interests. In 1962 William F. Buckley Jr.'s *National Review* urged the NAACP and CORE to "sink their teeth into a juicy civil rights campaign" in Palm Beach, Florida. There President John F. Kennedy frequented the all-white Palm Beach Country Club while residing at his winter estate, and conservatives were not alone in criticizing the president for his membership in the club. In the critical days leading up to the 1963 March on Washington, the insinuation that Kennedy, like Eisenhower, supported a segregated golf club in the South contributed to his administration's uneasy relationship with the civil rights movement. Kennedy also drew similar criticism when he golfed back home in Massachusetts. "I heard the Kennedys wouldn't allow any colored at their country club," wrote one disgruntled supporter to Martin Luther King Jr., presumably referring to the all-white Hyannisport Club, the president's home course located near his family's compound on Cape Cod.[61]

By the late 1960s a number of high-profile figures began to drop their associations with such clubs for the first time. At Kenwood Golf and Country Club some white members, led by the president of George Washington University, resigned over the club's banning of black guests. The issue erupted after the first mayor of Washington, D.C., Walter Washington, was not even allowed to visit. Meanwhile, Nixon continued to face criticism for frequenting all-white clubs as president but never enough to force a change in his golfing habits. In 1974, on the day after Nixon infamously resigned and boarded a helicopter on the South Lawn of the White House, new president Gerald Ford played eighteen holes at Burning Tree.[62]

Nevertheless, associations with all-white golf were starting to take their political toll. In 1970 the Senate rejected Nixon's nomination of G. Harrold Carswell to the Supreme Court because of Carswell's poor civil rights record, especially after it was learned the judge had helped avoid integrating golf in Tallahassee, Florida. "In 1956, while serving as a United States Attorney, Judge Carswell participated in converting a public golf course into a private, all-white country club," wrote Minnesota senator Walter Mondale, explaining his rationale for rejecting the nomination.[63] The NAACP and black leaders like Bayard Rustin agreed that the golf issue was enough to justify keeping Carswell off the court.

While white country clubs were under fierce attack in the late 1960s, another hallmark of the era's renewed black militancy was an increasingly global awareness that placed such domestic civil rights struggles in the context of a truly international movement. Many popular American sports were important battlegrounds over race but largely isolated from the rest of the world, while the period's largest controversies over race and sports were international, exemplified by the attempts to ban apartheid South Africa and Rhodesia from the Olympic Games. America's insular pastimes, especially baseball and football, fell off the radar in these debates, yet golf remained a controversial European import to Africa. The game's international dimension thus uniquely centered it in the global movement against racism during the period. African Americans such as W. E. B. Du Bois had long recognized golf's ties to global imperialism, particularly the British Empire, and some linked their attempts to access the game to a broader, global struggle for black golfers everywhere. As early as the 1930s, international stories of black or nonwhite golfers were virtually unnoticed in white America but appealed to African American sports fans. Black readers celebrated the story of Dominga Capati, a Filipina laundress who toiled on a sugar plantation in the 1930s while becoming one of Asia's top golfers. Hassan Hassanein, a former caddie from Cairo who was Egypt's greatest professional player, also drew particular interest from African Americans, enough that George May invited him three times to compete alongside UGA professionals at the Tam O'Shanter Open. Hassanein played throughout Europe and competed in the 1953 British Open.[64]

In addition, by the 1950s black fans were already commiserating with the plight of nonwhite golfers in South Africa. One of the first notable players was another former caddie, Rodney Ditsebe. "Ditsebe is to the residents of Kimberley, South Africa, what Ted Rhodes is to the Americans," announced the *Chicago Defender* in 1953.[65] Six years later another black South African golfer, Edward Sedibe, drew attention when he arrived unannounced at Scotland's Muirfield Links, borrowed a set of clubs, and became the first black man to compete in the British Open.[66] By the 1960s, South Africa's most accomplished nonwhite golfer was an ethnic Indian, Sewsunker "Papwa" Sewgolum. Sewgolum garnered sympathy in the American press after he beat 113 white players to win the 1963 Natal Open at the Durban Country Club, where he was barred from the clubhouse by the Group Areas Act. He instead accepted the winner's trophy outdoors in the rain while the white audience watched comfortably from inside. Meanwhile, the government-controlled South African Broadcasting Corporation canceled its planned national broadcast of the event and never reported the results, drawing scorn from antiapartheid activists in the United States.[67]

The game's global dimension thus allowed African Americans to celebrate accomplished nonwhite golfers from around the world, denounce racism outside the United States, and use the sport to boost Pan-African sentiment and international ties. For some, golf tourism heightened racial tension—as it did on St. Croix in 1972—but for others it elicited visions of a new age, one in which black tourists respectfully visited independent black nations and bonded over golf. By 1950 Haitian president Paul Magloire had forged a relationship with NAACP executive secretary Walter White, both men urging more American tourists to visit Haiti. Calling for the "right type" of travelers, meaning those with the "right type of attitude toward race," White envisioned a middle-class exchange that golf tourism suited perfectly.[68] *Chicago Defender* journalist Venice R. Spraggs echoed the calls, visiting the island in 1952, and when Magloire subsequently came to the United States in 1955, the black press noted Haiti's golf courses and highlighted its growing tourist economy. (In just five years, the number of visitors to the island increased from over 17,000 in 1951 to over 65,000 in 1956.) Other nations, including Mexico and Jamaica, also drew increased attention from black vacationers and golf tourists.[69]

With the arrival of more independent states, Africa itself soon emerged as a destination, and the exchange was mutual. Ghana's second ambassador to the UN, Alex Quaison-Sackey, was an avid player who looked for opportunities to golf in New York after joining the UN in 1959. A black pharmacist, Howard Reckling, and a Jewish attorney, Morris Levine, worked furiously behind the scenes to find a private club that was willing to host an integrated group featuring the Ghanaian and white UN ambassadors (nonwhite delegates from Thailand, India, and Ceylon reported similar problems finding courses near Manhattan). Levine finally arranged for the group to play at Hampshire Country Club in Westchester County, barely avoiding what would have been an embarrassing situation: a black man with plenty of access to private golf in his African nation but none in New York City. Poppy Cannon—the white, South African wife of NAACP leader Walter White—lamented the ambassador's treatment and the overblown hysteria surrounding integrated golf in the United States: "Like the dread and forbidden topic of intermarriage, the golf question makes everyone uncomfortable."[70]

Ironically, America's black golfers usually had an easier time playing abroad, including in Africa. Chartered black heritage tours proliferated in the 1960s and 1970s, embodying the optimism of the civil rights movement and the growing number of African Americans who could afford international travel. The tours were organized by groups like the NAACP and often featured politically prescient trips to newly independent African nations; Senegal, Gambia, Ghana, Sierra Leone, and Liberia were popular destinations (many black Americans, including Martin Luther

King Jr. and his wife, visited Ghana for its 1957 independence ceremony). Yet for many travelers some of the first black heritage tours were international golf excursions that catered to large groups of black players. These too were quite symbolic politically but even more so socially, displaying America's black golfers worldwide. Two corporations, Pepsi-Cola and American Airlines, were the first to sponsor annual trips, and others followed; the American Airlines tours drew 300 to 450 African American participants (the airline also sponsored the UGA).[71]

However, the Pepsi International Golf Tour (IGT) was the first (beginning in 1962) and ran for over fifteen years. Advertising in black newspapers, the Pepsi trips signed up thousands of black golfers for excursions all over the world; they included celebrities like Jim Brown and Jackie Robinson, who attended several times and served as the tour's honorary chairman. At first Caribbean destinations, such as Puerto Rico (1963) and the Bahamas (1965), were popular. They were followed by more distant locales like Spain (1967), Venezuela (1972), Kenya and Tanzania (1973), and East Asia (1974). The groups were quite large, ranging from the 334 participants who went to the Bahamas to the 485 who traveled to Venezuela, and the black press applauded all of the trips, especially the 1973 outing to Africa that drew 375. That tour included golf at various courses in Nairobi and Dar es Salaam, culminating in a trophy ceremony emceed by W. Beverly Carter Jr., "our Black ambassador to Tanzania," *Jet* proudly announced. (Carter later became the first black ambassador-at-large in American history).[72] These excursions drew high-profile participants like Robinson but also featured plenty of die-hard golf enthusiasts from more modest means, such as Max Stanford Sr.

The IGT trips were the brainchild of Earl Jackson, a black travel agent who was first exposed to golf in the 1930s while caddying as a child in rural Farmville, Virginia. After moving to New York City and becoming a police officer, Jackson transitioned into the travel industry and eventually established IGT, his own agency. IGT appointed area representatives from black clubs nationwide to recruit for its numerous golf trips, including domestic and international tours. One was Maggie Hathaway in Los Angeles, who annually updated her readers on the trips and encouraged them to sign up. Stanford was another, recruiting Philadelphia-area golfers for the excursions and attending some himself.[73] (The 424 who went to Spain in 1967, including Robinson and UGA women's champion Ann Gregory, had no idea FBI agents were tracking their trip over concerns about the Stanford family.) Even the UGA became involved in international golf travel after it effectively dissolved as a pro tour in 1975, continuing for a few years as a black golf outing. The Chicago Women's Golf Club organized a group of 168 who traveled to the Bahamas in 1978, while another UGA group went to Puerto Rico the following year. But IGT remained the clear leader; by 1973 Earl Jackson's travel firm was one of only two black travel agencies in the nation grossing more than a million dollars annually.[74]

Thus a new era of black pride meant staking a greater claim to golf both at home and abroad, and for many casual fans that was not possible unless black professional players achieved equality at the game's highest level. The 1960s were pivotal years in the civil rights movement that coincided with a dramatic rise in the popularity of professional golf. For the first time it became a legitimate spectator sport competing with baseball, football, and basketball for fan attention and dollars. As the popularity of golf soared, especially on television, the PGA experienced its own movement of democratization in keeping with the spirit of the times. Though perhaps not particularly "grassroots," a surge of working-class and lower middle-class fans nevertheless embraced golf in the 1960s, especially by celebrating a new generation of players who appeared less elitist and more accessible than the pros of the past. No one personified this new image more than Arnold Palmer, who drew many of these fans to the game and was the era's most popular player. (Palmer's voracious supporters were first dubbed "Arnie's Army" at the 1958 Masters.)

By that point the battle between black professionals and the PGA and USGA had begun to turn, thanks to earlier efforts by players like Charlie Sifford, Howard Wheeler, and Bill Spiller. Refusing to leave the first tee at the 1952 San Diego Open or being dragged out of the locker room at the 1952 Phoenix Open, Spiller personified "Black Power" on the links before the term was even coined: no professional who came after him would ever rival his militancy. These black competitors had won substantial access to PGA and USGA tournaments, but the barriers remained high. Throughout the 1950s, USGA public links tournaments continued to bar black participants. Whites in Washington, D.C., protested vocally in 1951 when the district public links championship was integrated there for the first time. Elsewhere, black golfers continued to be barred from their local USGA public links qualifying tournaments, most notably in Toledo, Ohio (1956); Jacksonville, Florida (1958, 1959); and Lisle, Illinois (1959).[75] (In Jacksonville it was Fred Hampton, the former policeman turned golf advocate, who was banned from a qualifier.)

The USGA's 1959 U.S. Amateur Public Links Championship exemplified how discrimination in competitive golf was more uncertain than the clear-cut "barriers" African Americans faced in other sports. While some black players in Illinois and Florida were barred from entering their local qualifiers, in Seattle, Washington, Bill Wright not only qualified for the championship without any fuss, but he went on to win it. Wright was a twenty-three-year-old student at Western Washington College when he shocked the golf world and became the first African American to win a USGA championship. He accomplished the feat by beating 150 players in the finals at the Wellshire Municipal Golf Course in Denver, Colorado. Although the tournament was an amateur event and the victory received relatively little attention (Wright did go on to a career in golf, becoming a club and teaching professional), it was nevertheless important. Some in the black press, including *Ebony*, joined fans in celebrating the achievement. More importantly, the victory highlighted a growing chasm between USGA and PGA policies on race. In previous eras the two organizations were relatively in step, but by 1960 the PGA's "Caucasian clause" looked more conservative than ever; not only had Wright won a USGA national championship, but he did it at a time when African Americans were still barred from joining the PGA.[76]

That barrier was under renewed threat, too. By 1955 black players like Sifford, Spiller, and Ted Rhodes were already playing in a series of PGA events each year, including the Los Angeles Open and the Canadian Open. At the 1957 L.A. Open, Rhodes and Sifford were joined by another black pro from Dallas: twenty-three-year-old upstart Lee Elder. That year Sifford even won the Long Beach Open, an unofficial event that featured many of the PGA's top white professionals.[77]

Sifford's victory once again provided Bill Spiller an opportunity to speak out forcefully for an end to discrimination on the tour. Since being slighted in San Diego and Phoenix in 1952, Spiller struggled more than any other black professional to deal with the PGA's mistreatment and adjust to the world of white golf. "Everyone stared at you as if you were made from some kind of weird black plastic," he told *Ebony* when asked about his experience playing sporadic PGA events.[78] His militancy was also starting to alienate some fellow black pros: "He'd stand there all day with a sign saying that the tournament was unfair for excluding blacks," Sifford wrote in his memoir. "His attitude rubbed some people the wrong way, but I think he was on the right track. The only way any black men have ever gotten into this game was through being belligerent and adamant about playing. But Spiller turned off a lot of people, and once he got into tournaments, he could never quite deliver the goods to prove that he belonged out there with the best players."[79] Even the *Chicago Defender*, which championed the players' struggle to integrate the PGA, questioned the value of Spiller's behavior: "The obstacle that has stood in his path has been temperament—explosive and devastating."[80]

Five years after Joe Louis and the players publicly feuded with PGA head Horton Smith, Spiller once again confronted Smith after Sifford won the Long Beach Open in 1957. PGA sections in southern California and Michigan had voted to remove the Caucasian clause and urged the national body to amend the PGA's constitution (twice in the case of the southern California PGA, a powerful section), but Smith informed Spiller that the national body had voted down the proposals and had no further plans to take up the issue. Blacks could continue to receive sponsor invitations at particular PGA tournaments, but they would not be allowed membership to the PGA and would be denied its professional benefits, including job placement services and discounts on equipment. Seething with anger, Spiller denounced Smith and the PGA yet again in the press, accusing the executive body of "pulling a Faubus" on him two months after Arkansas governor Orval Faubus had tried to stop the integration of Little Rock's Central High School. "The PGA prevents us from making a living at our chosen profession, either through its Caucasian clause or gentleman's agreement," he exclaimed.[81]

Thus, for the rest of the 1950s the players established a routine that mimicked segregation in college sports, participating in some events in California, the Midwest, and Canada before stepping away from the tour once it headed south. Despite his growing frustrations, Spiller managed to forge some positive relationships with white pros, including leading southern players like Jimmy Demaret, Byron Nelson, and Sam Snead: "I thought Byron Nelson was the greatest golfer who ever lived," he later said.[82] But by 1960, on the eve of the PGA's integration, Spiller was angrier and more dejected than ever, his golf career effectively over. In Los Angeles he shared his frustrations with Maggie Hathaway after unsuccessfully applying for a series of positions at various courses in the city. (One even turned him down when he applied for the menial position of course starter.) Later that year Spiller returned to the caddie ranks in a desperate bid to make ends meet, the ultimate indignity for a man who had competed alongside the best pros in the world. From there he slipped further into obscurity, his accomplishments on the course and militant fight with the PGA overshadowed by players like Sifford and Elder. By the 1980s he was living off his wife's income and slipping into dementia, waking in the middle of the night to curse the men who prohibited him from playing, grabbing a pistol he kept by his bed and vowing revenge. Spiller's son, who became an attorney in California, recalled how professional golf turned his father into the angriest man he ever met. "He was beyond bitter," William Spiller said, noting that his father's death in 1988 went completely unnoticed among golf fans and sports media: "Nobody was interested."[83] A small plaque at L.A.'s Chester L. Washington Golf Course was one of the few public tributes. "Man died with a broken heart," Hathaway told the *Los Angeles Times* in 1997. "He should have been the hero. But they made him the scapegoat."[84]

As Bill Spiller faded into obscurity, Charlie Sifford continued to shine in the world of white golf, taking advantage of his limited opportunities to play PGA events and endearing himself to white professionals and tour officials. One year after he won the Long Beach Open, Sifford returned to Ohio's Firestone Country Club for the PGA's 1958 Rubber City Invitational, where he was paired with a player half his age: eighteen-year-old Jack Nicklaus. It was Nicklaus's first PGA event, and the two bonded immediately. "Charlie and I were grouped together the first two rounds and we hit it off from the first tee and remained good friends ever since," Nicklaus remembered years later. "When I look back on that first round—me, a wide-eyed kid making my first swings and taking my first steps down the fairway in a tour event—I can't think of a better person to have walked side-by-side with than Charlie Sifford. He was kind, gracious and a true gentleman."[85] Nicklaus's father, who owned several drugstores in Ohio, sent Sifford a box of his cherished cigars after the tournament.

By 1960 Sifford remained the top black player in the country, and advocates considered him the most likely candidate to receive full access to the PGA and its professional events. He only had a reasonable chance of being invited to nineteen of the tour's forty-five annual stops, and there were still key tournaments outside the South that refused to include him (or any other black player).[86] None were more important than two California events: the Bing Crosby National Pro-Am at Pebble Beach and Bob Hope's inaugural Palm Springs Desert Golf Classic. For seven straight years Sifford had unsuccessfully applied to play at Pebble Beach. In January 1960, after both events turned Sifford down again, Jackie Robinson and Joe Louis publicly protested, insisting that Sifford's professional record warranted the invitations and highlighting how PGA racism remained entrenched in California, well outside the Deep South. Louis even telegrammed Vice President Richard Nixon, while Robinson railed against the PGA in the *Chicago Defender*: "Golf is the one major sport in America today in which rank and open racial prejudice is allowed to reign supreme," he wrote.[87] Crosby responded with surprise, insisting he was unaware of the PGA's Caucasian clause, which ultimately prohibited black participants in his tournament because the Pebble Beach event required that all professionals in the field have PGA membership. "This never came up before—it never occurred to me," the entertainer told the press. "They are all alike to me." Insisting he harbored "no bigotry of any kind," Crosby's words were not enough to satisfy Robinson, who assailed him for associating his name with an "un-American" golf tournament.[88] (Maggie Hathaway would later insist that Crosby was indeed naive about the exclusion. "The only thing I've ever regretted is that I picketed Bing Crosby's tournament," she said in 1997. "I found out later that he was trying to help blacks get into the tournament, but he couldn't do anything with the PGA.")[89]

A breakthrough came in March 1960 after California attorney general Stanley Mosk publicly asked the PGA to provide a rationale for banning Sifford from tournaments in the state without violating his civil rights. The organization responded by agreeing to grant Sifford status as an "approved tournament player." The designation, which allowed players an alternative path to membership and provided tournament eligibility, was nevertheless not full membership, and in November the national body again voted 64-17 to reject the southern California PGA's request to eliminate the Caucasian clause. Mosk was outraged and threatened to sue.[90]

The organization now faced overwhelming national pressure to desegregate and remove the clause. Jackie Robinson noted that the policy kept the doors open for rampant discrimination at courses outside the South and in any golf organization that insisted on PGA membership as a requirement for eligibility. This included the Metropolitan Golf Association, one of the largest amateur associations in the country, with member courses in New York, New Jersey, and Connecticut. Having the PGA's Caucasian clause help exclude African Americans from Metropolitan tournaments was a "quiet but effective" way for "the ugly specter of American apartheid" to permeate northern courses, Robinson wrote. It was "white supremacy, northern style."[91] New York's State Commission on Human Rights soon told the association it was no longer allowed to stage tournaments in the state. Meanwhile, New York attorney general Louis Lefkowitz and officials at Cornell University stepped in to prevent a professional tournament at Cornell's golf course from requiring PGA membership. While most PGA corporate sponsors remained silent, New York's Rheingold Beer took a public stand by inviting black professionals to the celebrity tournament it sponsored, even though the event was supposed to require PGA membership. Moreover, all of this pressure began to hit the PGA in its pocketbook: in California rumors swirled that Mosk's threat had forced the tour to abandon plans to hold the 1962 PGA Championship in Los Angeles.[92] By the time the PGA held its national meeting in November 1961, the sentiment that prompted an overwhelming rejection of integration months earlier had shifted dramatically. A combination of black professionals already successfully competing in PGA events, threats from public officials in California and New York, and increasingly bad press finally moved the body to eliminate the Caucasian clause: the PGA and its tour were officially desegregated. "The Professional Golfers Association's Caucasian only clause is dead. Good!" proclaimed the *Los Angeles Sentinel*.[93]

While the decision had substantial long-term implications, most fans judged PGA integration each week with their own eyes by following the black players who were already competing, especially Charlie Sifford. (Sifford himself would not earn full PGA membership until 1964, three years later.) In January and February 1961 he integrated the Bing Crosby National Pro-Am at Pebble Beach and Bob Hope's Palm Springs Golf Classic, the two major California tour stops that had remained closed to black professionals. "[I] found no discrimination," he told the *Chicago Defender*. "Bing Crosby treats me wonderful. And they were fine to me at Palm Springs."[94] The biggest test of all came in April, when Sifford was notified one week in advance that he had made the field for the 1961 Greater Greensboro Open: for the first time an African American would play a PGA event in the South. Returning to his native North Carolina, Sifford had plenty of supporters. Yet the atmosphere in Greensboro was tense, especially regarding race and golf. Just months earlier the historic student sit-ins had been launched, and the Greensboro Six golf trespassing case had reached the Supreme Court. In fact, the initial idea to invite Sifford came from George Simkins, the local NAACP president, leader of the Greensboro Six, and outspoken advocate for integrating Greensboro's public courses. Simkins pressed organizers at the private Sedgefield Country Club to invite Sifford. Having the local golf hero return to desegregate the first PGA event in the South was an opportunity tournament director Mose Kiser could not pass up.

Sifford was aware of the political and social significance of his visit when he arrived: he was directly sponsored by the NAACP and Simkins, and sportswriters covering the event noted the connection to the Greensboro Six. "Was I surprised when they accepted my application?" he remarked. "Man, I had to be surprised."[95] Many whites were as well, and some voiced their disapproval. The tension peaked after hundreds of black spectators arrived at Sedgefield on the tournament's first day and watched Sifford shoot 68, topping the leaderboard. He had integrated a southern tour event in dramatic fashion, delivering one of the finest rounds of his career despite the intense pressure. As he sat on the lead that night, congratulatory telegrams poured in from around the country, including from Bob Hope and Bing Crosby. Then the telephone rang with an anonymous caller: "You'd better not bring your black ass out to no golf course tomorrow if you know what's good for you, nigger," said the voice on the other end. "We don't allow no niggers on our golf course." Kiser, the tournament's director, also received threats: "Someone wrote a letter to me saying, 'If you love your young children, don't let them play in the front yard by themselves.'"[96] That weekend police pulled several hecklers, including one man whose voice Sifford recognized as the caller, off the course for yelling racial epithets and throwing beer cans. He finished the tournament in fourth place, his best performance at a tour event since finishing second to Billy Casper at the 1960 Orange County Open Invitational in Costa Mesa, California. But under the circumstances it was among the best performances of his life, one that drew far more press coverage to race and golf than anything else that year (including the PGA's decision to rescind the Caucasian clause). And rather than present a false narrative of golf integration in Greensboro, Sifford's appearance only emboldened the ongoing, local fight for equality: soon after the tournament George Simkins and the NAACP sued Sedgefield for discrimination, even as Sifford returned annually during the 1960s to play the Greensboro Open.[97]

Now technically a thirty-eight-year-old rookie on the PGA circuit, Sifford continued to face discrimination and exclusion. He drove all the way to Texas for the next scheduled stops, only to be rejected in Houston and San Antonio. When he eventually accessed more southern tournaments later in the decade, he continued to receive heckling and racial slurs from some fans. On one occasion a patron even kicked his ball off the green at an event in Dallas.[98] Through it all, Sifford remained cautious with the press and kept most thoughts to himself. "It won't advance me to talk about it," he told a sportswriter after his debut in Greensboro. "It won't advance anything else."[99] Meanwhile, his relationship to white professionals on tour continued to flourish, and many of the top players spoke up on his behalf. "I get on just fine on the tour," he told the *Chicago Defender* in 1961. "People like Gary Player, Arnold Palmer, I get on with. When I have to leave them in the South they think it's a damn shame. Gary has told me 'that's a damn shame, a disgrace,' when I have to drop out."[100] As was the case for Bill Spiller, several southern pros also befriended Sifford.

Contrary to popular history, the desegregation of the PGA—and the efforts of players like Spiller, Rhodes, and Sifford—helped dozens of black professionals play on the PGA and LPGA circuits: at least thirty-one men and seven women since 1960. Some of these players participated sparingly, while others enjoyed long and visible careers. The second African American to join the tour after Charlie Sifford, Ray Botts, went on to play eighty-six events (his last in 1986) and an additional eighty-seven more on the Senior PGA Tour. These included tournaments like the Bing Crosby National Pro-Am, where Botts was paired with star pitcher Sandy Koufax during the 1967 event at Pebble Beach.[101] Even Sifford's nephew, Curtis Sifford, played for thirteen years on the tour after he joined in 1969. Some who joined later in the 1970s achieved even greater longevity and success.

Desegregation also allowed black women to access the LPGA Tour. Although only two joined in the 1960s (Althea Gibson in 1963 and Renee Powell in 1967), both drew considerable attention, especially Gibson. She had already earned fame in the 1950s by becoming the world's top female tennis player, breaking the color barrier in international tennis and winning the French Open (1956), U.S. Open (1957, 1958), and Wimbledon (1957, 1958). Gibson also reached numerous fans beyond sports by publishing her 1958 memoir, *I Always Wanted to Be Somebody*, and appearing often on television in the late 1950s and 1960s. A multisport talent, she learned to play golf after enrolling at Florida A&M in 1949, winning a match at Tuskegee University's tournament for black college golfers. Even though she dominated international tennis, by 1958 Gibson was openly hinting that she planned to leave her primary sport in order to play golf professionally. She earned very little prize money or sponsorships playing tennis, and a professional women's tennis tour did not exist. Golf was the more popular sport, and it offered her the potential to earn more money

Table 4. African Americans Competing on the PGA and LPGA Tours, 1960–2016

Name	Year	Name	Year
Charlie Sifford	1960	Nathaniel Starks	1973
Rafe "Ray" Botts	1961	Calvin Peete	1975
Gordon Chavis	1962	Jim Thorpe	1976
Pete Brown	1963	Bobby Stroble	1976
Althea Gibson	1963	Ron Terry	1976
William Wright	1964	Lee Carter	1979
James Black	1965	Al Morton	1981
James Walker Jr.	1965	Tom Woodard	1981
Lee Elder	1967	Adrian Stills	1985
Renee Powell	1967	Walter Morgan (Senior Tour)	1991
Henry Baraben	1968	LaRee Sugg	1995
George Johnson	1968	Tiger Woods	1996
Howard Brown	1969	Timothy O'Neal	2002
Curtis Sifford	1969	Joseph Bramlett	2011
Cliff Brown	1970	Shasta Averyhardt	2011
James "Jim" Dent	1970	Sadena Parks	2015
Charlie Owens	1970	Cheyenne Woods	2015
Chuck Thorpe	1972	Harold Varner III	2016
Al Green	1973	Ginger Howard	2016

Some records indicate that two additional African American players, Willie Brown and Richard Thomas, also participated in PGA tournaments. See McDaniel, *Uneven Lies*, 167.

competing among the top forty women on the LPGA Tour than she could make by being the best amateur tennis player in the world. Later that year she formally announced her retirement from tennis.[102]

By 1961 Gibson was winning UGA women's events and slowly improving her golf game. She received some instruction from Ann Gregory, the top black female player at the time, and participated in a number of celebrity pro-ams and exhibitions. In 1962 she joined Gregory, Joe Louis, and Jackie Robinson for a match at Chicago's Pipe O' Peace course, where whites had shot at a group of black players nine years earlier. (The course was renamed after Louis in 1986.)[103] Playing nonstop for three years, she appeared in her first LPGA tournament in 1963 and joined the tour full time in 1964, at age thirty-seven. Gibson went on to play every LPGA event for the next six years, her fame attracting new fans to women's golf and challenging segregation at various tour stops. While the PGA was often perceived as a barrier for black men trying to compete in PGA professional tournaments, the LPGA Tour was organized and governed almost entirely by the players themselves, and throughout the 1960s Gibson's peers and her tour rallied around her and rejected sites that practiced discrimination. Several times the LPGA refused to play tournaments at country clubs that barred Gibson from their clubhouses, including the popular Babe Zaharias Open in Beaumont, Texas: when members of the Beaumont Country Club grumbled over her participation in 1964, the LPGA moved the event to another course in town.[104]

Gibson ultimately found some success but did not make significant money as a professional golfer. Her best performances on the LPGA Tour were third place at the 1967 Pacific Ladies Classic in Eugene, Oregon, and second place at the 1970 Len Immke Buick Open in Columbus, Ohio. Despite finishing in the top fifty on the LPGA money list five times (her highest ranking was twenty-seventh in 1966), she struggled to afford traveling around the country and at one point even asked Maggie Hathaway if the Beverly Hills NAACP would help sponsor her. She cut back on tournaments in 1970 and eventually retired from professional golf in 1978. Although Gibson's golf accomplishments fell far short of her tennis exploits, her previous fame and willingness to travel and play in every tour event drew attention to the LPGA and its willingness to confront discrimination more directly than its male counterpart. Of course, she also had considerable skills as well, centered on a powerful swing that contrasted sharply with the 1950s popular celebration of Ann Gregory and Babe Zaharias as talented "feminine" golfers. "That girl hits just like a man," said Jerry Volpe, the white pro at New Jersey's Englewood Country Club (Volpe gave lessons to Gibson and helped her become Englewood's only African American member). Gibson regularly drove the ball over 200 yards and occasionally exceeded 300 yards with a tailwind, longer than some men in PGA events at the time. "My style of play was aggressive, dynamic, and mean," she later said.[105]

As Althea Gibson became the first African American to play on the LPGA Tour, she joined Maggie Hathaway and Ann Gregory as the three most important advocates for black women in golf. The three were mutual friends who engaged in numerous struggles around the country. After integrating the USGA national championships in 1956, Gregory continued to play in USGA tournaments and confront discrimination in the amateur ranks. She was denied access to the players' banquet following the 1959 U.S. Women's Amateur at Congressional Country Club in Bethesda,

Althea Gibson and Jackie Robinson at the North-South Golf Tournament, Miami Springs Golf Course, February 23, 1962 (AP Photo).

Maryland; four years later at the 1963 championship, a fellow competitor mistook her for a maid at Taconic Golf Club in Williamstown, Massachusetts. Gregory even had to fight for access to her local municipal course back home in Gary, Indiana. One day she refused to play the nine holes for black golfers at Gleason Park, paid her greens fees, and began playing the eighteen-hole layout instead. Stunned officials watched in silence but did nothing, and Gleason Park never again segregated its public golfers.[106]

Meanwhile, Hathaway trumpeted the success of both Gregory and Gibson in her newspaper columns, all while she continued to organize NAACP golf lawsuits on behalf of black women and promoted youth golf programs among black girls in Los Angeles. In 1956 she led a group of women that sued for access to the city's public links tournaments and in the 1960s publicly challenged white women's golf clubs to invite more black women into their ranks. In 1971 Hathaway even stood up to some men in the black Western States Golf Association who opposed her strategy of trying to integrate the women's clubs. Spurned by the association, she watched as a brief but intense gender war erupted between black men and women over the prospect of uniting with white clubs and scheduling integrated tournaments at L.A.'s Western Avenue Golf Course. It was a bitter feud, with the tension of black nationalism and integration played out in the world of municipal golf; at one point black women were having their cars vandalized while they played, with golf tees nailed into their tires. Yet Hathaway was unintimidated, regularly updating her readers in the *Los Angeles Sentinel* and publicly challenging all those who she thought stood between black women and the game, whether they were L.A.'s top city officials and swankiest white country clubs or managers at predominately black golf courses and certain black men in the Western States Golf Association.[107]

As Gibson, Gregory, and Hathaway struggled to integrate women's golf, a new generation of black women emerged in the late 1960s to take advantage of the hard-fought opportunities. One was Renee Powell, who grew up playing on Clearview Golf Course, the historic public course her father, William, built and operated in Ohio. William crafted miniature clubs for his daughter when she was three years old, and by her teen years he recognized her immense talent and helped her enter junior tournaments. In 1960 fourteen-year-old Renee was already winning UGA women's titles, and at eighteen she won the 1964 UGA women's championship. She then joined the elite golf program at Ohio State University, eventually becoming the first African American, male or female, to captain a major university's golf team. In 1967 Renee Powell was the second black player to join the LPGA Tour, where she played for thirteen years and achieved a bit more success than her predecessor Gibson (Powell earned approximately $39,000 in LPGA events, her best performance a fourth-place finish at the 1972 Lady Errol Classic).[108] Powell was also the first black female pro to play extensively overseas, winning the 1973 Kelly Springfield Open in Queensland, Australia, and conducting golf clinics and exhibitions throughout East Asia and Africa on behalf of the U.S. State Department. A brief marriage to a Briton took her to England, where in 1979 she became the first black woman to serve as a golf professional in the United Kingdom after the Silvermere Club, located just outside London, hired her to be its head pro. She would later receive significant recognition in the British golfing world, most notably in 2015 when she was among the first seven women to ever receive membership in the Royal and Ancient Golf Club of St. Andrews. Powell came back to the United States in 1984 and became head pro at Seneca Golf Course in Cleveland, Ohio, before returning to Clearview in 1990 and taking over her father's course. She had been shaped both by the challenges he had faced confronting segregation and by her own experience as a pioneer in women's professional golf. "Believe me," wrote William Powell of his daughter. "She has her own story to tell from a different generation and a different gender."[109]

Despite the emergence of Renee Powell, Althea Gibson, and the twelve black men who played on the PGA circuit in the first ten years after desegregation, most fans in the 1960s kept the spotlight on Charlie Sifford. By the time he integrated the Greensboro Open in 1962, he was the face of black golf and still considered the best black player in the country. As networks began to experiment with prerecorded, made-for-television golf matches, supporters questioned why he was left out. In 1963 Jackie Robinson challenged ABC's *All-Star Golf* and its sponsor, the Reynolds Aluminum Company, for failing to feature Sifford on the show.[110] The most successful televised golf program, *Shell's Wonderful World of Golf*, was far more elaborate. Airing on NBC from 1961 to 1970, it featured two or three popular pros competing in matches at exotic courses around the world. (Viewers in 1968 watched Johnny Pott and Chi Chi Rodriguez duel at St. Croix's Fountain Valley Golf Club, four years before the infamous massacre.)[111] Watched by some 15 million people each week, *Wonderful World of Golf* reached a substantial audience and allowed fans to engage selected participants more than television coverage of a standard PGA event and its large field of players. In 1966 Sifford finally received his first invitation, facing off against Australian Bruce Devlin at the Royal Selangor Golf Club in Malaysia. Three years later he was featured again in a three-way match with Doug Sanders and Dave Thomas at Singapore's Island Country Club. The increased respect and exposure also generated more income. Having earned only $17,000 in seven years of tournament play before joining the PGA, Sifford made $200,000 over the next seven.[112]

Many fans, certain that Sifford would be the first African American to win an official PGA event, were therefore shocked in 1964 when the distinction went instead to Pete Brown. Winner of the 1961 and 1962 UGA Opens, Brown was a Mississippi native who joined the PGA circuit in 1963, the fourth black player to do so. He had grown up caddying for whites at Jackson's municipal course, played for the first time when he was fifteen years old, and suffered through a series of debilitating physical ailments (for two years in the late 1950s he was diagnosed with nonparalytic polio).[113] Overcoming both segregation and injury, he made history just eighteen months after joining the tour when he traveled to play in the fourth annual Waco Turner Open. Turner, the event's founder, was a wealthy Oklahoma oil executive with plans to promote an extensive golf resort in an obscure location: rural Burneyville, Oklahoma, one mile from the Texas border. Needing par on the event's final hole to win, Brown was "scared to death" but calmly sank a pressure putt for the victory.[114]

Pete Brown's historic win at the 1964 Waco Turner Open was quickly overlooked, even by some black fans. Just five years later the *Chicago Defender* was incorrectly reporting that Sifford had been the first African American to win an official PGA event, even as Brown proved his victory was no fluke: he played for seventeen years on the PGA's tour and won again at the 1970 Andy Williams–San Diego Open.[115] Although some black fans celebrated Brown's victory, two factors helped it fade from memory: the overwhelming attention given Sifford and the tournament's obscurity. Waco Turner's planned golf mecca quickly fell apart, and the PGA never again returned to Burneyville. Today drivers on Interstate 35 see little more than open land as they cross the Oklahoma-Texas border; few realize the significance as they pass one of the more unlikely spots in the history of African Americans and professional sports.

Brown's achievement also faded because three years later, Sifford, too, became an official winner on tour. After winning another unofficial event, the 1963 Puerto Rico Open, he won his first full PGA tournament at the 1967 Greater Hartford Open. Starting the final round five strokes off the lead, Sifford shot 64 to win by one shot—"to the roars of the crowd which had cheered him through out," reported the *Chicago Defender*.[116] At the trophy ceremony he thanked his fellow white competitors on tour, insisting the racism he experienced in the sport had always come from nonplayers. Finally obtaining his first tour win at the age of forty-four, Sifford recognized just how long and arduous the journey had been. "There have been many times I've wanted to quit, but my wife, Rose, would never let

Jack Nicklaus and Pete Brown at the 1967 Bing Crosby National Pro-Am (*Ebony*, May 1967).

me give up," he said tearfully. "I'll play this game as long as I can walk."[117] Two years later he won the 1969 Los Angeles Open, his second and final official PGA victory. It marked the peak of his golfing career and national popularity. The win was particularly celebrated by African Americans in Los Angeles, where Sifford had relocated permanently from Philadelphia. The city of Watts declared a "Charlie Sifford Day," honoring him with a parade and banquet emceed by Olympic champion Wilma Rudolph.[118]

Yet despite all of Charlie Sifford's success and popularity, the face of PGA integration failed to earn one elusive honor: an invitation to compete in the Masters. Moreover, by 1968 another black PGA newcomer, Lee Elder, was starting to draw fan attention away from Sifford. Born in Dallas,

Texas, Elder moved to Los Angeles as a teen to live with his aunt. At age sixteen he impressed Joe Louis when the two battled in a 1950 UGA amateur tournament, and he joined the inner circle of golfers supported by Louis and Ted Rhodes.[119] After a brief stint in the army, Elder started regularly playing the UGA pro circuit in 1961 and dominated the black tour. He took four of five UGA national championships from 1963 to 1967, and in 1966 alone he won eighteen of twenty-two consecutive tournaments. Elder's first UGA National victory came at Langston Golf Course in Washington, D.C., where he developed a long association. In the early 1960s he taught golf at the facility, and from 1978 to 1981 he served as manager.

In 1967 Elder became the eighth black player to qualify for the PGA circuit; unlike the others, he made an immediate splash. On the final day of the 1968 American Golf Classic, the rookie Elder matched the world's top player, Jack Nicklaus, shot for shot down the stretch at Firestone Country Club in Akron, Ohio. An estimated gallery of 23,000 and millions of television viewers watched the men duel for the title in what some consider the most exciting finish in the tour's history. On the fifth extra hole of a sudden-death playoff, Nicklaus dropped an eight-foot birdie putt to win in dramatic fashion. But it was Elder's performance that drew historic accolades; never before had so many fans watched a black golfer compete, and by the end most were rooting squarely for the underdog. "I showed the greatest golfer in the world that I could hit a few licks too," Elder said.[120] The performance landed him on the cover of *Golf Digest*, the first African American to achieve the honor (notably, the magazine's cover would never feature Sifford). UGA president Max Stanford Sr. told the magazine that "Elder did more for Negro golf in 45 minutes than everybody else put together had done in 45 years," likely the only time *Golf Digest* ever featured commentary from someone tracked by the FBI for subversive activity. And Elder followed up the performance with consistently strong, steady play. He was ranked the third straightest hitter on tour in 1968, and *Ebony* not only lauded the duel with Nicklaus but also noted that Elder made nine straight tournament cuts during the season, a record for tour rookies. Landing an endorsement deal with Faultless Golf, he was also the first black player featured in a national advertising campaign, including ads in *Golf Digest*. It was a deal that far surpassed any of the sponsorships offered Ted Rhodes or Charlie Sifford.[121]

While Sifford was undoubtedly the face of desegregation in professional golf during the 1950s and early 1960s, Elder became the world's top black golfer right as the new phase of racial tension and black militancy

Lee Elder and Arnold Palmer share an umbrella at the 1973 Greater New Orleans Open (*Jet*, April 12, 1973).

reached its breaking point. Fans watched as his rookie season unfolded alongside the tumultuous summer of 1968. In April he was in North Carolina for the Greater Greensboro Open when Martin Luther King Jr. was assassinated.[122] In August, two weeks after millions watched Elder's exciting duel with Nicklaus, violence erupted in the streets of Chicago at the Democratic National Convention. That October, while the tour was in Las Vegas, the summer Olympics opened in Mexico City amidst global protests targeting South Africa's participation. Sprinters Tommie Smith and John Carlos were suspended from the U.S. track team and expelled from the games after they displayed a "Black Power salute" during their medal ceremony. Professional golf was now touring a nation that was experiencing over 100 instances of mass urban unrest and violent protest, and Elder was regularly thrust into racial controversies. Two issues in particular, the South Africa protest and the desegregation of the Masters, eventually defined his relationship to the movement and made him the iconic pro golfer of the Black Power generation.

Golf was a major battlefield in the controversy over apartheid. In 1969 the *Chicago Defender* called Elder a "man in the middle" after black anti-apartheid protesters targeted the PGA Championship in Dayton, Ohio.[123] The game had grown dramatically in southern Africa, producing a number of leading white professionals who sought to compete in PGA events in the United States, most notably Bobby Locke (who dominated the tour in 1947), Gary Player (who made his American debut at the 1957 Masters and won his first PGA event the next year), and Harold Henning (who joined the tour in 1965). Meanwhile, regimes in both South Africa and Rhodesia hardened their commitment to segregation, prompting an escalation of racial violence and upheaval in the late 1960s. There, too, as in St. Croix and throughout the African Diaspora, golf was both a symbol of white colonialism and apartheid and a target of black resistance. *Sports Illustrated* reported that black guerrillas in Rhodesia "had prompted the adoption of two new rules at the golf club in Centenary.... The first rule 'allows a stroke to be played again if interrupted by gunfire or sudden explosion,' while the second enjoins players to check the holes for land mines before putting."[124] In the United States, Black Power groups celebrated the news that activists were disrupting white golf in Africa. "The European settlers still attempt to cling to their luxuries," joked the Student Organization for Black Unity. "But the game just ain't the same."[125]

The all-white South Africa PGA, which tried to help its professionals gain attention abroad, soon faced its own challenge from black golfers at home. In 1972 the South African government, attempting to keep its white golfers from being banned at international tournaments, announced that it would allow a few integrated, international tournaments to take place in the country. One organization representing South Africa's black golfers responded that it refused to participate in such tournaments, denouncing the move as tokenism designed to parade a few black players at select tournaments in order to secure the standing of South Africa's white golfers worldwide. Once again, American Black Power groups, such as the Student Organization for Black Unity, supported the move: "Black golfers in South Africa refuse to be used," the organization proudly announced.[126]

As the battle over race and golf escalated in Africa, the arrival of African Americans and white South Africans on the PGA circuit created the opportunity for symbolic clashes. Understanding that the success of white Africans on tour left it open for criticism, the PGA formally recognized South Africa's black golf organization in 1963, a move that meant little beyond the realm of public relations, for few black golfers in South Africa had any chance of qualifying for competition in the United States.[127] It was therefore up to black Americans like Charlie Sifford and Lee Elder whether or not they would speak for Africa's black golfers in the United States. Down the stretch at the 1969 L.A. Open, Sifford faced off against

Harold Henning, birdieing the first hole in a sudden-death playoff with Henning to earn his second tour victory. Many fans immediately recognized the symbolism: "It is ironic that Sifford scored his 'most important' tournament victory against an opponent from a country where blacks are not allowed to compete in bigtime golf," announced *Jet*.[128] Two months later *Sports Illustrated* concurred: "The fact that Charlie Sifford happened to beat Harold Henning who happened to be a product (if not necessarily a practitioner) of South African apartheid was not lost on American black men. . . . Negro newspapers were calling Charlie Sifford the epitome of Black Is Beautiful."[129] Sifford himself seemed to relish achieving a pressure-packed victory over a South African. "I wanted to prove to myself that I could play and to others that a Negro could play successful tournament golf," he told *Golf Digest*.[130] Yet in other ways he resented efforts to turn the 1969 L.A. Open into a Pan-African victory. "Intrepid white reporters were making him uncomfortable (and uncooperative) by pressing him for quotes on everything racial from Nat Turner's confession to Muhammad Ali's conviction," claimed *Sports Illustrated*. "His mail was up to 200 letters a week."[131] Henning, for his part, was gracious in defeat but politely refused to comment when asked about apartheid after the loss to Sifford. "I'm a golfer, not a politician," he responded.[132]

While Henning and Sifford managed to deflect the issue somewhat, Lee Elder and Gary Player could not. As South Africa's most accomplished golfer and a fan favorite at PGA events, Player faced the most severe criticism from the antiapartheid movement. While he was paired with Jack Nicklaus during the 1969 PGA Championship, black protesters threw ice in his face and attempted to physically assault him (he still managed to finish second in the tournament). Two years later black congressman Charles Diggs called for a federal investigation of U.S. relations with South Africa, arguing that Player "had no business making money in America," while in Boston the NAACP organized a boycott of the tour's 1971 Massachusetts Classic over the participation of Player and Henning.[133] Throughout the 1960s, Player had clearly supported the white regime in South Africa. "I am of the South Africa of [Prime Minister] Verwoerd and apartheid," he declared in his 1966 book *Grand Slam Golf* (published in London),

> a nation which is the result of an African graft on European stock and which is the product of its instinct and ability to maintain civilized values and standards amongst the alien barbarians. . . . Many people

draw comparisons between South Africa and the United States with regard to the coloured problem. They say we should give all the natives equal rights. It seems to me that the coloured people in the United States were given equal rights a century ago, but still see the need to fight for them today. . . . The American Negro is sophisticated and politically conscious. He was "imported" into the United States and has long lost contact with Africa. He has become an integral part of a western community, with its habits and attitudes. . . . The African may well believe in witchcraft and primitive magic, practise ritual murder and polygamy; his wealth is in cattle. More money and he will have no sense of parental or individual responsibility, no understanding of reverence for life or the human soul which is the basis of Christian and other civilised societies. . . . I have no evidence that I live in a police state, a "Hitler state," and people who write these things, and read and believe them, are doing a disservice to the progress of people everywhere. . . . A good deal of nonsense is talked of, and indeed thought about, "segregation." Segregation of one kind or another is practised everywhere in the world. . . . We in South Africa recognize this and believe that our races should develop separately, but in parallel.[134]

The apartheid government, particularly its Department of Information, saw in Player an opportunity to sanitize its image abroad with help from one of the world's top golfers at the zenith of his career. As the antiapartheid movement grew, Player became more reluctant to speak openly on the issue, especially in the United States. "I'm not getting involved in politics," he told the press after hecklers disrupted him again at the 1971 U.S. Open.[135] Yet he refused to criticize the apartheid regime and thereby left his previous comments and actions to stand for themselves.

At the same time, Player reached out to his fellow black competitors, and they began to defend him publicly. Charlie Sifford, Pete Brown, and George Johnson (who joined the tour in 1968) all spoke out on his behalf. "You couldn't ask for a finer man than Gary Player," said Sifford in 1971. "He's helped me so many times I've stopped counting."[136] Player also eventually struck up a long-term friendship with Maggie Hathaway after the two first met at the 1975 Masters: "He's done a lot for young black golfers that people don't know about," she later said in 1997. "He has to work harder than most to prove he's not a racist."[137] Player's longtime caddie, New Orleans native Alfred "Rabbit" Dyer, also came to his defense in the black press. Dyer would spend over twenty years caddying for the South

African and made history in 1974 when he became the first African American to caddie at the British Open, helping Player win the tournament for the third time. (Dyer was the first African American to caddie in the South African Open as well.) He told *Black Sports* that Player was "a caddie's friend, a real Christian and religious guy."[138]

At some point along the way—whether influenced by his interaction with African American golfers like Sifford and Hathaway, pressured by antiapartheid demonstrators, or both—Gary Player slowly had a change of heart. "It's hard to go back, I can't say what year it was when I suddenly realized," he later said in 2005. "We were brainwashed when we were young people just like the Germans before the war."[139] But in 1970, when the pressure from activists was strong and he still supported the regime, Player invited prominent African American golfers to visit South Africa and proposed a series of matches to benefit the United Negro College Fund. *Afro-American* called it a "cheap move" and criticized the idea: "No matter how 'likeable' a fellow Gary Player may be, he still is a representative of that racist nation and is a goodwill ambassador for it in this country." Black tennis star Arthur Ashe, locked in his own battle with the South African government over refusals to let him play in tournaments there, called Player's idea "a farce" and told *Jet* he feared for the golfer's life "the way things are going in the United States."[140] For many black Americans, Player was a legitimate, logical target of protest in response to South Africa's snubbing of Ashe, regardless of the kind words he received from his black PGA peers. "No Ashe, No Player," one protester wore on his shirt at a tour stop outside San Diego. Although the United Negro College Fund initially declined Player's offer and Sifford was openly skeptical of the idea, at least one such event did take place in 1972, when Player was joined by Lee Elder, Pete Brown, and black comedian Flip Wilson for a pro-am at the Old Dominion Golf Club in Newport News, Virginia.[141]

Player's invitation for black golfers to visit Africa also faced a backlash but proved more successful. In 1971 he encouraged Elder to make the trip to South Africa and participate in the South African PGA Championship in Johannesburg.[142] Although many black Americans were rightly skeptical, insisting that Player was using Elder to provide damage control for his own image and the apartheid regime, some whites in South Africa were also troubled by the invitation. Elder was unsure if he would accept, and golf writers like Maggie Hathaway encouraged him to proceed cautiously with the decision. "We do hope Lee Elder is not making a mistake going to South Africa to play to prove that Gary Player loves blacks in America," she wrote.[143] Elder finally agreed to the trip in August 1971 and was immediately flooded with both accolades and criticism from the black community. One of the more influential antiapartheid organizations, the American Committee on Africa, tried to dissuade him from going both publicly and in private meetings: "You say . . . that you do not want to be involved in politics," the group wrote Elder in an open letter. "But racism, here or in South Africa, is something that we are all involved in, like it or not."[144] Many in the black press agreed. "Neither was Nat King Cole a politician when he got slapped in Alabama some years back by people who believed in apartheid in this country," proclaimed the *New York Amsterdam News*.[145] Elder's decision also received a mixed reception in Africa. The Rhodesia Golf Union reported that some black fans were excited about the potential of him visiting their nation as well. However, South African activist Dennis Brutus testified to the U.S. House of Representatives that such visits would only aid the apartheid regime, noting that Player still refused to speak up for black golfers in his own country.[146]

However, once he was committed to the trip, Elder was undeterred. In November–December 1971 he spent three weeks in Africa, including stops in Liberia, Uganda, Nigeria, and Kenya, all sponsored by the U.S. State Department and designed to assuage the many Africans upset over his decision to play in South Africa. In each nation he met with heads of state and played exhibition matches, often in rudimentary conditions. "Uganda was the only country with grass on the greens," he recalled later.[147] As the trip continued, Elder responded to his detractors. "I play golf anywhere I am invited," he told the press in Nairobi shortly before heading to South Africa. "I believe my playing may help the black man there. It may open the door for other things to come later on. It may even lead to the South Africans allowing their own black men to play in former all-white tournaments."[148] Days later he and other black South African golfers participated in the PGA Championship at Johannesburg's Huddle Park, the first tournament in that tour's history to feature black Africans competing alongside whites. It was also the first to be played before an integrated gallery, as Elder had agreed to participate only after the government assured him it would suspend the PGA's usual policy of segregating spectators. Paired with Player during the first two days of the tournament, Elder's group attracted huge crowds, an estimated 5,000 the first day and 10,000 the next. "I thought about Dr. Martin Luther King's death," he told the *New York Times* when he returned from the trip. "I wondered if some crackpot would decide not to want me there."[149] But in the end

Elder had no complaints over the tournament, other than finishing fifteen strokes off the lead. He praised the fans, Player, and the South Africa PGA but, significantly, was unafraid to tell local golf writers that he had no plans to return until apartheid was abolished. (He also asked to meet the imprisoned Nelson Mandela but was denied.) "I felt like I really left something permanent there in South Africa," he later said.[150] The following week public attention surged again after he won the Nigerian Open, beating a field that included eight members of the British Ryder Cup team and becoming the first African American to win a major international tournament.

Elder's 1971 trip has long been slighted in the popular history of black athletes who traveled to Africa or confronted apartheid, overshadowed by subsequent events like Arthur Ashe's 1973 visit to South Africa or the 1974 "Rumble in the Jungle"—Muhammad Ali's landmark fight with George Foreman in Zaire. But it was Elder who broke new ground, for his controversial visit predated the others, and, in the end, he refused to be anyone's pawn, be it the apartheid regime, the South Africa PGA, Gary Player, or antiapartheid organizations. Elder made the trip on his own terms and established a long-term relationship with the region, and some who initially denounced the visit quickly changed their perspective. In 1975 *Jet* acknowledged that Elder had helped build a new seminary in Durban and raised $20,000 for black golf and education programs in South Africa. "Thanks to Elder, there are 40 Black professional South African golfers," the magazine proclaimed, "which is about four times as many as the U.S. can boast."[151] On the other hand, Elder refused to meet the demands of more fervent antiapartheid activists, establishing a lifelong friendship with Player and opposing U.S. economic sanctions on South Africa. He also returned in 1989, eighteen years after his historic trip, again unafraid to speak his mind. "So many dignitaries have been here and nothing has been said against them because they don't speak out about what changes have been made here," he told the press at Johannesburg's Randpark Golf Club. "But I'll certainly say it. I truly feel and hope and pray that apartheid will be abolished. . . . It's on its way out, it really is."[152] By the 1980s his stance, though understandably far too moderate for most activists, stood out compared with the actions of other PGA Tour pros. In 1981 Player established the richest golf tournament in the world, known as the "Million Dollar Challenge." An annual event at his Gary Player Country Club in Sun City, South Africa, the event attracted several of the tour's best players, including Jack Nicklaus, Lee Trevino,

Johnny Miller, and Raymond Floyd, all of whom defied the international sports boycott of the regime and warnings from the U.S. State Department in order to participate.[153]

Ironically, throughout Elder's 1971 visit the most common question he received from African golf fans (black and white) was not about apartheid, golf, or discrimination in Africa. Instead it was the same question American fans were contemplating. "Everywhere we went, people asked about the Masters," his wife, Rose, told the *New York Times*.[154] Elder himself used the success of the Africa trip to speak out against the most symbolic racial barrier that remained on the U.S. tour: "If a place like South Africa can invite a black golfer, I can't see why the Masters can't open its doors." Five months later Gary Player joined the chorus of professionals and fans who wondered aloud if a black player would ever receive an invitation to Augusta National. "With the number of good Black players increasing on the tour, I think it is a shame that none has enjoyed the experience," he was quoted in *Jet*.[155]

A generation after its inauguration in 1934, the Masters was clearly the world's most prestigious golf tournament by the late 1960s, and it continued to stand as a strong symbol of golf elitism, race, and power in the South. "What is it really like to be a member of Augusta National?" *Golf Digest* asked in 1967. "For certain, you will play one of the world's most famous—and best—golf courses. . . . You will associate with men of influence and power. . . . You will move in an atmosphere redolent with courtly, ante-bellum manners."[156] By then Augusta's roughly 200 members included former president Dwight Eisenhower and Georgia governor Carl Sanders. (Sanders was on the course when aides informed him of President John F. Kennedy's assassination in 1963.)[157]

Not only were the club's membership and rituals shrouded in mystery, but equally confusing were the qualifications professionals had to meet in order to receive a coveted invitation to the Masters. As was evident in the snubbing of Charlie Sifford, winning a PGA event did not automatically qualify one before 1972, and the club exercised considerable control over what was the smallest field of any major event. Many fans were certain that Elder's achievements warranted an invitation: he beat an elite field to win the 1971 Nigerian Open, placed in the top thirty at both the U.S. Open and the PGA Championship that year, and finished the 1973 season thirtieth on the PGA money list. Eighteen U.S. congressmen even formally asked Augusta National to invite "the most prominent black golfer" and urged the tournament to take "affirmative action" (a phrase still unfamiliar to many Americans in 1973). But club chairman Clifford Roberts rejected the request, calling it "discrimination in reverse." Elder, too, declined the congressmen's help, insisting he did not want to be a test case in one of the first popular controversies over affirmative action. He told the press he would refuse an invitation unless it was achieved "on merit."[158]

Elder and most golf fans thus knew that a victory in a PGA event was likely his only chance to secure a historic invitation to the Masters, and he faced intense pressure to secure one. In September 1972 he came agonizingly close, losing a sudden-death playoff to Lee Trevino at the Greater Hartford Open. The Mexican American Trevino, often dubbed the "Merry Mex" or "Supermex" in the press, faced his own struggles navigating the world of white golf. Although he later traveled to apartheid South Africa and competed in Gary Player's Million Dollar Challenge, Trevino also boycotted the Masters in 1970, 1971, and 1974 because he felt uncomfortable with the atmosphere at Augusta National. "I really felt bad," he said just after sinking an eighteen-foot birdie to beat Elder. "He wants so bad to get into the Masters, but . . . I wouldn't let my wife beat me if I could help it."[159]

Like Trevino, many players thought highly of Elder and recognized how significant it would be for a black pro to play the Masters. But the constant pressure and spotlight began to wear on the tour's African Americans, ultimately undermining their solidarity. "Everybody knows they discriminate so maybe the PGA should take a stand, do something, or say something about it," Sifford said in 1973.[160] Within a year, however, he had grown tired of talking about the issue. "It's getting to where none of them want to come to the press tent anymore," the PGA's media liaison said of the black players. Jim Dent, a former caddie at Augusta National who in 1970 became the fourteenth African American to join the tour, put it more bluntly. "To hell with the Masters," he spat back at a sportswriter. "If I win a tournament, that's my Masters."[161]

In April 1974 Elder finally broke through and secured his first PGA victory, beating Englishman Peter Oosterhuis in a playoff to win the Monsanto Open in Pensacola, Florida. Security guards immediately escorted him to the clubhouse of the Pensacola Country Club (he had started to receive threats, especially at tour events in the South). Getting his first win was special, but the golf world immediately recognized what was most significant about the victory: within minutes Clifford Roberts phoned from Augusta and announced that Elder would be invited to the 1975

Masters. For a week the golfer pondered whether or not to accept the invitation. To turn it down would be one of the more powerful rebukes from a black athlete in history but would also potentially doom his career.[162]

Eventually Elder indicated he would participate, but he still had to wait nearly a year before the next Masters was scheduled to take place. For the remainder of 1974 and early 1975 he was showered with accolades, overwhelmed with offers to speak, and bombarded with media requests, as well as occasional threats. He received major attention despite the fact that his victory in Florida and the Masters invitation came two weeks after black baseball star Hank Aaron broke Babe Ruth's homerun record, what many considered a major milestone in the history of race and sports. But nothing in the sporting world could overshadow the significance of Elder's achievements and the anticipation over integrating the Masters. "Move over Hank Aaron," the *Chicago Defender* announced. "There's enough room in the spotlight for at least two people."[163]

Support for Elder was particularly strong in Washington, D.C., where he resided and spent much of his time when not playing. Mayor Walter Washington gave him a key to the city, and President Gerald Ford, another in the long line of avid presidential golfers, provided more attention than any black golfer would ever receive from a sitting president. Elder and Ford played a round at Congressional Country Club (which they would do at least once more while Ford was president), and Ford also appeared with Elder at Langston Golf Course, D.C.'s historic black links. In December 1974 the president even attended a reception honoring Elder at the Washington Hilton, telling the audience that he, too, was waiting in anticipation for the next Masters. "Next April when Lee is a participant, I am going to be watching on that television set, pulling for Lee to show them that the guy that makes it one year can also win the tournament," Ford said. "I don't think many people will remember 1975 as the year that Jerry Ford was President, but they will remember that 1975 was the year that Lee Elder won the Masters."[164]

While the integration of the Masters promised to be a landmark moment in American sports, the attention lavished on Elder angered those who felt he was taking the place of more deserving players, especially Charlie Sifford. When supporters declared that Elder was "the Jackie Robinson of Golf," Sifford rejected the notion. "Elder deserves to be rewarded for what he has done," he said. "But no black golfers like it."[165] Soon the two were rumored to be feuding, and Elder went public with accusations that fellow black players were jealous he would be the first to play at Augusta National. "I've sensed resentment from fellow Blacks ever since I came on tour," he told *Jet*. "And if you think that all of them were happy for me when I qualified for the Masters, you got to be kidding. There is so much hatred and resentment among the Black golfers on the PGA tour that it's a shame. If another brother had been the first to make the Masters, hey, I would have been among the first to congratulate him and push him on."[166] The two subsequently tried to make amends at an event honoring Elder in Chicago, but the tension remained. "The people we are fighting are Jack Nicklaus and Arnold Palmer," Sifford joked. But Elder again insisted there was animosity among the tour's seven African Americans: "I'm not naming any names, but I've heard that some of them are down on me because I qualified.... But can I help it if I achieve something that I worked so hard for, for so many years?"[167]

Three months before Elder appeared in the 1975 Masters, fifty-two-year-old Sifford announced his retirement from playing regularly on the PGA tour. "The tour just isn't fun anymore," he said.[168] Always a bit uncomfortable with his relationship to black fans and other black golfers, Sifford insisted the decision had nothing to do with Elder or the integration of the Masters, which was likely true. Still, the timing was significant. He went on to play successfully on the Senior PGA Tour, even winning the 1975 Senior PGA Championship, but still a Masters invitation never came. "I really don't think [Cliff] Roberts likes me," he told the press.[169] The snubbing would be the biggest disappointment in Sifford's remarkable career. Despite all his accomplishments, golf's most important black player would never participate in its most important tournament. Refusing to even visit the course, Sifford never stepped foot on Augusta National.

Meanwhile, Elder was the center of attention when he arrived for the Masters in April 1975. A crush of reporters covered his every move, including a few black sportswriters and photographers who managed to get in. The *Chicago Defender* complained that Augusta National "had all but openly barred the black press from covering the event."[170] Maggie Hathaway, denied a press pass to cover the tournament for the *Los Angeles Sentinel*, finally obtained credentials through a Los Angeles radio station. Ninety-nine percent of the estimated 40,000 spectators were white; however, a few black fans were on hand. They included football star Jim Brown, who traveled with Hathaway to Augusta and only got past the gate after comedian Jackie Gleason stepped in to help and Brown gave an autographed photo to the caddiemaster. They arrived just in time to see

Lee Elder arrives at Augusta National for the 1975 Masters (Associated Press).

Elder on the first tee, and Hathaway fainted as she watched him hit his opening drive: "I don't know whether it was exhaustion or excitement."[171] She awoke inside the course medical facility next to where Gary Player was receiving treatment, and the two met for the first time.

Unlike other tournaments, the Masters required that players be assigned one of Augusta National's black caddies and not bring their own. Among the few African Americans on site, the caddies were openly appreciative of the moment, especially Elder's caddie, thirty-six-year-old Henry Brown. Brown had asked four years earlier to be paired with Elder should the golfer ever be invited to the event. Having faced months of scrutiny and admitting that the previous year's attention had negatively affected his game, Elder arrived with his wife looking tired. "I'll be glad when it's all over," she said. They rented two houses for the week in an effort to fool the press but also because Elder had received threats in the months before. He was also supported by the nearby black Paine College, the same institution whose students and faculty had protested Eisenhower's visit to Augusta National fifteen years earlier. When a local restaurant refused to serve Elder, Paine's president offered to have the college prepare his meals for the week.[172]

After shooting a respectable 74-78, missing the cut by four strokes, Elder seemed happy to have the experience behind him. He opened up with reporters in the parking lot, indicating he was relieved to have made it through the previous months. He was hopeful that he would return to Augusta soon with better play, and he did. He went on to compete in three more Masters from 1977 to 1979, making the cut each time and finishing in the top twenty in 1977 and 1979. He also won three more PGA Tour events (the 1976 Houston Open, the 1978 Greater Milwaukee Open, and the 1978 Westchester Classic), in 1979 became the first African American to play in the Ryder Cup, and continued to receive accolades from the black community. In 1977 a star-studded gala in his honor was held in Los Angeles, featuring Mayor Tom Bradley and comedian Redd Foxx.[173]

Meanwhile, on October 6, 1978, as Elder finished the most successful season in his career, viewers of the daytime talk series *The Mike Douglas Show* were introduced to yet another promising black golfer. Two-year-old Eldrick Tont Woods, called "Tiger," joined his father, Earl, Bob Hope, and actor Jimmy Stewart on stage. At first the audience laughed as the toddler shied away. But then little Tiger swung a driver as long as him and made perfect contact, drawing a gasp from Hope and cheers from the audience. Next came a putting showcase: "You got any money?" Hope jokingly asked the kid, offering a nickel if he made a three-foot putt. Tiger picked up the ball, moved it within an inch of the hole, then knocked it in. The crowd roared.

6

THAI PEOPLE DON'T GET HATE MAIL
Race and Golf in the Age of Tiger Woods

MAY 1997—LECANTO, FLORIDA

Charlie Sifford and Lee Elder watch Tiger Woods hit practice shots. The three men then stroll along a golf course, talking among themselves.

"Thank you, Mr. Sifford," comes the voice of Woods. "Thank you, Mr. Elder. I won't forget. You were the first. I refuse to be the last."

They walk, slow-motion, down a "dreamy fairway" as Woods continues: "You are the man, Mr. Sifford. You are the man, Mr. Elder. I won't forget. There's a jacket in Augusta with my name on it. There's a jacket in Augusta with your soul in it."

The commercial, the third television spot in a massive advertising campaign launched by Nike, Inc., after it signed an endorsement deal with Woods, would debut the following month during the 1997 U.S. Open. The same words appeared in print ads as well, including black publications like *Ebony* and *Black Enterprise*.

Tiger Woods, soon to be the richest athlete in history and one of the most recognizable men on the planet, was a savvy, confident professional who embraced his immense talent and understood the significance of his story to the historical black civil rights movement. But he was also a twenty-one-year-old proud of his unique, multiracial family and insistent that no one but himself had a right to claim his racial identity.

Money (an estimated $40 million, to start) certainly helped solidify the message. But no amount could completely erase such a public contradiction: Tiger Woods called himself "Cablinasian"; Nike called him "Black."[1]

Almost 50 million people saw Tiger Woods win the Masters in 1997, by far the most to ever watch a golf tournament.[2] Yet what viewers first embraced as a simple, compelling story has since grown increasingly hard to understand. The 1997 Masters—a triumphant, even unifying event in its day—with time has become a complicated moment in American history.

The uncertainty was always lying beneath the surface. By the time twenty-one-year-old Woods teed it up that weekend, won by twelve shots, and memorably embraced his father on the eighteenth green, at least thirty African Americans had already participated in thousands of PGA tour events in the previous forty-five years. Six had combined to win twenty-six times on tour (including Woods himself, who already had three victories under his belt). Four had already competed in the Masters a combined twenty-two times since Lee Elder's debut in 1975, finishing as high as eleventh place in the tournament (again including Woods, who was making his third appearance). Augusta National had already integrated its membership as well, inviting the first African American to join the club seven years before. In short, 50 million people knew they were watching something special in April 1997, and somehow historic because of Woods's race, yet despite the overwhelming media coverage there never was a consensus on why.

For some the 1997 Masters was the culmination of what came before, the pinnacle of a decades-long battle to provide African Americans full access to the nation's most privileged game, a symbol, of course, for the modern civil rights movement. Yet for others the event was a celebration of the future, a watershed for what promised to follow: a flood of black golfers who would change the game. Not so much a culmination of the civil rights movement, it was instead a multiracial victory that questioned the traditional black/white binaries of the past, one of the first "postracial" moments in popular culture. The moment likely belongs somewhere between these two narratives, an ill fit for either. When they watched Woods, most of those 50 million spectators channeled figures like Jackie Robinson, and in doing so they pulled the 1997 Masters back to 1947, further than it ever belonged. But ensuing years have witnessed an intriguing shift: Woods, and the popular discussion of race he invoked, as a precursor to figures like Barack Obama, pushing the 1997 Masters forward, to 2017 and beyond.

Woods was unique to African American golf from the start. He had no experience with the two institutions that were key to the black professionals that came before him: caddying and the UGA. A child prodigy, he won his first amateur event—the Junior World Golf Championships (for boys ten and under)—at age eight and went on to win twenty more amateur tournaments, including three straight U.S. Amateurs from 1994 to 1996 and the 1996 NCAA National Championship while playing for Stanford University, before he turned professional at age twenty. In 1989, thirteen-year-old Woods participated in a pro-am with twenty PGA professionals and shot a score good enough to beat eight of them. By the time he was twenty-nine, the same age when Bill Spiller first picked up a club, Tiger Woods had already won forty-six PGA Tour events and been ranked the world's number one golfer for over seven years. Although his family was not particularly wealthy, Woods had a thoroughly middle-class, California upbringing far removed from that of the generations of black pros who were introduced to golf as caddies in the South. The story of his early development in golf was thoroughly white, at least by the standards of the 1970s. "The white kids in the suburbs have nothing to do *but* take lessons," lamented Howard University golf coach John Organ in 1973, two years before Woods was born. "Their parents give the kids lessons because they know, in this game, you've got to learn the basics early."[3]

While Woods launched his career as a member of Stanford University's golf team, historically black colleges and universities (HBCUs) struggled to keep their teams black. Eddie Payton, older brother of NFL star Walter Payton, took over the men's and women's golf programs at Jackson State University in 1985. Realizing that no HBCU had ever been invited to the NCAA golf championships, he helped establish the Minority Collegiate Golf Championship in 1987, an annual tournament that the PGA took over in 2006. Under Payton, the men's team at Jackson State became the first HBCU squad to compete in the NCAA Men's National Golf Championships in 1995, the same year that Woods, a freshman at Stanford, was named Pac-10 Player of the Year and an NCAA First Team All-American. In 1999 the women's team at Jackson State became the first to compete in the NCAA Women's National Golf Championships. But while millions soon debated whether Woods was "a black golfer," far fewer noticed that Jackson State, like other HBCUs, no longer fielded "a black team." Four of the five starters on Payton's historic 1995 squad were white. "Some people question why we don't have more black kids," he said soon after. "If we did, we wouldn't be competitive."[4] At the 2012 PGA Minority Collegiate Golf Championship, neither the winning men's team (the University of Texas Pan-American) nor the women's (Bethune-Cookman University)

Tiger Woods, 15, and his father, Earl Woods, after Tiger won the 1991 U.S. Junior Amateur Championship at Bay Hill Club in Orlando, Florida (USGA).

had a single African American on its roster. Bethune-Cookman's team featured white students from Austria, Denmark, and Great Britain. Renee Powell once pressed a sponsor to donate golf equipment to three HBCUs in order to help colleges "where minority kids were struggling," only to be surprised when she discovered that all of the golfers were white. Some celebrated this shift as a positive sign of integration. "Payton's teams are rainbow coalitions of whites and blacks, Americans and foreigners," *Sports Illustrated* proclaimed in 2009.[5] And many players agreed with that sentiment. "All the brothers get accepted to the big white schools to play basketball," one of three white Australians on the Jackson State team said in 1996. "Here all the white guys get accepted to play golf. What's the difference?"[6]

Nevertheless, the declining number of African Americans on black college golf teams seemed to challenge the notion that the 1997 Masters was a turning point for race and golf. Woods himself, matriculating in predominately white schools, communities, and golf programs, avoided such debates over the future of historically black institutions such as HBCUs and their golf teams. ("Still got the letter I sent him," Payton recalled of his efforts to recruit Woods. "Never really had a chance, but it was worth trying.")[7] Moreover, by the time Woods was born in 1975, the most important historically black institution for professional golfers, the UGA, was nearly finished as a pro golf tour, though it continued to organize events into the 1980s. The black players on the PGA Tour during Woods's early life were the last to come through the black tour, but there were still a number of them. They included winning professionals from the 1960s like Pete Brown, who played on the PGA and Senior PGA circuits into the 1990s, and Lee Elder, who as late as 2004 was still playing senior events. A handful of others, including brothers Jim and Chuck Thorpe, parlayed UGA success in the 1970s into PGA appearances. Jim won 27 of 33 UGA tournaments in 1970, and Chuck took 25 of the 32 UGA events he entered from 1971 to 1973. Chuck played sporadically on the PGA and Senior PGA tours until the late 1990s, while Jim enjoyed a far more successful PGA career. "The first time I played with Arnold Palmer, I literally could not get my ball to stay on the tee," he recalled. "And knowing he was watching me just made it worse."[8] Nevertheless, Jim won three times on the PGA Tour in the mid-1980s, earned $2 million, finished tied for fourth at the 1984 U.S. Open, and competed in the Masters six times, finishing in the top twenty in 1985. He subsequently had even more success on the Senior PGA Tour from 2000 to 2007, winning thirteen events and earning an additional $14 million; by 2007 he ranked seventh in career earnings on the senior circuit.

Bobby Stroble and Charlie Owens were the last two players to parlay UGA success into PGA careers. In 1975 Stroble finished third at one of the last UGA Nationals, subsequently competing in 19 events on the PGA Tour and 133 more on the Senior Tour. Owens won 23 of the 41 UGA events he entered, including the 1974 and 1975 UGA Nationals, and went on to play more often in PGA events; in 1986 he even won 2 tournaments on the Senior Tour. His unorthodox play also drew considerable attention. Like Howard Wheeler decades before, Owens played with a cross-handed grip, and during the 1980s he was the first PGA Tour pro to use a long "belly" putter in competition, a controversial club that became common in the 1990s and 2000s.[9]

Thus, rather than Woods's victory at the 1997 Masters, perhaps his birth in 1975 was the real watershed moment in the history of black professional golf. The decline of the UGA in the early 1970s corresponded with the height of black participation on the PGA circuit, with as many as eleven African Americans participating at once. George Johnson played 177 events from 1968 to 1985. Jim Dent, the former Augusta caddie, played 450 from 1970 to 1989 and then made $9 million on the senior tour over the next twenty years, winning 12 times. Like Jim Thorpe, Dent was placed among the top ten all-time earners among seniors. The two men were even mistaken for each other at senior events. Thorpe was paired with Tom Watson and tied for the lead heading into the final round of the 2001 Senior PGA Championship when the starter stepped to the microphone and introduced him to the gallery as Jim Dent. "Why the hell couldn't he say Tiger Woods?" Thorpe blurted back.[10] (The joke, of course, was clear, but the irony lost on the gallery that day was that Woods would never be mistaken for a fellow black competitor because there would *be* no other black competitors.) Another African American pro, Walter Morgan, played the Senior Tour from 1991 to 2004 and won three times. Led by Morgan, Thorpe, and Dent, there was thus a period in the 1990s and early 2000s when a group of black players was a major force on the senior circuit, another important fact the Woods narrative overshadowed.

Woods was certainly a child prodigy who drew special attention because of his race as well as his skills. By age five he had appeared on more television shows, including *That's Incredible*, CBS Sports, and *The Today Show*. In 1982 he received a feature spread in *Ebony*. "This is one of the first Black golfers with natural skills whose parents have the means to get pro instructions that even exceed those afforded Jack Nicklaus in his formative years," Earl Woods proudly said of his son. "We are willing to pay the price." Representatives from CBS Sports told him they were committed to covering his son's development "all the way to the 18th green at Augusta Country Club." Tiger was six.[11] Soon other African American publications, from *Jet* to *Black Enterprise*, were following the child's development.[12] Thus the story line was formed by the time Woods turned ten in 1985: he could be an African American golfer on the PGA Tour more special than the dozens who came before him. Why? Because he had the potential to one day lead the tour and be the best player in the world.

Never mind that ten-year-old Tiger could already turn on the television and watch a black man dominate the PGA Tour. Although distinguishing the top player was a controversial science, Calvin Peete was certainly among the contenders. He won eleven times from 1982 to 1986, more than anyone else. The unofficial McCormack Golf Rankings listed him among the top ten golfers in the world in 1984, as did the inaugural Official World Golf Ranking when it debuted in April 1986. Moreover, only five of the ten on that first Official World list had been playing full time on the U.S. tour. (The top three, Bernhard Langer, Seve Ballesteros, and Sandy Lyle, all played full time in Europe.) By the end of that season, Peete had tallied twelve career PGA Tour victories and earned $2 million, placing him seventeenth on the all-time earnings list. He also beat Jack Nicklaus for the 1984 Vardon Trophy, awarded to the player with the lowest stroke average for the season. "I've passed that stage of wanting to establish myself as an excellent black player. I want to be recognized as a professional golfer," he said after winning the prestigious Players Championship in 1985.[13] Peete's status as the hottest player in golf was hampered only by his inability to win one of the four major tournaments (which limited his world-ranking points as well). But he came close, finishing eleventh at the 1986 Masters, fourth at the 1983 U.S. Open, and third at the 1982 PGA Championship. Remarkably, not once did he play in the British Open, perhaps the only top-ten player in modern golf never to play one of the major championships in his career. Only five other people had secured more PGA victories since World War II without winning a major.

Not only was Calvin Peete the best African American on the PGA Tour before the arrival of Tiger Woods, but he also had a compelling life story that the *Los Angeles Times* dubbed "one of the most remarkable in all of sports."[14] A native of Detroit, Peete was born in 1943 and grew up in crushing poverty, one of his father's nineteen children. He dropped out of school in the eighth grade. He fell out of a tree when he was twelve and severely fractured his left elbow; for the rest of his life he was unable to straighten the mangled arm. From working on farms and orchards in Florida to selling clothes and jewelry out of his station wagon, Peete never saw a golf club until 1966, when he was twenty-three. That summer friends invited him to a fish fry but ended up taking him to the links instead. Two years later he joined the millions of television viewers who watched Lee Elder and Jack Nicklaus duel down the stretch at the 1968 American Golf Classic. "That really inspired me," he said. "A black man going against the greatest player of all time."[15] Seven years later he made it through on his third trip to PGA qualifying school, earning a tour card in 1975 at age thirty-two; he still had never even heard of the Masters, but five years later in 1980 he became the second African American to play the tournament. Unlike Lee Elder before him and Tiger Woods later, Peete refused to play nice when it came to "honoring" Augusta National or its tournament. After shooting a deplorable 87 during the third round of the 1983 Masters, he angrily insisted the event meant no more to him than any other. "Tradition, they can keep it," he fired back at a reporter. "Asking a black man about the tradition of the Masters is like asking if he enjoyed his forefathers being slaves."[16]

Peete's incredible story paralleled that of the older generation of black professionals who struggled to overcome long odds. His late arrival to golf rivaled that of Bill Spiller, and his background was the antithesis of Woods's. "His story is Dickensian in its down-and-out beginnings and American in its particular obstacles and eventual rewards," proclaimed the *New York Times* after his passing in April 2015 (which was overshadowed by the response to Charlie Sifford's death two months earlier).[17] Because a high school diploma was required to join the American Ryder Cup squad, Peete had to pass an equivalency test in 1982 in order to participate, going on to be a member of the 1983 and 1985 teams. Yet nothing symbolized the humble beginnings and extreme obstacles more than his own withered arm. A fundamental tenet for right-handed golfers is that one's left arm must remain straight, yet with a permanently bent left elbow and without golf lessons, Peete fashioned a swing that was deadly accurate. For ten consecutive seasons (1981–90) he led the PGA Tour in driving accuracy, a feat no other player has come close to matching. He remains the straightest driver in tour history. Ironically, just as black journalists were beginning to tout the promise of young Tiger Woods, they were also heralding Peete's reign atop the tour. Publications like *Jet* and *Ebony* celebrated the man who went "from migrant worker to the Masters," and various black clubs and organizations honored his achievements.[18]

Juxtaposed with Woods's, Calvin Peete's success counters the popular understanding of race and golf that appeared after 1997. An alternative counternarrative begins to emerge: It is Peete's career, and not that of Woods, that marks the pinnacle of black golf in American history. The

Calvin Peete competes in the 1983 Bob Hope Desert Classic in Palm Springs, California (AP Photo/Lennox McLendon).

peak of black engagement with the game occurred during the 1970s and early 1980s, represented by the number of black professionals playing PGA events, the brief period of rapid economic growth in the black community, and the social optimism surrounding the game immediately after integration in the 1960s. And a moment like the Sunday in July 1982 when *Ebony* celebrated Jim Thorpe and Calvin Peete for winning two tournaments on the same day (Thorpe the Canadian PGA Championship, Peete the PGA's Greater Milwaukee Open) reflects the broader historical context of black golf better than Woods's victory at the 1997 Masters. "In recent years, changing lifestyles have seen the emergence of Blacks on the golf course," *Black Sports* magazine announced two years before Woods was born, in a 1973 golf fashion spread that proudly insisted that "the Black man's usual panache can prevail on the greens as prominently as it does elsewhere." A broader context of black optimism in the early 1970s fueled the idea that African Americans were transforming golf with "that unmistakable spirit indicative of the Black peacock."[19] The head of the fledgling UGA, Porter Pernell, agreed with such a sentiment: "The opportunities for young golfers are unlimited," he said. "They have more recognition, and it's much easier for them to play than it was five or ten years ago."[20]

In some ways, then, the crisis of race and golf in the 1990s was not the long-term, historical lack of black access to the game but, rather, a more immediate concern: a new generation of African Americans threatened with losing the level of access their community had already fought for and obtained by the 1970s. This is the key context to understanding the rise of Woods. When Woods was born in 1975, nearly a dozen black players could tee it up on the PGA Tour. By the early 1980s that number was halved, and by 1997 there was one. Many black fans and players, including Calvin Peete, felt as if they were slowly watching the game slip away. "Black golfers are an endangered species on the PGA Tour," Peete told *Sports Illustrated* in 1990 as he neared retirement. "In three to five years we will probably be extinct."[21] The emergence of Woods would make his statement both ironic and accurate.

Many African Americans saw this decline at the elite level as a reflection of a broader loss of access to golf, itself a symptom of growing racial discrepancies in wealth, lagging wages, and the deterioration of predominately black neighborhoods. There are no definitive studies that quantify whether the number of black golfers kept pace in the 1970s and 1980s, and the statistics that do exist are complicated by the fact that the popularity of golf in general grew rapidly during the period. More likely the total number of African American players continued to grow while their overall ratio declined. In 1990 *Sports Illustrated* cited one study arguing that the number of black golfers had tripled during the 1980s to nearly 500,000. The National Golf Foundation (NGF) reported 649,000 "African-Americans actively playing golf in 1990," up from 360,000 four years earlier.[22] Yet despite those impressive gains, black golfers were still losing ground; the same study noted they constituted just 2.3 percent of players in the United States.

Whether or not the actual numbers supported their assertion, many black fans perceived the dwindling number of African Americans on the PGA Tour as reflecting broader trends. Publications like *Ebony* affirmed the connection, both highlighting the decline of black professionals and encouraging more readers to play the game. "Black kids now live three blocks away from golf courses," Peete told the magazine in 1982. "The exposure is there."[23] Not only did some see the decline of golf as indicative of troubling changes in black neighborhoods; they also lamented the loss of a way to combat rising crime, urban decline, and racial unrest. The investigations launched by President Lyndon Johnson's Kerner Commission, charged with uncovering the causes of the 1960s race riots, included interviewing city recreation departments and probing the cost of municipal golf (in Cincinnati, Ohio, the head of the department insisted that "prices were very reasonable" and "many of the young Negroes if they were interested in golf could afford to play with no problem").[24]

It is no coincidence that the height of black presence in PGA events during the mid-1970s coincided with the emergence of junior golf programs aimed at black youth in the inner cities. Many pros, such as Lee Elder and Charlie Sifford, noted that golf lacked programs for serious black players and was falling behind other sports at high school and university levels. As evident in the rise of Arthur Ashe, even tennis had done a better job establishing organizations to reach black youth, particularly in the South. Elder organized his own youth program and began to talk openly about making golf affordable to African Americans. "Many black kids look up to Elder as an example," reported Tony Fusaro, the golf coach at historically black South Carolina State College in 1973.[25] Later Calvin Peete established a scholarship fund specifically for potential black college golfers, while Earl Jackson's IGT established a junior flight to promote youth play on its golf excursions. Another advocate for junior golf, Lenwood Robinson Jr., emerged in Chicago; from 1975 to 1979 his Chicago Urban Junior Golf Association attracted hundreds of black youth and forged a landmark alliance with the city's main golf body, the Chicago District Golf Association.[26] A larger organization soon formed in Phoenix, Arizona. Founded by Bill Dickey, a black real estate executive, the National Minority Junior Golf Scholarship Association went on to provide more than 1,000 scholarships (and $3 million) to minority golfers over the next thirty years. Efforts like these, which percolated in the mid-1970s and early 1980s, marked what *Golfweek* dubbed a "grass-roots minority golf movement."[27] Moreover, such junior programs tended to be more inclusive than caddying because they encouraged the participation of black girls as well as boys.

As courses that traditionally catered to urban black neighborhoods began to struggle with financial difficulties and rising crime rates, golf advocates who came to their defense found themselves engaged in much broader social commentary. "It seems there is no neutral territory that is safe from youthful killers in this city," Maggie Hathaway lamented in 1974 after two teenagers in south Los Angeles robbed a foursome on Western Avenue Golf Course, shooting and killing one.[28] In Cleveland, one *Call and Post* reader urged the black community to use golf in the fight against urban decline: "It is rare to see a youngster who has taken up the game of golf who has a criminal record. He is generally too involved in the progress of his game that he doesn't have time to think of criminal activity. . . . [Young blacks] may never become professional golfers, but it will make better citizens out of them. They can find out what kind of human beings they really are, how they can adjust to pressure, and how they can concentrate on the game of golf regardless of what their concerns and goals in life may be."[29]

Not everyone was on board with public golf as a useful response to urban decline and deindustrialization, especially regarding money. By the 1970s Atlanta's black leaders were fighting over whether to repair Bobby Jones Municipal, the historic course involved in *Holmes v. Atlanta*. Maynard Jackson, the first black mayor of a major southern city, insisted there were better ways to spend dwindling development funds in order to serve Atlanta's "poorer neighborhoods." Yet his biracial city council objected, passing an ordinance that forced him to fix the course.[30] While most golfers, black or white, saw some positives in bringing more black players to the game (especially in distressed neighborhoods), there were plenty of cynics. "The sentiment commonly held in the golf universe is that getting more inner-city minorities can only be a good thing," wrote Scott Stossel in the *New Republic* after Woods emerged. "One could argue that there is something implicitly racist about all this. What no one is openly stating is the belief that, if only this effete 'white' game can be imported to the inner-city, then black kids can be 'civilized' in a socially appropriate way.... In this view, the imposition of golf represents a kind of cultural imperialism."[31]

For generations, black caddies symbolized this critique of golf as white imperialism. By the 1970s, however, those who wanted to recruit more African Americans to the game cited one major factor inhibiting their efforts: the decline of caddying. "I learned by caddying, but now we ride in golf carts," said Howard University golf coach John Organ in 1973, as black colleges strived to recruit more talented players.[32] The critique grew stronger in the ensuing decades. At a 1993 SCLC event, Calvin Peete warned that removing caddies from the game was severely limiting opportunities for young African Americans to play. Jim Thorpe, Tiger Woods, and numerous other professionals eventually agreed: "It really bothers me to know there were more black players on the tour in the late 1960s and early '70s than there are today," Thorpe said in 2007, citing "the loss of caddie programs" as one factor.[33] For various reasons, including the advent of the golf cart and a desire to lower costs, caddying declined in popularity at courses around the country. On the PGA Tour players began to employ their own full-time caddies who traveled with them, rather than relying on local caddies at each course. The Masters was one of the last tournaments that prohibited players from bringing their own caddies; the requirement that participants use one of Augusta National's baggers was dropped in 1983. For years fans had recognized and celebrated the unique knowledge Augusta's caddies brought to the tournament and its players. When Art Wall Jr. dramatically came from behind to win the 1959 Masters over Arnold Palmer, he publicly attributed the victory to his black caddie for the week, Henry Hammond.[34] If the embrace of Earl and Tiger Woods on the eighteenth green nearly forty years later was meant to invoke a racial transformation at Augusta, most viewers failed to notice a more dramatic shift. When Tiger was a child, fans still saw only black caddies at the Masters; now nearly every bagger was white (including Tiger's). Sportswriters in 1997 fawned over the fact that "black Augusta caddies" and "African-American employees" watched intently as Woods conquered the tournament (just as they had celebrated Lee Elder when he integrated the event), but they, too, did not recognize the significance: Augusta's black caddies were now standing and watching, not caddying.[35]

Even more insulting was the fact that as caddying declined in popularity after the 1970s, the job itself became more respected, lucrative, and white. "Caddying, once perceived as a menial job, has become a vocation for the college-educated and failed professionals who are lured by the astronomical purses driven by Woods's immense popularity," announced the *New York Times* in 2012.[36] A few African Americans bridged this transformation and benefited from the profession's newfound respect and money. As late as 1976 almost thirty PGA pros still employed black caddies. Carl Jackson began bagging at Augusta National in 1958 at age eleven, working his first Masters three years later when he was fourteen. Jackson went on to caddie at the tournament a record fifty-four times until 2014, because 1984 and 1995 winner Ben Crenshaw continued to employ him rather than bring in an outsider. Crenshaw also worked with another black caddie, Emile Smith, who received residual payments from appearing in Buick commercials with his boss in the late 1970s and early 1980s. Smith even rejected an offer to be in commercials for Canon, Inc. "They only wanted to offer up-front money," he told *Sports Illustrated* in 1981.[37] When Raymond Floyd won the 1982 PGA Championship, the local press playfully noted that his longtime black caddie, Dolphus Hull, earned more money that week than famous golfers like Tom Watson or Jack Nicklaus did for making the cut. Hull insisted he deserved the share of Floyd's winnings: "He's the one who's swingin',' not me, but I'd say I'm 15 percent of his game."[38] Yet few black caddies were left by the time the money (and fame) increased dramatically in the 1990s.

For African Americans it was a bittersweet development; "Where did the black caddies go?" Maggie Hathaway lamented.[39] On one hand, the dwindling number signaled expanded opportunities for young African Americans and the end of a demeaning, symbolic profession that helped keep generations of black people in their place. Carl Jackson, the legendary Augusta caddie, saw some of these positives. By 2012 he was caddiemaster at a club in Arkansas (where all but one of the caddies was white) and insisting that young black golfers could now aim higher. "It would be my suggestion to try to be the player," he said. Yet Jackson and other African Americans still noted what the *New York Times* called a "bitter irony"—that "when the prize money was modest, they were the standard; when the money became huge, they became disposable."[40] Many in the black press agreed. "As a result of bypassing the opportunity to caddy, aspiring African American golfers are missing out on the opportunity of a lifetime," warned *Black Enterprise*, "to network and improve their game as golfers by watching and assisting other, more established, players."[41]

Even for those uninterested in playing, caddying had been a niche industry that helped some African Americans uplift their families. "Rabbit" Dyer grew up in a poor household in the Hollygrove neighborhood of New Orleans and started bagging at Metairie Country Club when he was nine. Later he caddied for Gary Player and managed to buy a house for his mother and put his son through Princeton University. The decline of the black caddie, while indicative of racial integration and social advancement, nevertheless allowed whites to turn a symbol of racial servitude into a more lucrative opportunity. Nothing symbolized the finality of this appropriation—and provided yet another image more accurate than the 1997 Masters—than the moment in 2015 when Woods's former white caddie, who made an estimated $11 million assisting him from 1999 to 2011, complained that the job made him feel like a "slave."[42]

Also lost in the hysteria surrounding the 1997 Masters was the fact that Augusta National and the PGA had already been forced to make substantial changes in response to recent protests against racial discrimination. It began seven years earlier, shortly before the 1990 PGA Championship at Shoal Creek Club in Birmingham, Alabama. Designed by Jack Nicklaus and opened in 1977, Shoal Creek was the state's top course and a private club with no African American or female members. The site had hosted numerous important tournaments, including the 1984 PGA Championship and the 1986 U.S. Amateur. But this time controversy erupted a month before the event after the club's founder, Hall Thompson, told a Birmingham newspaper that Shoal Creek would "not be pressured" into inviting black members. "I think we've said that we don't discriminate in every other area except the blacks," he clarified.[43] Black sportswriters and golf fans immediately responded with calls for a boycott. "Hall Thompson has told us what we already know," proclaimed the *Cleveland Call and Post*. "That at the core of exclusion in American society there remains racism. . . . The nation's country and private clubs are and have been the nation's strongest bastion of white power and exclusivity."[44] Both the SCLC's national head, Joseph Lowery, and its Birmingham chapter president, Rev. Abraham Woods, warned that Shoal Creek would be targeted by protests during the tournament, as did the NAACP. A majority of black golfers around the country voiced their approval as well; in New Jersey, the vice president of the historically black Freeway Golf Course, James Hughes, reported that its patrons supported the response. Some black fans also called on Jim Thorpe, the only African American scheduled to participate in the event, to boycott as well. (Thorpe responded that he "had a family to feed.") Calvin Peete, who had played his last major championship two years earlier, did not challenge Thorpe's decision but was more supportive of the protest, insisting that Thompson's statements "were directed not just at people in Birmingham, but all blacks in general."[45]

Yet the Shoal Creek controversy became an unusual moment in the history of racial integration and popular sports: the PGA would be forced to adopt a policy prohibiting tournaments at all-white private clubs because of action from groups like the SCLC and the NAACP, angry corporate sponsors, and black golf fans—but not actual black PGA players, who were virtually gone by 1990. In their place were a few white golfers whose supportive voices would have to serve as ironic substitutes. Most notable was South African Gary Player: "If I was in those peoples' shoes I would also demonstrate."[46]

Birmingham's SCLC leader, Rev. Abraham Woods, was spokesman for the protest. Woods and Mayor Richard Arrington (the first African American to hold that position) met with Thompson in the tense weeks leading up to the tournament, as a series of sponsors—IBM, Toyota, Honda, and Anheuser-Busch—announced they were pulling $2 million in television ads from coverage of the event on ABC and ESPN, an implicit acknowledgment that by the 1990s companies sponsoring the PGA Tour derived 25 percent of their revenue from African Americans. Finally, just days before the event, Thompson and Shoal Creek capitulated and struck a deal with the SCLC: the club gave membership to its first African American, Louis Willie Jr., and in exchange Woods called off the demonstration. The 1990 PGA Championship went on as planned with no disruption. (It turned out to be a generally unexciting tournament; little-known Australian golfer Wayne Grady was the winner, and Jim Thorpe missed the cut.) Notably, the PGA would never return to Shoal Creek, although four years later in 1994 Tiger Woods participated with the Stanford University golf team in an intercollegiate tournament at the club. A freshman at the time, Woods and his teammates discussed the controversy (some jokingly called the club "Soul Creek") as demonstrators once again gathered outside the gates, the first time Woods played an event targeted by racial protest. After Woods shot 67 to win the tournament, Hall Thompson greeted him as he walked off the eighteenth green: "You're a great player, I'm proud of you. You're superb."[47]

For some observers the Shoal Creek protest was a minor affair that exposed racial tokenism and exemplified how the historic civil rights organizations were floundering by the 1990s. As historian Glenn Eskew notes, all of the Birmingham leaders, including Abraham Woods, involved in the controversy had participated in negotiations when the SCLC's Birmingham movement caught the world's attention in 1963. The man Shoal Creek invited for membership, Louis Willie Jr., had no interest in golf and worked closely with businessman A. G. Gaston, the city's noted black moderate who initially rejected King and the SCLC in 1963. For Eskew, the image of Abraham Woods and SCLC demonstrators now threatening to lie down in front of golf carts to achieve tokenism at Shoal Creek revealed "the absurdity of the entire affair," how movement activists had turned to "desegregation of country clubs by multinational corporate pressure," and the ultimate "legacy of bourgeois reform."[48] Indeed, all of Birmingham's private country clubs had an estimated 6,000 white members and 2 black members in 1990; now, with the integration of Shoal Creek, there were 3 blacks. By 2005 one prominent black lawyer in town estimated the club still had only a handful of African Americans (former U.S. secretary of state Condoleezza Rice became a member in 2009). "This hardly sounds like the stuff of social revolution," *Sports Illustrated* announced weeks after the controversy. "And it certainly is small change when compared with the uprisings that raged in the streets of Birmingham during the spring and summer of 1963. . . . The summer of 1990 in Birmingham has seen another kind of revolution altogether, one that has been utterly peaceful, yet powerful enough to threaten one of this country's last bastions of white supremacy—the private golf club."[49]

The protest was indeed a "powerful" moment in the game's history, one that rippled through the world of golf and recalled the significant fight to integrate Birmingham's municipal links in the 1960s and *Shuttlesworth v. Gaylord*. Not only did the PGA Tour never return to Shoal Creek; it also announced that none of its tournaments would ever again take place at a private club unless it was racially integrated. Some sites, like Baltusrol Golf Club in New Jersey, responded immediately by integrating their memberships, while others balked. In Monterey, California, the 250-member Cypress Point Club refused to invite an African American and was promptly dropped from helping host the AT&T Pebble Beach National Pro-Am (formerly the Bing Crosby National Pro-Am). Also dropped were Butler National Golf Club outside Chicago, which had hosted the Western Open for seventeen years, and Old Warson Country Club in St. Louis, scheduled to host a senior tour event the following year. (Old Warson admitted its first black member soon after in 1991, by 2012 Butler National had also integrated, and Condoleezza Rice has been a member of Cypress Point since at least 2013.) Overall, at least eleven country clubs initially chose to remain exclusively white and forgo hosting PGA or USGA events, although some of these, including the Merion and Aronimink Golf Clubs in Pennsylvania, integrated within a few years.[50]

Moreover, the PGA was forced to make such a dramatic gesture at a time when some public schools in the South still refused to confront blatant racism in golf and caved to discrimination at private country clubs. In 1981 the NAACP in Monroe, Louisiana, denounced St. Frederick Catholic High School for agreeing to bench the two black players on its golf team for a match against public schools at all-white Morehouse Country Club. The Louisiana High School Athletic Association refused to intervene, and ten years later state officials again offered little reaction when the school was asked to bench its black golfers for a 1991 match at Caldwell Parish Country Club. This time St. Frederick supported its players and boycotted the event, but to the outrage of its supporters, the two public schools it was scheduled to face went ahead and competed anyway. One was the all-white golf team at nearby Jena High School, where fifteen years later racial tension and violence sparked national protests after six black students (the "Jena Six") were convicted of beating a white classmate.[51] The PGA's decision in Birmingham also helped publicize and embolden the numerous other local battles to integrate America's country clubs that flared in the late 1980s and early 1990s. African Americans filed discrimination complaints and lawsuits targeting sites across the country, including Friendly Hills Country Club (Whittier, Calif.), the Olympic Club (San Francisco), and the Highland Golf and Country Club (Indianapolis).[52]

Most significant for casual golf fans, the Shoal Creek protest also led directly to racial integration at Augusta National. Not only was Hall Thompson Shoal Creek's founder; he was also a member at Augusta, and the controversy in Alabama directly prompted discussion among the membership over whether or not it would join Shoal Creek and invite its first African American member. The debate was reported to be tense, unique to the club: unlike the others, Augusta National had complete control over the Masters and was not beholden to the PGA Tour's new policy banning tour stops at all-white clubs. (Granted, the tour could still have imposed a number of other penalties, like disassociating itself from the Masters or desanctioning the event as a major, but it threatened nothing of the sort.) Nevertheless, two months after the protests—and for the first time in its fifty-seven-year history—Augusta National invited a black member: Ron Townsend, a television executive and 15-handicap "golf nut" from Potomac, Virginia. The *New York Times* dubbed him "the Jackie Robinson of country-club golf."[53]

Thus, lost in the attention surrounding Tiger Woods's victory at the 1997 Masters was the fact that another Woods—Rev. Abraham Woods, head of the SCLC in Birmingham—had played the key role in prompting Augusta National to integrate its membership seven years earlier. The idea of the 1960s Birmingham movement transitioning into a 1990s protest for "bourgeois reform" certainly warranted some cynicism; but no one could discount that golf had played an important role in the original movement, and now the threat of direct, mass action had prompted an immediate and lasting response from the PGA Tour and the USGA. Proclaimed one *New York Times* sportswriter, "1990 will go down as the year in which golf was finally held accountable for the racially exclusionary membership practices of many of its private clubs."[54] Arthur Ashe used even loftier words, calling the success of the Shoal Creek protest "a watershed in the social dynamics of America."[55] Indeed, since 1990 Americans have no longer been able to turn on their televisions and watch U.S. golf tournaments take place at all-white country clubs.

Of course, despite the uncertainty of its meaning and the misleading narratives that surround it, the 1997 Masters remains an indelible moment in the history of race and sports, one that historians will likely reinterpret for generations. And Tiger Woods is a singular athlete in history. His more recent fall from grace—involving a series of injuries, poor play, a high-profile divorce, and tabloid scandals from sex addiction to rumors of performance-enhancing drugs—is, sadly, among the more common elements of his celebrity. Athletes from Jack Johnson and Babe Ruth to Joe Louis and Lance Armstrong have lived such tumultuous public lives and faced similar declines in fan support for over a hundred years. The historical uniqueness of Woods was his ability to seamlessly transition from child prodigy to richest athlete in history. Few children in American life—be it in sports, politics, or society—have ever matched, or even exceeded, the level of expectation that surrounded young Tiger. And no other athlete has ever dominated and changed his or her game the way he did in the late 1990s and early 2000s. "He is the prohibitive favorite for as long as he lives," quipped a fellow competitor, Tom Lehman, after the 1997 Masters.[56]

Woods was heralded by supporters who insisted that his emergence marked the beginning of a sea change in golf. He had unique potential to dominate the game, but more importantly, his significance lay in the fact that a generation of minority players promised to emerge in his wake. Many black fans and sportswriters joined this chorus, which peaked after the 1997 Masters in an optimistic surge that, in hindsight, proved woefully misguided. "Tigermania" on this front meant much more than Woods. "This young man has lit the torch for golf," proclaimed one *Atlanta Daily World* editorial. "One decade from now, we [African Americans] should have at least 10 such players with the developed talent of Tiger Woods to compete in pro golf."[57] Black journalists announced the potential "end of white supremacy" in the game, while many black fans (and some predominately black high schools) reported a dramatic surge in the number of youth interested in playing.[58] "There are already reports of young Blacks taking up golf," noted the *Philadelphia Tribune* days after the 1997 Masters. "The spectators at golf tournaments are quickly transforming from a sea of mainly white faces to an increasing rainbow of colors."[59] The *Los Angeles Sentinel* announced that the victory was an "unparalleled moment" in history: "World Has New Black Superhero," it headlined.[60]

Along with fans and the press, plenty of golf insiders and former players were also caught up in the moment. William Powell wrote that Woods was a "victor for all times" who "transcended" generations: "Tiger has made a quantum jump for the sport of golf and in the process [broke] every barrier in [his] path."[61] Lee Elder hinted that the 1997 Masters made Woods a civil rights figure as significant as any other athlete in history. "It might have more potential than Jackie Robinson breaking into baseball," he said. "No one will ever turn their head again when a Black walks to the first tee."[62] Though Charlie Sifford and Woods had a closer relationship, Sifford was more measured and skeptical, in keeping with his style. He grew frustrated with the hype surrounding the 1997 Masters and ridiculed the comparisons to other integrating figures. Starting in the 1960s Sifford had long rejected those who labeled him the "Jackie Robinson of golf," and not always out of deference. "My job is tougher than Jackie's ever was," he said in 1961. "First off, he had a set salary. I have no sponsor and have to finance my own way. . . . Additionally, Robinson had a team backing him up. I'm playing alone."[63] Thirty-five years later, the flood of attention and questions about Woods, Robinson, and Sifford quickly grew annoying. "I'm hot again 'cause of Tiger Woods," Sifford told one reporter shortly after the debut of his Nike ad with Woods. "Everybody wants to make a big deal about it, 'cause Tiger Woods is involved. But there's nothing in it for me, is there?"⁶⁴ Jim Thorpe, another of the older black PGA pros, was among the few at the time who predicted that Woods would never match Jack Nicklaus's record eighteen major championships (which, as of 2017, he has not). "This isn't anything like Jackie Robinson," he said. "That road's been paved.... Tiger's got it made."⁶⁵ Nevertheless, even the most cynical observers found themselves caught up in Tigermania. "Golf... is beginning to look more like America: diverse, multicultural, and middle class," admitted the liberal *New Republic* in an essay outlining the major socioeconomic and racial barriers that remained in the sport, as well as the tokenism of racial integration at private country clubs. Still the magazine proclaimed that there was "no longer a single, obvious golfer type" now that "Woods has helped make golf cool." More affordable than watching professional hockey, golf was "no longer a rich man's game."⁶⁶

The emergence of Woods indeed corresponded with an increase in the number of African American golfers during the 1990s. Estimates were hard to nail down but pointed to substantial growth. A 1994 report from the NGF indicated that the number of African American players had doubled in the previous ten years and reached nearly 700,000. Four years later the National Minority Golf Foundation claimed the number had grown to 4 million during the six-year period surrounding the rise of Woods. Even if that number is inaccurate, or if participation subsequently dropped after 2000, the proportion of African American players seems to have increased in the twenty years since the 1997 Masters. A 2014 estimate indicated that there were 1.3 million black players in the United States out of 25.7 million total. That would mean a ratio of over 5 percent, less than the proportion of Americans who identified exclusively as black on the 2010 U.S. Census (13 percent) but more than double the NGF's 1990, pre-Tiger estimate that 2.3 percent of U.S. golfers were African American.⁶⁷ Of course, the direct relationship between Woods and levels of black interest in golf, as opposed to broader factors such as economic growth, was never clear. (No one spoke of a "Calvin Peete effect" helping triple black participation during the 1980s, for instance.) But the promises attached to Woods were unprecedented, especially his potential to draw more popular black interest. "With his participation in junior golf clinics, his immense media following, and his stunning ability, he should do more to bring minorities into golf than anyone ever," proclaimed the black *American Legacy*.⁶⁸ In November 1997, seven months after Woods won the 1997 Masters, the World Golf Foundation partnered with the PGA

Tour, the LPGA, the PGA, the USGA, and the Masters to establish the First Tee, a youth golf organization that has worked with more than 10 million young people through in-school and after-school programs. Three years later Joe Louis Barrow Jr. (son of the famed boxer) became its chief executive officer, one of golf's few black executives.[69]

Woods certainly did inspire a surge of interest in golf, including among African Americans, and he overwhelmingly became the face of the game. A 2014 report estimated that the PGA Tour stood to lose $15 billion per year (and suffer a 30 percent drop in television ratings) without his participation, especially at major events like the Masters and even after his popularity dropped after 2009. Yet within a decade of the 1997 Masters, the promises of Tigermania were starting to crumble, and the flood of elite minority players turned out to be more like a trickle. The number of African Americans taking up golf likely doubled in the 1990s (and may have grown much more than that), but the blatant, visible lack of minorities on the PGA Tour highlighted the discrepancy between the hype generated by the 1997 Masters and reality. Some observers channeled the discussions surrounding Charlie Sifford and black PGA players in the late 1960s, arguing that Woods's success failed to have a broader effect because African Americans still lacked ownership in the game, as there were few black-owned golf courses and equipment manufacturers. Others noted the irony that women's golf and the LPGA Tour experienced one of the more dramatic racial shifts in sports history, as a tide of Asian and Asian American females took up golf and dominated the professional circuit. One year after the 1997 Masters, far fewer Americans were paying attention when twenty-one-year-old Se-Ri Pak, the lone Korean player on the LPGA Tour, won the 1998 LPGA Championship. Within ten years there were forty-five Koreans on the tour, along with numerous other Asians and Asian Americans, such as Michelle Wie; eventually the LPGA was generating more television revenue in South Korea than in the United States. Pak had "changed the face of golf even more than Tiger Woods," wrote one sportswriter.[70] Perhaps future historians will craft a very different narrative of race and sports, one that situates Woods as the leading Asian American player at a time when the Asian Diaspora dramatically appropriated and transformed modern golf.

Here Woods offered yet another unique contribution to history, for black athletes with such popularity had never insisted they weren't black. From the beginning, both Earl and Tiger hesitated to talk with the press about race. Earl's own sporting achievements paralleled the postwar civil rights movement far more than his son's golf career. At Kansas State University in 1952 he became the first African American baseball player in the Big Seven Conference. Traveling with the team, he often had to room separately at segregated hotels; his coach once refused to play a game in Mississippi after the opposing coach asked that Earl stay on the bus.[71] After college he joined the army, and as for many black veterans during the period, his military service provided new opportunities to confront segregation. He joined the first generation of black servicemen who successfully fought for full integration in the military, including recreational activities. As late as 1963, nine years after Earl enlisted, a federal report noted that 19 percent of golf courses adjacent to army installations and 29 percent adjacent to navy facilities remained racially segregated. Nevertheless, Earl was introduced to golf at age forty-two while stationed at Brooklyn's Fort Hamilton in 1972. Just three years before his son's birth, he took up the game at Dyker Beach Golf Course, formerly the Bath Beach Club. (He learned at the very course where some sixty years earlier the first African American golf pro, John Shippen, had offered lessons.) At age three, Tiger would also play for the first time on a course adjacent to a military facility; after the family moved to southern California, he shot 48 over nine holes at the Seal Beach Navy course in Cypress.[72]

As evident in his 1982 remarks to *Ebony*, Earl clearly identified his son as black and attached significance to Tiger's race. Moreover, he began teaching his son at a unique moment when black sportswriters optimistically mused that a transformative golfer was poised to emerge from the community. Unlike in the past, this black player promised to benefit from the early start that whites had enjoyed. "Who knows, maybe you'll discover a black Arnie Palmer or Babe Didrikson wandering about the streets of Watts," Maggie Hathaway told black parents in Los Angeles in 1969.[73] New York City's *Black Sports* put it even more bluntly in 1973, right as Earl took up the game in Brooklyn and two years before Tiger's birth: "Let's hope someone will 'get it going' because there are thousands of young Blacks who could learn to play golf. Maybe one day very soon, one could win the Masters; one could be the equal or better of Jack Nicklaus. But unless a lot more is done to practically snatch little Black babies from the crib to put them on the greens—no one will ever know."[74] Earl certainly considered his son's achievements in this vein, and he continued to do so until his death in 2006. "I wanted Tiger to have black friends," he said. "I would have liked it if he had a black caddie. But hell, he's a suburban kid."[75] (Woods did employ an African American caddie when he competed in his first Masters as an amateur in 1995, but he never did so as a professional.)

Like his father, Tiger also at times publicly affirmed those who celebrated him as an African American whose accomplishments belonged in the historical narrative of black civil rights. Woods first met Charlie Sifford in 1991, shortly after the Shoal Creek protests, and when Sifford published his memoir the following year, a seventeen-year-old Woods offered a generous cover blurb: "The pain, suffering and sacrifice experienced by Mr. Sifford in being a lonely pioneer for black golfers on the PGA Tour will never be forgotten by me. His successes and personal conduct will provide a blueprint and inspiration for myself and other aspiring black tour players."[76] Woods later provided the foreword for Pete McDaniel's 2000 book *Uneven Lies: The Heroic Story of African-Americans in Golf*, while both he and the Tiger Woods Foundation, established with his father in 1996, supported scholarships honoring black pioneers like Sifford and William Powell. Woods also visited courses that were historically important to black golfers, like Cedar Crest in Dallas, and gave speeches to minority junior golf organizations (though much to the chagrin of some, neither Woods nor President Barack Obama ever visited the most historic course: Washington's Langston Golf Course).[77]

Woods also made several overtures as public interest peaked at the 1997 Masters. When it became clear he was going to win by a wide margin, reporters and tournament organizers quickly contacted Lee Elder in Florida and flew him to Augusta for Woods's final round that Sunday. At the press conference following his victory, Woods praised a tearful Elder and the other black players who came before him. "I was the first one to ever win, but I wasn't the pioneer," he said. "Charlie Sifford, Lee Elder, Ted Rhodes—those are the guys who paved the way for me. I was thinking about them last night and what they've done for me and the game of golf. Coming up 18, I said a little prayer of thanks to those guys."[78] Augusta National's lone black member, Ron Townsend, embraced Earl Woods on the course and congratulated him on his son's achievement. In subsequent years Tiger freely shared personal stories of encountering racism in his life, most notably a harrowing tale from childhood that he publicly retold on multiple occasions and that was published in basketball star Charles Barkley's collection of conversations with prominent Americans, *Who's Afraid of a Large Black Man?* According to Woods, on his first day of kindergarten in Anaheim, California, he was lashed to a tree by older students, spray-painted with racial slogans, and pelted with rocks. Woods was accused of fabricating the incident (his former kindergarten teacher hired attorney Gloria Allred and demanded he retract the story, which he did not).[79]

Nevertheless, there were also early signs that Woods was unwilling to accept the simple, traditional notion that he was a black athlete confronting white supremacy in sports. "Golfer Tiger Woods Says He's Not Black," *Jet* bristled in April 1995 after Woods, then a freshman at Stanford, debuted at Augusta National. "[He] recently began correcting people who call him Black."[80] Woods also drew criticism when he declined to meet Jackie Robinson's family and President Bill Clinton right after the 1997 Masters. As many reporters noted (especially in the black press), his victory came two days before the fiftieth anniversary of Robinson's debut with the Brooklyn Dodgers and the integration of Major League Baseball in 1947. Like most American presidents, Clinton was a huge golf fan and telephoned Augusta that Sunday to congratulate Woods and invite him to fly with the president to New York for a commemoration event at Shea Stadium. Woods declined and instead appeared at the opening of two celebrity restaurants in Florida and South Carolina; then he traveled to Cancun, Mexico, for a vacation. "It would have been better to ask me before," he said of Clinton's invitation.[81] The White House downplayed the decision—"the president certainly understands," Clinton's spokeswoman said—and Clinton had lofty words for Woods's achievement: "Have your dreams and live for them," he told the crowd. "Think about Tiger Woods."[82] (Ironically, the president was still on crutches after injuring himself in a fall at golfer Greg Norman's house.) But the twenty-one-year-old Woods had seemed to snub both the U.S. president and Jackie Robinson, a significant moment that spoke to his uneasiness with the Robinson comparison and hinted that perhaps his politics were more in line with the conservative country club scene. One black sportswriter called out "sport's new Wunderkind" for his lack of "common sense."[83] However, it was more than just the rash judgment of an overwhelmed young man. The following year Woods surprised a predominately black crowd in Atlanta (and the black press) when he criticized Clinton at an event honoring Alfred "Tup" Holmes. "The Tiger Woods Foundation is all about hope. We need to give kids hope," he said. "Look at today's society. We have crime, we have our president. Unfortunately, our role models are few and far between these days."[84]

Most Americans first encountered Woods's racial identity one week after the 1997 Masters, when he appeared on the popular *Oprah Winfrey*

Show and introduced a term no none had ever heard of. "Growing up, I came up with this name: I'm a 'Cablinasian,'" he told Winfrey, who asked if it bothered him when people referred to him as African American. "It does," he responded. Woods noted that the word, a blend of Caucasian, Black, Indian, and Asian, was his chosen racial identity. "I'm just who I am, whoever you see in front of you."[85] The remark immediately touched a nerve, with passionate reactions prompting a conversation about multiracial identity more prolonged than any American pop culture had ever produced. Although most African Americans reacted negatively, many came to young Woods's defense, including some older fans who had celebrated him as a Jackie Robinson–like figure but now affirmed his decision to spurn the labels of "black" or "African American." Earl Woods spoke up for his son. "If you're seven-eighths Irish and one-eighth Indian, you're Irish," he told *Golf Magazine*. "If you're seven-eighths Irish and one-eighth black, you're black. Why is that?"[86] At age eighty-six, Maggie Hathaway not only lived long enough to see Woods win the 1997 Masters (she died in 2001) but also continued to support him in the black press. "The national press hounds him about his race, whether he is black or white," she told the *Los Angeles Sentinel*. "He should say both."[87] Other black editorials insisted the remark was not the sign of a young man "struggling with racial identity" but, rather, proved that Woods had "matured in his thinking about race" and was thus poised to represent the future struggle for civil rights better than anyone.[88] "Tiger Woods represents the new race paradigm in our culture," read one editorial in the *Philadelphia Tribune*. "Living proof that we must, at long last, begin to define the issue beyond Black and white."[89] One fan, calling himself "of total African American heritage," wrote a letter to the *Los Angeles Sentinel* defending Woods from his black critics. "Tiger knows the struggle to be black in America. Let's not cause him to be racially attacked from two fronts," he warned. "Those blacker than thee, love to point fingers."[90]

Yet these supporters were a minority; future historians will likely be surprised that a public figure as late as 1997 faced such severe criticism for making a relatively simple assertion about his race. Woods was hit with a negative popular backlash that began immediately and continued for years. Comedians like Chris Rock and Dave Chappelle mocked the idea that he (or any other black person) could deny he was African American, while diverse black publications—from the *Philadelphia Tribune* to *Reggae Roots International*—criticized the assertion and insisted that Woods was "black, like it or not."[91] Even his close friend Charles Barkley pressed him to embrace a more traditional identity: "I tell him that Thai people don't get hate mail, black people do," he said. (Indeed, Woods first received racist correspondence while at Stanford and continued to do so after he turned professional.)[92] After Augusta National began renovating its course in 2002, Barkley led a vocal group of fans who accused the club of racism and "Tiger-proofing" the links to prevent Woods from winning more Masters.

Critics who pressured Woods to embrace a traditional black identity pointed to the traditional racism that remained in elite golf. After winning a PGA Tour event in 1994, white South African pro David Frost was asked if the rise of Nelson Mandela would lead to more black players in golf-crazed South Africa. "Blacks like the active sports," he responded. "Golf's too still for them."[93] (Seven years later Earl Woods would raise eyebrows when he compared his son to Mandela.) Although Jack Nicklaus financially supported Maggie Hathaway's programs for minority golfers in Los Angeles and was long praised by Sifford, Elder, and other black players, he also responded to a question about race and golf in 1994 by insisting that "Blacks have different muscles that react in different ways."[94] But the remarks that drew the most attention came shortly after the 1997 Masters, when white pro Fuzzy Zoeller joked to CNN about what Woods might serve at the following year's Masters Champions Dinner: "He's doing quite well, pretty impressive. That little boy is driving well and he's putting well. He's doing everything it takes to win. So, you know what you guys do when he gets in here? You pat him on the back and say congratulations and enjoy it and tell him not to serve fried chicken next year. Got it.... Or collard greens or whatever the hell they serve."[95] Zoeller, unlike Gary Player, was also among the white players who responded apathetically to the Shoal Creek protests seven years before: "I think our job is to go down there and play golf," he said in 1990. "I don't have anything to do with politics."[96]

For many observers, "Cablinasian" was therefore not the thoughtful musings of a young man considering his own identity; it was a weak, immature, and even selfish response to classic white racism. "Let me respectfully point out to Mr. Woods that it wasn't his Asian ancestry, his Indian roots or, Lord knows, his Caucasian-ness that drew Mr. Zoeller's nasty humor," wrote one black journalist. "Rather it was the fact of being black."[97] The *Philadelphia Tribune* dryly noted that Zoeller "did not include" Thai food in his comments, while black and white sportswriters chided Woods for making his own racially charged jokes, which *Gentle-*

men's Quarterly printed in an unflattering feature just before he won the 1997 Masters.[98] But arguably the most powerful rebuke came from Joseph Lowery, head of the SCLC. Seven years after the organization founded by Martin Luther King Jr. had fought to integrate Shoal Creek, Augusta National, and all other PGA Tour sites, Lowery dubbed Woods a "growing cub" and, once again, reminded the young golfer that Zoeller's suggested menu "did not include chicken *chow mein*, just chicken."[99] Lowery and the SCLC continued to press for racial equality in golf and to celebrate Woods, but by 2000 they were resigned to the fact that he would not provide a prominent voice for any of the historic civil rights organizations.

Such criticism on the left continued to mount as Woods dominated golf into the new millennium, overshadowing the times he did indeed embrace the legacy of black civil rights. Lost in the reaction to "Cablinasian" was the rest of the 1997 *Oprah Winfrey Show* interview, which featured a heartfelt conversation with the daughter of Ted Rhodes and Woods insisting again that he had faced racism while growing up, alluding directly to the kindergarten story: "I got kicked off golf courses numerous times and was called some pretty tough names," he said. "[I was] tied to a tree, had rocks thrown at me. I was bleeding when I came home. Pop said, 'That's the way it is; you're in a neighborhood where you're the only one.'"[100]

Uncertain about the relationship between Woods and racial equality in golf, fans soon got a clearer understanding of his position on a related issue after activists turned their attention to gender discrimination at America's country clubs. In 2002 the National Council of Women's Organizations, headed by political psychologist Martha Burk, launched a protest against Augusta National's all-male membership. Burk was joined by several historic civil rights groups, including Jesse Jackson's Rainbow PUSH Coalition and King's oldest son, Martin Luther King III. Unlike the Shoal Creek controversy, this movement did not achieve an immediate response from Augusta National or the PGA, and, notably, it garnered far less popular support. Not until 2013 would Augusta National admit its first female members (former secretary of state Condoleezza Rice and financier Darla Moore). Maryland's Burning Tree Club, longtime choice of many golfing presidents, still has no female members and does not even allow female guests. Burning Tree has turned away women from Supreme Court Justice Sandra Day O'Connor to female secret service agents. (During the 2012 presidential campaign, both Barack Obama and Mitt Romney called on the club to reverse its policy, while House Speaker John Boehner came under fire for joining.)[101]

Woods first stepped into the fray at the 2002 British Open, held at Scotland's all-male Muirfield Links. Asked about the exclusion of women, he made it clear where he stood: private clubs that excluded females "were entitled to set up their own rules," he said. Once again his critics responded forcefully. Black political scientist Ron Walters lamented that Woods, now racked with "cultural confusion," had officially become "a terrible wasted resource" for African Americans and equality. As opposed to athletes like Charlie Sifford, Muhammad Ali, and Arthur Ashe (men "secure in their identity and connected with the legacy of civil rights," wrote Walters), Woods had instead chosen to join the other preeminent black athlete of his day in taking a different course. "Rather, he appears, like Michael Jordan, to be cautious in doing anything that would interfere with the economics of his position," Walters concluded. "The pressure of fan appeal, the endorsements for consumer products, the public appearances, the reception of his peers and the golf establishment, all challenge him to accept its culture."[102]

Woods indeed seemed to follow Jordan's model of presenting a public image that was relatively conservative, apolitical, and silent on the issue of race. The two met shortly after the 1997 Masters, and Jordan brought Woods into his inner circle of friends, which included Charles Barkley. And both men shared a common source for much of their income: Nike, Inc. Jordan's landmark 1984 endorsement deal with the company netted him more money than any athlete in history (by one estimate it continues to earn him $100 million per year). "[Tiger] looked to pattern himself after Michael," said a former Nike executive in 2001, "and the way Michael so carefully stays in that gray area—that in-between area where everything is neutral."[103] Woods signed a $40 million, five-year deal when he turned pro in 1996, far more lucrative than any golfer had ever received. In 2001 he renewed for more than $100 million, and estimates place his subsequent 2006 and 2013 Nike contracts in similar realms.

Nike made both Jordan and Woods the richest athletes in history, but there was one important difference: it joined the diverse chorus of civil rights groups and fans who insisted that Woods was black. The company launched a furious advertising push soon after he signed in 1996. The most memorable national television spot from the campaign is still considered a landmark advertisement in the industry. It featured diverse children from around the world repeating the simple phrase "I'm Tiger Woods." Often mistaken as Nike's debut ad with Woods, "I'm Tiger Woods" was actually the second of three national spots the company produced surrounding the 1997 Masters. More notable was the first, which clearly referenced Woods as African American and celebrated him as golf's Jackie Robinson. It ran on ESPN while Woods made his professional PGA Tour debut at the Greater Milwaukee Open in September 1996 and again throughout that weekend's NFL games on Fox and ABC's *Monday Night Football*. Set over images of Woods winning his U.S. Amateur titles, the ad featured him delivering a short monologue: "There are still courses in the U.S. I am not allowed to play because of the color of my skin. Hello world. I've heard I'm not ready for you. Are you ready for me?"[104] Critics assailed both Woods and Nike over the ad's bold assertion that Woods faced the same kind of historical discrimination as African Americans before him. One *Washington Post* columnist demanded that Nike provide a list of courses where Woods was not allowed to play because he was black, dubbing the campaign "discordant, dishonest and even vile." Jim Thorpe, the only other African American on tour in 1996, also expressed dismay at the lines (which he assumed Nike had "come up with"): "I personally don't think Tiger's ever been turned away from a golf course because of the color of his skin."[105] Calvin Peete and Jim Dent both agreed: "I really don't think Tiger knows what race is all about," Dent said.[106]

Woods promptly defended both the ad and his relationship with Nike, insisting he had personally approved the entire project. Earl Woods undoubtedly influenced the affair as well, though it was difficult to know to what extent. Earlier that year he had hired attorney John Merchant to serve as Tiger's lawyer and work with sponsors. Four years before, Merchant had become the first African American to serve on the USGA's Executive Committee, and he also served briefly as head of the Tiger Woods Foundation. But Merchant was fired in December, three months after the ad debuted; Tiger said the decision was his, while Merchant insisted he was dismissed by Earl. Regardless, the controversy surrounding race and Nike's relationship with Tiger likely played a role in the shake-up. According to one report, Merchant was under the impression that $1 million of the $40 million from the Nike deal would go to support junior golf, specifically the National Minority Golf Foundation that Merchant helped establish. Earl intervened and asked that he be given the money directly so he could personally decide what was distributed to junior or minority golf. Merchant also claimed later that he forcefully warned Tiger to avoid Michael Jordan and Charles Barkley. "I told him, 'Stay away from that son of a bitch [Jordan],'" he told *Vanity Fair* in 2010, "because he doesn't have anything to offer to the fucking world in which he lives except playing basketball, which he did yesterday. . . . Are they his black role models? You've got to be kidding me."[107]

Nike pressed on unperturbed while Tiger's inner circle clashed. Rather than shy away, the company continued to explore race during the next two years of the campaign. While "I'm Tiger Woods" made no direct allusion to black civil rights, a third television spot—the July 1997 commercial featuring Woods, Lee Elder, and Charlie Sifford—delivered a less confrontational message but one still firmly linking Woods (and his race) to the historic movement. Unlike any of its Michael Jordan campaigns, Nike's presentation of Woods thus invoked overtly political advertisements (albeit mild) and a corporate campaign that branded his racial identity. The result was the systematic removal of Woods's Asian heritage (and his Thai-Chinese mother, Kultida) from his public image, the very thing the golfer himself said he feared when he introduced "Cablinasian" and asked the media to recognize his multiracial heritage. Nike put Woods and his saga on the minds of people around the world, but it was an incomplete story. Few fans heard, for example, that Kultida ("Tida") spoke Thai to him until he developed a stuttering problem in first grade, spent her own countless hours supporting his golf dreams, or handmade the iconic tiger head cover—with "Love from Mom" stitched in Thai—that they noticed in his bag. Few even knew what Tida looked like, even as images of Tiger and Earl flourished in the global media, starting with their embrace at the 1997 Masters (which she attended as well). Today Tiger is the most identifiable athlete in the world, but most fans would still struggle to recognize an image of his mother. In the words of Asian American studies scholar Leilani Nishimi, the Nike campaign helped him become an "undercover Asian."[108]

While Nike worked with Woods to limit the influence of "Cablinasian" on his endorsements and golf career, his call for multiracialism did help produce at least one major change. During the 1997 *Oprah Winfrey* appearance, Woods also discussed the uneasiness he felt as a child when forced to complete forms demanding he check one box that best described his race. "So I checked off African American and Asian," he said with some defiance. "Those are the two I was raised under and the only two I know."[109] In this vein the discussion of "Cablinasian" and racial classification could not have been timelier. One day before, the U.S. Congress had held a hearing to explore the federal government's measurement of race and ethnicity, featuring testimony from representatives of the Census Bureau and the Congressional Black Caucus. Soon Wisconsin Republican Tom Petri introduced H.R. 830, which sought to add a "multiracial" category on the U.S. Census. Petri called it the "Tiger Woods Bill," and many conservatives joined him in championing the cause. "Tiger Woods is not alone in wanting the racial background of both his parents and all his relatives reflected in how people describe him," said a representative from the right-wing American Enterprise Institute.[110] Meanwhile, the Congressional Black Caucus and most black organizations (including the NAACP and the SCLC) initially opposed the move, once again criticizing Woods for playing into the hands of conservative politics. "Individuals like Mr. Woods who designate themselves as multiracial on the census form will not reduce by any amount the discrimination they will face," announced black congresswoman Carrie Meek (D-Fla.).[111] Joseph Lowery, head of the SCLC, reacted even stronger: "Tiger's self-entitlement sends ... a helpful message in the controversy surrounding the proposal to add a mixed or 'multiracial' category in the U.S. census," he warned. "The census is not a social register."[112]

Although the "Tiger Woods Bill" failed to pass the House, by the end of 1997 proponents were starting to win over the naysayers. Black organizations began to support the change, calmed by Census Bureau reports predicting it would not lower the government's official count of "black Americans" and, in fact, had the potential to increase it. While the idea of a "multiracial" category was ultimately rejected, starting with the 2000 Census Americans were allowed to select multiple racial categories for the first time in history. Woods was the major pop culture figure in this debate, and he helped spark what many now recognize as a dramatic change in popular attitudes on multiracialism and identity. "Cablinasian," the idea of a young man crafting his own race, is not nearly as controversial as it was twenty years ago. "If Tiger Woods said that today, I don't think he would get the same flak," sociologist Ann Morning, who specializes in racial classification, said in 2013. "There has been a sea change in American thinking. . . . We're no longer looking at Barack Obama or Mariah Carey and automatically saying: 'Those are black people.'"[113]

In fact, without Tiger Woods the world might not have discovered that President Obama decided to mark just one box on his 2010 census form. ("It is official: Barack Obama is the nation's first black president," proclaimed the *New York Times*.)[114] In typical fashion, Woods has since talked little about the issue and never indicated how (or if) he responds to the census. Few have even bothered to ask, another testament to how quickly attitudes changed regarding the concept of race as personal (and even private) preference. "I think he feels like, you know, it's a cross of so many things," Woods's agent responded when asked about the new census in 2002. "He wouldn't say, 'This is how I feel.' Or, 'This is what my single heritage is.' I think Tiger feels like it's a wide array, a wide grouping."[115] According to those comments, Woods likely joined the 1 million other California residents (and 2.4 percent of Americans nationally) who marked more than one box in 2000. Perhaps this, and not a stroll with Elder and Sifford down Nike's immaculate fairways, will be his ultimate legacy.

ACKNOWLEDGMENTS

A number of individuals helped make this project happen, including some who provided valuable feedback on draft chapters and others who helped track down key information or rare images. I can't name everyone, unfortunately, but I would like to thank a few in particular, beginning with Chuck Grench and the staff at the University of North Carolina Press for their tremendous support and encouragement, as well as Jeffrey Sammons at New York University, whose critique of the manuscript proved especially helpful. I was also fortunate to establish contact with the USGA museum in Far Hills, New Jersey. Under the direction of Robert Williams and Susan Wasser, the USGA museum has made great strides collecting archival material and organizing events dedicated to African American golf history, culminating in their recent exhibit "More Than a Game"—probably the best on this subject to date. Susan especially went above and beyond in helping me with the project.

Thanks as well to the many who helped me locate black golfers and golf courses around the country, including Nancy Adgent at the Rockefeller Archive Center; Linden Anderson at the New York Public Library's Schomburg Center for Research in Black Culture; Christina Bryant at the New Orleans Public Library; Lucas Clawson at the Hagley Museum and Library in Wilmington, Delaware; Jack Eckert at Harvard University's Medical Library; Michael Green and the Iowa State University athletics department; Ellen Johnston at Georgia State University's archives; Gregory Kinney at the University of Michigan's Bentley Historical Library; Jennifer Morris at the Anacostia Community Museum in Washington, D.C.; Barbara Natanson at the Library of Congress; Bob Ozer and Ken Tiemann at Save Muny, a nonprofit group founded to preserve the Lions Municipal Golf Course in Austin, Texas; Adrianne Pierce at the Dallas Public Library's history archive; Yvonne Spura at Northwestern University's archives; Ronald J. Stephens at Purdue University; and Ben Wilson, former director of Africana Studies at Western Michigan University. I also received invaluable help from Melissa James and Anita Gordon at the Central Michigan University Library and from Susan Paton, my dear friend and assistant editor at the *Michigan Historical Review*.

Along with these and numerous other individuals, research grants from the National Endowment for the Humanities and Central Michigan University provided financial support for the project. I'm greatly indebted to all of the above people and institutions. Humbly, I can only hope that this book is worthy of the time and resources they provided.

NOTES

Abbreviations in the Notes

ACOA Records	Records of the American Committee on Africa, Amistad Research Center, Tulane University, New Orleans, Louisiana
ADW	*Atlanta Daily World*
Ahmad Papers	Papers of the Revolutionary Action Movement, 1962–1996, edited by Muhammad Ahmad, Ernie Allen, and John H. Bracey (microform collection)
Amiri Baraka Collection	Komozi Woodard Amiri Baraka Collection, Auburn Avenue Research Library on African-American Culture and History, Atlanta-Fulton Public Library, Atlanta, Georgia
BAA	*Baltimore Afro-American*
BE	*Black Enterprise*
Bethune Papers	Mary McLeod Bethune Foundation Archive, Bethune-Cookman College, Daytona Beach, Florida
BP	*Black Panther*
BS	*Black Sports*
Bunche Collection	Ralph J. Bunche Oral Histories Collection, Moorland-Spingarn Research Center, Howard University, Washington, D.C.
CCP	*Cleveland Call and Post*
CD	*Chicago Defender*
CT	*Chicago Tribune*
CWNC	*Charleston Weekly News and Courier*
Eisenhower Papers	General Files, White House Central Files, Dwight D. Eisenhower Library, Abilene, Kansas
FBI Files	FBI Headquarters, Washington D.C.
GD	*Golf Digest*
GI	*Golf Illustrated*
GSM	*Golfers Magazine*
KG	*Kalamazoo Gazette*
LAS	*Los Angeles Sentinel*
LAT	*Los Angeles Times*
NAACP Records	Part II: Legal File, National Association for the Advancement of Colored People Records,

	Manuscript Division, Library of Congress, Washington, D.C.
NJG	*Norfolk Journal and Guide*
NYA	*New York Age*
NYAN	*New York Amsterdam News*
NYT	*New York Times*
PC	*Pittsburgh Courier*
PT	*Philadelphia Tribune*
SCLC Records	Records of the Southern Christian Leadership Conference, 1954–1970, King Library and Archive, Martin Luther King Jr. Center for Nonviolent Social Change, Atlanta, Georgia
Secretary of War Records	Records of the Secretary of War, Records of the Office of the Assistant Secretary of War, Entry 188: Civilian Aide to the Secretary-Subject File (General Correspondence [Judge Hastie], 1940–1948), RG 107, National Archives, College Park, Maryland
SI	*Sports Illustrated*
Simkins interview	George Simkins, interviewed by Karen Kruse Thomas, April 6, 1997, Southern Oral History Program Collection, Wilson Library, University of North Carolina, Chapel Hill
TAG	*The American Golfer*
WP	*Washington Post*
USCCR Records	RG 453: Records of the United States Commission on Civil Rights, National Archives, College Park, Maryland

Preface

1. "40 Years Ago: A Drive down the Fairway for Integration," *NYT*, November 5, 1995, S11.

2. "Supreme Court: A Chance to Play," *Time*, November 21, 1955, 22. This book makes no distinction between golf "courses" and "links": both terms were popularly used as synonyms throughout the game's history in America.

3. Dittmer, *Local People*.

4. Morris, *Origins of the Civil Rights Movement*; Gilmore, *Gender and Jim Crow* and *Defying Dixie*; Brown-Nagin, *Courage to Dissent*; Kruse, *White Flight*.

5. From its establishment in 1916 until 1968, the PGA was an organization that served a range of "professional golfers," not just professional tournament players (including club pros, instructors, etc.). In 1968 the professional players

established the autonomous Tournament Players Division, which in 1975 was renamed the PGA Tour.

6. Gorn and Oriard, "Taking Sports Seriously."

Chapter 1

1. Sinnette, *Forbidden Fairways*, 26; McDaniel, *Uneven Lies*, 31–32; Kirsch, *Golf in America*, 101–2.

2. Kirsch, *Golf in America*, 2–3; Tyldesley, *Egyptian Games and Sports*, 21.

3. Sandiford, *Measuring the Moment*, 23.

4. Price and Rogers, *Carolina Lowcountry*; Sapakoff, "Birthplace of American Golf," C1.

5. Sapakoff, "Birthplace of American Golf," C4; Paquette, "Jacobins of the Lowcountry," 190.

6. Sinnette, *Forbidden Fairways*, 5.

7. "For the Young Folks," *KG*, December 5, 1878, 3; "Her Point of View," *NYT*, October 12, 1890, 13.

8. Kirsch, *Golf in America*, 3.

9. Sinnette, *Forbidden Fairways*, 10; Jones, "Historically Speaking," 12–13.

10. Mohr, "Son Invented Wooden Tee," B1; Slater, "First Black Faculty Members," 97.

11. Sinnette, *Forbidden Fairways*, 10.

12. Dyer, "George F. Grant," 24.

13. Reed, "Sports Notes," 21; "Tiny Golf Tees Can Send a Big Message."

14. Jones, "Historically Speaking," 13.

15. Newport, "Bringing Joe B. Back to Life"; "Joe Bartholomew, an Early Golfer and Golf Course Designer"; Sinnette, *Forbidden Fairways*, 26.

16. Cited in Abraham, "Making of Audubon Park," 40.

17. Rosse, "Golf from a Neurological Viewpoint," 279.

18. Woodson, *Negro Professional Man and the Community*, 314.

19. Gibbons and Stansbury, *Child Labor in Mississippi*, 7, 22.

20. *Golf, a Weekly Record of "Ye Royal and Aunceint" Game*, December 19, 1896, 214.

21. "Golf and Golfers in Brazil," *GSM*, January 1918, 26; Grandin, *Fordlandia*, 268, 281–83.

22. *GSM*, January 1920, 62.

23. "Young Virginian Makes Good," *NJG*, October 14, 1916, 1.

24. "My First Game," *TAG*, November 1914, 14.

25. "Daisy May's Idea of Golf," *CWNC*, November 23, 1898.

26. "U.S. Navy Atlantic Fleet Golf Links, at Guantanamo, Cuba," *TAG*, June 1915, 107.

27. "Western Department," *TAG*, May 1916, 51.

28. "Negro Boys Loose Golf Play Tension," *Ogden Standard-Examiner*, August 18, 1922.

29. Cousins, *Golfers at Law*, 87–88.

30. "So They Say," *CD*, April 10, 1956, 19.

31. "Sidelights on the National Open Golf Championship," *TAG*, October 1913, 614.

32. "Caddy's Mean Suggestion," *CD*, December 14, 1912, 5.

33. "Western Department," *TAG*, May 1915, 54.

34. "Eastern Pennsylvania Notes," *TAG*, March 1917, 401.

35. "Caddie's Return Shot," *CD*, February 15, 1913, 6.

36. Harbrecht, "For John D. Rockefeller, Golf Was Life"; Chernow, *Titan*.

37. "Rockefeller's Hard Shot," *BAA*, August 27, 1910, 7.

38. "Was Willing to Try It Again," *Liberal Democrat* (Liberal, Kans.), September 19, 1913, 9.

39. Martin, *Golf Yarns*, 43.

40. "Western Department," *TAG*, July 1917, 774.

41. Van Loan, *Fore!*, 247–60.

42. Farley, "That Old Black Magic," 14; Nnedi Okorafor-Mbachu, "Stephen King's Super-Duper Magical Negroes," *Strange Horizons*, October 25, 2004, http://strangehorizons.com/non-fiction/articles/stephen-kings-super-duper-magical-negroes/; Susan Gonzalez, "Director Spike Lee Slams 'Same Old' Black Stereotypes in Today's Films," *Yale Bulletin & Calendar* 29, no. 21 (March 2, 2001), http://archives.news.yale.edu/v29.n21/story3.html.

43. "No Federal Inquiry into Panic Resulting in Death of Seventy," *Daily Capital Journal* (Salem, Ore.), December 26, 1913, 4; "President Begins Work on Message," *Salt Lake Tribune*, January 8, 1914, 2; "Western Department," *TAG*, July 1918, 810.

44. "Negro Caddie Attains Fame," *GSM*, March 1915, 40–41.

45. Carney and Rosomoff, *In the Shadow of Slavery*, 166–67; "How Green Is Golf?" *GD*, May 2008, 22.

46. Starn, "Caddying for the Dalai Lama," 456–57.

47. "American Notes," *GI*, June 21, 1901, 256.

48. "Live Topics about Town," *New York Sun*, November 8, 1898, 7; Bantock, *On Many Greens*, 131–33; "Grace in Golf," *CWNC*, January 12, 1898; Kirsch, *Golf in America*, 6.

49. J. E. Moorland, "Some Significant Religious Events," *Annual Report: Hampton Negro Conference, 1904* (Hampton, Va.: Hampton Normal and Agricultural Institute, 1904), 110.

50. "Chautauqua Park Opened Near D.C.," *PT*, June 13, 1914, 1.

51. "Summer Resort for Negroes Planned," *KG*, September 29, 1915, 2; Stephens, *Idlewild*; Walker and Wilson, *Black Eden*.

52. "Douglas Park Invites Not Only Your Scrutiny but Your Cooperation as

Well," *PT*, December 11, 1915, 1; "Colored to Have Golf Links in New Jersey," *PT*, November 13, 1915, 4; "Golf Course at Atlantic City," *CD*, November 20, 1915, 7; Keels, *Sensations of the Mind*, 1. For more on the *Crisis* and Douglas Park, see Foster, "In the Face of 'Jim Crow,'" 143–45.

53. "Country Club Flag Raising," *CD*, July 27, 1918, 9.

54. "Race Men Open Country Club," *PT*, September 29, 1917, 1.

55. Kirsch, *Golf in America*, 22.

56. "Oregon," *CD*, June 15, 1918, 5; "Doing a Great Work," *CD*, July 27, 1918, 10; "A Rap," *CD*, December 26, 1914, 3.

57. "First Race Golf Tournament in America Played Here," *CD*, October 16, 1915, 7; "Reply to Golf Challenge," *CD*, November 6, 1915, 7; Sinnette, *Forbidden Fairways*, 13.

58. "McDougals Challenge Speedy," *CD*, October 23, 1915, 7; "Colored Golf Players," *NYA*, October 14, 1915, 6.

59. "Tournament Sidelights," *CD*, August 31, 1918, 9; "Golf Tournament," *CD*, August 24, 1918, 9; "W. Speedy and R. Ball in City Golf Championship Play at Jackson Park," *CD*, August 17, 1918, 9.

60. "Ball Not in Gold Tournament," *CD*, September 27, 1919, 11; Krist, *City of Scoundrels*.

61. Chicago Commission on Race Relations, *Negro in Chicago*, 277.

62. "Golf Items," *CD*, August 30, 1919, 11.

63. "Missouri," *CD*, October 6, 1917, 3; "Among the Golfers," *CD*, June 28, 1919, 11; "Golfers Garland and Burns Victors," *CD*, July 5, 1919, 11; "Fred Dixon Replies to Jessa L. Garland," *NYA*, August 28, 1920, 7.

64. "First Colored Man to Use Cobbs Creek's Golf Course," *PT*, October 4, 1919, 11.

65. Sifford, *"Just Let Me Play,"* 24, 27.

66. "What's in a Name?," *CD*, November 4, 1911, 1; "Personals," *CD*, May 6, 1911, 3; Manning, *Black Apollo of Science*, 151; Schuyler and Ingersoll, *Reminiscences of George S. Schuyler*, 15.

67. "Woe Confronts Women Golfers with High Heels," *CD*, September 7, 1912, 7; "Golf," *CD*, April 27, 1918, 12.

68. "Beverage for Summer Time," *CD*, September 2, 1911, 8; "Miss Kent Wins Honors on Golf Links," *CD*, September 23, 1916, 24; "Mrs. Adams Gives Golf Party," *CD*, August 31, 1918, 11; "Doing a Great Work," *CD*, July 27, 1918, 10.

69. "Woman's World," *BAA*, September 24, 1904, 3; "Woman's World," *BAA*, July 16, 1904, 6; "The Modern Woman," *BAA*, August 12, 1916, 7.

70. Higginbotham, *Righteous Discontent*. For more of a critique on the notion of the "politics of respectability" as empowering, see Gaines, *Uplifting the Race*.

71. "Therapeutics of Golfing," *BAA*, September 26, 1903, 6; "Play Best Exercise," *CD*, August 30, 1913, 4. For examples of advertisements, see *CD*, November 1, 1919, 14, 17, and *PC*, August 2, 1912, 5.

72. Marchand, *Advertising the American Dream*, xix.

73. "Charles Reese and Other Young Men Take to Golf," *CD*, May 22, 1915, 7.

74. Rowland, *Bert Williams*, 59.

75. E. F. Benson, "The Social Value of Golf," *Everybody's Magazine*, September 1901, 373; "The Social Advantages of Golf," *BAA*, September 21, 1901, 8.

76. "'African Golf' Cause of Negro's Demotion," *El Paso Herald*, March 20, 1919, 1; "Sullivan Sends New Year Message," *Labor Journal*, January 13, 1922, 3; "African Golf," *BAA*, December 29, 1928, 6.

77. "Eastern Department," *TAG*, January 1918, 407.

78. Kemble, *Blackberries*, 43; MacGregor, "Golliwog," 127; Faulkner, *Ethnic Notions*, 69.

79. "Is Enthusiastic over Golf," *BAA*, August 27, 1904, 5.

80. "White Sailors Disgrace City, State and Nation by Mob Rule," *PT*, August 17, 1918, 1; Muhammad, *Condemnation of Blackness*, 218.

81. "How He Employs His Vacation," *BAA*, August 13, 1910, 4.

82. "Mr. Child's Word Not Worth a Hill of Beans," *BAA*, December 5, 1931, 6.

83. "Horace McDougal, Golfer," *CD*, July 11, 1914, 4; *Negro Year Book*, 44.

84. Catalog number E209770-0, Ethnology Division, Department of Anthropology, Smithsonian Institution, National Museum of Natural History, Washington, D.C.

85. Stevens, "In the Eye of the Storm," 12–15; Kirsch, *Golf in America*, 5; Sinnette, *Forbidden Fairways*, 17; United States Golf Association, "John Shippen"; Greene, "Oscar Bunn," 97–100.

86. "General Sporting," *KG*, July 5, 1896, 3.

87. St. Laurent, "John Shippen," 17, 30.

88. "Outing's Monthly Review of Amateur Sports and Pastimes," *Outing*, October 1897, 88.

89. Bond, "Jim Crow at Play," 218–19.

90. Sinnette, *Forbidden Fairways*, 21; St. Laurent, "John Shippen," 30; Londino, *Tiger Woods*, 46.

91. "Coloured Champions," *The Golfer*, August 5, 1896, 110, cited in Bond, "Jim Crow at Play," 220; "Golf in America," *GI*, September 15, 1899, 402.

92. "Golf in America," *Golf*, January 22, 1897, 342; "Money and 'Trades,'" *BAA*, September 18, 1909, 7; "First Colored Man to Use Cobbs Creek's Golf Course," *PT*, October 4, 1919, 11.

Chapter 2

1. "Stork Club Champ," *Time*, November 23, 1942, 72; Smith, "Still Fighting Old Wars," 170–80; Goldstein, "Beau Jack," B8.

2. "Conspicuous Gains by Race Noted in Various Fields," *NJG*, December 31, 1927, 1.

3. "Mashie-Niblick," *CD*, May 30, 1931, 9.

4. "Dr. Deany on Golf Links," *CD*, May 18, 1918, 6.

5. "Russ's Corner," *CD*, November 18, 1950, 16; "Down the Fairway," *CD*, August 30, 1952, 18; Marchand, *Advertising the American Dream*, 172.

6. "Golf," *CD*, May 7, 1921, 11.

7. Harrison, *Colored Girls and Boys*, 231.

8. "Golf Club Growing," *BAA*, July 14, 1922, 1; "Harlemites Get First Golf Club for Enthusiasts," *CD*, July 22, 1922, 8.

9. "A Negro Golf Club," *New York Tribune*, July 23, 1922, 8, and *Dallas Express*, August 5, 1922, 4.

10. "Negro Country Club Prospers in New Jersey," *KG*, July 31, 1922, 8.

11. For examples of advertisements, see *NYAN*, July 25, 1923, 4; *CD*, July 14, 1923, 8; "Golf Club Social," *CD*, March 8, 1924, 12; "N.Y. Club Stages Tourney," *CD*, August 2, 1930, 9; and *National Colored Tournament*, newsreel, Fox News, July 12, 1925, Fox News Story A7928, Moving Image Research Collections, University of South Carolina Library, Columbia.

12. "New Country Club," *CD*, April 26, 1924, 19; "Harlemites Buy Site for First Golf Club," *CD*, July 30, 1927, 9; "Race Firm Buys Site in Maine," *PC*, September 10, 1927, 1.

13. "Brooklynite Buys Top Shares in $250,000 Resort," *Jet*, May 27, 1954, 16; "Mink Fashion Show," *Jet*, August 20, 1953, 43. For a sample advertisement, see *Ebony*, November 1961, 108, and Molesworth, *And Bid Him Sing*, 274–75.

14. "Divine's Challenge to the Church," *PC*, March 27, 1937, 10; Fauset, *Black Gods of the Metropolis*, 93.

15. "Whites Fight to Halt Plan of Golf Club," *NYAN*, November 28, 1936, 1.

16. "Too Early for Leisure?," *NYAN*, December 26, 1936, 12; Donelson, "History of Golf in America."

17. "Bucks County to Have a New Country Club," *PT*, April 12, 1924, 1; "Wealthy Magnate Buys Farm for Country Club," *PC*, April 12, 1924, 1; McDaniel, *Uneven Lies*, 63.

18. Dawkins and Kinloch, *African American Golfers*, 24.

19. "Dawkins Wins Florida Golf Title," *CD*, September 22, 1928, 8; "Ballard Wins Hart Cup in Florida Golf Tournament," *CD*, September 13, 1930, 8.

20. Washington, "Recreational Facilities for the Negro," 280; "Lincoln Country Club Completely Annihilated by Flames," *ADW*, December 2, 1936, 1.

21. Rowan, *South of Freedom*, 153.

22. Cunningham and Cole, *Atlantic City*, 121; Lownes-Jackson, "Women and Business"; "Interracial Country Club Organized," *NYAN*, August 1, 1959, 1; "New Country Club," *NYAN*, August 8, 1959, 8. For advertisements, see *Jet*, October 15, 1959, 16, and *NYAN*, August 15, 1959, 6.

23. Borucki, "Golf," 310.

24. "An Endangered Legacy," *SI*, October 19, 1992, 14.

25. "Angry Contributors Halt Sale of Resort," *CD*, August 16, 1947, 7; "Through

the Years," *CD*, September 20, 1947, 20; "Nation's Golfers Start Annual Trek to Way Side Country Club," *CD*, May 22, 1948, 3.

26. "Californians Purchase Fine Country Club," *CD*, June 2, 1928, 7; Beasley, *Negro Trail Blazers of California*, 308; Alamillo, *Making Lemonade out of Lemons*, 24–25.

27. McDonald, *Mapledale Country Club*; "Hawkins, 'Father of Negro Golf,' Helped Pioneer UGA," *PC*, February 2, 1952, 20. Public or private, black-owned courses in America remain rare enough to this day that they continue to draw attention whenever they appear, such as Bull Creek Golf and Country Club in Louisburg, North Carolina (opened in 1996) or the short-lived Celebrity Golf Club International, a course outside Atlanta purchased by basketball legend Julius Irving in 2006. The magazine *African American Golfer's Digest* launched an initiative in 2014 encouraging players to visit the "African American Golf Trail"—a mixture of historic facilities (such as Freeway Golf Course) as well as newer black-owned courses like Bull Creek, College Park Golf Course (College Park, Ga.), Innisbrook Resort (Palm Harbor, Fla.), Sugar Creek Golf Club (Atlanta, Ga.), and Woodridge Golf Club (Mineral Wells, W.Va.).

28. "Britain's Negro Problem in Sierra Leone," *Current History* 21, no. 5 (February 1925): 693; "Worlds of Color," *Foreign Affairs*, April 1925, 435; Campbell, *Middle Passages*, 425; Hancock, *Citizens of the World*, 1–2.

29. *Crisis*, August 1926, 184, and October 1927, 271.

30. "The Segregated World," *World Tomorrow* 6, no. 5 (May 1923): 138; McDaniel, *Uneven Lies*, 61.

31. Jeffries, "Fields of Play," 267.

32. Du Bois, *On Sociology and the Black Community*, 235–36.

33. "The Future and Function of the Private Negro College," *Crisis*, August 1946, 253.

34. Elise Johnson McDougald, "The Task of Negro Womanhood," in Locke, *New Negro*, 371.

35. Boyd, *Wrapped in Rainbows*, 105, 113.

36. Johnson, *Along This Way*, 383.

37. "Nashville Poet Answers Schuyler's Charge against Under-Exercised Women," *PC*, August 1, 1936, 12; Miller, *Remembering Scottsboro*, 68.

38. "Aframerican Doing Pretty Well Writes H. L. Mencken in Mercury," *NJG*, May 25, 1929, A8.

39. "6,000 Elks Take St. Louis by Storm," *BAA*, August 31, 1940, 1; *PC*, June 3, 1939, 13; Skocpol, Liazos, and Ganz, *What a Mighty Power We Can Be*, 39.

40. "Golf in W. Va.—A La Nutter," *PC*, November 11, 1939, 17.

41. Wilkins and Mathews, *Standing Fast*, 82.

42. "Potato King Opens Estate to Golf Bugs," *PT*, April 4, 1929, 1; Wilkins and Mathews, *Standing Fast*, 82; "Race Relations in Missouri, 1940–1945," Records of

the Committee on Fair Employment Practices, pt. 1, Racial Tension File, 1943-1945, RG 228, National Archives, College Park, Md.

43. Ella Baker to Lucille Black, March 11, May 4, 1942, folder "Ella Baker, staff, 1940-1942," box A-572, NAACP Records, cited in Ransby, *Ella Baker and the Black Freedom Movement*, 120.

44. Farmer, *Lay Bare the Heart*, 52-54.

45. Griffiths, *Hot Jazz*, 22; "It's a Wow!," *BAA*, October 18, 1930, 1; "Are All Negroes Asleep?," *BAA*, August 30, 1930, A6.

46. Venutolo, "Shady Rest"; Starn, *Passion of Tiger Woods*, 5; *CD*, December 10, 1955, 7.

47. "Mashie-Niblick Shots," *CD*, August 8, 1931, 9; Davis, *Miles*, 24; "Down the Fairway," *CD*, June 12, 1954, 22; *CD*, October 1, 1949, 16; "Swing Stars Swing Different Instruments," *CD*, May 2, 1942, 23; "Mashie-Niblick Shots," *CD*, June 13, 1931, 8.

48. "Jimmie Lunceford Plays Golf, Sees Game at Poncey," *ADW*, August 10, 1937, 1; "Big Town: The Letter," *BAA*, March 29, 1952, 5; David Evans, liner notes to *Rare Jazz & Blues Piano*.

49. "Golfers Like Articles on Swig's Sports Page," *NYAN*, May 21, 1949, 11; "YMCA Golf Club Fought Par, Barriers," *NYAN*, October 30, 1965, 39.

50. "Why Midget Golf Swept Country," *Popular Science Monthly*, November 1930, 22-23.

51. For advertisements, see *NYAN*, November 19, 1930, 12, and December 3, 1930, 12; Mead, *Joe Louis*, 190; "Golfers to Hold Dance," *NYAN*, November 1, 1947, 9.

52. For advertisements, see *PT*, June 25, 1931, 3, July 16, 1931, 3, July 2, 1931, 2, and January 8, 1931, 10; Skaler, *Philadelphia's Broad Street*, 20.

53. For advertisements, see *PC*, October 25, 1930, A3, and June 13, 1931, 6; "Miniature Golf Course to Open Here Saturday" and "Business Possibilities Galore," *PC*, August 23, 1930, 1, 10.

54. "Are All Baltimore Negroes Asleep?," *BAA*, August 30, 1930, A6.

55. "Golf," *CD*, August 23, 1930, 9; *NYAN*, May 2, 1936, 15; "Golf Pro in Fine Form," *NYAN*, May 13, 1939, 19.

56. "Fore," *CD*, June 25, 1927, 9.

57. Cronin, *Century of Golf*, 224; "Woman Juror Blocks 'Jim Crow' Panel," *CD*, April 3, 1943, 9; "Mashie-Niblick," *CD*, March 21, 1931, 8; "Golf," *CD*, May 23, 1931, 9.

58. *BAA*, May 9, 1931, 2.

59. Writers' Program of the Work Projects Administration, *Survey of Negroes in Little Rock*, 59.

60. "99 Colored Homicides Reported," *ADW*, October 26, 1936, 1; "Man Critically Hurt in Tiff over Golf Balls," *ADW*, August 11, 1953, 1.

61. "Golf," *CD*, September 6, 1930, 9; "Mashie-Niblick," *CD*, April 11, 1931, 8.

62. "School Builds Golf Course," *CD*, September 13, 1930, 8.

63. "Mashie-Niblick," *CD*, August 15, 1931, 9.

64. McCloy, *Negro in France*, 253.

65. "Business Possibilities Galore," *PC*, August 23, 1930, 10.

66. See advertisements in *LAS*, December 31, 1959, A9; *NYAN*, June 7, 1952, 32, and May 17, 1958, 24; and *NJG*, May 8, 1954, E6G.

67. Marchand, *Advertising the American Dream*, 38.

68. Brown, *Correct Thing to Do*, 55.

69. For example, see *BAA*, May 13, 1939, 18; *PT*, January 17, 1935, 7; and *CCP*, February 14, 1942, 10-B.

70. Col. C. O. Sherrill, "Public Golf at the Capital of the Nation," *Bulletin of the Green Section of the U.S. Golf Association*, February 23, 1923, 37–38; "Two New Golf Links to Open This Summer," *WP*, May 13, 1924, 3; Kirsch, *Golf in America*, 84.

71. Jones, *Recreation and Amusement*, 31–32; "Golfers Have Day on Links," *BAA*, July 30, 1920, 1; Kirsch, *Golf in America*, 84; Dawkins and Kinloch, *African American Golfers*, 28; Savage, *African American Historic Places*, 139.

72. "Muny Golf Course for Negroes Open," *WP*, June 8, 1924; "Two New Golf Links to Open This Summer," *WP*, May 13, 1924, 3.

73. Jones, *Recreation and Amusement*, 31–32.

74. "Capt. and Mrs. Clayton Win Golf Championship," *CD*, October 25, 1924, 10; Williams, *Torchbearers of Democracy*, 406n134; Daly, *Not Only War*. See also the Victor Daly Papers, Schomburg Center for Research in Black Culture, New York Public Library, New York.

75. *BAA*, July 3, 1926, 2; Gritter, *River of Hope*, 68; Jones, *Recreation and Amusement*, 50.

76. "Dedication Ceremonies of Anacostia Recreation Camp for Negro Soldiers," September 20, 1941, 3, folder "Anacostia Recreation Camp," Secretary of War Records.

77. "Three Golfers Escorted by Police Play a Game," *CD*, July 5, 1941, 3; "Six Cops Guard Golfers," *BAA*, July 5, 1941, 1; "Interior Department Frets over Brown's Golf Action," *ADW*, July 9, 1941, 1.

78. Cited in Kirsch, *Golf in America*, 149.

79. "Praise for Ickes," *BAA*, August 9, 1941, 4.

80. "Expect End of Bias in DC Public Play Centers," *CD*, May 2, 1942, 4; "Capital Spotlight," *BAA*, November 27, 1943, 4; "District Board Rejects Interior Dept. Offer," *ADW*, July 15, 1949, 1.

81. "Litter Louna Park," *BAA*, June 14, 1930, 6.

82. Mitchell, *Reminiscences of Clarence Mitchell*, 17, 21; Wells, Buckley, and Boone, "Separate but Equal?"

83. Farrar, *Baltimore Afro-American*, 185; "Pat to Pansy," *BAA*, October 11, 1930, 18; "Golf Prexy," *BAA*, January 28, 1939, 17; "Golf Champ," *BAA*, Septem-

ber 2, 1939, 21; "Action at Maryland Open Golf Tournament," *BAA*, September 9, 1939, 23.

84. Dawkins and Kinloch, *African American Golfers*, 137.

85. Hughes, *Collected Works of Langston Hughes*, 10:175; "Colored Golf Players Lose Course Rights," *Baltimore Sun*, June 10, 1942, 26; "Golf Verdict Attacked by City," *Evening Sun*, June 29, 1942; "Negro Golf Dispute Ends," *Baltimore Sun*, April 22, 7; Farrar, *Baltimore Afro-American*, 185.

86. "Memorandum Supporting Application of Charles R. Law for the Right to Play Golf on Any Municipal Golf Course," in "Golf Courses, 1947–1952," box B-64, NAACP Records; "Sues to Stop Race Ban on Golf Course," *CD*, January 3, 1948, 6; "Baltimore Sued on Golf Parks," *BAA*, December 27, 1947, 1; Williams, *Thurgood Marshall*, 79.

87. "Baltimore Judge Rules Out Bias in Public Golf Links," *ADW*, July 17, 1948, 1; "One Judge for, One against Jim Crow," *ADW*, July 21, 1948, 1.

88. "U.S. Judge Kills Golf Segregation," *BAA*, June 19, 1948; "Baltimore Golf Links Open to All," *BAA*, June 26, 1948, 1; "Baltimore Adopts New Golfing Scheme," *ADW*, July 24, 1948, 1.

89. "Half Million Dollar Suit Demands End of Jim Crow," *BAA*, September 18, 1948, 1; *Law v. Mayor and City Council of Baltimore*, 78 F. Supp. 346 (D. M.D., 1948).

90. "Boy, 19, Killed in Public Park," *BAA*, October 8, 1949, 1; "The Carroll Park Tragedy and the Segregation Question," *Baltimore Sun*, October 6, 1949, in Subject File, 1942–1987, box 35, folder "Linwood Matthews Baltimore Park Situation, 1949," Bayard Rustin Papers, Manuscript Division, Library of Congress, Washington, D.C.

91. Wells, Buckley, and Boone, "Separate but Equal?," 165; Maryland Commission on Interracial Problems and Relations, *American City in Transition*, 213.

92. "Richmond Fares Better Than Norfolk," *NJG*, July 30, 1938, 8.

93. "Readers Say," *NJG*, June 7, 1930, 10; "Colored People's Resort," *NJG*, September 24, 1927, 14; "A Plea for Fair Play," *NJG*, August 4, 1923, 8; "A Fundamental Need," *NJG*, April 11, 1931, A6.

94. "The Memorial Park Golf Course Matter," *NJG*, July 13, 1946, B10.

95. "Norfolkians Turn to Golf for Recreational Pleasure," *NJG*, August 17, 1946, 11; "Golf Enthusiasts Encouraged Players," *NJG*, July 16, 1949, 16; *NJG*, June 25, 1949, C24; "Guide's Open Championship Golf Tournament," *NJG*, July 10, 1948, 11F; Brooks and Starks, *Historically Black Colleges and Universities*, 160.

96. Robertson, *Fair Ways*, 69; "Mashie-Niblick," *CD*, July 25, 1931, 9; "Mashie-Niblick," *CD*, August 1, 1931, 8; "Golf Course for Negroes Planned by Realtors," *Dallas Morning News*, April 3, 1927, 1; "Good News from Hades," *PC*, May 21, 1927, 20.

97. "500 Families Move to New Suburb Housing Settlement at Houston, Tex.," *CD*, October 10, 1942, 7.

98. Franklin D. Roosevelt, "Remarks at a Schoolhouse Dedication, Warm

Springs, Georgia," March 8, 1937, in Smith, *Builders of Goodwill*, 82; Kirsch, *Golf in America*, 123.

99. "Skilled WPA Jobs," *CCP*, May 9, 1940, 12.

100. "Bare Justice—Nothing More," *NJG*, December 16, 1933, 6.

101. "The Chamber's Fine Gesture," *ADW*, July 1, 1935, 6; "Is Nobody Interested?," *ADW*, November 20, 1935, 6; "Don't Let This Harvest Pass!," *ADW*, July 15, 1938, 6; "Time Marches On," *ADW*, July 10, 1938, 4.

102. "Atlanta Parks Offer Limited Opportunities for Negroes," *ADW*, January 30, 1949, 1.

103. "Negro Businessmen of New Orleans," *Fortune*, November 1949, 114.

104. Campanella, *New Orleans City Park*, 62; Ingham and Feldman, *African-American Business Leaders*, 54–58; Kirsch, *Golf in America*, 101–2; Sinnette, *Forbidden Fairways*, 27–30; McDaniel, *Uneven Lies*, 30–33.

105. "Race Caddy Slain on Course," *PC*, June 11, 1927, 1.

106. "Caddy Pleads for Life, Claims Slaying Accident," *ADW*, January 20, 1943, 1; "Slayer, 27, Never Played in Golf Tourneys: Miller," *ADW*, November 26, 1942, 1; "New Death Date for Golf Caddy," *ADW*, August 3, 1943, 1.

107. Crouse, "Treasure of Golf's Sad Past," A1.

108. "Stork Club Champ," *Time*, November 23, 1942, 72; Smith, "Still Fighting Old Wars," 170–80; Goldstein, "Beau Jack," B8.

109. "Beau Jack Reverts to Type," *BAA*, April 27, 1946, 14.

110. Sullivan, *Hardest Working Man*, 51.

111. "Former Caddie Gets Life Prison Term in Slaying," *ADW*, May 19, 1939, 1; Goodman, *Stories of Scottsboro*, 94.

112. "'Black Chile,' Raskob Caddy, Is a Natural," *Milwaukee Journal*, November 25, 1928, 3; "Raskob Adopts Kid," *BAA*, December 1, 1928, 1.

113. File 1180, John J. Raskob Papers, Hagley Library, Wilmington, Del.; "Orphan Caddy Wins Job with Auto Financier," *CD*, December 1, 1928, 2; "He Gets a 'Break,'" *CD*, December 8, 1928, A10.

114. "Keeping Eyes on the Ball," *PC*, March 22, 1930, 10.

115. Bagwell, *Jekyll Island Club*, 85.

116. "Caddy Master Equals Golf Course Record," *CD*, April 21, 1928, 8; White, "Morris Alexander," 30–33.

117. Mohr and Krupa, *Golf in Denver*, 73; "Prejudice Rampant in Denver Again," *PC*, September 14, 1940, 1.

118. "Mashie-Niblick," *CD*, June 25, 1932, 8; "Annual Prom Given by Golf Association," *CD*, March 17, 1934, 8; "Marshall Retains Golf Title," *CD*, September 12, 1931, 8; "Oscar Clisby Wins Medal in Eagle Golf Tournament," *California Eagle*, August 11, 1938, 5-A.

119. Lewis, "Maggie Hathaway," B3; "25th NAACP Image Awards Silver Anniversary Voting Process," *Crisis*, November/December 1992, 9; Smith, "Maggie Hathaway," 50.

120. "Tee Time," *LAS*, October 21, 1976, B3; *LAS*, September 23, 1948, 22.

121. "Who Needs Lessons?," *BAA*, June 27, 1936, 4.

Chapter 3

1. "Canadian Open Lead Shared by 4 Americans," *CT*, July 10, 1953, 2; "Unknown in Canadian Golf Lead," *St. Petersburg Times*, August 18, 1955, 14; "Negro Ties Golf Record in Canada," *PC*, August 20, 1955, 1; "Philly Pro Leading Canadian Open," *PT*, August 20, 1955, 1; Sifford, *"Just Let Me Play,"* 71–74.

2. Reed, "Blacks in Golf," 20; Warren, "Blacks in the World of Golf," 6.

3. For a list of key clubs, see Henderson, *Negro in Sports*, 431–32; Dawkins and Kinloch, *African American Golfers*, 23; Sinnette, *Forbidden Fairways*, 73; McDaniel, *Uneven Lies*, 56; and "Western States Golf Assn.," *LAS*, March 4, 1982, B4.

4. "Shady Rest Club to Stage an Open Golf Championship," *PT*, June 27, 1925, 1; "Washington Man Wins the National Golf Championship" *CD*, September 11, 1926, 11; *National Colored Tournament*, newsreel, Fox News, July 12, 1925, Fox News Story A7928, Moving Image Research Collections, University of South Carolina Library, Columbia.

5. "Hawkins, 'Father of Negro Golf,' Helped Pioneer UGA," *PC*, February 2, 1952, 20; "Western Golfers Will Invade East," *CD*, August 28, 1926, 10; Johnson, *Heroines*, 14; McDonald, *Mapledale Country Club*.

6. "Shippen Is Victor over NY Golfers," *CD*, July 17, 1926, 10; "Shippen Wins Golf Honors on July 4," *NYAN*, July 6, 1932, 9; "St. Nicholas Golf Club to Hold Tournament on Local Links in September," *NYA*, August 28, 1926, 6; Dawkins and Kinloch, *African American Golfers*, 42.

7. "Southerner Wins National Golf Championship," *CD*, September 6, 1930, 1; "Honor Golf King with Stag Whist," *CD*, October 29, 1927, 6; "Golf," *CD*, September 7, 1929, 9; "A Double Win for Chicago," *CD*, August 30, 1941, 22.

8. "Pat Ball Appointed Pro at Palos Park Golf Course," *CD*, May 13, 1939, 8; "Move Over Old Golfers, There's a Crop of Good Young Players Coming," *CD*, February 16, 1952, 16; Dawkins and Kinloch, *African American Golfers*, 54.

9. "Porter Washington Wins National Golf Championship," *CD*, September 8, 1928, 8; "Golf," *CD*, May 25, 1929, 9.

10. "Purple Golfers Drop Match to Cardinals," *Daily Northwestern*, May 22, 1923, 2; Paulison, *Tale of the Wildcats*, 114; "Southerner Wins National Golf Championship," *CD*, September 6, 1930, 1; "Mid-West Golf Championship at Casa Loma," *CD*, September 14, 1929, 9; "Warms Up for UGA Nat'l Amateur Here," *CD*, August 17, 1940, 22.

11. "Marshall Retains Golf Title," *CD*, September 12, 1931, 8; "Cliff Strickland Is National Open Golf Champion," *CD*, September 2, 1939, 10.

12. "Can 'Down Home' Boys Repeat?," *CD*, August 6, 1938, 9; "Mashie-Niblick," *CD*, July 11, 1931, 8.

13. Dawkins and Kinloch, *African American Golfers*, 48; "Mashie-Niblick," *CD*, June 20, 1931, 8; "It's News to Me," *CD*, August 29, 1931, 8.

14. "Mashie-Niblick," *CD*, May 16, 1931, 8; "Alabama Golfer Wins National Open at N. York," *CD*, September 28, 1935, 15; "Solomon Hughes Wins Joe Louis' Open Tourney," *CD*, July 28, 1945, 7; Jones, "Caucasians Only," 384.

15. "John Dendy, Morehouse Soph, Wins Dixie Golf Title," *ADW*, July 5, 1934, 1; McDaniel, *Uneven Lies*, 47–48, 52–53.

16. "Hartsfield Holds Lead at Half-way Mark of Tourney," *ADW*, July 5, 1937, 1; "Hartsfield Leads in Southern Open at Halfway Mark with 122," *ADW*, July 3, 1946, 1; "Hartsfield Cards 57 to Set Pace in Southern Open," *ADW*, July 2, 1946, 1; "Hugh Smith Is Winner in Atlanta Open," *CD*, September 18, 1943, 17; "Reject Golfer in Big Tourney," *NYAN*, June 25, 1938, 1; "Ralph Alexander Seeks Double Win at Southern Open Tourney," *Memphis World*, June 29, 1954, 7; "Pennsylvania Open Drawing Star Golfers," *CD*, September 3, 1938, 9; "The Stuff Is Here," *CD*, August 30, 1941, 24.

17. Sinnette, *Forbidden Fairways*, 91; Sifford, *"Just Let Me Play,"* 28–29.

18. Sifford, *"Just Let Me Play,"* 29; "The Fairview Golf Club Top Philly Pioneer," *PT*, January 1, 1963, 17.

19. "Georgia Youth Wins Golf Crown," *CD*, September 9, 1933, 9.

20. Sifford, *"Just Let Me Play,"* 29; Barrett, *Miracle at Merion*, 143.

21. "Golf Champion," *ADW*, September 14, 1935, 7.

22. "U.S. Colored Champion in Australia," *Sydney Referee*, August 3, 1939, 18; "Splendid Golf by Visitor," *Queensland Times*, May 18, 1939, 15; "Touring Comedy Artists to Play at Woombye," *Nambour Chronicle and North Coast Advertiser*, May 19, 1939, 3; "Golf," *Dubbo Liberal and Macquarie Advocate*, June 1 1939, 3.

23. "The Stuff Is Here," *CD*, July 22, 1939, 9.

24. "Splendid Golf by Visitor," *Queensland Times*, May 18, 1939, 15; "Exhibition Match," *Kalgoorlie Miner*, September 11, 1940, 3. For more on Radcliffe's Australia tour, see "A Visiting Golfer," *Wellington Times*, April 27, 1939, 6; "Champion U.S.A. Player to Visit Dubbo," *Dubbo Liberal and Macquarie Advocate*, May 2, 1939, 5; *Kalgoorlie Miner*, September 21, 1940, 7; "U.S. Golfer-Vaudeville Star at Glenelg Today," *Adelaide Advertiser*, July 2, 1940, 7; "U.S.A. Golfer at Practice," *Brisbane Courier-Mail*, July 26, 1939, 14; and "Sportlight," *Perth Daily News*, September 18, 1940, 21.

25. Johnson, *Heroines*, 21–23; "Mashie-Niblick," *CD*, September 19, 1931, 9; "Women to Play in Joe Louis Open," *CD*, June 1, 1946, 11.

26. "Golf Star Seeks to Divorce Cruel Mate," *CD*, January 12, 1935, 13; Johnson, *Heroines*, 23–24.

27. Johnson, *African American Woman Golfer*, 72.

28. Warren, "Blacks in the World of Golf," 5.

29. "Mrs. Wilson in Tam O'Shanter," *CD*, August 26, 1944, 7; "Woman Juror Blocks 'Jim Crow' Panel," *CD*, April 3, 1943, 9.

30. "Club President," *CD*, June 1, 1940, 24; "Former Champions in 1940 U.G.A. Golf Tourney," *CD*, August 10, 1940, 23; Kirsch, *Golf in America*, 174.

31. "Louis 'Ups' Golf Monies; Bars Gals from Playing," *CD*, May 31, 1947, 11.

32. Louis, *My Life Story*, 110, 181.

33. "Negro Golfer Plans to Sue over Ousting," *NYAN*, May 30, 1936, 1; "Corbin Breaks Color Bar in Michigan Open Meet," *CD*, August 12, 1939, 9.

34. Louis, *My Life Story*, 138–39; Starn, *Passion of Tiger Woods*, 5; McKenna, "Links to the Past"; "Champion Joe Louis Gets Ready for His Golf Tourney," *CD*, July 5, 1941, 22; "Denby, Hartsfield, Searles in Tam O'Shanter Open," *CD*, July 18, 1942, 20; Sinnette, *Forbidden Fairways*, 39–40.

35. "Dr. Remus Robinson in Louis' Open Golf Meet," *CD*, July 26, 1941, 24; Young, "Black Athlete in the Golden Age of Sports," 116; "Joe Louis Will Sue 'Ebony,'" *PC*, May 25, 1946, 1.

36. "Wins Joe Louis Golf Tourney," *CD*, August 12, 1939, 9; "Georgian Wins U.G.A. Open," *CD*, August 31, 1940, 22; "Detroit Okays Rackham Course for Louis Tourney," *CD*, March 29, 1941, 22; "Clyde Martin Wins Joe Louis Open Tourney," *CD*, August 23, 1941, 24.

37. "Willie Mosely's Golf Appointment Hailed," *PC*, February 10, 1951, 14; City Commission Committee, "Rackham Golf Course Historic District Proposal."

38. Roberts, *Joe Louis*, 224; Jones, "Caucasians Only," 384; "S-Sgt. Joe Louis Thrills Soldiers," *CD*, August 5, 1944, 7.

39. "Joe Louis in Golf Tourney," *CD*, July 13, 1940, 23; Dawkins and Kinloch, *African American Golfers*, 68; Louis, *My Life Story*, 110; "Joe Louis Wins Eastern Amateur Golf Tournament," *CD*, August 16, 1947, 11; "Joe Louis Wins Own Invitational Golf Tourney," *CD*, September 11, 1948, 10; "Memorial Amateur Golf Tournament in Indianapolis Gets UGA Under Way," *PC*, June 28, 1952, 25.

40. "Louis 'Ups' Golf Monies," *CD*, May 31, 1947, 11.

41. "Joe Louis Offers $2,500 Purse for Annual Golf Meet," *ADW*, May 23, 1947, 1; "Golf Crown to Wheeler," *CD*, September 14, 1946, 11; "United Golf Association Arranges Summer Tournament Swing," *PC*, May 27, 1950, 23.

42. Sifford, *"Just Let Me Play,"* 40–41.

43. Dawkins and Kinloch, *African American Golfers*, 65, 69; "On The Ball at 50th Annual UGA Golf Tournament," *NYAN*, September 4, 1976, D18.

44. "Joe Louis' Golf Pro Takes Houston Open with Par 253," *CD*, July 3, 1948, 11.

45. "Ball Is Cook County Golf Champ Again," *CD*, August 4, 1934, 17; Dawkins and Kinloch, *African American Golfers*, 156; "National Open Golf Play to Start Saturday," *CD*, September 1, 1928, 9.

46. "Wheeler and Radcliffe Win Interracial Match," *CD*, September 10, 1938, 10.

47. Sifford, *"Just Let Me Play,"* 32; Sinnette, *Forbidden Fairways*, 93; "Howard Wheeler, Moss Moye Win Golf Crowns," *CD*, September 10, 1938, 9.

48. "Negro Golfers Win Fight," *NJG*, August 11, 1928, 1; "Writer Raps Golf Offi-

cials but Praises Ball and Stout," *BAA*, August 11, 1928, 13; "'Good Sports,' Golfers Bow Their Heads," *PT*, August 9, 1928, 1.

49. "'Good Sports,' Golfers Bow Their Heads," 1.

50. *PT*, September 13, 1928, 16.

51. "Fay Says," *CD*, August 11, 1928, 8.

52. *PT*, August 30, 1928, 16; Canton, *Raymond Pace Alexander*.

53. "US Golf Body Bars Robert Ball," *CD*, May 20, 1933, 8; "U.S. Golf Association Returns 3 Entry Fees," *CD*, May 27, 1939, 10.

54. Cronin, *Century of Golf*, 224; "Reject Golfer in Big Tourney," *NYAN*, June 25, 1938, 1; "Mashie-Niblick Shots," *CD*, June 11, 1932, 9.

55. "Negro Golfers Welcomed in $15,000 Open," *CD*, June 6, 1942, 19.

56. "Wheeler Wins $200 Prize at Tam O'Shanter Open," *CD*, August 1, 1942, 21; "Capital Spotlight," *BAA*, July 25, 1942, 4; Barrett, *Miracle at Merion*, 143.

57. Strege, *When War Played Through*, 169; "Sgt. Joe Louis Playing in All-American Open," *CD*, July 24, 1943, 11; "Negro Pros Fail in Tam O'Shanter Open," *CD*, July 31, 1943, 11; "Louis, Seven Others Fail in Golf Test," *CD*, July 31, 1943, 11; "Walter Speedy, Pioneer Golfer, Dies Suddenly," *CD*, December 4, 1943, 11.

58. "Women's Golf Champ Has Daughter Who'd Rather Play Piano," *CCP*, September 1, 1951, 1-A; "Mrs. Wilson in Tam O'Shanter," *CD*, August 26, 1944, 7; "Down the Fairway," *CD*, August 13, 1955, 10; "Joe Louis Shoots 79 in Tam O'Shanter," *CD*, August 14, 1948, 10; "Private Searles Is 22nd in Tam O'Shanter Open," *CD*, September 2, 1944, 7.

59. "Golfers Eye Joe Louis Open," *CD*, July 14, 1945, 7; "Down the Fairway," *CD*, May 22, 1954, 22.

60. "Scratching the Surface after 100 Years," *NJG*, July 8, 1939, 8.

61. "Why Are the Major Leagues Silent on the Negro?," *CCP*, December 12, 1942, 20; "White Baseball Champions," *BAA*, September 2, 1944, 4.

62. Winn, "Leaders of Afro-American Nashville," 1; Sinnette, *Forbidden Fairways*, 84–85.

63. *CD*, September 10, 1957, 24.

64. Sinnette, *Forbidden Fairways*, 85–87; "First Black Pro Golfer Dead at 56," *LAS*, July 10, 1969, A1.

65. Sifford, *"Just Let Me Play,"* 38.

66. "Rhodes Fires Record 62 to Win Robinson Open," *CD*, August 6, 1949, 15; Dawkins and Kinloch, *African American Golfers*, 77; "United Golf Association Arranges Summer Tournament Swing," *PC*, May 27, 1950, 23.

67. "UGA Golf Champs to Defend Laurels Starting This Month," *PC*, June 14, 1952, 26; "Down the Fairway," *CD*, July 17, 1954, 22; Wiggins, *African Americans in Sports*, 299; "DeVoe Named to Golfcraft Staff," *Tee-Cup*, October–December, 1956, 3.

68. Sinnette, *Forbidden Fairways*, 89; "First Negro Golf Pro Ted Rhodes Succumbs," *CCP*, July 12, 1969, 11-B; Winn, "Leaders of Afro-American Nashville," 2.

69. Sifford, *"Just Let Me Play,"* 44.

70. Ibid., 10–11, 14.

71. Ibid., 19, 21.

72. Goldstein, "Charlie Sifford," B17; "UGA Golf Champs to Defend Laurels Starting This Month," *PC*, June 14, 1952, 26.

73. "Sifford Is Selling Golf Clubs," *CD*, February 16, 1956, 22. That same year Jimmie DeVoe became the third black pro to land a deal, this time with California-based Golfcraft, Inc. See "DeVoe Named to Golfcraft Staff," *Tee-Cup*, October–December 1956, 3.

74. "'Light as a Feather'—Sifford," *Tee-Cup*, October–December 1957, 5; "Rhodes Fires 283 to Win $4,000 Louis Tourney," *CD*, September 10, 1949, 14; "Greensboro OK Surprises Charlie Sifford," *CD*, April 22, 1961, 23.

75. "Rhodes Finishes 12th in Tourney," *CD*, January 21, 1950, 16; Sifford, *"Just Let Me Play,"* 37; "Lee Elder Plays It Cool," *GD*, December 1968, 28; "The Man: Charlie Owens," *BS*, July 1973, 24; "After 38 Years, Blacks Still Not Invited to Masters," *Jet*, May 4, 1972, 53.

76. Sifford, *"Just Let Me Play,"* 81, 83; "Benefit Fund for Golfers Established," *CD*, March 26, 1955, 10; Young, "Black Athlete in the Golden Age of Sports," 116, 118.

77. "The Stuff Is Here," *CD*, August 30, 1941, 24; McDaniel, *Uneven Lies*, 54.

78. "Down the Fairway," *CD*, September 23, 1950, 18.

79. Sinnette, *Forbidden Fairways*, 133–35; Barkow, *Gettin' to the Dance Floor*, 225, 228; Tramel, "Little-Known Story," B1.

80. Sinnette, *Forbidden Fairways*, 134; Barkow, *Gettin' to the Dance Floor*, 227.

81. "Russ' Corner," *CD*, March 31, 1951, 16; Sifford, *"Just Let Me Play,"* 48, 67.

82. "Thelma Cowans Plotting Victorious Swing East in Golf Title Defense," *CD*, May 20, 1950, 18; "Wheeler Tops Nation's Pro Golfers," *CD*, September 6, 1947, 11; Johnson, *Heroines*, 32–37.

83. "Down the Fairway," *CD*, September 11, 1954, 10.

84. "Down the Fairway," *CD*, September 29, 1956, 17; "Down the Fairway," *CD*, October 6, 1956, 17; "Sifford Wins Meet On Putting," *CD*, November 23, 1957, 23.

85. Ashe, *Hard Road to Glory*, 135; Johnson, *Heroines*, 38–41; Glenn, "Playing through Racial Barriers," 4–8.

86. Cayleff, *Babe*; "Women's Golf Champ Has Daughter Who'd Rather Play Piano," *CCP*, September 1, 1951, 1-A.

87. "Golf Experts Believe Ann Gregory Is Greatest of the Women Champs," *CD*, October 14, 1950, 18.

88. "Ted Takes a Golf Club, Makes Name for Self," *CD*, August 27, 1949, 1; "Golfer or Not—He's Still Champ," *CD*, August 10, 1946, 13.

89. Barkow, *Gettin' to the Dance Floor*, 230; Kirsch, *Golf in America*, 137.

90. McDaniel, *Uneven Lies*, 48; Kennedy, *Course of Their Own*, 20–21. Most sources list either 1916 or 1943 as the year for the addition of the formal "Cau-

casian clause," including Kirsch, *Golf in America*, 156; Sinnette, *Forbidden Fairways*, 125; Dawkins and Kinloch, *African American Golfers*, 153; Barkow, *History of the PGA Tour*, 98; Gabriel, *Professional Golfers' Association Tour*, 129; Hudson, *Women in Golf*, 105; and Jones, "Caucasians Only," 386. The confusion likely originated from a PGA official history published in 1975; see Graffis, *The PGA*, 236.

91. Barkow, *Gettin' to the Dance Floor*, 232.

92. "Dewey Brown," 31–34; Sinnette, *Forbidden Fairways*, 30–33.

93. "James R. 'Jimmie' DeVoe, PGA," *PGA Magazine*, March 2013, insert 1; Wexler, "Los Angeles Open," D8; Cayleff, *Babe*, 134.

94. Barkow, "One Man's Mission," 18; Tramel, "Little-Known Story," B3; "Rhodes Finishes 12th in Tourney," *CD*, January 21, 1950, 16; Barkow, *Gettin' to the Dance Floor*, 234.

95. "The Nineteenth Hole," *PC*, January 24, 1948, 6; "Color Test for Golf," *LAS*, January 22, 1948, 5; "Requested to Quit 'White' Golf Meet," *LAS*, January 15, 1948, 1; "Golfers Fight Jim Crow Tournament on West Coast," *CD*, January 31, 1948, 3; "Rhodes Makes National Open," *CD*, June 11, 1949, 14; Tramel, "Little-Known Story," B3; Barkow, *Golden Era of Golf*, 114–15.

96. Jones, "Caucasians Only," 386–88.

97. "Louis Puts Blast on Bing for Golf Tournament Barrier," *PT*, January 25, 1949, 1.

98. Cited in Kennedy, *Course of Their Own*, 56–57.

99. "Joe Louis Declares War on Jim Crow Golf," Associated Negro Press, January 14, 1952; "Joe Louis Presses Fight against PGA," *ADW*, January 15, 1952, 1.

100. "Joe Louis Declares War on Jim Crow Golf," Associated Negro Press, January 14, 1952; "Joe Louis to Challenge PGA Tourney Bias," *CD*, January 19, 1952, 1.

101. "Louis in Border Open; PGA Bars Bill Spiller," *LAS*, January 17, 1952, A1.

102. "Providing Recreational Facilities," *ADW*, January 22, 1952, 6; "Golf: The Last Frontier," *PC*, January 26, 1952, 8.

103. "PGA Gives Joe Louis Permission to Play in San Diego Golf Meet," *ADW*, January 16, 1952, 1; Barkow, *Gettin' to the Dance Floor*, 232.

104. Barkow, *Gettin' to the Dance Floor*, 232–33.

105. Tramel, "Little-Known Story," B3; Sinnette, *Forbidden Fairways*, 127–29.

106. "Joe Louis Wins First Battle against Jim Crow Golf," Associated Negro Press, January 21, 1952; "How Joe Louis Upset PGA Race Ban," *CD*, January 26, 1952, 1; "Louis in Border Open; PGA Bars Bill Spiller," *LAS*, January 17, 1952, A1; "Still the Champ!," *NYAN*, January 19, 1952, 14.

107. "PGA Votes Death of Race Golf Ban," *BAA*, January 26, 1952, 1.

108. Sifford, *"Just Let Me Play,"* 66–67; Barkow, "One Man's Mission," 21–22.

109. Sifford, *"Just Let Me Play,"* 67.

110. "Golf Club Members Claim Jim-Crow Responsible for Closing of Shower

Rooms at Highland Park," *CCP*, May 31, 1947, 1-A; "No Showers Today, Boys," *CCP*, May 31, 1947, 1-A; "Down the Fairway," *CD*, September 11, 1954, 10.

111. "Down the Fairway," *CD*, August 29, 1953, 23; "Down the Fairway," *CD*, August 21, 1954, 10; Barkow, *Gettin' to the Dance Floor*, 234.

112. "Golf Pays Debt to a Real Pro," *Ebony*, April 1969, 49.

113. "Canadian Open Lead Shared by 4 Americans," *CT*, July 10, 1953, 2; "Unknown in Canadian Golf Lead," *St. Petersburg Times*, August 18, 1955, 14; "Negro Ties Golf Record in Canada," *PC*, August 20, 1955, 1; "Philly Pro Leading Canadian Open," *PT*, August 20, 1955, 1; Sifford, *"Just Let Me Play,"* 71-74.

114. "Down the Fairway," *CD*, June 7, 1952, 18; Cronin, *Century of Golf*, 224-25.

115. Jones, "Caucasians Only," 389-91; "Down the Fairway," *CD*, June 11, 1955, 10; "Thelma Cowans Beats Ann Gregory in Flint," *CD*, July 30, 1955, 11; "Down the Fairway," *CD*, July 2, 1955, 10.

116. "21st UGA Golf Session Set for Toledo Feb. 22-23," *PC*, February 23, 1952, 27.

117. "Down the Fairway," *CD*, July 10, 1954, 22; "Rhodes Will Not Defend Title in Louis Tourney," *CD*, August 13, 1949, 15; "Rhodes Fires 283 to Win $4,000 Louis Tourney," *CD*, September 10, 1949, 14.

118. "U.S. Court Integrates Jekyll Island Resort," *ADW*, June 13, 1964, 1; "Georgia Island Told to Lift Color Bars," *NYT*, July 28, 1964, 12; Bagwell, *Jekyll Island*, 103; McDaniel, *Uneven Lies*, 56.

119. "Rhodes Makes National Open," *CD*, June 11, 1949, 14.

120. Barrett, *Miracle at Merion*, 144; Kennedy, *Course of Their Own*, 31; "Howard Wheeler Focuses Eyes on 1952 National," *CD*, June 30, 1951, 18.

121. "Bowling Bias Is Target of Drive," *PT*, March 29, 1949, 1; "Started Golf on Doctor's Orders, Thelma Is Now National Champ," *CD*, September 27, 1947, 12; "Amateur Champ Recalls Sis Is Bitterest Rival," *CD*, May 20, 1950, 18.

122. "Eoline Thornton Upsets Golf Queen," *LAS*, October 2, 1952, A1; "4 Girls Fail in Pasadena Golf Tourney," *CD*, November 18, 1950, 17; "Down the Fairway," *CD*, July 10, 1954, 22.

123. Stevens, "The Natural," 50, 52; Johnson, *Heroines*, 43; Sinnette, *Forbidden Fairways*, 106-7.

124. "Calls Off Golf Meet over Bias," *PT*, June 20, 1959, 1.

125. "Racial Barriers Still Up in Golf, Jackie Declares," *NJG*, April 20, 1957, 1.

126. Owens, *Blackthink*, 140.

127. "Rhodes Fires 283 to Win $4,000 Louis Tourney," *CD*, September 10, 1949, 14; "Down the Fairway," *CD*, August 20, 1955, 10; "Paramount Will Film Golf Tourney at Two," *ADW*, July 3, 1935, 1; Rader, *American Sports*, 307, 309.

128. "The First Negro Elected Judge," *Literary Digest*, November 29, 1924, 12; "Pioneer Golf Club Makes Society Bow," *CD*, April 12, 1930, 5; "Hodge, Nashville Ace, Shoots Tourney Course in Par Score," *CD*, September 9, 1933, 9.

129. "Mashie-Niblick," *CD*, September 24, 1932, 8; "Rhodes Favored to Lift Wheeler's UGA Title," *CD*, August 27, 1949, 15; "Down the Fairway," *CD*, August 20, 1955, 10; "Warms Up for UGA Nat'l Amateur Here," *CD*, August 17, 1940, 22; "Mayor Will Present UGA Golf Trophies," *CCP*, September 1, 1951, 1-A.

130. "Ickes Okays National Golf Tournament," *CD*, April 25, 1942, 21; "No National UGA Play," *CD*, August 8, 1942, 19.

131. "Golf," *CD*, July 3, 1926, 8; "Joe Puts Gloves Down for Clubs," *CD*, July 3, 1948, 10; Curl, *Jersey Joe Walcott*, 101.

132. "Joe Louis in Angel City Golf Tourney," *CD*, November 8, 1941, 4.

133. Rowan, *Wait till Next Year*, 29, 226; "Robinson Enters UCLA and Students Are Happy," *CD*, September 16, 1939, 8; Robinson and Smith, *Jackie Robinson*, 10, 105; Tygiel, *Baseball's Great Experiment*, 60.

134. "Is My Mixed Marriage Mixing Up My Kids?," *Ebony*, October 1966, 124; "Sammy's Golf Tournament Highlighted Sports Life," *Jet*, June 4, 1990, 50; Image PA2005-4/219-2.5, Marion Butts Collection, Texas/Dallas History & Archives, Dallas Public Library, Dallas; "Freeway Golf Tour May 5," *NYAN*, May 2, 1970, 37.

135. "Women's National Golf Champion and Trophies," *CD*, October 5, 1940, 22; "Cliff Strickland Is National Open Golf Champion," *CD*, September 2, 1939, 10.

136. Branchik and Davis, "Black Gold," 44; "Down the Fairway," *CD*, August 14, 1954, 22; "Record Golf Tourney Slate Set for 1963," *CD*, April 13, 1963, 20; Greer, "Consuming America."

137. "Down the Fairway," *CD*, September 10, 1955, 10. For the Seagram's advertisement, see *CD*, June 26, 1954, 6; "Tee Time: 1976 Summer Tournaments," *LAS*, May 27, 1976, B3.

138. "Tournament Attraction for Society," *CD*, September 5, 1931, 6; "United Golfers' Ass'n Gives Awards at Dance," *CD*, September 18, 1937, 14; "Seneca Crowded as 400 Golfers Play in UGA," *CCP*, September 1, 1951, 1-A.

139. "The Stuff Is Here," *CD*, August 21, 1937, 21; "Seneca Crowded as 400 Golfers Play in UGA," 1-A; "Atlanta Round-Up," *CD*, July 14, 1951, 4; Wiggins, *African Americans in Sports*, 328.

140. "To Play National Golf Tourney on Ponka Pog Links," *CD*, April 12, 1941, 23; "The Pat Balls Win Two Golf Championships," *CD*, August 30, 1941, 22.

141. "Louis Heads List in 39th UGA Nationals," *CD*, June 5, 1965, 18; "Thomas Takes UGA Pro Title," *CD*, September 19, 1959, 24.

142. "Golf Moguls Must Select Tourney Site," *CD*, December 3, 1955, 10.

143. "Joe Louis' Golf Pro Takes Houston Open with Par 253," 11; "Down the Fairway," *CD*, June 11, 1955, 10, Kennedy, *Course of Their Own*, 142.

144. Dawkins and Kinloch, *African American Golfers*, 51; "Los Angeles Bars Club at Muny Course on 'Segregation,'" *Tee-Cup*, April–June 1956, 1; "Jimmie DeVoe's Golf Quiz," *Tee-Cup*, October–December 1956, 5; "'Light as a Feather'—Sifford," *Tee-Cup*, October–December 1957, 5.

145. "My Toughest Fight," *Our Sports*, June 1953, 30.

146. "National Golf Tournament in Chicago during September," *CD*, August 19, 1922, 10.

147. "Howard Wheeler, Miss Moye Win Golf Crowns," *CD*, September 10, 1938, 9; "Ann Gregory, Don Jarrard Win Vehicle City Amateur Golf Titles," *PC*, July 31, 1954, 21; "Rhodes Fires 283 to Win $4,000 Louis Tourney," *CD*, September 10, 1949, 14; "Down the Fairway," *CD*, August 21, 1954, 10.

148. "UGA Plans 41st Tourney for Miami August 21-26," *CD*, August 5, 1967, 15; "Midwest District Golfers Assn. Holds Tournament," *PC*, July 6, 1974, 9; Kennedy, *Course of Their Own*, 215.

149. "A Few Closed Doors," *CD*, June 17, 1950, 17.

150. Robert C. Morris to Walter White, March 16, 1953, box A-237, NAACP Records.

151. Langston Hughes, "Brainwashed," in Hughes, *Return of Simple*, 117-19.

152. Pollock and Riley, *Barnstorming to Heaven*, 15-16; Fuse and Miller, "Jazzing the Basepaths," 119-40.

153. Quoted in McDaniel, *Uneven Lies*, 55; Kennedy, *Course of Their Own*, 159.

154. "Expect Record Entry for UGA Tourney," *CD*, August 24, 1957, 24; "UGA Faces Battle for Its Life," *CD*, February 16, 1957, 24.

155. "Down the Fairway," *CD*, April 25, 1953, 23.

156. "Unnecessary and Undesirable Negroes," *PC*, January 28, 1956, A1.

157. Sifford, *"Just Let Me Play,"* 39, 53.

158. Ibid., 50.

Chapter 4

1. "Students Picket Ike at Jim-Crow Golf Club," *PT*, December 13, 1960, 1; Stroud, *In Quest of Freedom*, 94-95; "News from the States," *Student Voice* (Student Nonviolent Coordinating Committee), December 1960, 2; "Paine Students Worked to End Segregation," *Augusta Chronicle*, February 6, 2005, 1.

2. Whitaker, *Race Work*, 77; "Major Teate Gives Army Post Lessons in Golfing," *CD*, February 5, 1938, 9; Kryder, *Divided Arsenal*, 72-73; "Dedication Ceremonies of Anacostia Recreation Camp for Negro Soldiers," September 20, 1941, 3, folder "Anacostia Recreation Camp," Secretary of War Records.

3. "Plan Summer Sports at Camp Bragg, N.C.," *CD*, April 17, 1943, 20; "Discrimination against Fort Bragg's Colored GIs," *NJG*, June 2, 1951, 1; "Army Ignores Truman Order," *BAA*, June 2, 1951, 1; "Army Man's Chief Takes Great Pride in his Golfing Wins," *CCP*, September 1, 1951, 1-A.

4. Moss, *Kingdom of Golf*, 158-59; W. I. Gibson to James Evans, October 5, 1944, folder "Negro Athlete Troupe, [September 1944-March 1945]," Secretary of War Records.

5. "Howard Wheeler Wins D.C. Golf Championship," *CD*, August 29, 1942, 9; "Winners in Shady Rest Golf Tourney," *BAA*, July 17, 1943, 23.

6. "Hale America Tourney Hitlerizes Seven Golfers," *CD*, May 30, 1942, 20;

"Golf for 'Whites Only,'" *PC*, June 13, 1942, 11; "What the People Say," *CD*, June 6, 1942, 14.

7. "Ministers Hit Fascist Golf Club," *CCP*, June 15, 1946, 1-A.

8. Kater, *Different Drummers*, 37, 124; *Come ci vorrebbero* (1944 propaganda poster), Republic of Salò Collection, The Wolfsonian—Florida International University Museum, Miami Beach; "PGA Continues Ban on Negro Pro Golfers," *CD*, November 25, 1950, 18.

9. "Portland Boy 2d in Oregon Golf Play," *CD*, October 5, 1929, 9; *The Gopher* (University of Minnesota Yearbook), vol. 45 (1932), 303; Dawkins and Kinloch, *African American Golfers*, 94; "Roddy Is Favorite in Big 10 Golf Play," *CD*, May 17, 1930, 8; "Southerner Wins National Golf Championship," *CD*, September 6, 1930, 1; "J. Dendy 1937 Champion in Golf Tourney," *CD*, September 11, 1937, 21.

10. Kaye, *Pussycat of Prizefighting*, 98; Reed, "Blacks in Golf," 20; "Robinson, Crosby Are Finalists in U. of M. Golf Play," *CD*, June 14, 1930, 8; Jones, "Past Greats," 67.

11. "Carver Wins High School Golf Crown," *ADW*, May 14, 1953, 2.

12. Reed, "Blacks in Golf," 20; "Build 9-Hole Golf Links at Lincoln," *CD*, September 27, 1930, 9; "Down the Fairway," *PT*, April 7, 1932, 11.

13. "Simpson Golf Team Wins from Florida A. and M.," *CD*, April 5, 1930, 8; Williams, "Negro in Golf," 53; "Morehouse Is S.I.A.A. 1938 Golf Champ," *CD*, May 21, 1938, 9; "'Skegee Hosts College Golf," *CD*, April 29, 1950, 17; "Atlanta Golfers Win Three Titles at Tuskegee," *ADW*, July 10, 1939, 1.

14. "Mashie-Niblick," *CD*, February 28, 1931, 9; "Wilberforce Wins Intercollegiate Golf Team Match," *CD*, May 15, 1937, 14; "Wilberforce Golfers Win," *CD*, May 29, 1937, 14; Strege, *When War Played Through*, 213.

15. Wendell Davis oral history, series III, box 15, folder 173, National Visionary Leadership Project interviews and conference collection, American Folklife Center, Library of Congress, Washington, D.C.

16. "Alphas Tee Off on Picnic Date," *CD*, August 22, 1953, 13; "Joseph Williams Joins Parade of Famcee Stars," *CD*, May 10, 1952, 18.

17. Nösner, *Clearview*, 56.

18. Ibid., 61; Goldstein, "Bill Powell," B6.

19. Nösner, *Clearview*, 2, 21; Winerip, "His Most Powerful Drive," 14.

20. "Negro Golfers Seek to Use City Course," *CD*, September 25, 1948, 2; "Ask Permission to Use Course," *CD*, October 29, 1949, 14; "Shreveport Is a Wide-Awake Unusual City," *CD*, October 14, 1950, 19; Joint Committee for the Survey of Shreveport's Negro Community, *Shreveport Story*, 73; "Four Atlanta Golfers Seek Right to Play on City Links," *ADW*, July 20, 1951, 1; "Miss. Golfer Demand [sic] Use of Public Links," *CD*, April 5, 1952, 4; "Seek Entry to Columbus City Golf Course," *ADW*, September 16, 1954, 1; "Desegregation of Macon City Golf Course Is Sought," *ADW*, April 5, 1961, 1; "Macon Counters Are Desegregated," *ADW*, November 1, 1961, 1.

21. Petition, May 25, 1964, folder "Louisiana 1964," box 141, series I, Records of Andrew J. Young, Program Director, 1961–1964, pt. 4, Records of the Program Department, SCLC Records.

22. *Travelguide* (New York: Travelguide, Inc., 1949), 11, 16, 51, 95; *Travelguide* (New York: Travelguide, Inc., 1952), 1; and *Grayson's Travel and Business Guide* (Los Angeles: Grayson's Guide, Inc., October 22, 1949), 12, 82, in folder 7, "Travel—General Guides—Pamphlets," box 380, series 11, Race relations, 1923–1965, Claude A. Barnett Papers, Chicago History Museum, Chicago, Ill.; *The Negro Motorist Green Book* (New York: Victor H. Green, 1949), 30, Travel Literature Collection, Henry Ford Museum, Dearborn, Mich.

23. Mohr and Krupa, *Golf in Denver*, 95; "Clark v. Sherman," *Race Relations Law Reporter*, Spring 1962, 308–10.

24. "Flash News in Brief," *BAA*, October 19, 1957, 1.

25. Hope, *Equality of Opportunity*, 67.

26. "Public Opinion," *PC*, September 7, 1946, 3.

27. "Gary Negroes Invite Whites to Play Golf," *CD*, August 9, 1947, 1.

28. "'Tutt' Holmes Adds Another Golf Plum," *ADW*, July 6, 1938, 5; "Morehouse Is S.I.A.C. 1938 Golf Champ," *CD*, May 21, 1938, 9; "Wins S.I.A.C. Golf Crown," *CD*, May 27, 1939, 8; "Color Line Bars Southern Golf Champ 'Tut' Holmes," *CD*, July 1, 1939, 10.

29. Brown-Nagin, *Courage to Dissent*, 117; Kirsch, *Golf in America*, 154; "Brilliant Performances at Tuskegee Meet," *ADW*, May 13, 1939, 1; "Holmes Wins Forest City Golf Tournament," *CD*, September 2, 1939, 8; "Brings Glory to Atlanta," *ADW*, July 8, 1940, 1; "Holmes Takes His Fourth Amateur Crown," *ADW*, July 5, 1939, 1.

30. Ashe, *Hard Road to Glory*, 530–31; "Wheeler Tops Nation's Pro Golfers," *CD*, September 6, 1947, 11; "Louis Has Never Won His Own Golf Tourney," *CD*, July 24, 1948, 11; "Down the Fairway," *CD*, June 5, 1954, 22; Clay, "Breaking Par against Racism," 110.

31. Clay, "Breaking Par against Racism," 109–10.

32. "Four Atlanta Golfers Seek Right to Play on City Links," *ADW*, July 20, 1951, 1; Brown-Nagin, *Courage to Dissent*, 117.

33. "NAACP Legal Defense and Educational Fund, 1954 Summer Report," 7, folder "NAACP Board of Directors, Sept.–Dec. 1954," pt. 3, Subject Files, 1939–1955, Bethune Papers; "Mayor Pushes Plan for Negro Golf Course," *ADW*, August 18, 1953, 1; "Negro Golf Course Budget Attacked at Council Meet," *ADW*, January 20, 1953, 1.

34. "Court Keeps Races Apart," *NJG*, July 17, 1954, 1; NAACP Press Release, box A-237, NAACP Records.

35. Clay, "Breaking Par against Racism," 108–9; "Judge Sloan's Decision Should Be Given a Chance," *ADW*, July 16, 1954, 4.

36. Motley, *Equal Justice*, 69.

37. Woofter, *Southern Race Progress*, 161; Lewis, *W. E. B. Du Bois*, 427; Ellis, *Race Harmony and Black Progress*.

38. "'Separate but Equal' Doctrine Seen in Golf Course Decision," *ADW*, July 9, 1954, 1.

39. John Calhoun to Robert L. Carter, December 26, 1955, box A-237, NAACP Records.

40. "NAACP to Consider Action on Golf Suit, Shooting, Beating at Parley," *ADW*, July 13, 1954, 1; "NAACP Votes $1,800 to Appeal Suit," *ADW*, July 20, 1954, 1.

41. Talmadge, *You and Segregation*, 29.

42. "Georgia Views Varied on Tech in Sugar Bowl," *New Orleans Times-Picayune*, December 6, 1955, 29.

43. "Text of Golf Case Ruling," *ADW*, December 24, 1955, 1; Kruse, "Politics of Race and Public Space," 613, and *White Flight*, 117–23.

44. "Court Keeps Races Apart," *NJG*, July 17, 1954, 1; "'Concessions' Made in Golf Suit," *ADW*, July 7, 1954, 1; "Segregation Barriers Fall at City Golf Courses without Incidents," *ADW*, December 25, 1955, 1; "Four Atlanta Golfers Seek Right to Play on City Links," *ADW*, July 20, 1951, 1.

45. "Danville Puts Bias before Tolerance," *NJG*, February 25, 1956, 1; "Golf Course Closed in Bias Row," *CD*, February 20, 1956, 21.

46. "Bares Result of Survey on Golf Desegregation," *ADW*, December 8, 1955, 1; "Atlanta Received Final Order to Desegregate Public Golf Courses at Once," *ADW*, December 23, 1955, 1.

47. Clay, "Breaking Par against Racism," 110; "There Is a Responsibility," *Atlanta Journal Constitution*, December 26, 1955 (with margin comments), box A-237, NAACP Records.

48. "Atlantans Play Golf," *BAA*, December 31, 1955, 1.

49. Clay, "Breaking Par against Racism," 109; "Without Incident," *ADW*, December 27, 1955, 6.

50. Young, "Black Athlete in the Golden Age of Sports," 116.

51. "Negroes Play Golf without Incident on 2 City Courses," *Atlanta Journal Constitution*, December 25, 1955, 4–A; Clay, "Breaking Par against Racism," 109.

52. "Cancel Negro Golf Tourney in Atlanta over Jim Crow," *CD*, July 27, 1959, 24; "A Grievous Setback to Tolerance," *ADW*, July 28, 1959, 6; "Golf Group Meets to Vote on Issue," *ADW*, July 23, 1959, 1; "Man Threatened on Golf Course, 3 Shots Fired," *ADW*, October 25, 1960, 1.

53. "Down the Fairway," *CD*, June 20, 1953, 23.

54. "Atlantans Play Golf," *BAA*, December 31, 1955, 1.

55. "Golf Suit Figures Express Satisfaction with Outcome," *ADW*, November 8, 1955, 1.

56. John Calhoun to Robert L. Carter, December 26, 1955, box A-237, NAACP Records.

57. "Cong. Diggs to Give Emancipation Address," *ADW*, January 1, 1956, 1.

58. "Court Order Marks New Era in Atlanta's Golf History," *ADW*, December 27, 1955, 1.

59. "Mass Pressure and Indiscriminate Efforts Are Ill-Advised," *ADW*, May 10, 1960, 6.

60. "Dixie Fumes over New Supreme Court Ruling," *CD*, November 19, 1955, 1.

61. "This Looks Like a Segregation Bill," *ADW*, January 18, 1956, 6; "Georgia House Passes Bill to Permit City Golf Links Sale," *ADW*, January 26, 1956, 1; Azarian and Fesshazion, "State Flag of Georgia."

62. Motley, *Equal Justice*, 145; Brown-Nagin, *Courage to Dissent*, 324; *Holmes v. Danner*, 191 F. Supp. 394 (M.D. G.A., 1961).

63. Clay, "Breaking Par against Racism," 110, 112; Rapoport, *Immortal Bobby*, 296; "City to Name Park Honoring Alfred 'Tup' Holmes Saturday," *ADW*, August 19, 1983, 1.

64. "Bar Harlemites from Golf Course," *New York Amsterdam Star-News*, June 7, 1941, 1; "Hubert Delaney, Wilkins Losers in Rights Suit," *ADW*, June 6, 1941, 1; *Delaney v. Central Valley Golf Club*, 28 N.Y. Supp. (2d) 932 (1941).

65. "Bill Bars Bias on Golf Links," *New York Amsterdam Star-News*, May 23, 1942, 1; "Bans Discrimination in Sports Promotion," *BAA*, May 16, 1942, 22; Moss, *Golf and the American Country Club*, 154.

66. "Barring 3 Costs Golf Club $750," *BAA*, August 16, 1947, 1; "Harlemites Sue Ritzy Golf Club," *NYAN*, May 24, 1947, 1; "Dr. Arthur Logan, 2 Others Win $1,000 Anti-Bias Award," *NYAN*, August 9, 1947, 1; "N.Y. Law Balks Lily-White State Championships," *CD*, June 13, 1942, 21.

67. Dresser, *African Americans on Martha's Vineyard*, 85; "Creating a Racquet," *BE*, July 1989, 54.

68. "Third Suit Filed in Kankakee Shores Row," *ADW*, September 29, 1949, 1; "Churchmen Preach Tolerance, Operate Jim Crow Golf Course," *CD*, February 8, 1947, 11.

69. "Massachusetts Joins Fight on Jim Crow in Public Places," *CD*, August 26, 1950, 7.

70. "Barred: He Sues Golf Course Owner," *CCP*, August 15, 1942, 1; "Gillespie, Lucas Seek Ban on Bias at Exclusive Lake Shore Golf Club," *CCP*, October 16, 1948, 1-A; "Court Rules against 'Private' Golf Club," *CCP*, January 28, 1950, 1-A.

71. Thurgood Marshall to Chester Gillespie, January 26, 1950, "Amended Motion for New Trial," *Gillespie v. Lake Shore Golf Club*, June 8, 1949, and "Race Barrier Lifted at Cleveland Golf Links," Press Release, January 26, 1950, box B-64, NAACP Records; *Gillespie v. Lake Shore Golf Club*, 91 N.E.2d 290, 292 (Ohio Ct. App., 1950).

72. "Churchmen Preach Tolerance, Operate Jim Crow Golf Course," *CD*, February 8, 1947, 11.

73. Klein, "Walk in the Park with Jimmy Comiskey," 1; *New Orleans City Park Improvement Association v. Detiege*, 358 U.S. 54 (1958); "New Orleans Negroes

Sue for Recreation," *CD*, November 26, 1949, 1; "Court Agrees to Hear Golf Suit," *CD*, August 18, 1951, 1.

74. "Park Bias Ban Stands," *LAS*, October 23, 1958, A1; "NAACP Argues 6 Cases in Federal Court," *CD*, February 1, 1958, 21.

75. "Park Integrated," *BAA*, June 6, 1964, 1.

76. "Federal Court's Ruling on Use of Public Golf Courses," *NJG*, November 24, 1951, A16.

77. "Former Portsmouth Mayor James Holley Dies at 85," *Virginian-Pilot*, October 6, 2012; *Holley v. City of Portsmouth*, 150 F. Supp. 6 (1957); "Holley, III v. City of Portsmouth," *Race Relations Law Reporter*, June 1957, 609–11.

78. Stricklin, *Links, Lore, and Legends*, 85; "City to Build Houston Course," *CD*, September 11, 1948, 13.

79. "Baltimore Will Mix Schools," *PC*, June 12, 1954, 1; Pitre, *In Struggle against Jim Crow*, 72; Lavergne, *Before Brown*, 180; Haurwitz, "State Panel Recommends Muny"; Kaufmann, "Fighting for Their Course," 30–33.

80. *Beal v. Holcomb*, 193 F.2d 384 (1951); "Court Rules Houston Must Open Golf Courses to Negroes," *ADW*, December 29, 1951, 1.

81. "Baltimore Will Mix Schools," *PC*, June 12, 1954, 1; "Dixie Dilemma Deepens," *CD*, June 19, 1954, 1.

82. "NAACP Legal Defense and Educational Fund Monthly Report, October 1954," 9–10, folder "NAACP Board of Directors, Sept.–Dec. 1954," pt. 3, Bethune Papers; Loth and Fleming, *Integration North and South*, 90; "Extols Corpus Christi's Fine Race Relationships," *PC*, June 12, 1954, 29; "Corpus Christi Beat Court Decision by Two Years," *CD*, June 5, 1954, 7; "San Antonio Ends Public Segregation," *CD*, March 31, 1956, 1; "Golf Courses Opened to Negro Players," *ADW*, June 12, 1954, 1; Housewright, "Course Cares about 1 Color Only," 33A.

83. "Statement of G. B. Wadzeck, Superintendent of Schools, San Angelo, Tex.," in U.S. Commission on Civil Rights, *Conference on Education*, 52; "City Can Find Much Evidence of Successful Golf Desegregation," *ADW*, November 29, 1955, 1.

84. *Fayson v. Beard*, 134 F. Supp. 379 (E.D. Tex., 1955); Robertson, *Fair Ways*.

85. "Negro Golfers Seek to Use City Course," *CD*, September 25, 1948, 2; "Miami Decrees Negro Golf Day," *CD*, May 7, 1949, 14; "Miami Plans Golf Course," *CD*, August 20, 1949, 3.

86. Harry T. Moore, "1950 Annual Report to Florida NAACP Branches," November 24, 1950, folder "Florida NAACP Conference of Branches," pt. 3, Bethune Papers; "The Florida Golf Case," *BAA*, October 28, 1950, 4; "Supreme Court Scraps Racial Rule in Golf," *NJG*, October 21, 1950, 1; "Supreme Court Hits Jim Crow on Golf Course," *CD*, October 28, 1950, 18; *Rice v. Arnold*, 340 U.S. 848 (1950).

87. G. E. Graves Jr. to Franklin H. Williams, April 15, 1950, and I. C. Mickens to Thurgood Marshall, May 6, 1950, box B-64, NAACP Records; "Florida Shuns

High Court Order in Golf Bias Case," *ADW*, December 12, 1951, 1; "U.S. Court OKs Golf Jim Crow," *CD*, March 15, 1952, 13.

88. "Old JC Arguments Useless, Miami Told," *BAA*, March 23, 1957, 1; *Ward v. City of Miami*, 151 F. Supp. 593 (S.D. Fla., 1957). Another member of the group was local civil rights leader Theodore Gibson; see "Father Theodore R. Gibson," *Crisis*, February 1961, 92.

89. "City of Miami Files Counter Golfer's Suit," *CD*, May 26, 1956, 11; "Miami Golf Course Is Integrated," *ADW*, April 18, 1958, 1; Daniel H. Pollitt, "The President's Powers in Areas of Race Relations," 27, folder "Southern Regional Council, March 9, 1961–April 4, 1962," box 009, series 1, "Alphabetical Files, 1956–1962," White House Staff Files of Harris Wofford, John F. Kennedy Presidential Papers, John F. Kennedy Presidential Library, Boston, Mass.; "West Palm Beach Golf Course Opens," *ADW*, April 20, 1958, 1; "Golf Course Integration Goes Smooth," *CD*, October 13, 1959, 3.

90. "City Can Find Much Evidence of Successful Golf Desegregation," *ADW*, November 29, 1955, 1.

91. "Plan Injunction on Jacksonville's Golfing Setup," *ADW*, June 29, 1958, 1; "Closes City Golf Courses to Evade Mandate of Court," *ADW*, April 3, 1959, 1; Wolcott, *Race, Riots, and Roller Coasters*, 171; Cox, "Frank Hampton Sr. Leaves Legacy."

92. Motley, *Equal Justice*, 257; *Hampton v. City of Jacksonville, Florida*, 304 F.2d 320 (5th Cir., 1962); "Jacksonville Club Must End Discrimination," *ADW*, January 29, 1963, 1; "What's New in the Law," *American Bar Association Journal* 48, no. 9 (September 1962): 866–67.

93. *Wimbish v. Pinellas County, Florida*, 342 F.2d 804 (1965); "Baltimore Will Mix Schools," *PC*, June 12, 1954, 1; Motley, *Equal Justice*, 254.

94. Beeler, "Race Riot in Columbia, Tennessee," 49–61; King, *Devil in the Grove*; "2 Sue for Use of Golf Links," *CD*, August 11, 1951, 5; "Negro Councilman Defends Jimcrow Golf Link Stand," *ADW*, December 7, 1952, 1; "Looby-Lillard Feud Rages in Nashville, Tenn.," *CD*, December 13, 1952, 2; "Transcript of Tape-Recorded Interview with Alexander Looby," November 29, 1967, 28, RJB 90, Bunche Collection.

95. "Judge Says Nature Approves Jim-Crow," *CCP*, November 29, 1952, 1-A; "Federal Judge Says Birds, Animals All Practice Jim-Crow," *PT*, November 29, 1952, 1; "Judge Oks Segregated Golf Course," *CD*, December 6, 1952, 13.

96. Z. Alexander Looby to Walter White, December 23, 1952, box A-237, NAACP Records.

97. "Nashville Answers Suit, Plans Jim Crow Course," *CD*, December 6, 1952, 18; "NAACP Legal Defense and Educational Fund Monthly Report, February 1954," 9, folder "NAACP Board of Directors, Jan–June 1954," pt. 3, Bethune Papers; "Bias Fades on Golf Course," *ADW*, February 14, 1954, 1; *Hayes v. Crutcher*, 137 F. Supp. 853 (M.D. Tenn., 1956).

98. "Drop Golf Race Ban for Tourney," *CD*, February 25, 1956, 1; "Appeal Delays Memphis Parks Desegregation," *ADW*, June 20, 1962, 1; U.S. Commission on Civil Rights, *Civil Rights U.S.A.*, 139.

99. *Sweeney v. City of Louisville*, 102 F. Supp. 525 (1951); "Kentucky Bias Bars Appealed," *ADW*, March 5, 1949, 1; "Flashes," *PT*, February 26, 1949, 1; Young, "Black Athlete in the Golden Age of Sports," 116.

100. *Sweeney v. City of Louisville*, 102 F. Supp. 525 (1951); "NAACP Legal Defense and Educational Fund Monthly Report, May 1953," 1-2, folder "NAACP Board of Directors, Jan-June 1953," pt. 3, Bethune Papers; "Citizens Tell Mayor Louisville Unfair to Group with Jim Crow," *ADW*, July 16, 1948, 1; "Federal Judge Orders End to Biased Golf Facilities," *ADW*, September 20, 1951, 1.

101. "NAACP Legal Defense and Educational Fund Monthly Report, May 1954," 9-10, folder "NAACP Board of Directors, Jan-June 1954," pt. 3, Bethune Papers; "City Can Find Much Evidence of Successful Golf Desegregation," *ADW*, November 29, 1955, 1; Loth and Fleming, *Integration North and South*, 88; U.S. Commission on Civil Rights, *50 States Report*, 172. Desegregating Louisville's other public arenas required Carter and the NAACP to continue with the case all the way to the U.S. Supreme Court in *Muir v. Louisville Park Theatrical Ass'n.*, 347 U.S. 971 (1954).

102. "3 Florida Negroes Seek U.S. Ruling on Public Links," *Montgomery Advertiser*, November 9, 1955; "Augustus v. City of Pensacola," *Race Relations Law Reporter*, August 1956, 681; *Augustus v. City of Pensacola*, Fed. Supp. N. D. Fla. (1956); "Court Orders Pensacola to Let Negroes Play Golf," *CT*, May 25, 1956, 5; "Flash News in Brief," *BAA*, April 26, 1958, 1; "Pensacola Course Opens Fairways to All Golfers," *BAA*, June 2, 1956, 1; "Court Makes Golf Course Open to All," *CD*, June 9, 1956, 17.

103. Motley, *Equal Justice*, 118; *Augustus v. Board of Public Instruction of Escambia County Florida*, 306 F.2d 862 (1962).

104. "Greensboro Proposes Separate Links to Meet Golf Course Issue," *NJG*, March 12, 1949, 1; "Greensboro Golf Course Being Cleared," *NJG*, November 19, 1949, B5; "Denied Permission to Play Municipal Golf Course," *NJG*, April 9, 1949, 13; "Carolina Notebook," *NJG*, February 26, 1949, 15; Dawkins and Kinloch, *African American Golfers*, 148; McDaniel, *Uneven Lies*, 94-96; Kirsch, *Golf in America*, 155.

105. Simkins interview, 3.

106. "Greensboro Golfers Guilty of Trespassing," *Charlotte News*, December 4, 1956; "Supreme Court Agrees to Rule on Sentences in Racial Golf Case," *ADW*, January 13, 1959, 1; "Six Jailed for Defying Dixie's Golf Course Ban," *CCP*, December 24, 1955, 1-A; "Supreme Court Takes N.C. Golf Case under Advisement," *ADW*, October 22, 1959, 1; "Six Use NC City Course; Arrested," *NJG*, December 17, 1955, 1; "Convicted for Playing Golf," *CD*, February 11, 1956, 17; "Calls Closing

of Golf Course 'Stupid' Irresponsible," *ADW*, January 4, 1956, 1; "Seek Review of Titles Hinge Convictions of 6 in Greensboro," *ADW*, November 28, 1958, 1.

107. George Simkins to Gloster B. Current, August 27, 1956, box A-109, group III, NAACP Records.

108. Gloster B. Current to George Simkins, August 22 and October 18, 1956; see also memorandum and notes from June 22, 1956, all in box A-109, pt. III, NAACP Records.

109. "Park Board Relaxes Ban," *BAA*, July 7, 1951, 1.

110. Balkin, *What* Brown v. Board of Education *Should Have Said*, 48; Sinclair, *International Relations Theory and International Law*, 98; *Simkins v. City of Greensboro*, 246 F.2d 425 (4th Cir., 1957).

111. Simkins interview, 4. See also box II, Gillespie Park Golf Course, Dr. George Simkins Jr. Collection, F. D. Bluford Archives and Special Collections, North Carolina A&T State University, Greensboro.

112. *Wolfe v. North Carolina*, 364 U.S. 177 (1960); "Greensboro's 'Golfers' Lose in High Court," *NJG*, July 2, 1960, 1.

113. "Greensboro, N.C., Desegregation Figure Honored," *ADW*, November 20, 1958, 1; "Greensboro Smoke Screen," *NJG*, July 6, 1957, 1; Simkins interview, 4.

114. George Roach, interviewed by Eugene E. Pfaff, November 17, 1978, 2, and Jo J. Spivey, interviewed by Eugene E. Pfaff, May 30, 1979, 2, Greensboro Voices Oral History Project, Greensboro Public Library, Greensboro, N.C.

115. U.S. Commission on Civil Rights, *Equal Protection of the Laws in North Carolina*, 208-9; *Simkins v. Moses H. Cone Memorial Hospital*, 323 F.2d 959 (1963).

116. Simkins interview, 3.

117. "Wasted Money," *NJG*, December 15, 1956, 8; "NAACP Legal Defense and Educational Fund Monthly Report, October 1954," 9, and "NAACP Legal Defense and Educational Fund Monthly Report, February 1955," 5, folder "NAACP Board of Directors, Sept.-Dec. 1954," pt. 3, Bethune Papers; Memoranda and NAACP Press Release, January 17 1954, box A-237, NAACP Records; "Lawyers in Charlotte Golf Case," *NJG*, November 22, 1952, A7. The U.S. Supreme Court refused to review the decision. See *Leeper v. Charlotte Park and Recreation Commission*, 350 U.S. 983 (1956); "Judge Decides Negro Players May Use City Golf Course," *Charlotte News*, December 4, 1956, 1; "Charlotte Golf Course Segregation Is Ended," *Charlotte Observer*, December 5, 1956, 1.

118. "Transcript of Tape-Recorded Interview with Fred Alexander," August 1968, 3, RJB 407, and "Transcript of Tape-Recorded Interview with Kelly Alexander," February 5, 1969, 5, RJB 399, Bunche Collection.

119. "Gastonia Facility Open to All," *NJG*, December 22, 1956, 1; "The Civil Rights Crisis: A Synopsis of Recent Developments," Southern Regional Council, July 26, 1963, 14, folder "Southern Regional Council Reports, 1963-1964," box

139, series I, Records of Andrew J. Young, Program Director, 1961–1964, pt. 4, SCLC Records.

120. Loth and Fleming, *Integration North and South*, 89; "The School Decision and the South," *New South* (Southern Regional Council), July–August 1956, 2; Korstad and Lichtenstein, "Opportunities Found and Lost," 804; "High Point Drops Golf Course Bars," *NJG*, March 3, 1956, 1; "20 Golfers Quit over Race Issue," *CD*, December 3, 1955, 10.

121. "14 Negroes Try Segregated SC Golf Fairways," *CD*, November 25, 1958, A22.

122. "It Can Be Done!," *BAA*, June 3, 1961, 1; "Fight Stepped Up to End Bias on Golf Course," *ADW*, April 19, 1961, 1; *Cummings v. City of Charleston*, 288 F.2d 817 (1961).

123. "Second Golf Case Ready," *BAA*, January 14, 1956, 1; "Turned Back at Columbus Golf Course," *ADW*, January 5, 1956, 1; Luker and Richardson, *Historical Dictionary of the Civil Rights Movement*, 87.

124. "Dr. Brewer Died for Justice!," *PC*, February 25, 1956, 1; "Doctor Slain in Georgia," *NJG*, February 25, 1956, 1; "NAACP Leader Shot to Death!," *CCP*, February 25, 1956, 1-A; "Doctor-Civic Leader Killed in Go. Store," *BAA*, February 25, 1956, 1.

125. Sampson, "Augusta vs. the World," 164.

126. Branch, *Parting the Waters*, 213; "Transformation of the Racial Views of Harry Truman," 28.

127. Morrow, *Black Man in the White House*, 24–25, 43, 161–63.

128. Michael Nelson, "White House Life," in Nelson, *Guide to the Presidency*, 1521.

129. Folder 124-A-1, "School-Arkansas Initial (2)," box 920, Eisenhower Papers.

130. "Speak Up Ike," *NYAN*, September 28, 1957, 8.

131. "Little Rock Shows Gain Following Integration Trend," *ADW*, September 1, 1963, 1; Wallach and Kirk, *Arsnick*, 17; *Freeman v. City of Little Rock*, E.D. Ark., W. Div., No. LR-62-C-40 (1963).

132. "Strictly Personal," *Augusta Courier*, October 7, 1957, 1.

133. "Ike Gets Friendly Welcome in Augusta," *ADW*, November 16, 1957, 1.

134. "President Eisenhower and Augusta," *ADW*, November 23, 1958, 4.

135. Folder 124-A-1, "Segregation 1960 (5)," box 914; folder 124-A, "Negro Affairs 1960," box 910; and folder 124-A-1, "School Decision-Pro (5)," box 917, Eisenhower Papers.

136. Langston Hughes, "Golfing and Goofing" and "Four-Way Celebrations," in Hughes, *Collected Works of Langston Hughes*, 109, 130; Langston Hughes, "Promulgations," in Hughes, *Simple's Uncle Sam*, 163.

137. "No Priority," *NYAN*, March 9, 1957, 6; "Turns Back on Group," *PT*, March 12, 1957, 8; "'I Cannot Do It'—Ike," *BAA*, February 9, 1957, 1; "Notes That Eisen-

hower Plays Golf in Georgia," *PC*, July 27, 1957, B3; "Eisenhower Evasive on Mob Rule Issue," *NJG*, February 16, 1957, 8.

138. "Ike Plays Golf; Youths for Integration Rebuffed," *CD*, November 1, 1958, 1; "Ike Too Busy to Meet NCNW," *PC*, November 29, 1958, 1.

139. "Ike Thanks UGA for Honors; Plans for 33rd Tourney Set," *Carolina Times*, August 15, 1959, 7; "Eisenhower Is Honorary UGA Member," *Carolina Times*, August 8, 1959, 7.

140. "Fight Stepped Up to End Bias on Golf Course," *ADW*, April 19, 1961, 1.

141. "Southeastern Georgia Crusade for Voters Report," 2, folder 10, "Southeastern Georgia Crusade for Voters Report 1964," box 130, pt. 3, SCLC Records; Clark, "Literacy and Liberation," 119; Boynton, *Student Protest Movement*, 6; Tuck, *Beyond Atlanta*, 128; "Savannah Drops More Racial Bars," *NJG*, July 15, 1961, 1; "The City of Savannah Sets a Pace," *ADW*, March 8, 1961, 6.

142. "West Side Golf Club against Golf Course for Negroes Only," *Jackson State Times*, March 9, 1955; "Plan to Build Jim Crow Park in Miss. Blasted," *ADW*, January 24, 1959, 1.

143. Oral History, Mr. Fred Clark Sr., 5, Center for Oral History and Cultural Heritage, University of Southern Mississippi, Hattiesburg.

144. "Interview with Aaron Henry," September 28, 1968, 19, RJB 326, Bunche Collection.

145. "Freedom Fighters Sexually Abused," *BAA*, June 15, 1963, 1; "The Civil Rights Crisis: A Synopsis of Recent Developments," Southern Regional Council, July 26, 1963, 11, folder "Southern Regional Council Reports, 1963–1964," box 139, series I, pt. 4, SCLC Records.

146. "Tribune Trophy to Vernice Turner in NAACP-WHAT Golf," *PT*, July 18, 1961, 1; "Help for 'Riders,'" *PT*, August 15, 1961, 4.

147. Ralph Abernathy sermon text, November 22, 1962, folder 15, "Sermon—'Trying to Get Home Without Jesus' Oct. 1961," box 58, series I, Records of the Treasurer, pt. 2, Records of the Executive Director and Treasurer, SCLC Records.

148. "Sewanee Sit-ins," folder 36, "Episcopal Society for Cultural and Racial Unity 1962," box 3, series 1, Correspondence, 1958–1968, pt. 1, Records of the President's Office, SCLC Records; "President Leading Sit-in," *BAA*, April 21, 1962, 1.

149. Joseph Lowery, Keynote Address at SCLC's Eighth Annual Convention, Savannah, Georgia, September 30, 1964, 12, folder 6, "President's Report-1964," box 130, pt. 3, Records of the Public Relations Department, SCLC Records.

150. Cotton, *If Your Back's Not Bent*, 73; "Jackie Robinson Says," *NJG*, July 13, 1963, 6.

151. "Transcript of Oral Interview with Reverend Wyatt Tee Walker," October 11, 1967, 11, RJB 56, Bunche Collection.

152. "WSB-TV newsfilm clip of Dr. Martin Luther King Jr. and reverend C. S.

Hamilton speaking to a mass meeting, Augusta, Georgia, 1962 April 3," reel 1012, 1:45/04:37, and "WSB-TV newsfilm clip of Dr. Martin Luther King Jr. speaking of African American civil rights, including voting rights, Augusta, Georgia, 1962 April 2," reel 0051, 00:00/09:29, WSB-TV Newsfilm Collection, Walter J. Brown Media Archives and Peabody Awards Collection, University of Georgia Library, Athens.

153. "King 'Masters' Augusta," SCLC Press Release, April 4, 1962, folder 7, "Apr. 1962," box 120, pt. 3, SCLC Records.

154. Lipsey, "King of Clubs," 12.

155. "Dr. Anderson, Irked by Decision, Renews Fight," *BAA*, February 23, 1963, 1; Lokos, *House Divided*, 107; Brunswick Corporation, *Annual Report*, 14.

156. Smith, "Albany's White," B1.

157. Lipsey, "King of Clubs," 14.

158. "Jack Nicklaus Visits MacGregor's Georgia Plants," *Coach & Athlete*, June 1963, 40.

159. Lipsey, "King of Clubs," 15.

160. "Transcript of Oral Interview with Reverend Wyatt Tee Walker," 90, Bunche Collection.

161. Eskew, *But for Birmingham*, 206; Abernathy, *And the Walls Came Tumbling Down*, 233.

162. Eskew, *But for Birmingham*, 72; "Birmingham Gives Negro Citizens Seventh Park Site," *ADW*, August 3, 1948, 1.

163. "City May Give Race Golf Course," *ADW*, February 23, 1952, 1; "Begin Work on $78,000 Birmingham Golf Site," *CD*, April 5, 1952, 5; "Golf Course Is Named for Mayor," *CD*, March 14, 1953, 5.

164. "Race Law Mars Dixie Series," *CD*, September 22, 1958, 24; "Birmingham and Houston," *PC*, June 12, 1954, 22; City Code, Montgomery, Alabama (1958 Supplement), 89, and City Code of Selma, Alabama (1956 Supplement), 2, in folder "State and City Ordinances (1)," 306 D, Records of Burke Marshall, Attorney, Civil Rights Division, 1961–1965, Record Group 60, General Records of the Department of Justice, 1790–2002, National Archives, College Park, Md.

165. "Opens All Parks to Everybody," *BAA*, November 4, 1961, 1; *Shuttlesworth v. Gaylord*, 202 F. Supp. 59 (N.D. Ala., 1961); *Moorhead v. City of Fort Lauderdale*, 152 F. Supp. 131 (1957).

166. "Freedom Now!," transcript of 1963 Pacifica Radio documentary, in McKinney, *Exacting Ear*, 168.

167. "Martin Luther King Reports Birmingham 'Living Up to Agreement,'" SCLC Press Release, July 17, 1963, folder 18, "Jul. 1963," box 120, pt. 3, SCLC Records; "The Civil Rights Crisis: A Synopsis of Recent Developments, II," Southern Regional Council, July 26, 1963, 1, folder "Southern Regional Council Reports, 1963–1964," box 139, series I, pt. 4, SCLC Records; "Albany Quiet after Business Shutdown," *ADW*, June 23, 1963, 1.

168. "Golf New Headache for Mobile," *CD*, April 22, 1958, A6; "Mobile Won't Integrate Course; Can't Afford Two," *ADW*, April 22, 1958, 1; "Mobile Gets Order from U.S. Court to Integrate Links," *BAA*, March 25, 1961, 1; *Sawyer v. City of Mobile*, 208 F. Supp. 548 (1961); Wolcott, *Race, Riots, and Roller Coasters*, 171.

169. "Racial Situation, Mobile Division, March 31, 1961," file 157-6-61-5, FBI Files.

Chapter 5

1. Askia Muhammad Toure, "'All African People Are Prisoners of War!' An Interview with Muhammad Ahmad," 4–5, folder "Muhammad Ahmad, Biographical (1)," series 1, Muhammad Ahmad (Max Stanford), Biographical Material, 1968–1995, The Black Power Movement, pt. 3, Ahmad Papers.

2. "Two Held, Five Sought in Virgin Isl. Killings," *NYAN*, September 16, 1972, A1; Krajicek, "Slaughter in Paradise," 42.

3. Griffin, "Murder on the Green," 4; Greaux, "Fountain Valley Put V.I. Golf in Unwanted Spotlight."

4. Griffin, "Murder on the Green," 4; Hansen, *Difficult Par*, 346–47.

5. Griffin, "Murder on the Green," 9.

6. Ibid., 6; "Hunt Killer-Bandits on St. Croix," *CD*, September 9, 1972, 1; Greaux, "Fountain Valley Put V.I. Golf in Unwanted Spotlight."

7. Griffin, "Murder on the Green," 6; Krajicek, "Slaughter in Paradise," 42.

8. "Intercommunal News: Innocent Brothers Held for Virgin Islands Golf Club Murders," *BP*, April 14, 1973, 9; "Virgin Islands 5 Tortured," *BP*, May 19, 1973, 10; "Two Arrested in Eight Virgin Island Murders," *ADW*, September 12, 1972, 1.

9. Greaux, "Fountain Valley Put V.I. Golf in Unwanted Spotlight."

10. "Black St. Croix," *Black News*, May 1, 1973, 36, in 1126832-000, 157-HQ-25073-EBF, Section 511, May 1, 1973–May 19, 1978, FBI Files.

11. "Virgin Islands: U.S. Official Tortured V.I. 5," *BP*, July 7, 1973, 11; "Virgin Islands 5 Tortured," *BP*, May 19, 1973, 10.

12. Griffin, "Murder on the Green," 7.

13. Krajicek, "Slaughter in Paradise," 42.

14. "Hijacker, Alone in Jet Restroom, Emerged with Gun, Official Says," *NYT*, January 2, 1985; Day, "30 Years after Massacre"; Pennington, "Fountain Valley Killer"; Krajicek, "Slaughter in Paradise," 42.

15. Griffin, "Murder on the Green," 7–8; "Rockresorts Solid Once Again," *CT*, February 15, 1987.

16. "The Seale-Brown 14-Point Program to Rebuild Oakland," *BP*, May 12, 1973, 4.

17. "Udin Writes to Brothers, Sisters," *PC*, June 10, 1972, 8.

18. "Hekima Ana: RNA Citizen," *Southern Patriot*, May 1972, in 1127197-000, HQ 157-9079, Section 55, 7/20/73–8/1/73, FBI Files.

19. "State Democratic Leader Operates Segregated Country Club!!," *Black*

New Ark, April 1973, 8, in "Black New Ark, Volume 2, April–June 1973," series XV, Serial Publications, 1968–1984, box 9, folder 9, Amiri Baraka Collection.

20. "Did You Know?," *Crusader*, June 5, 1961, 5, 8; Tyson, *Radio Free Dixie*, 201–2; Williams, *Negroes with Guns*, xix.

21. Max Stanford Jr., "On the Death of My Father: Maxwell Curtis Stanford, Sr.," March 1969, 2–3, folder "Muhammad Ahmad (Max Stanford), Writings, 1969," series 2, "Muhammad Ahmad (Max Stanford), Writings, 1962–1991," Ahmad Papers.

22. Johnson, *African American Woman Golfer*, 92; Shapiro, "For Years, Black Golfers' Best Club," A1; 100-152759, 100-441765, November 6, 1964, 42, "FBI File on Muslim Mosque, Inc.," Section 6, Aug.–Sep. 1964, FBI Files; Sinnette, *Forbidden Fairways*, 94; "Death Ends Career of Max Stanford," *Washington Afro-American*, January 21, 1969, 21.

23. "Black Golf Club Has Expansion Plans," *Outlook* (Office of Minority Business Enterprise), September 1970, 6; "Great Golf," *PT*, April 26, 1975, 15.

24. "$125 Stolen from Golfer Killed by Lightning," *PT*, June 18, 1957, 1; Askia Muhammad Toure, "'All African People Are Prisoners of War!' An Interview with Muhammad Ahmad," folder "Muhammad Ahmad, Biographical (1)," series 1, Muhammad Ahmad (Max Stanford), Biographical Material, 1968–1995, The Black Power Movement, pt. 3, Ahmad Papers.

25. NY-1058999, 100-399321, Section 3, 1957–1958, 85, "FBI File on Malcolm X," FBI Files.

26. "Muslim Chief's Son to Make Phila. His New Home Base," *PT*, September 26, 1964, 1; "Golf: The Fairview Golf Club Top Philly Pioneer," *PT*, January 1, 1963, 17; 100-152759, 100-441765, November 6, 1964, 42, "FBI File on Muslim Mosque, Inc.," Section 6, Aug.–Sep. 1964, FBI Files.

27. "Wonderful Woman," *PT*, April 7, 1970, 8.

28. Countryman, *Up South*, 139–40, 234; Joseph, *Waiting 'til the Midnight Hour*, 59–60, 103, 182.

29. FBI Memorandum, 12/13/66, folder "FBI File on Maxwell C. Stanford (Muhammad Ahmad), 1964–1967," series 4, "FBI File on Maxwell C. Stanford (Muhammad Ahmad), 1964–1975," Ahmad Papers.

30. Tyson, *Radio Free Dixie*, 290, 297; Ogbar, *Black Power*, 79.

31. "Poverty in the Caribbean," *Inner-City Voice* (Detroit), February 1970, 14.

32. "Tee Time," *LAS*, October 16, 1969, B3, and March 5, 1970, B4; "Hit Expert's Attack on Black Capitalism," *Jet*, January 22, 1970, 4; Hartmann, *Race, Culture, and the Revolt of the Black Athlete*, 138–39.

33. "Opportunities for Young Blacks," *BS*, July 1973, 71; "Tee Time," *LAS*, August 7, 1969, B4; "Race and Salesmanship," *NJG*, December 8, 1962, 8; "Negroes Fail to 'Tee Off' with Kroydon Clubs," *PT*, July 21, 1962, 1. For a sample Sifford-Kroydon ad, see "Swing with a Winner!," *LAS*, August 31, 1961, B11.

34. "Tee Time," *LAS*, July 17, 1969, B3.

35. "Tee Time," *LAS*, July 1, 1971, B4; Dyson, *Mercy, Mercy Me*, 53n16.

36. "Night Riders Raid Home," *BAA*, September 7, 1963, 1.

37. "Letter of the Week," *CCP*, August 8, 1964, 9-B; "Bias Rampant in Ohio!," *CCP*, December 10, 1960, 1-A; "Golf Club Bias Fight Now Headed for Court," *CCP*, February 11, 1956, 1-A; "Legal Sandtraps at Manikiki Golf Course," *CCP*, July 25, 1959, 2-C; "Manikiki to Become Public Links," *CCP*, August 29, 1959, 2-C.

38. "Down the Fairway," *CD*, May 10, 1952, 18; "Julian Black Sues Golf Club," *CD*, October 30, 1954, 1.

39. Rowan, *Wait till Next Year*, 319; Rampersad, *Jackie Robinson*, 412–13.

40. Cavanaugh, "Remembering Jackie Robinson," WC13.

41. Rampersad, *Jackie Robinson*, 413; folder 28, "Pheasant Valley Golf and Country Club, Lewisboro, N.Y., 1966–1967," box 4, Jackie Robinson Papers, Manuscript Division, Library of Congress, Washington, D.C.; "Upstate Golf Club Hit by Bias Charge," *NYAN*, January 22, 1966, 1; "Interracial Golf Club Put in the Rough by Town Zoners," *NYAN*, October 29, 1966, 1; "Jackie Heads Country Club in New York," *NJG*, October 29, 1966, 1; "Court Order Halts Golf Play," *NYAN*, November 5, 1966, 1; "Golf Club Fight Heads for SCHR," *NYAN*, January 14, 1967, 1.

42. Hirsch, *Willie Mays*, 469–71; "Willie Mays vs. Jackie Robinson Concerning Civil Rights Remark," *ADW*, March 16, 1968, 1. Two years later Mays also became a member of the Sharon Heights Golf and Country Club in Menlo Park, California; see "Mays Accepted in Exclusive Calif. Golf Club," *Jet*, March 5, 1970, 48.

43. "Tee Time," *LAS*, December 18, 1969, B3.

44. "Tee Time," *LAS*, June 12, 1969, B3; "Golf Course Named in Discrimination Suit," *LAS*, July 17, 1969, A1.

45. B. H. Netherland to Walter White, April 19, 1952, box A-237, NAACP Records; "Knoxville Drops Golf Course Bias," *CD*, March 29, 1952, 1; "Barred from Golf Course, Minister Promises to Return," *BAA*, October 24, 1959, 1; "Knoxville Golfers Ready to Sue for Use of Course," *CD*, May 10, 1952, 16; "Knoxville Bars Negro Golfers," *CD*, October 15, 1959, 30.

46. "Golfers Win Greensboro Golf Appeal," *CD*, July 13, 1957, 23; "On Leasing Virginia State Parks and Municipal Golf Courses," *NJG*, August 25, 1951, 14; U.S. Commission on Civil Rights, *Civil Rights U.S.A.*, 176; "Second Golf Case Ready," *BAA*, January 14, 1956, 1.

47. "State Summary of Recent Segregation Laws," December 1956, 306B: Files of W. Wilson White, Assistant Attorney General, Civil Rights Division, 1958–1959, Record Group 60, General Records of the Department of Justice, 1790–2002, National Archives, College Park, Md.; Loth and Fleming, *Integration North and South*, 88; "Huntsville, Ala. Links Opened to Negroes," *ADW*, February 21, 1956, 1.

48. "Will Sell Links for Half Price to Avoid Integration," *ADW*, July 11, 1957, 1; "Florida City Sells Course to Void Edict," *CD*, July 20, 1957, 11; *Griffis v. City of Fort Lauderdale*, 104 So.2d 33 (1958); Dawkins and Kinloch, *African American Golf-*

ers, 151; "U.S. Asked to Cite Golf Club for Contempt," *ADW*, January 25, 1963, 1; "Jacksonville Club Must End Discrimination," *ADW*, January 29, 1963, 1.

49. "Dr. Holley Tried to Open Course in the Sixties," *NJG*, April 13, 1988, 1; "Golf Champ in Portsmouth," *NJG*, September 6, 1975, 1; "U.S. Probing Jim Crow Golf Club in Portsmouth," *NJG*, April 26, 1975, 1; "Commission Urges City Take Over Jimcro Golf Links," *NJG*, October 9, 1976, 1.

50. "Good News in Race Relations," *NJG*, February 10, 1988, 2; "Jimcro Golf Club Shames City," *NJG*, July 24, 1976, 1; "Bide-A-Wee Controversy Grows though Course Opens to Public," *NJG*, April 13, 1988, 1; "Bide-A-Wee Actions Draw New Ire from Community," *NJG*, April 4, 1990, 1.

51. "Do the Farm Programs in Your Area Discriminate?," 2, folder 2, "Farm Programs—c. 1965," box 145, series II, Records of Randolph T. Blackwell, 1963–1966, pt. 4, Records of the Program Department, SCLC Records.

52. "8 Congressmen Delay Loan for All-White Miss. Golf Club," *BAA*, August 16, 1969, 1; "Golf Loan Cancellation Demanded," *BAA*, December 20, 1969, 1; "3 Members Win for Miss. Club," *BAA*, December 6, 1969, 1.

53. *CBS Evening News*, October 17, 1969, Television News Archive, Vanderbilt University, Nashville, Tenn.

54. "FHA Golf Loans Termed 'Racist,'" *BAA*, August 22, 1970, 1; folder "Mississippi-Field Reports [1966–1967]," entry 22, Records Relating to Special Projects, 1960–1970, USCCR Records.

55. "Whose Hand Is Out?," *CD*, August 13, 1969, 17.

56. "Golf Courses—Michigan," *Race Relations Law Reporter*, October 1957, 1046; Dawkins and Kinloch, *African American Golfers*, 151.

57. "All Race Barriers Down at Miami's City-owned Sites," *NJG*, March 31, 1962, 1; "Miami Golf Course Is Integrated," *ADW*, April 18, 1958, 1; "Expect Attempt to Desegregate Integrated Course's Clubhouse," *ADW*, May 3, 1958, 1.

58. "NAACP Legal Defense and Educational Fund Monthly Report, April 1953," 6, folder "NAACP Board of Directors, Jan–June 1953," pt. 3, Bethune Papers; "Golf Courses" (handwritten notes), box A-237, NAACP Records.

59. "Freedom Fighters Sexually Abused," *BAA*, June 15, 1963, 1.

60. Tennessee Commission on Human Relations, "Tennessee's Needs for Human Relations Laws," February 1966, 2, folder "Tennessee-Commission Housing Relations [1965–1967]," USCCR Records; *U.S. v. Central Carolina Bank and Trust*, 431 F.2d 972 (1970); Dawkins and Kinloch, *African American Golfers*, 144; *Wesley v. City of Savannah*, 294 F. Supp. 698 (1969).

61. "On the Palm Beach Frontier," *National Review*, April 10, 1962, 241; Katharine Knap to Martin Luther King, April 17, 1964, folder 14, "Jun. 1964," box 11, series 1, pt. 1, SCLC Records.

62. "D.C. Country Club Bias," *CD*, March 6, 1969, 17; "He Just Wanted to Golf," *BAA*, August 10, 1968, A4; Van Natta, *First Off the Tee*, 80.

63. "Minn. Senator Casts a 'No' Vote on Carswell," *PT*, February 10, 1970, 8; "Nixon Tiptoes Back into 19th Century," *PT*, February 7, 1970, 8; "Carswell Is Unfit," *CD*, February 26, 1970, 21; "Last Chance to Keep Carswell off Supreme Court," *BAA*, March 21, 1970, 1.

64. "Wins P.I. Open Golf Tourney," *CD*, February 12, 1938, 24; "Hassanein Returns for Another Try," *CD*, August 7, 1954, 22; "Hassan Hassanein Returns for Tourney," *CD*, July 9, 1955, 10.

65. "Rodney Ditzebe [sic], South African Golf Champ," *CD*, April 11, 1953, 23.

66. "S. African Golfer Finds British Greens Too Tricky," *Jet*, July 23, 1959, 16; "S. African Golfer Gets a Break," *Pacific Stars and Stripes*, June 18, 1961, 23; "Non-European Golf," *South African Golf*, July 1961, 7; "England's First Negro Golf Pro," *Jamaica Gleaner*, June 20, 1961, 19; Corcoran, *Duel in the Sun*, 6.

67. "Apartheid in Sports: South African Racial Policies Seen as a Contradiction to Athletic Ideal," *NYT*, October 15, 1963, 64; Booth, *Race Game*, 60–61, 66.

68. Gill, *Beauty Shop Politics*, 89; Polyné, "Modernizing the Race," 75.

69. "Hail the Republic of Haiti," *CD*, February 12, 1955, 4; Gill, *Beauty Shop Politics*, 89; "Back from Mexico," *CD*, April 9, 1955, 11; "A Tough Hole on Kingston Course," *CD*, April 16, 1955, 11.

70. "Golf and Marriage," *NYAN*, June 9, 1962, 11; "Alex Quaison-Sackey—UN President," *Crisis*, January 1965, 32.

71. "Special Interest Tours," *BE*, April 1977, 56.

72. "Travelogue," *Jet*, October 4, 1973, 59; "Pioneer Woman Golfer Enters Puerto Rico Tourney," *Jet*, January 17, 1963, 55; "D.C. Dominates Golf Meet," *NJG*, August 15, 1964, A24; "Jackie Robinson with 334 at Pepsi Golf Tourney," *Jet*, July 22, 1965, 54; "Prize Time," *Jet*, August 19, 1965, 55; "Paris Scratchpad," *Jet*, December 1, 1966, 28; "Society World," *Jet*, August 31, 1972, 38; "International Tourney," *LAS*, September 23, 1976, B3. For sample ad, see *CCP*, January 20, 1968, 7-B.

73. "TCB: Earl Jackson," *BS*, September 1973, 22, 68–69; "Tee Time," *LAS*, March 13, 1969, B3, and June 12, 1969, B3; *Jet*, August 3, 1967, 28, 54.

74. "TCB: Earl Jackson," *BS*, September 1973, 22; Johnson, *African American Woman Golfer*, 124; "Chicago Women Host Successful UGA Play," *CD*, September 2, 1978, 17.

75. "Hate Protest Fails to Halt Golf Tourney," *Washington Afro-American*, October 2, 1951, 1; "Toledo Golf Club Accuses Council of Public Links Qualifying Bias," *CD*, July 14, 1956, 17; "4 Negro Golfers Refused Tickets on Two Courses," *ADW*, June 25, 1958, 1; "Four Fight Nat'l Golf Meet Bias," *CD*, June 17, 1959, 22; "Bar Chicago Golfers in Nat'l Publinx Play," *CD*, June 27, 1959, 23.

76. Mohr and Krupa, *Golf in Denver*, 92; Young, "Black Athlete in the Golden Age of Sports," 114; "Student Wins Major Golf Title," *CD*, July 20, 1959, 1; "At 23, He's a 'First,'" *NJG*, July 25, 1959, 1.

77. "Down the Fairway," *CD*, January 19, 1957, 17; "Russ' Corner," *CD*, Janu-

ary 23, 1954, 24; "Sifford and Rhodes Get Golf Cash," *CD*, January 21, 1956, 17; Wexler, "Los Angeles Open," D8; "Negro Wins Major Golf Tournament," *NJG*, November 16, 1957, 1.

78. Young, "Black Athlete in the Golden Age of Sports," 114.

79. Sifford, *"Just Let Me Play,"* 48.

80. "Golfers Expect Charles Sifford, Bill Spiller to Grab 1950 Titles," *CD*, June 17, 1950, 17.

81. "Golfer Charges Links Bias," *LAS*, November 14, 1957, A1.

82. Barkow, *Gettin' to the Dance Floor*, 229, 232; Sinnette, *Forbidden Fairways*, 135.

83. Tramel, "Little-Known Story," B3; Barkow, "One Man's Mission," 23.

84. Plaschke, "He Went Down Swinging," S7.

85. "Jack Remembers Pioneer."

86. "Jackie Robinson," *CD*, March 7, 1960, 35.

87. "Jackie Robinson," *CD*, February 29, 1960, A11.

88. "Jackie Robinson," *CD*, March 7, 1960, 35.

89. Harvey, "Militant Maggie Hathaway," S8.

90. Dawkins and Kinloch, *African American Golfers*, 157–58; "PGA Facing Court Action," *CD*, December 17, 1960, 23.

91. "Jackie Robinson," *CD*, March 14, 1960, A11, and April 12, 1960, A11.

92. "SCAD Opens MGA to Negro Golfers," *NYAN*, July 2, 1960, 1; "Jackie Robinson," *CD*, August 29, 1960, 11; "SCAD 'Tees' Off," *NYAN*, July 30, 1960, 10; "PGA—In Step," *LAS*, November 23, 1961, A6.

93. "PGA—In Step," *LAS*, November 23, 1961, A6; "PGA-Color Line," *CCP*, June 3, 1961, 4-B.

94. "Charley Sifford Proving Popular Golf Path-Finder," *CD*, February 25, 1961, 24.

95. "Greensboro OK Surprises Charlie Sifford," *CD*, April 22, 1961, 23.

96. Sifford, *"Just Let Me Play,"* 121; Alexander, "At Wyndham Golf," B1.

97. "19 Years Is a Long Time to Be in the Rough," *BS*, July 1973, 32; "Church Blasts Laid to N.C. Klan," *BAA*, May 21, 1966, 1.

98. Sifford, *"Just Let Me Play,"* 127–34.

99. "New Respect for Tan Golfers," *NJG*, April 22, 1961, 1.

100. "Greensboro OK Surprises Charlie Sifford," *CD*, April 22, 1961, 23; "Charley Sifford Proving Popular Golf Path-Finder," *CD*, February 25, 1961, 24.

101. Dawkins and Tellison, "Golf," 61; "Big Time Golf: Pete Brown Hurls His Challenge," *Ebony*, May 1967, 130.

102. Gray and Lamb, *Born to Win*, 138, 140; "Too Little Fanfare for Althea," *CD*, June 11, 1956, 11.

103. "Althea Wins Chippers' Golf Tourney," *CCP*, July 29, 1961, 5; Gray and Lamb, *Born to Win*, 142; "Althea Gibson, Joe Louis to Play in Golf Tourney," *CD*, June 19, 1962, 2.

104. Robertson, *Fair Ways*, 79; *GD*, November 1967, 79.

105. Gray and Lamb, *Born to Win*, 137, 147; Denney, "Althea Gibson"; Johnson, *Heroines*, 73.

106. Sinnette, *Forbidden Fairways*, 107–9; Kirsch, *Golf in America*, 175; Glenn, "Playing through Racial Barriers," 4–8.

107. "Women's Golf Club Seeks County Ban," *LAS*, May 17, 1956, A1; "Lady Golfers Level Charges at WPLGA," *LAS*, October 11, 1956, A1; "Tee Time," *LAS*, December 16, 1971, B3.

108. Goldstein, "Bill Powell," B6; "Letters from Readers," *CCP*, September 16, 1961, 2-C; "Will Compete in UGA Junior Golf Tourney," *CCP*, July 30, 1960, 5-C.

109. Nösner, *Clearview*, 117; Sinnette, *Forbidden Fairways*, 118–19; Crouse, "Prejudice Challenged a Path," D1; "Black Female Golf Pro, 32, Wins Posh Spot in England," *Jet*, January 25, 1979, 50; "British Club Hires Renee Powell," *Sarasota Herald-Tribune*, January 3, 1979, 4-C; McDaniel, *Uneven Lies*, 80–81.

110. "The Way the Ball Bounces," *PT*, March 23, 1963, 4; "Negroes and TV Golf," *NJG*, March 30, 1963, 6.

111. "Pro Golfers to Be Featured in St. Croix," *Virgin Islands Daily News*, March 17, 1967, 9; "St. Croix Defeats Local Golf Team," *Virgin Islands Daily News*, May 11, 1968, 9.

112. "Sifford Defeated in TV Golf Duel," *Washington Afro-American*, February 8, 1966, 13; "Sifford to Meet Sanders in Match," *BAA*, January 25, 1969, 16; Young, "Black Athlete in the Golden Age of Sports," 118.

113. "Pete Brown Hurls His Challenge," *Ebony*, May 1967, 130; "Pete Brown Makes T of C History," *LAS*, April 8, 1965, A1.

114. "Invited to Colonial Meet," *NJG*, May 9, 1964, 1; "Pete Brown Wins Golf Tourney in Oklahoma," *CD*, May 4, 1964, 21.

115. "Elder's a Man in the Middle," *CD*, August 16, 1969, 25; "Brown Takes First in Open Golf Tournament," *LAS*, February 5, 1970, A1; "Hungry Pete Brown Wins $30,000 Golf Pot," *NJG*, February 7, 1970, 1.

116. "Sifford Moves into Golfdom's Limelight," *CD*, August 26, 1967, 17.

117. *GD*, November 1967, 77.

118. "Sifford Wins $20,000 in Golf's Pot o' Gold," *CCP*, January 18, 1969, 1-A; "A Day for Sifford in Watts," *LAS*, February 6, 1969, A1.

119. "Elder Joins Golfing Elite," *CD*, August 24, 1968, 16; "Down the Fairway," *CD*, September 11, 1954, 10.

120. "Top Black Golfer Misses Masters," *CD*, March 26, 1974, 26; "Negro Star Thrills World of Pro Golf," *CCP*, August 17, 1968, 1-A; "Lee Yields in Overtime," *NJG*, August 17, 1968, 1; "Elder Wins $12,187," *PT*, August 13, 1968, 1.

121. "Lee Elder Plays It Cool," *GD*, December 1968, 30; "Lee Elder, Hottest Sophomore in Pro Golf," *Ebony*, September 1969, 62. For a sample advertisement, see *GD*, June 1969.

122. "Casper Wins Greensboro Open by 4 Shots," *CT*, April 9, 1968, C3.

123. "Elder's a Man in the Middle," *CD*, August 16, 1969, 25.

124. "Scorecard," *SI*, April 23, 1973, 13.

125. "Wherever We May Be," *African World*, May 19, 1973, 2, in 1126832-000, 157-HQ-25073-EBF, Section 511, May 1, 1973–May 19, 1978, FBI Files.

126. "Black Golfers in S. Africa Refuse to Be Used," *African World*, September 16, 1972, 11, in "The African World, Volume 2, July–September 1972," series XV, Serial Publications, 1968–1984, box 9, folder 1, Amiri Baraka Collection.

127. "African Golfers to Play in PGA Meets," *CD*, March 7, 1963, 26.

128. "$20,000 at Los Angeles Open," *Jet*, January 30, 1969, 53; "Sifford Picks Up $20,000 in L.A. Open," *NJG*, January 18, 1969, 1.

129. "Call Back the Years," *SI*, March 31, 1969, 56.

130. "What They Are Saying," *GD*, March 1969, 91.

131. "Call Back the Years," *SI*, March 31, 1969, 56.

132. "$20,000 at Los Angeles Open," *Jet*, January 30, 1969, 53.

133. Hall, *Arthur Ashe*, 119, 135; "NAACP Plan Sports Protest," *Boston Globe*, July 15, 1971, in series 1, Administration, 1952–1972, box 1, Interoffice Memoranda, 1952–1972, folder "Interoffice Memoranda, July, 1971," ACOA Records.

134. Player, *Grand Slam Golf*, 7–11; Monbiot, "Comment & Debate," 31; Booth, *Race Game*, 59.

135. Kennedy, *Course of Their Own*, 211; Sanders, *South Africa and the International Media*, 68, 234.

136. Kennedy, *Course of Their Own*, 212; "Gary Player Is Heckled over Apartheid Policy," *NYT*, June 18, 1971, 46; Hall, *Arthur Ashe*, 156.

137. Harvey, "Militant Maggie Hathaway," S8.

138. "Black Caddies," *BS*, May 1976, 25–26.

139. Buckley, "Player for All Time," 12.

140. "Go Home, Gary Player," *BAA*, April 11, 1970, 4; "Fears for Safety of S. African Golfer's Life in U.S.," *Jet*, April 9, 1970, 52.

141. "S.A. Golfer Is Target of Protest," *BAA*, May 2, 1970, 1; "College Fund Declines S. African Golfer's Offer," *Jet*, April 30, 1970, 55; "2 Negroes Support Benefit Golf," *NYT*, March 12, 1970, 70; "Flip Wilson OD Golf Meet Headliner," *NJG*, May 6, 1972, A25.

142. "Black Golfer Elder Gets South African Invitation," *Jet*, July 15, 1971, 48.

143. Kennedy, *Course of Their Own*, 211.

144. ACOA to Lee Elder, August 23, 1971, series 3, Programs and Activities in African Countries, 1948–1987, box 102, folder 21, "Cultural Boycott: memoranda, articles, correspondence, and press releases and clippings, 1971–1972," ACOA Records. See also George Hauser letter, June 29, 1971, series 1, box 1, folder "Interoffice Memoranda, June, 1971," ACOA Records, and "Black Pro Golfer Agrees to Compete in S. African Event," *NYT*, August 19, 1971, 48.

145. "Going to South Africa," *NYAN*, September 4, 1971, B-12.

146. "Africans for Rhodesian Circuit," news clipping, July 14, 1971, series 3,

box 103, folder 52, "Sports boycott, Lee Elder (golf): press clippings, 1971," and "Dennis Brutus, Testimony before Digg's Sub-Comm on Africa, House," February 4, 1970, 35, folder 54, "Sports boycott, Gary Player (golf): press clippings," ACOA Records.

147. Leonard, "Elder Made Bold Play in South Africa."

148. "S. Africa No Worry to Elder," *CD*, November 27, 1971, 34.

149. "Elder Hopeful of Bid to Masters," *NYT*, December 21, 1971, 48; "Three, at 280, Will Play Off in South African Pro Golf," *NYT*, November 28, 1971, S11.

150. Leonard, "Elder Made Bold Play in South Africa"; "18 Years Later, Lee Elder Sees Some Welcomed Changes in South Africa," *LAT*, March 26, 1989, Sports-6.

151. "Masters Pressure Off," *Jet*, November 27, 1975, 47.

152. "18 Years Later, Lee Elder Sees Some Welcomed Changes in South Africa," *LAT*, March 26, 1989, Sports-6.

153. Levinson and Christensen, *Encyclopedia of World Sport*, 156; Hall, *Arthur Ashe*, 254. In November 1983 Johannesburg newspapers reported that Calvin Peete, the PGA Tour's top black pro at the time, had agreed to participate in the 1983 Million Dollar Challenge the following month, although Peete never did. See "South African Report," *NYT*, November 3, 1983, B21.

154. "Elder Hopeful of Bid to Masters," *NYT*, December 21, 1971, 48.

155. "After 38 Years, Blacks Still Not Invited to Masters," *Jet*, May 4, 1972, 53.

156. "What It's Really Like to Belong to Augusta National," *GD*, April 1967, 36.

157. Carl Sanders, interviewed by Thomas H. Baker, May 13, 1969, 5, AC 78-76, Interview 1, LBJ Presidential Library Oral Histories, LBJ Presidential Library, Austin, Tex.

158. "Top Black Golfer Misses Masters," *CD*, March 26, 1974, 26; "Elder, Sifford, Dent in PGA's Top 100 '73 List," *Jet*, December 27, 1973, 80; Sampson, "Augusta vs. the World," 166; "Elder: 'Won't Accept Masters Invite,'" *PC*, April 14, 1973, 1.

159. "Trevino 'Sorry' for Lee Elder," *CD*, September 6, 1972, 25.

160. "19 Years Is a Long Time to Be in the Rough," *BS*, July 1973, 34.

161. "Masters 'Quiz' Tires Black Pros," *CD*, March 4, 1974, 24.

162. "Elder Sheds Doubt on Masters Invite," *CD*, April 23, 1974, 2; McDaniel, *Uneven Lies*, 116.

163. "Elder Makes Masters Bid," *CD*, April 22, 1974, 1; "How Lee Elder Won the Monsanto Open," *LAS*, April 25, 1974, A1; "Elder Says Attention Hurts His Golf Game," *CD*, April 3, 1975, 32.

164. "268—Gerald R. Ford, Remarks at a Reception Honoring Professional Golfer Lee Elder, December 1, 1974," in *Gerald R. Ford*, 675; "Elder Sets Sight on Masters," *CD*, June 29, 1974, B2; "Masters Pressure Off," *Jet*, November 27, 1975, 47; *The Best of Golf Digest, 1950-1975* (New York: Simon and Schuster, 1975), 161; "Ford Plays a Round of Golf at Congressional Club," *NYT*, July 26, 1976, 13.

165. "'Lee Elder Day' Irks Sifford," *CD*, June 29, 1974, 1.

166. "Words of the Week," *Jet*, August 22, 1974, 32.

167. "Elder Wants More Kids in Golf," *CD*, July 2, 1974, 30.

168. "Sifford Quits PGA, Takes Club Pro Spot," *CD*, January 23, 1975, 36.

169. "Masters Founder Uses 'Simple Logic,'" *CD*, April 14, 1975, 30; "Portrait of a Golf Pioneer," *CCP*, July 6, 1963, 10-C.

170. "Achievement Drawbacks," *CD*, January 28, 1975, 7.

171. McDaniel, *Uneven Lies*, 78–79.

172. "Rose, Lee Elder Eye Masters End," *CD*, April 9, 1975, 29; "Black Caddy Chose Elder 10 Years Ago," *CD*, April 9, 1975, 28; Leonard, "Elder Changed the Face of the Masters," D11; McDaniel, *Uneven Lies*, 116.

173. "Elder Lost Out but Proved He's a 'Pro,'" *CD*, April 14, 1975, 28; "Elder Wins a Big One," *NYAN*, August 26, 1978, A1; "Elder Wins $60 Gs," *LAS*, August 24, 1978, A1; "Stars Sing & Dance for Lee Elder," *LAS*, February 10, 1977, A1.

Chapter 6

1. "New Nike Ad with Tiger Woods, Lee Elder, and Charlie Sifford," *Sports Business Daily*, May 15, 1997; "Changing History's Course," *Hartford Courant*, July 20, 1997, K1; "Thanks to Tiger, Elder Getting into TV Ad Act," *CT*, June 01, 1997, C-13; "Golf Legend Praises Tiger on Success, Loyalty to Game," *PT*, June 30, 2000, 1C; *Ebony*, July 1997, 7; *BE*, September 1997, 9.

2. "Wow! That Ball Is Going, Going . . . Shhhh!," *NYT*, April 20, 1997, E2; "Woods Draws Masters Ratings Up," *Free Lance-Star*, April 16, 1997, B5.

3. "Opportunities for Young Blacks," *BS*, July 1973, 74; "Can Black Golfers Come to the Fore?," *SI*, July 9, 1990, 86.

4. "Eye of the Tiger," *SI*, May 27, 1996, C18; "First Rate Effort," *Jet*, December 22, 1986, 46; "Payton Set to Retire as Jackson State's Golf Coach," *Jackson Clarion-Ledger*, June 24, 2016, clarionledger.com/story/sports/college/jackson-state/2016/06/23/payton-set-retire-jackson-states-golf-coach/86309154/; "National Headliners," *Jet*, June 10, 1996, 10; "History-Making Golf Team," *Jet*, May 21, 2001, 49.

5. "Eddie Payton Establishes Own Legacy as Jackson St. Golf Coach," *SI*, November 6, 2009, si.com/more-sports/2009/11/06/payton; "Not a Black-and-White Issue for HBCUs," *Fox Sports*, May 6, 2012, foxsports.com/golf/story/historically-black-colleges-winning-without-minorities-051612.

6. "Eye of the Tiger," *SI*, May 27, 1996, C18.

7. "Eddie Payton Establishes Own Legacy as Jackson St. Golf Coach," *SI*, November 6, 2009, si.com/more-sports/2009/11/06/payton.

8. Yocom, *My Shot*, 170; Sinnette, *Forbidden Fairways*, 181; "Black Pros," *BS*, July 1973, 54; Ashe, *Hard Road to Glory*, 141.

9. "Cross-Handed Star Cops UGA National Golf Title," *BAA*, August 30, 1975, 9; "The Man: Charlie Owens," *BS*, July 1973, 24; Fields, "Owens an Overlooked

Pioneer," 17; Page, "Love, Hate Relationship with Golf," 1C; Owens and Smith, *I Hate to Lose*.

10. Yocom, *My Shot*, 171.

11. "Golf Champ at Six," *Ebony*, November 1982, 96.

12. "Black Teen Golfer Wins U.S. Amateur Title," *Jet*, August 26, 1991, 48; "Teeing Off," *BE*, August 1992, 97; "Tiger Woods Captures 2nd Amateur Championship," *Jet*, August 31, 1992, 47; "Tiger Woods Becomes First Black to Win U.S. Amateur," *Jet*, September 12, 1994, 51.

13. "Calvin Peete's Mission . . . The Masters," *LAT*, April 11, 1985, C-14; "Peete Returns to the Ranks of Leaders," *NYT*, March 27, 1988, S4; Weber, "Calvin Peete," A28.

14. "Calvin Peete's Mission . . . The Masters," *LAT*, April 11, 1985, C-14.

15. Ibid.

16. Ibid.

17. Weber, "Calvin Peete," A28.

18. "From Migrant Worker to the Masters," *Ebony*, July 1980, 104; "George Johnson Wins Benefit Black Golf Meet," *Jet*, January 17, 1980, 50; "Black Golfer Wins $36,000," *CCP*, July 21, 1979, 1-A; "Calvin Peete Wins $162,000 in Tournament Championship," *Jet*, April 22, 1985, 48; "Peete Conquers Master's Course Despite Himself," *Jet*, May 7, 1984, 46.

19. "Golf Fashions," *BS*, July 1973, 42; "A Double Victory for Black Golfers," *Ebony*, October 1982, 102.

20. "Opportunities for Young Blacks," *BS*, July 1973, 74.

21. "Can Black Golfers Come to the Fore?," *SI*, July 9, 1990, 86.

22. "Teeing Off," *BE*, August 1992, 97; "Can Black Golfers Come to the Fore?," *SI*, July 9, 1990, 86.

23. "A Double Victory for Black Golfers," *Ebony*, October 1982, 104.

24. "Interview with B. J. McGuinnis of the Cincinnati Recreation Department," 3, reel 0438, Field team interviews, September 1967, box 1, series 59, Subject Files of Robert Conot, pt. V, Records of the National Advisory Commission on Civil Disorders (Kerner Commission), "Civil Rights during the Johnson Administration, 1963-1969" (Frederick, Md.: University Publications of America, 1987), microfilm collection.

25. "Opportunities for Young Blacks," *BS*, July 1973, 74; "Elder Wants More Kids in Golf," *CD*, July 2, 1974, 30; Hall, *Arthur Ashe*, 28-29, 44.

26. "Calvin Peete Scholarships to Assist Black Golfers," *Jet*, April 23, 1984, 50; "TCB: Earl Jackson," *BS*, September 1973, 69; "Golf 'School' Opens to Help Youngsters," *CD*, February 8, 1975, 18; "Local Golf Club to Hold 6-Week School for Kids," *CD*, May 10, 1975, 17; Robinson, *Skins and Grins*, 104.

27. Schupak, "Dickey, 84, Elevated Minority Golf," 9; "Playing Power Sports Leads to Power Jobs," *PT*, October 7, 1988, 7A.

28. "Death on the Eighth Green," *LAS*, May 30, 1974, A1.

29. "Golf, a Game of Relaxation," *CCP*, March 8, 1984, 9-A.

30. "Council OKays Plans for Bedford-Pine Area Development Project," *ADW*, March 20, 1975, 1.

31. "The Golfing of America," *New Republic*, August 3, 1998, 19.

32. "Opportunities for Young Blacks," *BS*, July 1973, 70, 74.

33. Yocom, *My Shot*, 173; "Calvin Peete Visits SCLC Women's Golf Tournament," *ADW*, June 17, 1993, 8; Crouse, "Treasure of Golf's Sad Past," A1.

34. "New Golf Champ Gives Caddy Credit for Victory," *NJG*, April 11, 1959, 1.

35. "Woods Tears Up Augusta and Tears Down Barriers," *NYT*, April 14, 1997, C7.

36. Crouse, "Treasure of Golf's Sad Past," A1.

37. "It's Money in the Bag," *SI*, May 4, 1981, 39; "Black Caddies," *BS*, May 1976, 26.

38. "Caddy 'Worth' 15% of PGA Check," *Oklahoman*, August 9, 1982.

39. "Golf Pioneer Maggie Hathaway Retires," *LAS*, February 15, 1996, B1.

40. Crouse, "Treasure of Golf's Sad Past," A1.

41. "Where We Once Roamed," *BE*, September 2002, 126.

42. Williams, *Out of the Rough*, 210; "Tiger Woods Could Sue Kiwi Caddy Steve Williams over Tell-all Book," *Sunday Star-Times* (N.Z.), November 8, 2015; Reed, "Black Golf Caddy," 61.

43. Eskew, *But for Birmingham*, 339; "Shoal Creek," *SI*, August 6, 1990, 14.

44. "Shoal Creek and Racism," *CCP*, August 9, 1990, 4-A; "Golf Clubs on Notice," *PT*, August 10, 1990, 2A; "Shoal Creek Controversy," *LAS*, August 2, 1990, B3; "PGA, Caught in the Trap," *LAS*, August 2, 1990, B1.

45. "Gary Player Sides with PGA Protesters," *LAT*, July 30, 1990, C-11; "Black Golfers Hail Withdrawal of PGA Sponsors," *PT*, July 31, 1990, 1A.

46. "Gary Player Sides with PGA Protesters," *LAT*, July 30, 1990, C-11.

47. Strege, *Tiger*, 89; Eskew, *But for Birmingham*, 340; "The Golfing of America," *New Republic*, August 3, 1998, 19.

48. Eskew, *But for Birmingham*, 339–40.

49. "The Gates Open," *SI*, August 13, 1990, 54; Glennon Threatt, interviewed by Kimberly Hill, June 16, 2005, 46, Southern Oral History Program Collection, Wilson Library, University of North Carolina, Chapel Hill; Pennington, "Hall Thompson," B11.

50. "Cypress Point Drops PGA Tour Event Instead of Changing Its Rules," *NYT*, September 18, 1990, D26; Kirsch, *Golf in America*, 196; "Rice Flexing Soft Power to Break Golf's Barriers," *San Francisco Chronicle*, February 8, 2013, A13.

51. "Sports Snobbery," *BAA*, April 18, 1981, 4; "Off Course," *SI*, April 29, 1991, 15.

52. "Whittier Country Club Hit with Suit," *LAS*, March 14, 1985, A1; "Historic Club Faces Bias Lawsuit," *LAS*, November 19, 1987, A1; "Indiana Country Club Admits Black Chrysler Exec," *PC*, May 30, 1992, 1.

53. "Augusta's Rewarding 'Golf Nut,'" *NYT*, April 14, 1991, S1; Sampson, "Augusta vs. the World," 167.

54. "Top Achievers and a Turning Point: Golf," *NYT*, December 31, 1990, 40.

55. Shipnuck, *Battle for Augusta National*, 27.

56. "Tiger Woods 'Masters' the Augusta Masters," *ADW*, April 17, 1997, 1.

57. "Tiger Who?," *ADW*, April 20, 1997, 4; "First Black Wins U.S. Amateur Golf Crown," *PT*, August 30, 1994, 1A; "Tiger Woods Smashes Golf Records and Mean Stereotypes," *NJG*, April 30, 1997, 2.

58. "Blacks & Sports," *ADW*, May 4, 1997, 4; "Tiger Masters Golf's Legends," *PT*, April 15, 1997, 1A; "Bartram Girls Tee Off over Tiger," *PT*, April 22, 1997, 1A; "Number of Area Golfers on the Rise," *NJG*, August 7, 2002, 1.

59. "Tiger Woods Roars to Masters Victory," *PT*, April 18, 1997, 6A.

60. "Blacks Exult in Tiger's Win," *LAS*, April 17, 1997, A1.

61. Nösner, *Clearview*, 115.

62. "Tiger Woods Roars to Masters Victory," *PT*, April 18, 1997, 6A; "Woods Tears Up Augusta and Tears Down Barriers," *NYT*, April 14, 1997, C7.

63. "Charley Sifford Proving Popular Golf Path-Finder," *CD*, February 25, 1961, 24; "Big Time Golf," *Ebony*, May 1967, 138; Sifford, *"Just Let Me Play,"* 108.

64. "Changing History's Course," *Hartford Courant*, July 20, 1997, K1.

65. Rosaforte, *Tiger Woods*, 183; Yocom, *My Shot*, 174.

66. "The Golfing of America," *New Republic*, August 3, 1998, 18–21.

67. Roberson, "African American Culture," 801–2; "Catch the Flying Tiger," *BE*, September 1997, 80–82; "The Golfing of America," *New Republic*, August 3, 1998, 19; Sammons, "Black Golfers."

68. "Past Masters," *American Legacy*, Fall 1997, 44.

69. Kirsch, *Golf in America*, 237; McDaniel, *Uneven Lies*, 81. Others include USGA Secretary Sheila C. Johnson and USGA Executive Committee member Gregory B. Morrison. In 1992 John Merchant became the first African American to serve on the Executive Committee, while in 2010 Condoleezza Rice was named to the USGA's Nominating Committee. Former IBM executive Barbara Douglas joined the USGA Women's Committee in 1993 and served as chair from 2009 to 2010. Earnest Ellison Jr. served as PGA director of business and community relations from 1997 to 2013. See Sammons, "Black Golfers."

70. "Bivens' Missteps Starting to Add Up," *ESPN*, September 5, 2008, espn.com/golf/columns/story?id=3571125&columnist=adelson_eric; "The Coming Tiger Crash," *Golf Magazine*, April 20, 2014, golf.com/scorecard/2014/04/20/coming-tiger-crash-woods-absence-spells-trouble-golf-industry; "'Four!' Looking Out for a Black-Owned Golf Firm," *LAS*, February 27, 2003, A6.

71. Woods and McDaniel, *Training a Tiger*, xiv; Tramel, "Tiger Was Raised by a Wildcat," B-5.

72. President's Committee on Equal Opportunity in the Armed Forces, *Ini-*

tial Report, 45; "The City Game," Met Golfer, August–September 2007, 32; Woods and McDaniel, Training a Tiger, xvi–xvii.

73. "Tee Time," LAS, August 21, 1969, B3.

74. "Opportunities for Young Blacks," BS, July 1973, 75.

75. Callahan, His Father's Son, 109; Crouse, "Treasure of Golf's Sad Past," A1.

76. Sifford, "Just Let Me Play"; "Sifford Lands Endorsement with Woods," Lawrence Journal-World, May 8, 1997, 2C.

77. McDaniel, Uneven Lies, 8–9; "Tiger Woods' Gift Launches a New UMES Golf Management Scholarship Fund," Office of Public Relations, University of Maryland Eastern Shore, March 26, 2015; Nösner, Clearview, 103; Housewright, "Course Cares about 1 Color Only," 33A; "With Tiger, It's Reachable," WP, July 2, 2009, G3; "If He's Looking, Woods Could Find Redemption at a Historic Golf Course in D.C.," WP, December 9, 2009, B1; "Overtures to the Obamas," WP, February 9, 2009, B1.

78. "Tiger Woods Makes History at the Masters," Jet, April 28, 1997, 55, 59; Leonard, "Elder Changed the Face of the Masters," D11; "Tiger Masters Golf's Legends," PT, April 15, 1997, 1A.

79. Barkley and Wilbon, Who's Afraid of a Large Black Man?, 4; Zirin, "Tiger Woods Story That Actually Matters"; Callahan, His Father's Son, 108.

80. "Golfer Tiger Woods Says He's Not Black, Newspaper Reports," Jet, April 24, 1995, 8.

81. "Woods Master from Tee to Green, but Off-course Judgments Suspect," Baltimore Sun, May 15, 1997, 2C; "Tiger Woods Makes History at the Masters," Jet, April 28, 1997, 54.

82. "Clinton Honors Robinson," PC, May 3, 1997, 1.

83. "Woods Master from Tee to Green, but Off-course Judgments Suspect," Baltimore Sun, May 15, 1997, 2C.

84. "Woods Praises Alfred 'Tup' Holmes for Efforts," ADW, September 17, 1998, 1.

85. "Woods: I'm More Than Black," Chicago Sun-Times, April 22, 1997, 1.

86. Yocom, My Shot, 25

87. "Golf Pioneer Maggie Hathaway Retires," LAS, February 15, 1996, B1.

88. "A Sign of Hope," LAS, May 1, 1997, A6.

89. "Tiger Woods Represents the New Race Paradigm of Black Culture," PT, April 29, 1997, 6A.

90. "Tiger Woods . . . ," LAS, May 8, 1997, A6.

91. "Tiger Woods African American—Like It or Not," PT, April 29, 1997, 6A; "Editorial," Reggae Roots International 1, no. 3 (1997): 4.

92. "Too Far out of Bounds," Chicago Sun-Times, June 15, 2001, 94; Londino, Tiger Woods, 68; Starn, Passion of Tiger Woods, 79; "Sir Charles Accuses Ga. Golf Club of Practicing Racism against Woods," LAS, March 14, 2002, B2.

93. "Out of Bounds," *SI*, May 23, 1994, 14; "Too Far out of Bounds," *Chicago Sun-Times*, June 15, 2001, 94.

94. "Out of Bounds," *SI*, July 25, 1994, 16; Harvey, "Militant Maggie Hathaway," S8.

95. Dalmage, *Politics of Multiracialism*, 137.

96. "Gary Player Sides with PGA Protesters," *LAT*, July 30, 1990, C-11.

97. "Is There Room in This Sweet Land of Liberty for Such a Thing as a 'Cablinasian'?," *Baltimore Sun*, April 29, 1997, 11A.

98. "Tiger Woods African American—Like It or Not," *PT*, April 29, 1997, 6A; "Does Tiger Owe Black People an Apology for His Off-color Remarks?" *NJG*, May 14, 1997, 2; "Woods Master from Tee to Green, but Off-course Judgments Suspect," *Baltimore Sun*, May 15, 1997, 2C; "Tiger Woods Also Needs to Apologize for Distasteful Jokes," *NYT*, April 27, 1997, S2; "The Man," *Gentlemen's Quarterly*, April 1997, 196.

99. "'Tiger' On Course," *NJG*, May 21, 1997, 2; "The Amen Corner," *LAS*, September 21, 2000, A6.

100. "Woods: I'm More Than Black," *Chicago Sun-Times*, April 22, 1997, 1.

101. Shipnuck, *Battle for Augusta National*, 29–30, 246; "Letter to Augusta National Golf Club," *ADW*, October 3, 2002, 11; "A No (Wo)man's Land," *ESPN*, April 7, 2003, espn.com/golf/masters/story?id=1534920; "Boehner, Member of All-Male Golf Club, Steers Clear of Augusta Debate," *Talking Points Memo*, April 6, 2012, talkingpointsmemo.com/dc/boehner-member-of-all-male-golf-club-steers-clear-of-augusta-debate.

102. "Tiger Woods Retards Civil Rights," *LAS*, August 8, 2002, A6.

103. "Tiger's Brothers," *Newsweek*, June 17, 2001, 48–49; Lazenby, *Michael Jordan*, 234–44; "How Michael Jordan Still Makes $100 Million A Year," *Forbes*, March 11, 2015, forbes.com/sites/kurtbadenhausen/2015/03/11/how-new-billionaire-michael-jordan-earned-100-million-in-2014.

104. Rosaforte, *Tiger Woods*, 180; Callahan, *In Search of Tiger*, 143.

105. Rosaforte, *Tiger Woods*, 181–82.

106. "Changing History's Course," *Hartford Courant*, July 20, 1997, K1.

107. "The Temptation of Tiger Woods," *Vanity Fair*, May 2010, 156; "Loyalty Is Paramount in Woods's Inner Circle," *NYT*, April 3, 2010, D1; Londino, *Tiger Woods*, 106.

108. Nishimi, *Undercover Asian*, 41–62; Yu, "Tiger Woods at the Center of History"; Yu, "Tiger Woods Is Not the End of History"; and Yu, "How Tiger Woods Lost His Stripes," B5; Yocom, *My Shot*, 24; Rosaforte, *Tiger Woods*, 177.

109. "Woods: I'm More Than Black," *Chicago Sun-Times*, April 22, 1997, 1.

110. Younge, *Who Are We?*, 73; Nishimi, *Undercover Asian*, 44.

111. "Racial Confusion," *LAS*, May 15, 1997, A6

112. "'Tiger' On Course," *NJG*, May 21, 1997, 2.

113. "Ranks of Multiracial Americans Grows," *LAT,* June 13, 2013, AA4; Perlmann and Waters, *New Race Question,* 37.

114. "Asked to Declare His Race for Census, Obama Checks 'Black,'" *NYT,* April 3, 2010, A9.

115. "Will Tiger Ever Show the Color of His Stripes?," *ESPN,* May 22, 2002, espn.com/gen/s/2002/0521/1385355.html.

BIBLIOGRAPHY

Although there is no complete account of African American golf and its history, the subject has yielded a number of important studies, including some nonscholarly works and a few produced in disciplines other than history—notably journalism, sociology, and media studies. Several books were published shortly after Tiger Woods won the Masters Tournament in 1997, which sparked a brief, intense flurry of publications related to race and golf. Yet interest in the topic seemed to fade as quickly as it flourished, along with prophecies that Woods foreshadowed a flood of minority golfers around the world poised to take up the game and forever erase its elitism. (Another reason why the Jackie Robinsonization of Woods is itself now a historical phenomenon of the 1990s, one in need of the same kind of context and analysis recent history textbooks provide events like the O. J. Simpson trial and the beating of Rodney King.)

The literature that emerged alongside Woods includes a few introductory histories of African Americans in golf, most written by professional journalists and dedicated enthusiasts. One of the best is Calvin Sinnette's *Forbidden Fairways: African Americans and the Game of Golf*. Sinnette, an emeritus professor of pediatrics at Howard University, first took up the game in the 1950s while serving in Germany with the U.S. Air Force. Another scientist and frequent player, M. Mikell Johnson, published two titles on black women in the game, *Heroines of African American Golf* and *The African American Woman Golfer*, including background on several important female golf clubs founded by African American women around the country, as well as biographical portraits of prominent black female professionals. Also significant is *Skins & Grins*, by Lenwood Robinson Jr. Two journalists, Pete McDaniel and John Kennedy, also produced short titles for popular readers. McDaniel's *Uneven Lies: The Heroic Story of African-Americans in Golf*, a large-format hardcover full of excellent images, is particularly successful as a showpiece work on the history of black golf. McDaniel wrote for *Golf Digest* and worked closely with Woods on other publications; Woods even provided a foreword to *Uneven Lies* when it was published in 2000 (see Kennedy, *Course of Their Own*). While important works, none of these titles are comprehensive, and they tend to focus primarily on the biographies of black professional players. A few additional books probe unique, regional examples of African American contributions to golf, including Ellen Susanna Nösner's *Clearview*, a short biography of William J. Powell—the only African American to design, build, and operate his own golf course—and Robert J. Robertson's *Fair Ways*, a study of the legal battle to desegregate municipal golf courses in Beaumont, Texas.

Scholars from various academic disciplines have also weighed in on the subject of race and golf. Sociologists Marvin P. Dawkins and Graham C. Kinloch published *African American Golfers*, a helpful study of black golfers during the age of segregation, one of the few that tries to address the game's appeal to the broader black public alongside the stories of professional players. The two best comprehensive golf histories produced by historians, George Kirsch's *Golf in America* and Richard Moss's *The Kingdom of Golf in America*, both manage to devote several passages to African Americans but are understandably limited in their ability to go into greater detail. Finally, biographies of professional black golfers have proven popular with readers. There are over a dozen on Woods alone, but others were published as well. The earliest, Linda Jacobs's *Lee Elder: The Daring Dream*, is a 1976 biography of Elder meant to inspire young adults. The most important, Charlie Siffords's *"Just Let Me Play": The Story of Charlie Sifford* (1992), is highly underrated and should rank among the best memoirs from *any* black athlete in American history; it stands alongside influential biographies like Bill Russell's *Go Up for Glory* (1966) or Jackie Robinson's *I Never Had It Made* (1972).

In addition to this existing literature, the narrative also draws from a range of archival, newsprint, film, and manuscript collections. NAACP and American Committee on Africa organizational archives include stand-alone files on golfing figures and golf-related civil rights disputes. By the 1910s many African American newspapers featured weekly golf columns and covered black professionals and all-black golf clubs in Chicago, Pittsburgh, Baltimore, and Cleveland. From newspapers like the *Chicago Defender* and *Baltimore Afro-American* at the turn of the twentieth century to magazines like *Jet*, *Ebony*, and *Sports Illustrated* in the 1970s, the narrative draws heavily on the very same popular literature that most everyday fans and players used to frame their own understandings of the game; the intention is thus to introduce readers to black golf primarily with the same sources, and the same words, the black community first used to confront the issue. Along with the popular press, sporting archives such as those of the Amateur Athletic Foundation yield thousands of pages of evidence, ranging from comprehensive records of UGA-sponsored tournaments to short-lived black golf periodicals. Archived interview transcripts available in the National Visionary Leadership Project files and the Federal Writers' Project repository, both housed at the Library of Congress, as well as interview transcripts published in *Golf Digest* magazine, yield unique, rare stories of black Americans who encountered and shaped the game.

Primary Sources
Archives
Delaware
    John J. Raskob Papers, Hagley Library, Wilmington

Florida
- Mary McLeod Bethune Foundation Archive, Bethune-Cookman College, Daytona Beach
- Republic of Salò Collection, The Wolfsonian—Florida International University Museum, Miami Beach

Georgia
- Komozi Woodard Amiri Baraka Collection, Auburn Avenue Research Library on African-American Culture and History, Atlanta-Fulton Public Library, Atlanta
- Records of the Southern Christian Leadership Conference, King Library and Archive, Martin Luther King Jr. Center for Nonviolent Social Change, Atlanta
- WSB-TV Newsfilm Collection, Walter J. Brown Media Archives and Peabody Awards Collection, University of Georgia Library, Athens

Illinois
- Claude A. Barnett Papers, Chicago History Museum, Chicago

Kansas
- General Files, White House Central Files, Dwight D. Eisenhower Library, Abilene

Louisiana
- Records of the American Committee on Africa, Amistad Research Center, Tulane University, New Orleans

Maryland
- National Archives, College Park
  - General Records of the Department of Justice
  - Records of the Committee on Fair Employment Practices
  - Records of the Secretary of War
  - Records of the United States Commission on Civil Rights

Massachusetts
- John F. Kennedy Presidential Papers, John F. Kennedy Presidential Library, Boston

Michigan
- Travel Literature Collection, Henry Ford Museum, Dearborn

Mississippi
- Center for Oral History and Cultural Heritage, University of Southern Mississippi, Hattiesburg

New York
- Victor Daly Papers, Schomburg Center for Research in Black Culture, New York Public Library, New York

North Carolina
- Greensboro Voices Oral History Project, Greensboro Public Library, Greensboro

Dr. George Simkins Jr. Collection, F. D. Bluford Archives and Special Collections, North Carolina A&T State University, Greensboro

Southern Oral History Program Collection, Wilson Library, University of North Carolina, Chapel Hill

South Carolina

Moving Image Research Collections, University of South Carolina Library, Columbia

Tennessee

Television News Archive, Vanderbilt University, Nashville

Texas

Marion Butts Collection, Texas/Dallas History & Archives, Dallas Public Library, Dallas

LBJ Presidential Library Oral Histories, LBJ Presidential Library, Austin

Washington, D.C.

Ralph J. Bunche Oral Histories Collection, Howard University, Moorland-Spingarn Research Center

Ethnology Division, Department of Anthropology, Smithsonian Institution, National Museum of Natural History

FBI Headquarters

Library of Congress

American Folklife Center, National Visionary Leadership Project interviews and conference collection

Manuscript Division

National Association for the Advancement of Colored People (NAACP) records

Jackie Robinson Papers

Bayard Rustin Papers

Microfilm/Microform Collections

Papers of the Revolutionary Action Movement, 1962–1996. Edited by Muhammad Ahmad, Ernie Allen, and John H. Bracey. Microform collection.

Records of the National Advisory Commission on Civil Disorders (Kerner Commission). "Civil Rights during the Johnson Administration, 1963–1969." Frederick, Md.: University Publications of America, 1987. Microfilm collection.

Legal Cases

Augustus v. Board of Public Instruction of Escambia County Florida, 306 F.2d 862 (1962)

Augustus v. City of Pensacola, Fed. Supp. N. D. Fla. (1956)

Beal v. Holcombe, 193 F.2d 384 (1951)

Clark v. Sherman, Denver, C.O. (1962)

Cummings v. City of Charleston, 288 F.2d 817 (1961)
Delaney v. Central Valley Golf Club, 28 N.Y. Supp. (2d) 932 (1941)
Durkee v. Murphy, 181 Md. 259 (1942)
Fayson v. Beard, 134 F. Supp. 379 (E.D. Tex., 1955)
Freeman v. City of Little Rock, E.D. Ark., W. Div., No. LR-62-C-40 (1963)
Gillespie v. Lake Shore Golf Club, 91 N.E.2d 290, 292 (Ohio Ct. App., 1950)
Griffis v. City of Fort Lauderdale, 104 So.2d 33 (1958)
Hampton v. City of Jacksonville, Florida, 304 F.2d 320 (5th Cir., 1962)
Hayes v. Crutcher, 137 F. Supp. 853 (M.D. Tenn., 1956)
Holley v. City of Portsmouth, 150 F. Supp. 6 (1957)
Holmes v. City of Atlanta, 350 U.S. 879 (1955)
Holmes v. Danner, 191 F. Supp. 394 (M.D. G.A., 1961)
Jones v. Attridge and Martha's Vineyard Country Club, Martha's Vineyard, M.A. (1947)
Law v. Mayor and City Council of Baltimore, 78 F. Supp. 346 (D. M.D., 1948)
Leeper v. Charlotte Park and Recreation Commission, 350 U.S. 983 (1956)
Moorhead v. City of Fort Lauderdale, 152 F. Supp. 131 (1957)
Muir v. Louisville Park Theatrical Ass'n., 347 U.S. 971 (1954)
New Orleans City Park Improvement Association v. Detiege, 358 U.S. 54 (1958)
Rice v. Arnold, 340 U.S. 848 (1950)
Sawyer v. City of Mobile, 208 F. Supp. 548 (1961)
Shuttlesworth v. Gaylord, 202 F. Supp. 59 (N.D. Ala., 1961)
Simkins v. City of Greensboro, 246 F.2d 425 (4th Cir., 1957)
Simkins v. Moses H. Cone Memorial Hospital, 323 F.2d 959 (1963)
Sweeney v. City of Louisville, 102 F. Supp. 525 (1951)
U.S. v. Central Carolina Bank and Trust, 431 F.2d 972 (1970)
Ward v. City of Miami, 151 F. Supp. 593 (S.D. Fla., 1957)
Wesley v. City of Savannah, 294 F. Supp. 698 (1969)
Wimbish v. Pinellas County, Florida, 342 F.2d 804 (1965)
Wolfe v. North Carolina, 364 U.S. 177 (1960)

Newspapers and Periodicals
Adelaide Advertiser (Australia)
African American Golfer's Digest
African World
American Bar Association Journal
American Golfer
Atlanta Daily World
Atlanta Journal Constitution
Augusta Courier
Baltimore Afro-American
Baltimore Sun
Black Enterprise
Black New Ark
Black News
Black Panther
Black Sports
Boston Globe
Brisbane Courier-Mail (Australia)
Bulletin of the Green Section of the U.S. Golf Association
California Eagle

Carolina Times
Charleston Weekly News and Courier
Charlotte News
Charlotte Observer
Chicago Defender
Chicago Sun-Times
Chicago Tribune
Cleveland Call and Post
Coach & Athlete
Crisis
The Crusader
Current History
Daily Capital Journal (Salem, Ore.)
Daily Northwestern
Dallas Express
Dallas Morning News
Dubbo Liberal and Macquarie Advocate (Australia)
Ebony
El Paso Herald
Everybody's Magazine
Forbes
Foreign Affairs
Fortune
Free Lance-Star (Fredericksburg, Va.)
Gentlemen's Quarterly
Golf
Golf Digest
The Golfer
Golfers Magazine
Golf Illustrated
Golf Magazine
Golf, a Weekly Record of "Ye Royal and Auncient" Game
The Gopher (University of Minnesota yearbook)
Grayson's Travel and Business Guide
Hartford Courant
Inner-City Voice (Detroit)
Jackson Clarion-Ledger
Jackson State Times
Jamaica Gleaner
Jet
Kalamazoo Gazette
Kalgoorlie Miner (Australia)
Labor Journal
Lawrence Journal-World
Liberal Democrat (Liberal, Kans.)
Literary Digest
Los Angeles Sentinel
Los Angeles Times
Memphis World
Met Golfer
Milwaukee Journal
Montgomery Advertiser
Nambour Chronicle and North Coast Advertiser (Australia)
National Review
Negro Motorist Green Book
New Orleans Times-Picayune
New South (Southern Regional Council)
Newsweek
New York Age
New York Amsterdam News
New York Amsterdam Star-News
New York Sun
New York Times
New York Tribune
Norfolk Journal and Guide
Ogden Standard-Examiner
Oklahoman
Our Sports
Outing
Outlook (Office of Minority Business Enterprise)
Pacific Stars and Stripes
Perth Daily News (Australia)
Philadelphia Tribune
Pittsburgh Courier
Popular Science Monthly
Queensland Times (Australia)
Race Relations Law Reporter
Reggae Roots International

Salt Lake Tribune
San Francisco Chronicle
Sarasota Herald-Tribune
South African Golf
Southern Patriot
Sports Business Daily
Sports Illustrated
St. Petersburg Times
Student Voice (Student Nonviolent Coordinating Committee)
Sunday Star-Times (New Zealand)
Sydney Referee (Australia)
Tee-Cup
Time
Travelguide
Tuesday Magazine
Vanity Fair
Virgin Islands Daily News
Washington Afro-American
Washington Post
Wellington Times (Australia)
World Tomorrow

Books, Articles, Pamphlets, and Music

Abernathy, Ralph. *And the Walls Came Tumbling Down: An Autobiography*. New York: HarperCollins, 1990.

Annual Report: Hampton Negro Conference, 1904. Hampton, Va.: Hampton Normal and Agricultural Institute, 1904.

Bantock, Miles. *On Many Greens: A Book of Golf and Golfers*. New York: Grosset and Dunlap, 1901.

Barkley, Charles, and Michael Wilbon. *Who's Afraid of a Large Black Man?* New York: Penguin, 2005.

Barkow, Al. *Gettin' to the Dance Floor: An Oral History of American Golf.* New York: Athenaeum, 1986.

Beasley, Delilah L. *The Negro Trail Blazers of California*. Los Angeles: Times Mirror, 1919.

Boynton, G. R. *The Student Protest Movement: A Recapitulation*. Atlanta: Southern Regional Council, 1961.

Brown, Charlotte Hawkins. *The Correct Thing to Do, to Say, to Wear*. Boston: Christopher Publishing House, 1941.

Brunswick Corporation. *Brunswick Corporation Annual Report, 1961*. Chicago: Brunswick Corporation, 1961.

Chicago Commission on Race Relations. *The Negro in Chicago: A Study of Race Relations and a Race Riot*. Chicago: University of Chicago Press, 1922.

Clark, Septima P. "Literacy and Liberation." *Freedomways* 4, no. 1 (1964): 113–24.

Daly, Victor. *Not Only War: A Story of Two Great Conflicts*. Boston: Christopher Publishing House, 1932.

Davis, Miles. *Miles: The Autobiography*. New York: Simon and Schuster, 1989.

Du Bois, W. E. B. *On Sociology and the Black Community*. Chicago: University of Chicago Press, 1978.

Farmer, James. *Lay Bare the Heart: An Autobiography of the Civil Rights Movement*. New York: Arbor House, 1985.

Gerald R. Ford, 1974: Containing the Public Messages, Speeches, and Statements of the President, August 9 to December 31, 1974. Washington, D.C.: U.S. Government Printing Office, 1975.

Gibbons, Charles E., and Chester T. Stansbury. *Child Labor in Mississippi*. New York: National Child Labor Committee, 1928.

Harrison, William Henry, Jr. *Colored Girls and Boys Inspiring United States History*. Allentown, Pa.: Searle and Dressler, 1921.

Hope, John. *Equality of Opportunity*. Washington, D.C.: Public Affairs Press, 1956.

Hughes, Langston. *The Collected Works of Langston Hughes*. Vol. 8. Edited by Donna Akiba Sullivan Harper. Columbia: University of Missouri Press, 2002.

———. *The Collected Works of Langston Hughes*. Vol. 10. Edited by Christopher De Santis. Columbia: University of Missouri Press, 2001.

———. *The Return of Simple*. New York: Hill and Wang, 1994.

———. *Simple's Uncle Sam*. New York: Hill and Wang, 2000.

"Jack Remembers Pioneer and 2014 Presidential Medal of Freedom Winner Charlie Sifford," nicklaus.com/news/jack-remembers-charlie-sifford. February 4, 2015.

Johnson, James Weldon. *Along This Way: The Autobiography of James Weldon Johnson*. New York: Viking, 1933.

Joint Committee for the Survey of Shreveport's Negro Community. *The Shreveport Story*. Shreveport, La.: Council of Social Agencies, 1953.

Jones, William Henry. *Recreation and Amusement among Negroes in Washington, D.C.* Washington, D.C.: Howard University Press, 1927.

Keels, Thomassine Ringo. *Sensations of the Mind*. Vol. 2. Bloomington, Ind.: AuthorHouse, 2015.

Kemble, Edward. *The Blackberries and Their Adventures*. New York: R. H. Russell, 1897.

Locke, Alain, ed. *The New Negro: An Interpretation*. New York: A. and C. Boni, 1925.

Loth, David, and Harold Fleming. *Integration North and South*. New York: Fund for the Republic, 1956.

Louis, Joe. *My Life Story*. With Haskell Cohen and Chester L. Washington. New York: Duell, Sloan and Pearce, 1947.

Martin, Harry Brownlow. *Golf Yarns: The Best Things about the Game of Golf*. New York: Dodd, Mead, 1913.

Maryland Commission on Interracial Problems and Relations. *An American City in Transition: The Baltimore Community Self-Survey of Inter-Group Relations*. Baltimore: Maryland Commission on Interracial Problems and Relations, 1955.

McKinney, Eleanor, ed. *The Exacting Ear: The Story of Listener-Sponsored*

Radio, and an Anthology of Programs from KPFA, KPFK, and WBAI. New York: Pantheon, 1966.

Mitchell, Clarence. *The Reminiscences of Clarence Mitchell.* Alexandria, Va.: Alexander Street Press, 2003.

Morrow, E. Frederic. *Black Man in the White House: A Diary of the Eisenhower Years by the Administrative Officer for Special Projects, the White House, 1955-1961.* New York: Coward-McCann, 1963.

Motley, Constance Baker. *Equal Justice under Law: An Autobiography.* New York: Farrar, Straus and Giroux, 1998.

Negro Year Book, 1918-1919. Tuskegee, Ala.: Negro Year Book Publishing Co., 1919.

Owens, Charlie, and Ed Smith. *I Hate to Lose: How a Little-Known, Handicapped Black Man Beat the Best of the Best on the PGA Tour.* Bloomington, Ind.: iUniverse, 2008.

Owens, Jesse. *Blackthink: My Life as a Black Man and White Man.* New York: William Morrow & Co., 1970.

Player, Gary. *Grand Slam Golf.* London: Cassell, 1966.

President's Committee on Equal Opportunity in the Armed Forces. *Initial Report: Equality of Treatment and Opportunity for Negro Military Personnel Stationed within the United States.* Washington, D.C.: Government Printing Office, 1963.

Rare Jazz & Blues Piano. Document Records DOCD-5388, CD, 1995.

Robinson, Jackie. *I Never Had It Made: An Autobiography.* New York: G. P. Putnam's Sons, 1972.

Robinson, Jackie, and Wendell Smith. *Jackie Robinson: My Own Story.* New York: Greenberg, 1948.

Rosse, Irving. "Golf from a Neurological Viewpoint." *Journal of the American Medical Association* 31, no. 6 (1898): 279-80.

Rowan, Carl Thomas. *South of Freedom.* New York: Knopf, 1952.

Rowland, Mabel. *Bert Williams, Son of Laughter.* New York: English Crafters, 1923.

Russell, Bill, and William McSweeny. *Go Up for Glory.* New York: Berkley Books, 1966.

Schuyler, George, and William Ingersoll. *The Reminiscences of George S. Schuyler, 1962.* Alexandria, Va.: Alexander Street Press, 2003.

Sifford, Charlie. *"Just Let Me Play": The Story of Charlie Sifford.* With James Gullo. Latham, N.Y.: British American Publishing, 1992.

Stroud, Virgil. *In Quest of Freedom.* Dallas: Royal Publishing Co., 1963.

Talmadge, Herman. *You and Segregation.* Birmingham, Ala.: Vulcan Press, 1955.

U.S. Commission on Civil Rights. *Civil Rights U.S.A.* Washington, D.C.: Government Printing Office, 1962.

———. *Conference on Education before the U.S. Commission on Civil Rights, Nashville, TN, March 5, 1959*. Washington, D.C.: Government Printing Office, 1959.

———. *Equal Protection of the Laws in North Carolina: Report of the North Carolina Advisory Committee to the United States Commission on Civil Rights*. Washington, D.C.: Government Printing Office, 1962.

———. *The 50 States Report Submitted to the Commission on Civil Rights by the State Advisory Committees, 1961*. Washington, D.C.: Government Printing Office, 1961.

Van Loan, Charles E. *Fore! Golf Stories*. New York: George H. Doran, 1919.

Washington, Forrester B. "Recreational Facilities for the Negro." *Annals of the American Academy of Political and Social Science* 140, no. 1 (1928): 272–82.

Wilkins, Roy Ottoway, and Tom Mathews. *Standing Fast: The Autobiography of Roy Wilkins*. New York: Viking, 1982.

Williams, Robert F. *Negroes with Guns*. Detroit: Wayne State University Press, 1998.

Williams, Steve. *Out of the Rough*. New York: Penguin, 2015.

Woods, Earl, and Pete McDaniel. *Training a Tiger: A Father's Guide to Raising a Winner in Both Golf and Life*. New York: HarperCollins, 1997.

Woofter, Thomas J. *Southern Race Progress: The Wavering Color Line*. Washington, D.C.: Public Affairs Press, 1957.

Writers' Program of the Work Projects Administration in the State of Arkansas. *Survey of Negroes in Little Rock and North Little Rock*. Little Rock: Urban League of Greater Little Rock, 1941.

Yocom, Guy. *My Shot: The Very Best Interviews from Golf Digest Magazine*. New York: Harry N. Abrams, 2007.

Secondary Sources

Abraham, Nels. "The Making of Audubon Park: Competing Ideologies for Public Space." M.A. thesis, University of New Orleans, 2010.

Alamillo, Jose M. *Making Lemonade out of Lemons*. Champaign: University of Illinois Press, 2006.

Alexander, Chip. "At Wyndham Golf, Memories of a Trailblazing Player." *Raleigh News and Observer*, August 20, 2015.

Ashe, Arthur. *A Hard Road to Glory: A History of the African American Athlete*. Vol. 3. New York: Amistad Press, 1993.

Azarian, Alexander J., and Eden Fesshazion. "The State Flag of Georgia: The 1956 Change in Its Historical Context." Georgia Senate Research Office, August 2000.

Bagwell, Tyler E. *Jekyll Island: A State Park*. Charleston, S.C.: Arcadia, 2001.

———. *The Jekyll Island Club*. Charleston, S.C.: Arcadia, 1998).

Balkin, Jack, ed. *What* Brown V. Board of Education *Should Have Said*. New York: NYU Press, 2002.

Barkow, Al. *The Golden Era of Golf: How America Rose to Dominate the Old Scots Game*. New York: Thomas Dunne Books, 2000.

———. *The History of the PGA Tour*. New York: Doubleday, 1989.

———. "One Man's Mission." *Golf World*, January 18, 2008.

Barrett, David. *Miracle at Merion: The Inspiring Story of Ben Hogan's Amazing Comeback and Victory at the 1950 U.S. Open*. New York: Skyhorse Publishing, 2010.

Beeler, Dorothy. "Race Riot in Columbia, Tennessee, February 25–27, 1946." *Tennessee Historical Quarterly* 39, no. 1 (Spring 1980): 49–61.

Bond, Gregory. "Jim Crow at Play: Race, Manliness, and the Color Line in American Sports, 1876–1916." Ph.D. diss., University of Wisconsin–Madison, 2008.

Booth, Douglas. *The Race Game: Sport and Politics in South Africa*. London: Routledge, 1998.

Borucki, Wesley. "Golf." In *Encyclopedia of African American History*. Vol. 1. Edited by Paul Finkelman. Oxford: Oxford University Press, 2009.

Bowden, Tripp. *Freddie & Me: Life Lessons from Freddie Bennett, Augusta National's Legendary Caddy Master*. New York: Skyhorse Publishing, 2009.

Boyd, Valerie. *Wrapped in Rainbows: The Life of Zora Neale Hurston*. New York: Scribner, 2003.

Branch, Taylor. *Parting the Waters: America in the King Years, 1954–1963*. New York: Simon and Schuster, 1988.

Branchik, Blaine J., and Judy Foster Davis. "Black Gold: A History of the African-American Elite Market Segment." In *Proceedings of the Conference on Historical Analysis and Research in Marketing*. Vol. 13. 2007.

Britt, Grant. *Charlie Sifford*. Greensboro, N.C.: Morgan Reynolds, 1998.

Brooks, Erik, and Glenn L. Starks. *Historically Black Colleges and Universities: An Encyclopedia*. Santa Barbara, Calif.: Greenwood, 2011.

Brown-Nagin, Tomiko. *Courage to Dissent: Atlanta and the Long History of the Civil Rights Movement*. New York: Oxford University Press, 2012.

Buckley, Will. "Player for All Time." *The Observer*, July 10, 2005.

Callahan, Tom. *His Father's Son: Earl and Tiger Woods*. New York: Gotham, 2010.

———. *In Search of Tiger: A Journey through Golf with Tiger Woods*. New York: Three Rivers Press, 2004.

Campanella, Catherine. *New Orleans City Park*. Charleston, S.C.: Arcadia, 2011.

Campbell, James T. *Middle Passages: African American Journeys to Africa, 1787–2005*. New York: Penguin, 2007.

Canton, David A. *Raymond Pace Alexander: A New Negro Lawyer Fights for Civil Rights in Philadelphia*. Oxford: University Press of Mississippi, 2013.

Carney, Judith A., and Richard Nicholas Rosomoff. *In the Shadow of Slavery: Africa's Botanical Legacy in the Atlantic World*. Berkeley: University of California Press, 2009.

Cavanaugh, Jack. "Remembering Jackie Robinson, the Golfer." *New York Times*, April 27, 1997.

Cayleff, Susan E. *Babe: The Life and Legend of Babe Didrikson Zaharias*. Champaign: University of Illinois Press, 1996.

Chernow, Ron. *Titan: The Life of John D. Rockefeller, Sr*. New York: Random House, 1998.

City Commission Committee, City of Huntington Woods, Michigan. "Final Report: Rackham Golf Course Historic District Proposal." November 21, 2006.

Clay, Bobby. "Breaking Par against Racism." *Black Enterprise*, September 1996.

Corcoran, Michael. *Duel in the Sun*. New York: Simon and Schuster, 2010.

Cotton, Dorothy. *If Your Back's Not Bent: The Role of the Citizenship Education Program in the Civil Rights Movement*. New York: Atria Books, 2012.

Countryman, Matthew J. *Up South: Civil Rights and Black Power in Philadelphia*. Philadelphia: University of Pennsylvania Press, 2006.

Cousins, Geoffrey. *Golfers at Law*. New York: Knopf, 1959.

Cox, Jeremy. "Frank Hampton Sr. Leaves Legacy of Battles." *Florida Times-Union*, June 25, 2011.

Cronin, Tim. *A Century of Golf: Western Golf Association, 1899–1999*. Chelsea, Mich.: Sleeping Bear Press, 1998.

Crouse, Karen. "Prejudice Challenged a Path to St. Andrews." *New York Times*, July 13, 2015.

———. "Treasure of Golf's Sad Past, Black Caddies Vanish in Era of Riches." *New York Times*, April 3, 2012.

Cunningham, John T., and Kenneth D. Cole. *Atlantic City*. Charleston, S.C.: Arcadia, 2000.

Curl, James. *Jersey Joe Walcott: A Boxing Biography*. Jefferson, N.C.: McFarland, 2012.

Dalmage, Heather M., ed. *The Politics of Multiracialism*. Albany, N.Y.: SUNY Press, 2004.

Dawkins, Marvin P., and Graham C. Kinloch. *African American Golfers during the Jim Crow Era*. Westport, Conn.: Praeger, 2000.

Dawkins, Marvin P., and A. C. Tellison Jr. "Golf." In *African Americans and Popular Culture*. Vol. 2. Edited by Todd Boyd. Santa Barbara, Calif.: Praeger, 2008.

Day, Jim. "30 Years after Massacre, LaBeet's Fate Unknown." *St. Croix Source*, September 6, 2002.

Denney, Bob. "Althea Gibson: Breaking Down Barriers on the Court and the Course." PGA of America, February 23, 2015, pga.org/articles/althea-gibson-breaking-down-barriers-court-and-course.

"Dewey Brown: Superintendent, Professional, Gentleman." *Golf Superintendent*, July 1974.

Dittmer, John. *Local People: The Struggle for Civil Rights in Mississippi*. Urbana: University of Illinois Press, 1995.

Donelson, Dave. "History of Golf in America: Westchester, the Birthplace of Golf." *Hudson Valley Magazine*, 2013 Golf Guide.

Donovan, Richard E., and Joseph S. F. Murdoch. *The Game of Golf and the Printed Word, 1566-1985: A Bibliography of Golf Literature in the English Language*. Endicott, N.Y.: Castalio Press, 1988.

Dresser, Tom. *African Americans on Martha's Vineyard: From Enslavement to Presidential Visit*. Mount Pleasant, S.C.: History Press, 2010.

Dyer, Erv. "George F. Grant Gave the Golf World a Tee." *Crisis*, September/October 2007.

Dyson, Michael Eric. *Mercy, Mercy Me: The Art, Loves, and Demons of Marvin Gaye*. New York: Basic Books, 2004.

———. *The Michael Eric Dyson Reader*. New York: Basic Civitas Books, 2004.

Ellis, Mark. *Race Harmony and Black Progress: Jack Woofter and the Interracial Cooperation Movement*. Bloomington: Indiana University Press, 2013.

Eskew, Glenn T. *But for Birmingham: The Local and National Movements in the Civil Rights Struggle*. Chapel Hill: University of North Carolina Press, 1997.

Farley, Christopher John. "That Old Black Magic." *Time*, November 27, 2000.

Farrar, Hayward. *The Baltimore Afro-American, 1892-1950*. Santa Barbara, Calif.: Praeger, 1998.

Faulkner, Janette. *Ethnic Notions: Black Images in the White Mind*. Berkeley, Calif.: Berkeley Art Center, 1982.

Fauset, Arthur Huff. *Black Gods of the Metropolis: Negro Religious Cults of the Urban North*. Philadelphia: University of Pennsylvania Press, 2002.

Fields, Bill. "Owens an Overlooked Pioneer." *Golf World*, September 2007.

Forster, Dave, and Gary A. Harki. "Former Portsmouth Mayor James Holley Dies at 85." *Virginian-Pilot*, October 6, 2012.

Foster, Mark S. "In the Face of 'Jim Crow': Prosperous Blacks and Vacations, Travel, and Outdoor Leisure, 1890-1945." *Journal of Negro History* 84, no. 2 (Spring 1999): 130-49.

Fuse, Montye, and Keith Miller. "Jazzing the Basepaths: Jackie Robinson and African American Aesthetics." In *Sports Matters: Race, Recreation, and Culture*, edited by John Bloom and Michael Willard, 119-40. New York: New York University Press, 2002.

Gabriel, Mike. *The Professional Golfers' Association Tour: A History*. Jefferson, N.C.: McFarland, 2001.

Gaines, Kevin K. *Uplifting the Race: Black Leadership, Politics, and Culture in the Twentieth Century.* Chapel Hill: University of North Carolina Press, 1996.

Gill, Tiffany M. *Beauty Shop Politics: African American Women's Activism in the Beauty Industry.* Champaign: University of Illinois Press, 2010.

Gilmore, Glenda Elizabeth. *Defying Dixie: The Radical Roots of Civil Rights, 1919–1950.* New York: Norton, 2009.

———. *Gender and Jim Crow: Women and the Politics of White Supremacy in North Carolina, 1896–1920.* Chapel Hill: University of North Carolina Press, 1996.

Glenn, Rhonda. "Playing through Racial Barriers." *Sports Illustrated,* May 20, 1991.

Goldstein, Richard. "African-American Golf Pioneer Bill Powell Dies at 93." *New York Times,* January 2, 2010.

———. "Beau Jack, 78, Lightweight Boxing Champion in the 1940's." *New York Times,* February 12, 2000.

———. "Charlie Sifford, Who Shattered a Barrier of Race in the Sport He Loved, Dies at 92." *New York Times,* February 5, 2015.

Goodman, James. *Stories of Scottsboro.* New York: Vintage, 1994.

Gorn, Elliott J., and Michael Oriard. "Taking Sports Seriously." In *Major Problems in American Sport History,* edited by Steven A. Riess, 3–5. New York: Houghton Mifflin, 1996.

Graffis, Herb. *The PGA: The Official History of the Professional Golfers' Association of America.* New York: Thomas Crowell Company, 1975.

Grandin, Greg. *Fordlandia: The Rise and Fall of Henry Ford's Forgotten Jungle City.* New York: Picador, 2009.

Gray, Frances Clayton, and Yanick Rice Lamb. *Born to Win.* Hoboken, N.J.: John Wiley and Sons, 2004.

Greaux, Jean P., Jr. "Fountain Valley Put V.I. Golf in Unwanted Spotlight." *St. Croix Source,* September 6, 2002.

Greene, Baylis. "The Brief Golfing Life of Oscar Bunn." *Southampton Review* 9, no. 2 (Summer 2015): 97–100.

Greer, Brenna W. "Consuming America: Moss Kendrix, Coca-Cola, and the Identity of the Black American Consumer." *Coca-Cola Journey,* February 25, 2013.

Griffin, G. Elmer. "Murder on the Green: The Politics of Golf in the Eastern Caribbean." *Transition* 74 (1997): 4–15.

Griffiths, David. *Hot Jazz: From Harlem to Storyville.* Lanham, Md.: Scarecrow Press, 1998.

Gritter, Elizabeth. *River of Hope: Black Politics and the Memphis Freedom Movement, 1865–1954.* Lexington: University of Kentucky Press, 2014.

Hall, Eric Allen. *Arthur Ashe: Tennis and Justice in the Civil Rights Era.* Baltimore: Johns Hopkins University Press, 2014.

Hancock, David. *Citizens of the World: London Merchants and the Integration of the British Atlantic Community, 1735–1785*. Cambridge: Cambridge University Press, 1997.

Hansen, James R. *A Difficult Par: Robert Trent Jones Sr. and the Making of Modern Golf*. New York: Gotham, 2015.

Harbrecht, Douglas. "For John D. Rockefeller, Golf Was Life." Interview with Ron Chernow. *Bloomberg Business Week*, November 7, 2001, bloomberg.com/news/articles/2001-11-07/for-john-d-dot-rockefeller-golf-was-life.

Hartmann, Douglas. *Race, Culture, and the Revolt of the Black Athlete: The 1968 Olympic Protests and Their Aftermath*. Chicago: University of Chicago Press, 2003.

Harvey, Randy. "Militant Maggie Hathaway Never Quits Fighting for Her Cause." *Los Angeles Times*, February 27, 1997.

Haurwitz, Ralph K. M. "State Panel Recommends Muny for National Register of Historic Places." *Austin American-Statesman*, January 23, 2016.

Henderson, Edwin Bancroft. *The Negro in Sports*. Washington, D.C.: Associated Publishers, 1949.

Higginbotham, Evelyn Brooks. *Righteous Discontent: The Women's Movement in the Black Baptist Church, 1880–1920*. Cambridge: Harvard University Press, 1994.

Hirsch, James. *Willie Mays: The Life, the Legend*. New York: Scribner, 2010.

Housewright, Ed. "Course Cares about 1 Color Only: Greens." *Dallas Morning News*, December 22, 2002.

Hudson, David. *Women in Golf: The Players, the History, and the Future of the Sport*. Westport, Conn.: Praeger, 2008.

Ingham, John N., and Lynne B. Feldman. *African-American Business Leaders: A Biographical Dictionary*. Westport, Conn.: Greenwood, 1994.

Jacobs, Linda. *Lee Elder: The Daring Dream*. St. Paul, Minn.: EMC Corporation, 1976.

"James R. 'Jimmie' DeVoe, PGA." *PGA Magazine*, March 2013.

Jeffries, Hasan Kwame. "Fields of Play: The Mediums through Which Black Athletes Engaged in Sports in Jim Crow Georgia." *Journal of Negro History* 86, no. 3 (Summer 2001): 264–75.

"Joe Bartholomew, an Early Golfer and Golf Course Designer." aaregistry.org/historic_events/view/joe-bartholomew-early-golfer-and-golf-course-designer.

Johnson, M. Mikell. *The African American Woman Golfer: Her Legacy*. Westport, Conn.: Praeger, 2007.

———. *Heroines of African American Golf: The Past, the Present, and the Future*. Bloomington, Ind.: Trafford Publishing, 2010.

Jones, Guilford. "Historically Speaking: Dr. George F. Grant." *Black Sports*, July 1973.

Jones, Guilford. "Past Greats." *Black Sports*, July 1973.
Jones, Thomas B. "Caucasians Only: Solomon Hughes, the PGA, and the 1948 St. Paul Open Golf Tournament." *Minnesota History* 58, no. 8 (Winter 2003–4): 383–93.
Joseph, Peniel E. *Waiting 'til the Midnight Hour: A Narrative History of Black Power in America*. New York: Holt, 2006.
Kater, Michael H. *Different Drummers: Jazz in the Culture of Nazi Germany*. Oxford: Oxford University Press, 2003.
Kaufmann, Martin. "Fighting for Their Course." *Golfweek*, April 4, 2016.
Kaye, Andrew M. *The Pussycat of Prizefighting: Tiger Flowers and the Politics of Black Celebrity*. Athens: University of Georgia Press, 2007.
Kennedy, John H. *A Course of Their Own: A History of African American Golfers*. Lincoln: University of Nebraska Press, 2005.
King, Gilbert. *Devil in the Grove: Thurgood Marshall, the Groveland Boys, and the Dawn of a New America*. New York: HarperCollins, 2013.
Kirsch, George B. *Golf in America*. Urbana: University of Illinois Press, 2009.
Klein, Henry L. "A Walk in the Park with Jimmy Comiskey." *The Advocate* (Federal Bar Association, New Orleans chapter) 14, no. 3 (Spring 2004): 1.
Korstad, Robert, and Nelson Lichtenstein. "Opportunities Found and Lost: Labor, Radicals, and the Early Civil Rights Movement." *Journal of American History* 75, no. 3 (December 1988): 786–811.
Krajicek, David J. "Slaughter in Paradise." *New York Daily News*, July 17, 2005.
Krist, Gary. *City of Scoundrels: The Twelve Days of Disaster That Gave Birth to Modern Chicago*. New York: Broadway Books, 2013.
Kruse, Kevin M. "The Politics of Race and Public Space: Desegregation, Privatization, and the Tax Revolt in Atlanta." *Journal of Urban History* 31, no. 5 (July 2005): 610–33.
———. *White Flight: Atlanta and the Making of Modern Conservatism*. Princeton: Princeton University Press, 2005.
Kryder, Daniel. *Divided Arsenal: Race and the American State during World War II*. Cambridge: Cambridge University Press, 2001.
Lavergne, Gary M. *Before Brown: Heman Marion Sweatt, Thurgood Marshall, and the Long Road to Justice*. Austin: University of Texas Press, 2010.
Lazenby, Roland. *Michael Jordan: The Life*. Boston: Back Bay Books, 2015.
Leonard, Tod. "Elder Changed the Face of the Masters." *San Diego Union-Tribune*, April 5, 2015.
———. "Elder Made Bold Play in South Africa." *San Diego Union-Tribune*, April 5, 2015.
Lester, Robin. *Stagg's University: The Rise, Decline, and Fall of Big-Time Football at Chicago*. Urbana: University of Illinois Press, 1999.
Levinson, David, and Karen Christensen, eds. *Encyclopedia of World Sport: From Ancient Times to the Present*. Oxford: Oxford University Press, 1999.

Lewis, David L. *W. E. B. Du Bois, 1919–1963: The Fight for Equality and the American Century*. New York: Henry Holt, 2001.

Lewis, Jason. "Maggie Hathaway—Community and Civil Rights Activist." *Los Angeles Sentinel*, March 22, 2012.

Lipsey, Rick. "King of Clubs." *Sports Illustrated*, November 4, 1996.

Lokos, Lionel. *House Divided: The Life and Legacy of Martin Luther King*. New Rochelle, N.Y.: Arlington House, 1968.

Londino, Lawrence. *Tiger Woods: A Biography*. Westport, Conn.: Greenwood, 2010.

Lownes-Jackson, Millicent Gray. "Women and Business." In *Encyclopedia of African American Business*, vol. 2, edited by Jessie Carney Smith, 839. Westport, Conn.: Greenwood, 2006.

Luker, Ralph E., and Christopher M. Richardson. *A Historical Dictionary of the Civil Rights Movement*. Lanham, Md.: Rowman and Littlefield, 2014.

MacGregor, Robert M. "The Golliwog: Innocent Doll to Symbol of Racism." In *Advertising and Popular Culture*, edited by Sammy R. Danna, 124–33. Bowling Green, Ohio: Bowling Green State University Press, 1992.

Manning, Kenneth R. *Black Apollo of Science: The Life of Ernest Everett Just*. New York: Oxford University Press, 1984.

Marchand, Roland. *Advertising the American Dream: Making Way for Modernity, 1920–1940*. Berkeley: University of California Press, 1985.

McCloy, Shelby Thomas. *The Negro in France*. Lexington: University of Kentucky Press, 1961.

McDaniel, Pete. *Uneven Lies: The Heroic Story of African-Americans in Golf*. Greenwich, Conn.: American Golfer, 2000.

McDonald, Robert C. *Mapledale Country Club: The First Recorded American Negro Golf Course*. Stow, Mass.: Stow Historical Society, 1997.

McKenna, Dave. "Links to the Past." *Washington City Paper*, April 19, 2002.

Mead, Chris. *Joe Louis: Black Champion in White America*. Mineola, N.Y.: Dover Publications, 2010.

Miller, James A. *Remembering Scottsboro: The Legacy of an Infamous Trial*. Princeton: Princeton University Press, 2009.

Mohr, F. A. "Son Invented Wooden Tee for Golfing." *Syracuse Post-Standard*, February 17, 2003.

Mohr, Rob, and Leslie Mohr Krupa. *Golf in Denver*. Mount Pleasant, S.C.: Arcadia, 2011.

Molesworth, Charles. *And Bid Him Sing: A Biography of Countée Cullen*. Chicago: University of Chicago Press, 2012.

Monbiot, George. "Comment & Debate." *Guardian*, October 16, 2007.

Morris, Aldon. *The Origins of the Civil Rights Movement*. New York: Free Press, 1986.

Moss, Richard J. *Golf and the American Country Club*. Urbana: University of Illinois Press, 2007.

———. *The Kingdom of Golf in America*. Lincoln: University of Nebraska Press, 2013.

Muhammad, Khalil Gibran. *The Condemnation of Blackness: Race, Crime, and the Making of Modern Urban America*. Cambridge: Harvard University Press, 2010.

Nelson, Michael, ed. *Guide to the Presidency*. Vol. 2. 4th ed. Washington, D.C.: CQ Press, 2008.

Newport, John Paul. "Bringing Joe B. Back to Life." *Wall Street Journal*, December 10, 2010.

Nishimi, Leilani. *Undercover Asian: Multiracial Asian Americans in Visual Culture*. Champaign: University of Illinois Press, 2014.

Nösner, Ellen Susanna. *Clearview: America's Course*. Haslett, Mich.: Foxsong Publishing, 2000.

Ogbar, Jeffrey O. G. *Black Power: Radical Politics and African American Identity*. Baltimore: Johns Hopkins University Press, 2005.

Page, Rodney. "Love, Hate Relationship with Golf." *Tampa Bay Times*, February 19, 2009.

"Paine Students Worked to End Segregation." *Augusta Chronicle*, February 6, 2005.

Paquette, Robert L. "Jacobins of the Lowcountry: The Vesey Plot on Trial." *William and Mary Quarterly* 59, no. 1 (January 2002): 185–92.

Paulison, Walter. *The Tale of the Wildcats: A Centennial History of the Northwestern University Athletics*. Chicago: Northwestern University Alumni Association, 1951.

Pennington, Bill. "Hall Thompson, 87; Stirred Golf Controversy." *New York Times*, October 29, 2010.

Pennington, Shaun. "Fountain Valley Killer LaBeet Alive and Well in Cuba." *St. Croix Source*, April 23, 2015.

Perlmann, Joel, and Mary C. Waters, eds. *The New Race Question: How the Census Counts Multiracial Individuals*. New York: Russell Sage Foundation, 2005.

Pitre, Merline. *In Struggle against Jim Crow: Lulu B. White and the NAACP, 1900–1957*. College Station: Texas A&M University Press, 2010.

Plaschke, Bill. "He Went Down Swinging." *Los Angeles Times*, February 27, 1997.

Pollock, Alan J., and James A. Riley, eds. *Barnstorming to Heaven: Syd Pollock and His Great Black Teams*. Tuscaloosa: University of Alabama Press, 2006.

Polyné, Millery. "Modernizing the Race: Political and Cultural Engagements between African Americans and Haitians, 1930–1964." Ph.D. diss., University of Michigan, 2003.

Price, Charles, and George C. Rogers. *The Carolina Lowcountry Birthplace of American Golf, 1786.* Charleston, S.C.: Sea Pines Co., 1980.

Rader, Benjamin. *American Sports.* Upper Saddle River, N.J.: Pearson, 2009.

Rampersad, Arnold. *Jackie Robinson: A Biography.* New York: Ballantine Books, 1998.

Ransby, Barbara. *Ella Baker and the Black Freedom Movement: A Radical Democratic Vision.* Chapel Hill: University of North Carolina Press, 2003.

Rapoport, Ron. *The Immortal Bobby: Bobby Jones and the Golden Age of Golf.* New York: Wiley Press, 2005.

Rattray, Jeannette Edwards. *Fifty Years of the Maidstone Club: 1891–1941.* East Hampton, N.Y.: Maidstone Club, 1941.

Reed, Wornie L. "The Black Golf Caddy: A Victim of Labor Market Discrimination." *Challenge* 14, no. 1 (Spring 2008): 61–71.

———. "Blacks in Golf." *Trotter Review* 5, no. 1 (Winter 1991): 19–23.

———. "Sports Notes." *Trotter Review* 5, no. 3 (Fall 1991): 19–23.

Riess, Steven A., ed. *Major Problems in American Sport History.* New York: Houghton Mifflin, 1996.

Roberson, Venita. "African American Culture and Physical Skill Development Programs: The Effect on Golf after Tiger Woods." *Journal of Black Studies* 33, no. 6 (July 2003): 801–16.

Roberts, Randy. *Joe Louis: Hard Times Man.* New Haven: Yale University Press, 2012.

Robertson, Robert J. *Fair Ways: How Six Black Golfers Won Civil Rights in Beaumont, Texas.* College Station: Texas A&M University Press, 2005.

Robinson, Lenwood, Jr. *Skins and Grins: The Plight of the Black American Golfer.* Chicago: Chicago Spectrum Press, 1997.

Rosaforte, Tim. *Tiger Woods: The Makings of a Champion.* New York: St. Martin's, 1997.

Rowan, Carl T. *Wait till Next Year: The Story of Jackie Robinson.* With Jackie Robinson. New York: Random House, 1960.

Sammons, Jeffrey T. "Black Golfers: A Wake-Up Call before Your Next Tee Time." *African American Golfer's Digest*, africanamericangolfersdigest.com/black-golfers-a-wakeup-call-before-your-next-tee-time.

Sampson, Curt. "Augusta vs. the World." *Golf Magazine*, April 2003.

———. *The Masters: Golf, Money, and Power in Augusta, Georgia.* New York: Villard Books, 1998.

Sanders, James. *South Africa and the International Media, 1972–1979: A Struggle for Representation.* London: Routledge, 1999.

Sandiford, Keith Albert. *Measuring the Moment: Strategies of Protest in Eighteenth-Century Afro-English Writing.* Selinsgrove, Pa.: Susquehanna University Press, 1995.

Sapakoff, Gene. "The Birthplace of American Golf." *Charleston Post and Courier*, August 5, 2012.

Savage, Beth L., ed. *African American Historic Places*. New York: Wiley, 1994.

Schupak, Adam. "Dickey, 84, Elevated Minority Golf." *Golfweek*, October 26, 2012.

Shapiro, Leonard. "For Years, Black Golfers' Best Club Was Their Own." *Washington Post*, May 28, 1997.

Shipnuck, Alan. *The Battle for Augusta National: Hootie, Martha, and the Masters of the Universe*. New York: Simon and Schuster, 2007.

Sinclair, Adriana. *International Relations Theory and International Law: A Critical Approach*. Cambridge: Cambridge University Press, 2010.

Sinnette, Calvin. *Forbidden Fairways: African Americans and the Game of Golf*. Chelsea, Mich.: Sleeping Bear Press, 1998.

Skaler, Robert Morris. *Philadelphia's Broad Street: South and North*. Chicago: Arcadia, 2003.

Skocpol, Theda, Ariane Liazos, and Marshall Ganz. *What a Mighty Power We Can Be: African American Fraternal Groups and the Struggle for Racial Equality*. Princeton: Princeton University Press, 2008.

Slater, Robert Bruce. "The First Black Faculty Members at the Nation's Highest-Ranked Universities." *Journal of Blacks in Higher Education* 22 (Winter 1998–99): 97–106.

Smith, Gary. "Still Fighting Old Wars." *Sports Illustrated*, February 15, 1988.

Smith, Loran. "Albany's White a Legend in Club Making." *Albany Herald*, August 7, 2013.

Smith, R. J. "Maggie Hathaway." *Los Angeles Magazine*, December 2001.

Smith, S. L. *Builders of Goodwill: The Story of the State Agents of Negro Education in the South*. Nashville: Tennessee Book Co., 1950.

Starn, Orin. "Caddying for the Dalai Lama: Golf, Heritage Tourism, and the Pinehurst Resort." *South Atlantic Quarterly* 105, no. 2 (Spring 2006): 447–63.

———. *The Passion of Tiger Woods: An Anthropologist Reports on Golf, Race, and Celebrity Scandal*. Durham: Duke University Press, 2011.

Stephens, Ronald J. *Idlewild: The Rise, Decline, and Rebirth of a Unique African American Resort Town*. Ann Arbor: University of Michigan Press, 2013.

Stevens, Peter F. "In the Eye of the Storm." *Golf Journal*, June 1996.

———. "The Natural." *Golf Journal*, September 1998.

St. Laurent, Philip. "The Negro in World History—John Shippen." *Tuesday Magazine*, April 1969.

Strege, John. *Tiger: A Biography of Tiger Woods*. New York: Broadway Books, 1998.

———. *When War Played Through: Golf during World War II*. New York: Gotham, 2005.

Stricklin, Art. *Links, Lore, and Legends: The Story of Texas Golf.* Boulder, Colo.: Taylor Trade, 2005.

Sullivan, James. *The Hardest Working Man: How James Brown Saved the Soul of America.* New York: Gotham, 2009.

"Tiny Golf Tees Can Send a Big Message," Simpleecology.com/eco/golf-tees.

Tramel, Jimmie. "The Little-Known Story of Golf Pioneer Bill Spiller." *Tulsa World*, August 16, 2007.

———. "Tiger Was Raised by a Wildcat." *Tulsa World*, August 3, 2007.

"The Transformation of the Racial Views of Harry Truman." *Journal of Blacks in Higher Education* 26 (January 2000): 28–30.

Tuck, Stephen G. N. *Beyond Atlanta: The Struggle for Racial Equality in Georgia, 1940–1980.* Athens: University of Georgia Press, 2003.

Tygiel, Jules. *Baseball's Great Experiment: Jackie Robinson and His Legacy.* New York: Vintage, 1983.

Tyldesley, Joyce A. *Egyptian Games and Sports.* Oxford: Shire Publications, 2008.

Tyson, Timothy B. *Radio Free Dixie: Robert F. Williams and the Roots of Black Power.* Chapel Hill: University of North Carolina Press, 2001.

United States Golf Association (USGA). "John Shippen: A Golfing Pioneer," usga.org/articles/2016/02/john-shippen-a-golfing-pioneer.html. February 10, 2016.

Van Natta, Don, Jr. *First off the Tee.* New York: PublicAffairs, 2004.

Venutolo, Anthony. "Shady Rest in Scotch Plains Was First African-American Club of its Kind," blog.nj.com/ledgerarchives/2009/02/country_club_life.html.

Walker, Lewis, and Benjamin C. Wilson. *Black Eden: The Idlewild Community.* East Lansing: Michigan State University Press, 2007.

Wallach, Jennifer Jensen, and John A. Kirk, eds. *Arsnick: The Student Nonviolent Coordinating Committee in Arkansas.* Fayetteville: University of Arkansas Press, 2011.

Warren, Stanley. "Blacks in the World of Golf: Indianapolis Style." *Black History News and Notes* 15 (November 1983): 5–8.

Weber, Bruce. "Calvin Peete, 71, a Pioneer on the PGA Tour, Is Dead." *New York Times*, April 30, 2015.

Wells, James E., Geoffrey L. Buckley, and Christopher G. Boone. "Separate but Equal? Desegregating Baltimore's Golf Courses." *Geographical Review* 98, no. 2 (April 2008): 151–70.

Wexler, Daniel. "Los Angeles Open Has Been More 'Open' Than Most." *Los Angeles Times*, February 18, 2009.

Whitaker, Matthew C. *Race Work: The Rise of Civil Rights in the Urban West.* Lincoln: University of Nebraska Press, 2005.

White, Jane Baber. "Morris Alexander, Caddy Master and Golf Professional at Oakwood Country Club for Fifty-four Years, 1914–1967." *Lynch's Ferry*, Fall/Winter 2004/2005.

Wiggins, David. *African Americans in Sports*. London: Routledge, 2015.

Williams, Chad L. *Torchbearers of Democracy: African American Soldiers in the World War I Era*. Chapel Hill: University of North Carolina Press, 2013.

Williams, Juan. *Thurgood Marshall: American Revolutionary*. New York: Broadway Books, 2000.

Williams, L. J. "The Negro in Golf." *Negro History Bulletin* 15, no. 3 (December 1951): 52–54.

Winerip, Michael. "His Most Powerful Drive Was to Play, with Pride." *New York Times*, June 28, 1996.

Winn, Linda T. "Leaders of Afro-American Nashville: Theodore 'Ted' Rhodes, 1913–1969." Nashville Conference on Afro-American Culture and History, 1998.

Wolcott, Victoria W. *Race, Riots, and Roller Coasters: The Struggle over Segregated Recreation in America*. Philadelphia: University of Pennsylvania Press, 2012.

Woodson, Carter Godwin. *The Negro Professional Man and the Community, with Special Emphasis on the Physician and the Lawyer*. Washington, D.C.: Association for the Study of Negro Life and History, 1934.

Young, A. S. "Doc." "The Black Athlete in the Golden Age of Sports." *Ebony*, June 1969.

Younge, Gary. *Who Are We—And Should It Matter in the 21st Century?* New York: Viking, 2010.

Yu, Henry. "How Tiger Woods Lost His Stripes." *Los Angeles Times*, December 2, 1996.

———. "Tiger Woods at the Center of History." In *Sports Matters: Race, Recreation, and Culture*, edited by John Bloom and Michael Willard, 320–53. New York: New York University Press, 2002.

———. "Tiger Woods Is Not the End of History." *American Historical Review* 108 (2003): 1406–14.

Zirin, Dave. "A Tiger Woods Story That Actually Matters." *Nation*, April 5, 2010.

INDEX

Aaron, George, 88
Aaron, Hank, 233
Abernathy, Ralph, 181, 184
Able, Ella, 89, 98
Acorn Country Club (Va.), 45, 46, 47, 71
Adams, Dorsey, 59
Adams, George, 86, 100
Affirmative action, 231-32
"African golf," 29-30
African Methodist Episcopal (AME) Church, 3, 21-22. *See also* Churches; Ministers
Alabama, ix, 28, 80, 93, 117, 146, 179, 185, 200, 229. *See also* Alabama State College; Birmingham, Ala.; Montgomery, Ala.; Tuskegee Institute
Alabama State College, 145
Albany, Ga., 182-84
Alfred "Tup" Holmes Memorial Golf Course (Atlanta). *See* Black Rock Golf Course
Ali, Muhammad, xiii, xiv, 82, 190, 197, 226, 230, 265
All-American Open. *See* Tam O'Shanter Open
Allred, Gloria, 261
Alpha Golf Club (Chicago), 23, 85. *See also* Chicago, Ill.
Amateur golf: early black amateurs, 33; after World War I, 55, 82, 96-97, 100, 140, 149-50; after World War II, 119, 142, 151, 223, 239, 260. *See also* Interscholastic golf; Metropolitan Golf Association; U.S. Amateur; U.S. Amateur Public Links Championship; U.S. Women's Amateur
American Airlines, 133, 207
American Beach (Fla.), 45
American Committee on Africa, 229, 322

American Golf Classic (PGA), 223, 244
Anderson, Marian, 66-67
Andy Williams–San Diego Open (PGA). *See* San Diego Open
Anheuser-Busch, 133, 252
Apartheid, xiii, 204-5, 224-32. *See also* American Committee on Africa; Rhodesia; South Africa
Apex Country Club (N.J.), 46, 47
Apollo Theater (Harlem), 42, 55, 57, 58, 61
Arizona, 141. *See also* Phoenix, Ariz.; Tucson Open
Arkansas, 250. *See also* Little Rock, Ark.
Armed forces, 65, 123, 176, 223, 259, 321. *See also* World War I; World War II
Armour, Tommy, 99
Armstrong, Lance, 255
Armstrong, Louis, 55
Aronimink Golf Club (Philadelphia), 38, 254
Arvin, Alma, 114-15, 194
Ashe, Arthur, 228, 230, 247, 255, 265
Asheville, N.C., 26, 94, 112, 175
Asia, 205, 206, 207, 220, 258. *See also* "Cablinasian"; India; Thailand
Astaire, Fred, 112-13, 117
Atlanta, Ga., ix, xi, 60, 66, 73-74, 81, 88, 138, 145, 182, 280n27; integrating municipal courses, 148. *See also* Atlanta University; Black Rock Golf Course; Bobby Jones Municipal Golf Course; Clark College; Coca-Cola; East Lake Golf Club; Emory University; *Holmes v. Atlanta*; Jackson, Maynard; Morehouse College; Morris Brown College; New Lincoln Country Club; Piney Wood Country Club; Southern Open
Atlanta University, 33

(343)

Atlantic City, N.J., 21. *See also* Brigantine Hotel and Golf Course; Douglas Park (Atlantic City)
Audubon Park (New Orleans), 6–8, 93. *See also* Bartholomew, Joseph M.; Marshall, Edison
Augusta, Ga., 14–15. *See also* Augusta National Golf Club; Masters Tournament; Paine College
Augusta Country Club (Ga.), 14–15
Augusta National Golf Club (Ga.), 18, 40, 77–80, 81, 141, 183, 264; and Dwight D. Eisenhower, 177–80, 195, 203–4, 231, 235, 238, 242, 263; and integration of the Masters, 231–36; first black members of, 251, 254–55, 264. *See also* Augusta, Ga.; Masters Tournament
Augustus v. Board of Public Instruction of Escambia County Florida (1962), 170–71
Augustus v. City of Pensacola (1956), 170–71
Australia, 96–97, 220, 241, 252. *See also* Kelly Springfield Open
Averyhardt, Shasta, 216

Babe Zaharias Open (LPGA), 217
Bahamas, 207, 208
Baker, Ella, 53, 54, 181
Baker, Josephine, 61
Ball, Cleo, 88, 89, 97, 98
Ball, Robert (Pat), xii, 23–25, 59, 86, 88, 89, 93, 94, 96, 98, 101–4, 105, 123, 142
Ballesteros, Seve, 243
Baltimore, Md., xi, 28, 39, 61, 91, 165; integrating municipal courses, 68–71, 154, 172; and the UGA, 114. *See also* Baltimore Country Club; Coney Island Golf Links; Morgan College
Baltimore Country Club, 38
Baltusrol Golf Club (N.J.), 117, 253
Baraben, Henry, 216
Baraka, Amiri, 192
Barker, Beltram, 86

Barkley, Charles, 127, 260, 262–63, 265, 266–67
Barrow, Joe Louis, Jr., 258. *See also* Louis, Joe
Bartholomew, Joseph M., 1, 6–8, 9, 12, 18, 73, 74–76, 93, 162
Baseball, 60, 105–6, 120, 185, 205, 208, 259. *See also* Aaron, Hank; Mays, Willie; Negro Leagues; Robinson, Jackie; Ruth, Babe
Basie, Count, 55
Basketball, 22, 120, 185, 208, 241. *See also* Barkley, Charles; Jordan, Michael
Bath Beach Club (New York), 38, 259
Baton Rouge, La., 74, 162
Battistoni, Gene, 102
Beal v. Holcombe (1951), 163, 164–65, 167
Beaumont, Tex., 165, 217, 321. See also Babe Zaharias Open; *Fayson v. Beard*
Beavers, Louise, 131
Belafonte, Harry, 179
Bell, Charles T., 151, 155–56
Benny, Jack, 130
Benson, E. F., 29
Bermuda, 96, 99
Bermuda grass, 18
Bethesda, Md. *See* Burning Tree Club; Congressional Country Club
Bethune-Cookman University, 239–40
Beverly Country Club (Chicago), 23
Bide-A-Wee Golf Course (Portsmouth, Va.), 200–201
Bilbo, Theodore, 67
Bing Crosby National Pro-Am (PGA), 119, 120, 131, 211–12, 213, 215, 222, 253
Birmingham, Ala., 75, 151, 158, 178, 183–86, 251–55. *See also* Shoal Creek Club; *Shuttlesworth v. Gaylord*
Birth of a Nation, 17
Black, James, 91, 216
Black, Julian, 198
Black, Lucille, 54
Black Arts Movement, 192

Black Panther Party, 187, 190–92, 193, 196
Black Power, x, xiii–xiv, 187, 189, 192, 193, 196–98, 208, 223–24, 225
Black press, 29–30, 234–35, 322
Black Rock Golf Course (Atlanta), 75–77, 156–57, 159
Bobby Jones Municipal Golf Course (Atlanta), ix, 151, 153–56, 177, 183, 248
Bob Hope Desert Classic (PGA). *See* Palm Springs Desert Golf Classic
Boehner, John, 264
Bolling v. Sharpe (1954), 68
Booker T. Washington Country Club (Philadelphia), 44–45, 46, 47
Boston, Mass., x, xii, 3–7, 88, 112. *See also* Brae Burn Country Club; Harvard University; Mapledale Country Club; Massachusetts Classic; Ponkapoag Golf Club
Botts, Rafe "Ray," 138, 215–16
Bow, Clara, 48
Bowling, 203
Boxing. *See* Charles, Ezzard; Dempsey, Jack; Ivory, Frank; Jack, Beau; Johnson, Jack; Louis, Joe; Robinson, Sugar Ray; Wills, Harry
Boykins, Harvey, 130
Bradley, Tom, 59, 236
Brady, Mike, 15–16
Brae Burn Country Club (Boston), 15–16, 22
Bramlett, Joseph, 216
Brazil, 10
Brewer, Thomas, 176–77, 200
Bridge (card game), 64
Brigantine Hotel and Golf Course (Atlantic City), 44
British Open, 13, 205, 228, 243, 265
Brook Hollow Golf Club (Dallas), 72
Brown, Charlotte Hawkins, 60, 61
Brown, Cliff, 91, 216
Brown, Dewey, 117–18
Brown, Edgar George, 66–68
Brown, Howard, 216

Brown, James, 41, 80, 197
Brown, Jim, 196–97, 207, 234–35
Brown, Mary, 90, 105
Brown, Paris (Toomer), 66, 99
Brown, Pete, 90, 216, 221, 227, 228, 241
Brown v. Board of Education (1954), x, 71, 152, 154, 157, 158, 161, 164, 165, 166, 167, 168, 170, 172, 173, 185
Brutus, Dennis, 229. *See also* Apartheid
Buckley, William F., Jr., 203–4
Bunce Island, 50
Bunn, Oscar, 34–36, 38
Burk, Martha, 264
Burke, Jack, 13
Burke, Thomas, 128
Burke Golf Company, 108, 110, 197
Burning Tree Club (Md.), 177, 178, 179, 203, 204, 264
Burton, Harold, 67
Bush, Prescott, 104
Butler National Golf Club (Chicago), 253–54

"Cablinasian," xiv, 237, 261–64, 267–69
Caddying, xi, 6, 23, 49; origins of, 3, 9, 50; before World War I, 9–19, 28–29, 35, 117; at Augusta National, 40, 77–80, 232, 235, 242, 249–50; at black-owned courses, 43; after World War I, 54, 59, 75–77, 80–81, 88, 91, 146, 205, 207; and UGA players, 92, 93, 94, 105, 106, 109, 142, 210, 221; after World War II, 124, 180, 197, 239, 248–49; and gambling, 137–38; on the PGA Tour, 227–28, 249–51, 259–60. *See also* Golf clubs; Groundskeepers; Instructors
California, 160, 184, 200, 202, 210, 211, 239, 254, 260–61, 269. *See also* Bing Crosby National Pro-Am; Cypress Point Club; Los Angeles, Calif.; Oakland, Calif.; Orange County Open Invitational; Palm Springs Desert Golf Classic; Parkridge Country Club; San Diego, Calif.; San Fran-

cisco, Calif.; Seal Beach Navy Golf Course; Stanford University; Val Verde Resort
Calloway, Cab, 55
Campbell, Floyd, 55
Canada, 123, 131–33, 210. *See also* Canadian Open; Canadian PGA Championship; Labatt Open; Montreal Open; Toronto, Can.
Canadian Open, 84–85, 118, 209
Canadian PGA Championship, 246
Cannon, Poppy, 206
Capati, Dominga, 205
Cape May Golf Club (N.J.), 13
Capra, Frank, 131
Carey, Mariah, 268
Carlos, John, 224
Carnegie, Andrew, 14
Carroll Park Golf Course (Baltimore), 68–71
Carswell, G. Harold, 204
Carter, Herman J. D., 52
Carter, John Garnet, 57
Carter, Lee, 216
Carter, Robert L., 169–70
Carter, W. Beverly, Jr., 207
Casa Loma Country Club (Wisc.), 46, 88, 89, 93, 97
Casper, Billy, 214
Caucasian clause, 85, 116–19, 121–22, 209–13, 214, 289–90n90
Cedar Crest Golf Course (Dallas), 90, 114, 122, 130, 131, 134, 165, 260
Cedar Rapids Open (PGA), 124
Cedar River Golf Club (N.Y.), 47, 118
Champions Tour (PGA). *See* Senior PGA Tour
Chappelle, Dave, 262
Charles, Ezzard, 129
Charleston, S.C., 2–3, 56. See also *Cummings v. City of Charleston*
Charlotte, N.C., 109, 192, 193. See also Dr. Charles L. Sifford Golf Course; *Leeper v. Charlotte Park and Recreation Commission*; Sifford, Charlie

Chavis, Gordon, 216
Cheshire Country Club (Conn.), 21, 47
Chester L. Washington Golf Course (Los Angeles). *See* Western Avenue Golf Course
Chicago, Ill., x, xi, xii, 21, 22, 29, 31, 143; black players before 1920 in, 23–28, 39; after World War I, 41–42, 46–48, 53, 55, 56, 59, 60, 86, 92, 98; and UGA National, 96, 98–99, 128, 132–33, 135; after World War II, 142, 149, 234. *See also* Alpha Golf Club; Beverly Country Club; Butler National Golf Club; Chicago Golf Club; Chicago Urban Junior Golf Association; Chicago Women's Golf Club; Jackson Park Golf Course; Marquette Park Golf Course; McDougal, Horace; Medinah Country Club; Northwestern University; Palos Park Golf Course; Pipe O' Peace Golf Course; Ravisloe Country Club; Speedy, Nettie (George); Speedy, Walter; Tam O'Shanter Open; Wayside Country Club; Windy City Golf Association
Chicago Golf Club, 37
Chicago Seven, 190, 191, 224
Chicago Urban Junior Golf Association, 247–48
Chicago Women's Golf Club, 99, 115, 126, 208
Churches, 22, 28, 46, 160. *See also* African Methodist Episcopal (AME) Church; Ministers
City Park (New Orleans), 73, 74, 162
Civilian Conservation Corps (CCC), 65, 66, 73, 106, 193
Civil Rights Act (1964), 201, 203
Civil Rights Cases (1883), 31
Civil Works Administration (CWA), 73
Clark College, 131, 145
Clarke, Eural, 119
Clay, William L., 202
Clay v. U.S. (1971), 190
Clearview Golf Club (Ohio), 47, 146–47,

346) INDEX

219–20, 321. *See also* Powell, Renee; Powell, William
Cleveland, Ohio, xi, xii, 21, 59, 61, 85, 92, 128, 143, 150, 198, 248. See also *Gillespie v. Lake Shore Golf Club*; Highland Park Golf Course; Seneca Golf Course
Clinton, Bill, 192, 261
Clisby, Oscar, 82, 91
Cobb, James, 64
Cobbs Creek Golf Course (Philadelphia), 26, 88, 89, 90, 95, 102–4, 109, 133, 151. *See also* Fairview Golf Club
Cobo, Albert, 128
Coca-Cola, 131, 133
Cole, Nat King, 55, 59, 229
Colonial Country Club (Miss.), 180
Colonialism, xi, 49–50, 196, 205, 225
Colorado. *See* Denver, Colo.
Columbus, Ga., 148, 151, 176–77, 200
Commission on Interracial Cooperation, 153
Coney Island Golf Links (Baltimore), 55, 59, 60
Congressional Country Club (Md.), 99, 217–18, 233
Congress of African People, 192, 196
Congress of Racial Equality (CORE), 54, 192, 197, 198, 203
Connecticut, 21, 91, 198–99. *See also* Cheshire Country Club; Hartford, Conn.; Lee Haven Beach Club; Metropolitan Golf Association; Sammy Davis Jr.–Greater Hartford Open
Connie's Inn (Harlem), 43
Connor, Eugene "Bull," 185
Conyers, John, 201–2
Coolidge, Calvin, 64
Corbin, Louis Rafael, 99, 100, 101, 104
Cornell University, 64, 213
Corpus Christi, Tex., 165, 203
Cosell, Howard, 198–99
Cosmopolitan Golf Club (Los Angeles), 83, 85, 86, 111, 134, 136

Cottam, H. T., 8
Cotton, Henry, 96
Country clubs. *See* Golf clubs
Cowans, Thelma (McTyre), xii, 90, 105, 114–15, 116, 125–26, 194
Cox, Charles M., 48–49
Crenshaw, Ben, 183, 250
Crescent City Golf Club (New Orleans), 47, 74, 86
Cricket, 3
Cronkite, Walter, 202
Croquet, 20, 45
Crosby, A. D. V., 145
Crosby, Bing, 99, 117, 131, 142, 212, 213, 214. *See also* Bing Crosby National Pro-Am
Cruikshank, Bobby, 13
Cuba, 12, 191, 193, 196
Cudone, Carolyn, 126
Cullen, Countee, 44
Cummings v. City of Charleston (1961), 163, 175–76
Cypress Point Club (Calif.), 253–54

Dallas, Tex., xii, 43, 72, 86, 155, 165, 215. *See also* Cedar Crest Golf Course; Elder, Lee
Daly, Victor, 63–64
Dashy's Inn Golf Club (New York), 55
Davis, Kenneth E., 38
Davis, Miles, 41, 55
Davis, Sammy, Jr., 82, 130, 165. *See also* Sammy Davis Jr.–Greater Hartford Open
Dawes, Charles, 117
Dawkins, Ralph, 45
Dayton, Ohio, 104, 145, 224
Delaney, Hubert, 159–60
Delaney v. Central Valley Golf Club (1941), 159–60, 161, 163
Delaware, 80–81, 202
Demaret, Jimmy, 101, 117, 121, 142, 210
Dempsey, Jack, 129
Dendy, John Brooks, xii, 89, 94, 105, 112, 128

INDEX (347

Dent, Jim, 91, 108, 216, 232, 242, 266
Denver, Colo., 81, 148, 209
Depew, Chauncey, 102
Depew, Ganson, 102
De Priest, Oscar, 128
Detroit, Mich., xii, 20, 21, 85, 98, 104, 114, 128, 131, 198, 243. *See also* Joe Louis Open; Louis, Joe; Rackham Municipal Golf Course; Rouge Park Golf Course; Sweet, Ossian
Devlin, Bruce, 220
DeVoe, Jimmie, 59, 83, 112, 118, 124, 134
Dickey, Bill, 248
Diggs, Charles, 157, 201–2, 226
Dillard University, 74
Ditsebe, Rodney, 205
Dixon, Ike, 55
Dominican Republic, 5
Double V campaign, 142
Douglas Park (Atlantic City), 21, 30
Douglass Park (Indianapolis), 89, 91, 98, 145
Dr. Charles L. Sifford Golf Course (Charlotte), 175
Du Bois, W. E. B., 21, 41, 49–51, 205
Dudley, Ed, 119
Dufina, Frank, 34
Duncan, George, 13
Dunn, Willie, 35
Dyer, Alfred "Rabbit," 227–28, 251
Dyker Beach Golf Course (New York). *See* Bath Beach Club

Eastern Golf Association, 86
Eastern Open (UGA), 86, 100
East Lake Golf Club (Atlanta), 80, 94
Eckstine, Billy, 55, 56, 101, 107, 109, 111
Edison, Thomas, 34
Egypt, 2, 205
Eisenhower, Dwight D., 141, 177–80, 195, 203–4, 231, 235
Elder, Lee, xii, xiii, 90, 91, 92, 97, 108, 124, 137, 209, 211, 216, 247, 322; and PGA events, 222–24, 241, 244, 263; confronting apartheid and trip to Africa, 224–31; participating in the Masters, 231–36, 238, 244, 249; and Tiger Woods, 237, 256, 260, 267, 269
Eliot, Charles W., 4
Ellington, Duke, 55
Ellison, Ralph, 80, 81
Embargo Act of 1807, 2
Emory University, 159
England, 2, 9, 29, 31, 33, 36, 39, 97, 100, 146, 220. *See also* British Open; Silvermere Club
Evans, Chick, 117
Evers, Medgar and Myrlie, 180–81

Fair Employment Practices Committee (FEPC), 54
Fairview Golf Club (Philadelphia), 85–86, 181, 188–89, 193–96. *See also* Stanford, Max; Stanford, Max, Jr.; Stanford, Winnie
Farmer, James, 54, 75
Farmers Home Administration, 201–2
Farr, Mel, 197–98
Father Divine, 44
Faultless Golf, 223
Fayson v. Beard (1955), 163, 165, 185
Federal Bureau of Investigation (FBI), 187–87, 190–91, 194–96, 201, 207, 223
Federal Emergency Relief Administration (FERA), 73
Firestone, Harvey, 14
Firestone Country Club, 124, 211, 223. *See also* American Golf Classic; Rubber City Open
First Tee, 257–58
Fisk University, 145
Fitzgerald, Ella, 55
Flipper, Joseph Simeon, 22
Florida, 3, 52, 54, 59, 104, 158, 166, 168, 204, 237, 243, 260, 261, 280n27. *See also* American Beach; Bethune-Cookman University; Florida A&M College; Fort Lauderdale, Fla.; Jacksonville, Fla.; Lady Errol Classic; Miami, Fla.; Miami Beach, Fla.; Palm

Beach, Fla.; Pensacola, Fla.; *Wimbish v. Pinellas County, Florida*
Florida A&M College, 145, 146, 215
Floyd, Raymond, 231, 250
Fonda, Henry, 48
Football, 120, 128, 145, 185, 205, 208, 266. See also Brown, Jim; Farr, Mel; Payton, Walter; Washington, Kenny
Ford, Aaron L., 67
Ford, Gerald, 204, 232
Ford, Henry, 10, 14
Fordlandia (Brazil), 10
Foreman, George, 230
Forest Park (St. Louis), 26, 53, 55
Fort Lauderdale, Fla., 200. See also *Griffis v. City of Fort Lauderdale*; *Moorhead v. City of Fort Lauderdale*
Fort Wayne Open (PGA), 123-24
Foulis, James, 36
Fountain Valley massacre (Fountain Valley Golf Course), xiii, 189-92, 206, 220, 225
Fox News, 86, 87, 128
Foxx, Redd, 236
France, 61, 105
Freedom Riders, 181
Freeway Golf Course (N.J.), 46, 47, 91, 130, 194, 251, 280n27
Frelinghuysen, Joseph S., 38
Frick, Henry Clay, 38
Frost, David, 263
Funches, Ethel (Powers), xii, 90, 91, 194

Gambia, 206
Gambling, 30, 60, 96, 99, 102, 111, 137-39
Garden City Golf Club (New York), 38
Garland, Jessa, 26
Garvey, Marcus, 196
Gary, Ind., 115, 149, 218
Gaston, A. G., 253
Gaye, Marvin, 197-98
Gentlemen's agreement, 117, 210
Georgia, 72-73, 93, 112, 280n27. See also Albany, Ga.; Atlanta, Ga.; Augusta, Ga.; Columbus, Ga.; Jekyll Island Club; Macon, Ga.; Savannah, Ga.; University of Georgia
Ghana, 206-7
Gibson, Althea, xii, 59, 108, 125, 215-20
Gillespie v. Lake Shore Golf Club (1950), 161-63
Gleason, Jackie, 234-35
Golf clubs: workers and attendants, 10-11, 18-19, 73, 75, 112, 274-75n5; black-owned courses before 1920, 20-23; black-owned courses after 1920, 42-49, 54, 258, 280n27. See also Caddying; Groundskeepers; Instructors
Golliwog, 31, 32
Goodman, Benny, 198-99
Grady, Wayne, 252
Grant, George Franklin, 3-7, 31
Grayson's Travel and Business Guide, 148
Great Depression, 57, 60
Greater Greensboro Open (PGA), 213-15, 220, 224. See also Sedgefield Country Club
Greater Hartford Open (PGA). See Sammy Davis Jr.-Greater Hartford Open
Greater Milwaukee Open (PGA), 236, 246, 266
Great Migration, x, 10-11, 29, 41-42, 55, 60, 75, 93
Green, Al, 216
Greenbrier Resort (W.Va.), 8
Greensboro, N.C., 171-75, 176, 200, 213-14. See also Greater Greensboro Open; Sedgefield Country Club; Simkins, George; *Simkins v. City of Greensboro*; *Wolfe v. North Carolina*
Greensboro Six. See *Simkins v. City of Greensboro*; *Wolfe v. North Carolina*
Greenskeepers. See Groundskeepers
Gregory, Ann Moore, xii, 90, 91, 105, 115-16, 126, 207, 216-19
Griffin, Marvin, 157
Griffis v. City of Fort Lauderdale (1958), 163

INDEX (349

Griffith Park (Los Angeles), 82, 89, 129, 197
Griggs, John, 31
Grimké, Archibald, 5
Groundskeepers, xi, 8, 74. *See also* Caddying; Golf clubs; Instructors
Groves, Junius, 53
Groves Center Golf Course (Kansas City), 47, 53-54
Guilford, Jesse, 15
Gunter, Madison, 118-19

Hagen, Walter, 5, 6, 100, 104, 117
Haiti, 206
Halarack, Charles, 102, 135
Hale America National Open, 142
Hall, Fred "Tubby," 55
Hampton v. City of Jacksonville, Florida (1962), 166-67, 208
Harding, Warren G., 117
Harlan, John Marshall, 31
Harlem, N.Y., xi, 42-44, 59, 61, 64, 179, 195. *See also* Apollo Theater; Connie's Inn; Harlem Renaissance; Savoy Ballroom
Harlem Renaissance, xi, 42, 44, 49-57, 61. *See also* Harlem, N.Y.
Harleston Green (Charleston), 2-3
Harper, Chandler, 201
Hartford, Conn., 33
Hartsfield, William, 152, 154-57, 158
Hartsfield, Zeke, 94, 105, 124, 128, 137, 139
Harvard University, 4-5, 103
Hassanein, Hassan, 205
Hathaway, Maggie Mae, 82-83, 114, 197, 199-200, 207, 210, 211, 212, 217, 219, 227-29, 234-35, 248, 250, 259, 262, 263
Havemeyer, Theodore, 35-36, 39
Hawkins, Robert, 49, 86
Hayes v. Crutcher (1956), 167-68
Hazzard, Hoxie, 105
Hebert, F. Edward, 67
Height, Dorothy, 179

Henning, Harold, 225-26
Hicks, Betty, 126
Hicks, James, 56
Highland Park Golf Course (Cleveland), 73, 89, 122
Hill, Earl, 81, 124
Historically black colleges and universities (HBCUs). *See* Interscholastic golf
Hitler, Adolph, 67, 120, 142-43, 227
Hockey, 257
Hogan, Ben, 106, 118, 119, 138, 177
Holley, James, 164, 200-201. *See also Holley v. City of Portsmouth*
Holley v. City of Portsmouth (1957), 162-64, 185, 200-201
Holmes, Alfred "Tup," ix, 140, 149-59, 261. *See also Holmes v. Atlanta*
Holmes, Gary, ix
Holmes, Hamilton E., ix, 158-59
Holmes, Hamilton M., ix, 149, 151, 153, 155, 159
Holmes, Oliver, 151, 153, 155-56
Holmes v. Atlanta (1955), ix, xii, 74, 149-59, 161, 162, 163, 164, 165, 166, 167, 171, 173, 176, 177, 178, 185, 248. *See also* Holmes, Alfred "Tup"
Hoover, J. Edgar, 195
Hope, Bob, 100, 131, 142, 214, 236. *See also* Palm Springs Desert Golf Classic
Horne, Lena, 82
Horse racing, 3, 30
Houston, Charles Hamilton, 69
Houston, Tex., 72, 86, 101, 134, 155, 185, 214. *See also Beal v. Holcombe*; Houston Open
Houston Open (PGA), 236
Howard, Ginger, 216
Howard University, 26, 34, 62, 65, 164, 239, 249, 321
Hughes, Langston, 137, 179
Hughes, Solomon, 89, 93-94, 100, 101, 107, 119, 123
Hull, Dolphus, 250

Hunter, John F., 67
Hurston, Zora Neal, 52

Ickes, Harold, 65–67, 129
Idlewild, Mich., 21, 22, 47
Illinois, 115, 160, 208–9. *See also* Chicago, Ill.; Kankakee Shores Country Club; Sunset Hills Country Club
Improved Benevolent and Protective Order of Elks of the World (Black Elks), 53
India, 205, 206
Indiana, 115. *See also* Fort Wayne Open; Gary, Ind.; Indianapolis, Ind.; Indiana University
Indianapolis, Ind., xii, 90, 254. *See also* Douglass Park (Indianapolis); Meridian Hills Country Club
Indiana University, 145
Instructors, 22, 38, 59, 88, 101, 108. *See also* Caddying; Golf clubs; Groundskeepers
Insurance City Open (PGA). *See* Sammy Davis Jr.–Greater Hartford Open
Intercollegiate golf. *See* Interscholastic golf
International Sweethearts of Rhythm, 55
Interscholastic golf, 33, 38, 88, 129, 143–45, 180, 239, 252, 254, 259, 261, 263; historically black colleges and universities (HBCUs), 45, 46, 51, 60, 114, 145–46, 180, 215, 239–41, 247, 249. *See also* Amateur golf; *and individual schools*
Iowa, 3, 20, 149, 202. *See also* Cedar Rapids Open; Iowa University
Iowa University, 143
Isles Golf Club (Miss.), 16–17, 31
Ivory, Frank, 80–81

Jack, Beau, 40, 77–80, 81
Jackson, Carl, 250
Jackson, Eddie, 105
Jackson, Harry, 86, 87, 89
Jackson, Jesse, 264
Jackson, Lillie, 68, 69
Jackson, Maynard, 248
Jackson, Miss., 148, 180–81, 203, 221. *See also* Jackson State University; Millsaps College
Jackson Park Golf Course (Chicago), 23–25, 27–28, 41–42, 46
Jackson State University, 239–41
Jacksonville, Fla., xi, 134, 200, 208–9. See also *Hampton v. City of Jacksonville, Florida*; Lincoln Country Club (Jacksonville)
Jamaica, 12, 184, 196, 206
Jazz, 55
Jekyll Island Club (Ga.), 81, 124, 125
Jena Six, 254
Joe Louis Golf Course (Chicago). *See* Pipe O' Peace Golf Course
Joe Louis Open (UGA), 94, 98, 99, 100, 106, 108, 124, 128, 129, 135, 137. *See also* Louis, Joe
Johnson, George, 216, 227, 242
Johnson, Jack, 33, 255
Johnson, James Weldon, 41, 52, 53, 64
Johnson, Lyndon B., 247
Jolson, Al, 117, 131
Jones, Bobby, 40, 56, 77, 88, 94, 151. *See also* Augusta National Golf Club; Bobby Jones Municipal Golf Course; East Lake Golf Club
Jones, Carrie, 90, 98
Jones, Forrest, Jr., 145
Jones, Robert Trent, Sr., 189
Jones, William Henry, 62–63, 64
Jones v. Attridge and Martha's Vineyard Country Club (1947), 160, 163
Jordan, Michael, xiv, 127, 265, 266–67
Joseph M. Bartholomew Golf Course. *See* Pontchartrain Park Golf Course
Just, Ernest Everett, 26

Kankakee Shores Country Club (Ill.), 46–48, 49
Kansas, 100. *See also* Kansas City, Mo.; Kansas State University

INDEX (351)

Kansas City, Mo., xii, 53–54, 90, 131, 159. *See also* Groves Center Golf Course
Kansas State University, 259
Kelly, Edward Joseph, 128
Kelly Springfield Open (Australia), 219
Kemble, Edward, 30, 32, 143
Kendrix, Moss, 131
Kennedy, John F., 203–4, 231
Kentucky, 170. *See also* Louisville, Ky.
Kenya, 207, 229
Kerner Commission, 247
King, A. D., 186
King, Coretta Scott, 179, 206–7
King, Martin Luther, Jr., ix, 23, 148, 155, 179, 181–82, 184, 186, 190, 199, 201, 204, 206–7, 224, 229, 253, 264. *See also* Southern Christian Leadership Conference
King, Martin Luther, III, 264
King, Rodney, 321
Kirkwood, Joe, 5
Kleindienst, Richard, 190
Kolven (*kolf*), 1
Koufax, Sandy, 215
Kroydon Golf Company, 197
Ku Klux Klan (KKK), 48, 181
Kunstler, William, 190, 191

Labatt Open (PGA), 123
Ladies Professional Golf Association (LPGA), 125, 147, 180, 215–17, 219–20, 257–58; list of black participants, 216. *See also* Professional Golfers' Association; *and individual events*
Lady Errol Classic (LPGA), 219
La Guardia, Fiorello, 159
Lancaster, Burt, 48
Langer, Bernard, 243
Langford, John, 64–65
Langston, John Mercer, 65
Langston Golf Course (Washington, D.C.), 55, 64–65, 73, 90, 99, 100, 133, 142, 223, 233, 260
Las Vegas, Nev., 133
Lee, Howard, 5
Lee, Spike, 16
Lee Haven Beach Club (Conn.), 47
Leeper v. Charlotte Park and Recreation Commission (1956), 163, 175, 176
Lefkowitz, Louis, 213
Legend of Bagger Vance, 16
Lehman, Herbert, 160
Lehman, Tom, 255
Len Immke Buick Open (LPGA), 217
Lewis, Abraham Lincoln, 45
Lewis, Edward S., 68
Liberia, 206, 229
Lincoln Country Club (Atlanta). *See* New Lincoln Country Club
Lincoln Country Club (Jacksonville), 45, 47, 94, 145, 166
Lincoln Memorial Golf Course (Washington, D.C.), 62–63, 69
Lincoln University (Mo.), 145
Lincoln University (Pa.), 145
Lions Municipal Golf Course (Austin, Tex.), 164
Little Rock, Ark., 60, 178. *See also* Little Rock Nine; Shorter College
Little Rock Nine, 178, 179, 210
Locke, Bobby, 225
Locke, Alain, 51
Long Beach Open, 115, 209, 210, 211
Long Island (N.Y.), 19, 43. *See also* Maidstone Club; Manaqua Country Club; National Golf Links; Shinnecock Hills Golf Club
Lopez, Nancy, 183
Los Angeles, Calif., xii, 59, 61, 81–83, 91, 112–14, 125–26, 130–31, 133, 148, 213, 223, 236. *See also* Cosmopolitan Golf Club; Griffith Park; Hathaway, Maggie Mae; Long Beach Open; Los Angeles Open; Riviera Country Club; Vernondale Golf Club; Western Avenue Golf Course
Los Angeles Open (PGA), 113, 118, 119, 131, 200, 209, 222, 225–26. *See also* Riviera Country Club
Louis, Joe, xiv, 48, 57, 82, 93–94, 125, 161,

198, 216, 255; and UGA events, 99–101, 129, 133, 134, 151; and Tam O'Shanter Open, 105, 116; and Ted Rhodes, 107–8; and Bill Spiller, 112, 113; and PGA events, 118–22, 127, 210; and World War II, 142; and Charlie Sifford, 211–12; and Lee Elder, 223. *See also* Barrow, Joe Louis, Jr.; Joe Louis Open; Pipe O' Peace Golf Course

Louisiana, 23, 55, 67, 82, 93, 148, 254. *See also* Bartholomew, Joseph M.; Baton Rouge, La.; New Orleans, La.; Shreveport, La.

Louisville, Ky., 134, 146, 155, 158. *See also* Louisville Country Club; *Sweeney v. City of Louisville*

Louisville Country Club (Ky.), 13

Lowden, Frank, 25

Lowell, William, 5–6

Lowery, Joseph, 181, 251, 264, 268

LPGA Championship, 258

Lunceford, Jimmie, 56

Lyle, Sandy, 243

Macdonald, Charles Blair, 36

MacGregor Golf, 183

Mackay, John W., 19

Macon, Ga., 148

Madison Square Garden (New York), 59, 77

Maggie Hathaway Golf Course (Los Angeles), 83

Magloire, Paul, 206

Maidstone Club (N.Y.), 38

Maine, 43

Malcolm X, 190, 195

Manaqua Country Club (N.Y.), 43, 47

Mandela, Nelson, 230, 263

Mangrum, Lloyd, 108

Mangrum, Ray, 108, 112

Mapledale Country Club (Boston), 47, 48–49, 86–87, 88, 89

March on Washington (1963), 204

Marquette Park Golf Course (Chicago), 23, 28, 41, 46

Marshall, Edison, 89, 91, 93, 105

Marshall, Thurgood, xii, 69, 153–54, 155, 157, 162, 164, 167–68, 169, 172–73, 181

Martin, Clyde, 99, 100, 101, 105, 142

Maryland, 33, 91, 193. *See also* Baltimore, Md.; Bethesda, Md.; National Capital Country Club

Mason, Sanders, 94, 104

Massachusetts, 49, 72, 91, 161, 204, 218. *See also* Boston, Mass.; *Jones v. Attridge and Martha's Vineyard Country Club*

Massachusetts Classic (PGA), 226

Masters Tournament, xiii, 13, 78–80, 108, 120, 121, 182, 183, 208, 222, 224, 225, 227, 241, 243, 244, 249, 254, 257–58; and Lee Elder, 231–36, 244, 249; and Tiger Woods, 237, 238, 241, 242, 246, 249, 251, 255–67, 321. *See also* Augusta, Ga.; Augusta National Golf Club

May, George S., 104–5, 116, 118, 119, 128, 177, 205. *See also* Tam O'Shanter Open

Mays, Benjamin, 153

Mays, Willie, 199

McCard, Harry, 64

McCormick, Joseph Medill, 24

McDougal, Horace, 23, 33, 86, 88, 92, 142–43

McDougald, Elise, 51

McGuinn, Robert, 69

McLaurin v. Oklahoma State Regents (1950), 165

McLeod, Fred, 6–8

Meadowbrook Country Club (Raleigh, N.C.), 46, 47

Medinah Country Club (Chicago), 104, 124

Meek, Carrie, 268

Memorial Park Golf Course (Norfolk, Va.), 71–72, 162, 200

Memphis, Tenn., xii, 90, 134, 168–69

Mencken, H. L., 52–53

Merchant, John, 266–67, 317n69

INDEX (353

Meridian Hills Country Club (Indianapolis), 126
Merion Golf Club (Philadelphia), 125, 254
Metairie Country Club (La.), 1, 8, 18, 19, 251. *See also* Bartholomew, Joseph M.
Metropolitan Golf Association, 99, 212–13
Mexico, 206, 232, 261
Miami, Fla., xii, 134, 148, 167. *See also* Miami Beach, Fla.; Miami Springs Golf Course; *Rice v. Arnold*; *Ward v. City of Miami*
Miami Beach, Fla., 80, 165–66
Miami Springs Golf Course (Fla.), 91, 165–66, 202–3, 218
Michigan, 34, 59, 99, 115, 135, 160, 162, 201, 202, 210. *See also* Detroit, Mich.; Idlewild, Mich.; University of Michigan
Miles, Lizzie, 55
Miller, Johnny, 231
Miller High Life Open (PGA), 123
Million Dollar Challenge (South Africa), 230–31, 232
Millsaps College, 180
Mills Brothers, 59
Miniature golf, 56–62, 88, 98
Ministers, 21–22, 34, 81, 143, 151, 167, 181–82, 185–86. *See also* African Methodist Episcopal (AME) Church; Churches; Southern Christian Leadership Conference
Minneapolis, Minn., 94. *See also* St. Paul Open; University of Minnesota
Minnesota, 28. *See also* Minneapolis, Minn.
Minority Collegiate Golf Championship, 239–40
Mississippi, 9–10, 55, 67, 74, 80, 115, 117, 259. *See also* Isles Golf Club; Jackson, Miss.; Tupelo, Miss.
Missouri, 120. *See also* Kansas City, Mo.; Lincoln University (Mo.); St. Louis, Mo.
Mitchell, Billy, 56
Mitchell, Clarence M., 68
Mobile, Ala., 186–87. *See also Sawyer v. City of Mobile*
Mohansic Golf Course (N.Y.), 89, 93
Mondale, Walter, 204
Monsanto Open (PGA), 232–33
Montgomery, Ala., ix, 155, 185. *See also* Montgomery Bus Boycott
Montgomery Bus Boycott, ix, 155, 171, 179
Montreal Open (PGA), 123
Moore, Darla, 264
Moorhead v. City of Fort Lauderdale (1957), 163, 185
Morehouse College, 94, 131, 145, 153
Morgan, Walter, 216, 242
Morgan College (Baltimore), 68
Morris Brown College, 114, 145
Morrow, E. Frederic, 177
Morton, Al, 216
Mosk, Stanley, 212–13
Motley, Constance Baker, xii, 152–53, 159, 166–67, 169, 170–71, 181
Moye, Melanie, 89, 98
Muhammad, Elijah, 195
Muhammad, Wallace, 195
Muirfield Links (Scotland), 205, 265
Munich massacre (1972 Summer Olympic Games), 190

Nashville, Tenn., 106, 109, 151. *See also* Fisk University; *Hayes v. Crutcher*; Rhodes, Ted
Nassau Country Club (N.Y.), 10–11
National Association for the Advancement of Colored People (NAACP), x, xii–xiii, xiv, 5, 26, 53–54, 68, 69, 82, 180–81, 192, 193, 197, 199, 201, 206, 254, 268, 322; and the UGA, 133, 135, 137; and postwar municipal golf integration, 151, 157, 161–62, 165–68,

171–77, 184–86, 198, 202–3, 204, 219; and the Masters, 182; and the PGA/LPGA, 213–14, 217, 226, 251–55. *See also* Baker, Ella; Carter, Robert L.; Du Bois, W. E. B.; Hathaway, Maggie Mae; Johnson, James Weldon; Marshall, Thurgood; Motley, Constance Baker; White, Walter; Wilkins, Roy

National Capital Country Club (Md.), 38, 47, 50, 64–65

National Council of Negro Women, 179

National Council of Women's Organizations, 264

National Golf Foundation (NGF), 247, 257

National Golf Links (N.Y.), 38

National Minority Golf Foundation, 257, 266

National Minority Junior Golf Scholarship Association, 248

National Negro Council, 66

Nation of Islam (NOI), 195

Native Americans, 31, 34–36

Nebraska, 3. *See also* Omaha, Neb.

Negro Leagues (baseball), xii, 43, 102, 135, 137

Negro Motorist Green Book, 148

Nelson, Byron, 79, 105, 106, 142, 210

Nelson, Eugene C., 48

Netherlands, 1

Nevada. *See* Las Vegas, Nev.

Newark, N.J., 43, 102, 192

New Jersey, 5–6, 38, 45, 56, 117, 161, 198, 217. *See also* Apex Country Club; Atlantic City, N.J.; Cape May Golf Club; Freeway Golf Course; Metropolitan Golf Association; Newark, N.J.; Shady Rest Country Club; Somerset Hills Country Club; Spring Lake Golf Club

New Lincoln Country Club (Atlanta), 45–46, 47, 51, 56, 77, 94, 114, 133, 151, 152, 159

New Orleans, La., xi, 1, 6–8, 55, 74–76, 186, 224, 227, 251. *See also* Bartholomew, Joseph M.; City Park; Crescent City Golf Club; Dillard University; Marshall, Edison; Metairie Country Club; *New Orleans City Park Improvement Association v. Detiege*; New Orleans Country Club; Pontchartrain Park Golf Course; Xavier University

New Orleans City Park Improvement Association v. Detiege (1958), 162–63, 165

New Orleans Country Club, 74, 105

Newport Country Club (R.I.), 9

New York, 3, 4, 44, 57, 72, 161, 202. *See also* Cedar River Golf Club; Cornell University; *Delaney v. Central Valley Golf Club*; Long Island; Metropolitan Golf Association; Mohansic Golf Course; Nassau Country Club; New York, N.Y.; Pheasant Valley Country Club; Rising Sun Country Club; Shangri-La Resort; Syracuse University; Westchester Classic

New York, N.Y., xi, 8, 10–11, 19–20, 29; after World War I, 56, 57, 80, 85, 86, 88, 92, 99; and the UGA, 108, 112; after World War II, 206, 207. *See also* Bath Beach Club; Dashy's Inn Golf Club; Garden City Golf Club; Harlem, N.Y.; Madison Square Garden; United Nations; Van Cortlandt Park; Westchester Hills Golf Club

Nicklaus, Jack, 109, 145, 183, 211, 222, 223, 224, 226, 230, 234, 242, 243, 244, 250, 251, 257, 259, 263

Nigeria, 229. *See also* Nigerian Open

Nigerian Open, 97, 230, 231

Nike, Inc., xiv, 237, 256, 265–67, 269

Nixon, Richard, 177, 202, 203, 204, 212

Noone, Jimmie, 55

Norfolk, Va., 61, 71–72, 73. *See also* Memorial Park Golf Course; Norfolk State University; Portsmouth, Va.

Norfolk State University, 72
Norman, Greg, 183, 261
North Carolina, 13, 60, 62, 117, 142, 145, 175, 193, 203, 280n27). *See also* Asheville, N.C.; Charlotte, N.C.; Greensboro, N.C.; Pinehurst Resort; Raleigh, N.C.
North Carolina A&T College, 145
North Park Golf Course (Pittsburgh), 90, 91, 95, 110
Northwestern University, 33, 88, 92, 142, 143
Nutter, T. Gillis, 53

Oakhurst Links (W.Va.), 3
Oakland, Calif., 192. *See also* Black Panther Party; Richmond Open
Oakmont Country Club (Pa.), 13
Obama, Barack, 238, 260, 264, 268
O'Chier, Exie, 91
O'Connor, Sandra Day, 264
Official World Golf Ranking. *See* World Golf Ranking
Ohio, 67, 115, 178, 208, 247. *See also* American Golf Classic; Clearview Golf Club; Cleveland, Ohio; Dayton, Ohio; Firestone Country Club; Len Immke Buick Open; Ohio Northern University; Ohio State University; Rubber City Open; Wilberforce University
Ohio Northern University, 145, 146
Ohio State University, 145, 219
Oklahoma, 112, 138. *See also McLaurin v. Oklahoma State Regents*; Waco Turner Open
Old Warson Country Club (St. Louis), 253
Olmsted, Frederick Law, 8
Olmsted, John Charles, 8
Omaha, Neb., 149. *See also* Shalimar Country Club
O'Neal, Timothy, 216
Oosterhuis, Peter, 232
Open Championship. *See* British Open

Oprah Winfrey Show, 261–62, 264, 267
Orange County Open Invitational (PGA), 214
Oregon. *See* Pacific Ladies Classic; Portland, Oreg.
Ouimet, Francis, 10, 13, 15
Owens, Charlie, 91, 216, 241–42
Owens, Jesse, 127, 142

Pacific Ladies Classic (LPGA), 217
Padgham, Alf, 96
Paige, Satchel, 142
Paine College (Ga.), 180, 235
Pak, Se-Ri, 258
Palm Beach, Fla., 166, 203–4
Palmer, Arnold, 84–85, 123, 183, 208, 215, 224, 234, 241, 249, 259
Palmer Memorial Institute, 60, 61
Palm Springs Desert Golf Classic (PGA), 211–12, 213, 245
Palos Park Golf Course (Chicago), 46, 88, 89, 102
Pan-African Congress (1923), 49
Pan-Africanism, 49, 205–8, 226
Paramount Pictures, 128
Parkridge Country Club (Calif.), 47, 48–49
Parks, Rosa, ix, 155
Parks, Sadena, 216
Payton, Eddie, 239–41
Payton, Walter, 239
Pebble Beach National Pro-Am (PGA). *See* Bing Crosby National Pro-Am
Peete, Calvin, 216, 243–46, 247, 249, 252, 257, 266
Pennsylvania, 3, 117, 178, 191. See also Lincoln University (Pa.); Oakmont Country Club; Philadelphia, Pa.; Pittsburgh, Pa.
Pensacola, Fla., 186. See also *Augustus v. Board of Public Instruction of Escambia County Florida*; *Augustus v. City of Pensacola*; Monsanto Open
Pepsi-Cola. *See* Pepsi International Golf Tour

Pepsi International Golf Tour (IGT), 207, 247
Pernell, Porter, 197, 246
Perry, Edward, 44
Petri, Tom, 268
PGA Championship, 13, 85, 213, 224, 226, 231, 243, 250; Shoal Creek protest, 251-55, 260, 263, 264. *See also* LPGA Championship; Senior PGA Championship
PGA Tour, 84-85, 118-24, 208-15, 220-26, 230-36, 238-39, 241-47, 249-58, 260-267, 274-75n5; list of black participants, 216. *See also* Ladies Professional Golf Association; Professional Golfers' Association; Senior PGA Tour; *and individual events*
Pheasant Valley Country Club (N.Y.), 199
Philadelphia, Pa., xii, 31, 39, 56, 57, 61, 81, 86, 126-27, 138, 149, 179, 222. *See also* Aronimink Golf Club; Booker T. Washington Country Club; Cobbs Creek Golf Course; Fairview Golf Club; Merion Golf Club; Sifford, Charlie
Phoenix, Ariz., 86. *See also* National Minority Junior Golf Scholarship Association; Phoenix Open
Phoenix Open (PGA), 122, 208, 209
Pickett, Wilson, 124
Pierce, Samuel, 10-11
Pinehurst Resort (N.C.), 13, 18-19, 57
Piney Wood Country Club (Atlanta), 45, 47, 145
Pipe O' Peace Golf Course (Chicago), 157, 216
Pittsburgh, Pa., xii, 29, 57-58, 138. *See also* North Park Golf Course; Oakmont Country Club; South Park Golf Course
Player, Gary, xiii, 215, 225-32, 235, 251, 252, 263
Players Championship (PGA), 243
Plessy v. Ferguson (1896), 8, 31, 172

Ponkapoag Golf Club (Boston), 89, 90, 98, 133
Pontchartrain Park Golf Course (New Orleans), 74-76
Poor People's Campaign, 202
Portland, Oreg., 22, 86, 137, 143
Portsmouth, Va., 10-11, 200-201. *See also* Bide-A-Wee Golf Course; *Holley v. City of Portsmouth*; Norfolk, Va.
Potomac Park (Washington, D.C.), 60, 62-68, 90, 129, 133
Pott, Johnny, 220
Powell, Renee, xii, 91, 147, 215-16, 219-20, 240. *See also* Clearview Golf Club; Powell, William
Powell, William, 146-47, 149, 219-20, 256, 260, 321. *See also* Clearview Golf Club; Powell, Renee
Prairie View A&M College, 146
Price, Jack, 91, 135
Prince Hall Freemasonry, 60
Professional Golfers' Association (PGA), xi, 59, 83, 105, 106, 117-18, 225, 257-258, 274-75n5, 289-90n90; and World War II, 142-43. *See also* Caucasian clause; Ladies Professional Golf Association; PGA Tour; Senior PGA Tour
Puerto Rico, 207, 208. *See also* Puerto Rico Open
Puerto Rico Open, 221
Pullman porters, 11, 43, 112
Purcell, Henry, 3

Rackham Municipal Golf Course (Detroit), 85, 89, 90, 91, 99, 100, 198
Radcliffe, Frank, 96-97, 102, 105
Raleigh, N.C., 46
Randolph, A. Philip, 67, 179
Randolph, Luther "Red," 44
Raskob, John J., 80-81
Ravisloe Country Club (Chicago), 33
Rawlins, Horace, 33
Raynor, Seth, 8
Redding, Otis, 124

Reddy Tee, 5–6
Red Summer, 25
Renip, E. L., 41–42
Republic of New Africa, 192, 196
Revolutionary Action Movement (RAM), 187, 189, 193, 195–96. *See also* Stanford, Max, Jr.
Rheingold Beer, 213
Rhodes, Ted, xii, 90, 92, 94, 101, 106–9, 110, 111, 112, 135, 137, 139, 167, 205; and PGA events, 114, 116, 118, 119, 122–24, 143, 209, 215, 223, 260, 264; and U.S. Open, 124–25
Rhodesia, xiii, 204–5, 225, 229
Rice, Condoleezza, 253–54, 264, 317n69
Rice, Grantland, 10
Rice v. Arnold (1950), 163, 165–66
Richmond, Va., 45, 71. *See also* Acorn Country Club; Silver Rest Golf Club
Richmond Open (PGA), 118–20
Rickey, Branch, 116
Rising Sun Country Club (N.Y.), 44, 47
Riviera Country Club (Los Angeles), 118, 124, 200. *See also* Los Angeles Open
Rizzo, Frank, 195
Roberts, Clifford, 77, 232–33, 234. *See also* Augusta National Golf Club
Robinson, Jackie, xiv, 33, 59, 82, 106, 116, 121, 126–27, 129–30, 134, 135, 137, 142, 177, 179, 182, 198–99, 207, 211–12, 216, 218, 220, 233, 238, 255, 256–57, 261, 262, 266, 321, 322. *See also* Pheasant Valley Country Club
Robinson, Lenwood, Jr., 247–48, 321
Robinson, Sugar Ray, 93–94, 100, 108, 112, 129
Rock, Chris, 262
Rockefeller, John D., 14–15, 26, 29, 117, 189
Rockefeller, Laurance, 189, 190–91
Roddy, George, 143–45
Rodriguez, Chi Chi, 183, 220
Romans, 1, 30
Romney, Mitt, 264
Roosevelt, Franklin D., 66–67, 72–73, 75

Ross, Donald, 18–19, 23
Rouge Park Golf Course (Detroit), 90, 197–98
Rowan, Carl, 45
Royal and Ancient Golf Club of St. Andrews, 2, 39, 175, 220
Rubber City Open (PGA), 124, 211
Rudolph, Wilma, 222
Russell, Bill, 322
Rustin, Bayard, 204
Ruth, Babe, 233, 255
Ryder Cup, 230, 236, 244

Saltonstall, Leverett, 133
Sammy Davis Jr.–Greater Hartford Open (PGA), 123, 130, 221, 232
San Antonio, Tex., 72, 165, 214
Sandale Golf and Country Club (N.J.). *See* Apex Country Club (N.J.)
Sanders, Carl, 183, 231
Sanders, Doug, 220
San Diego, Calif., 86, 228. *See also* San Diego Open; Torrey Pines Golf Course
San Diego Open (PGA), 119–22, 131, 208, 209, 221
San Francisco, Calif., 86, 123, 148, 199, 254
São Paulo Golf Club (Brazil), 10
Sarazen, Gene, 6, 13, 96, 100, 104
Savannah, Ga., 2–3, 180, 203
Savannah Golf Club (Ga.), 2–3
Savoy Ballroom (Harlem), 57
Sawyer v. City of Mobile (1961), 186–87
Schuyler, George, 26–27, 52
Scotland, 1, 2, 9, 33, 36, 39, 50, 97. *See also* British Open; Muirfield Links; Royal and Ancient Golf Club of St. Andrews
Scott, Emmett J., 64
Scott, George C., 199
Scottsboro Boys, 80
Seagram Company, 131–33
Seal Beach Navy Golf Course (Calif.), 259

358) INDEX

Seale, Bobby, 192
Searles, Calvin, 105
Seattle, Wash., 86, 137, 209
Sedgefield Country Club (Greensboro, N.C.), 213–15. *See also* Greater Greensboro Open
Sedibe, Edward, 205
Seneca Golf Course (Cleveland), 90, 133, 220
Senegal, 206
Senior PGA Championship, 234, 242
Senior PGA Tour, 215, 234, 241, 242, 253. *See also* Senior PGA Championship
Sewgolum, Sewsunker "Papwa," 205
Shady Rest Country Club (N.J.), 23, 38, 42–43, 47, 50, 51, 52, 55, 58, 59, 61, 86–88, 89, 102, 128, 129, 142
Shalimar Country Club (Omaha), 47
Shamwell, Cecil, 66
Shangri-La Resort (N.Y.), 43–44, 47
Sharpe, Granville, 2
Shell's Wonderful World of Golf, 220
Sherrill, Clarence O., 62
Shinnecock Hills Golf Club (N.Y.), 34–36
Shippen, Cyrus, 34, 38
Shippen, John, xii, 34–39, 59, 86, 87–88, 102, 104, 124, 259
Shoal Creek Club (Ala.), 251–55, 260, 263, 264
Shorter College, 60
Shreveport, La., 148
Shuttlesworth, Fred, 185–86. See also *Shuttlesworth v. Gaylord* (1961)
Shuttlesworth v. Gaylord (1961), 163, 185, 186, 253
Sierra Leone, 50, 206
Sifford, Charlie, xii, 26, 56, 84–85, 90, 92, 107, 108, 109–11, 116, 125, 131, 133, 137, 175, 180, 194, 197, 244, 247, 322; and Howard Wheeler, 94, 95–96, 102; and Joe Louis, 101; and Ted Rhodes, 109; and Bill Spiller, 114, 209–10; and Thelma Cowans, 115; and PGA events, 122–24, 201, 208–16, 220–22, 223, 225–28, 231, 258, 263; and gambling, 138–39; and Lee Elder, 232, 233–34; and Tiger Woods, 237, 256–57, 260, 265, 267, 269
Sifford, Curtis, 215, 216
Siler, Julia (Towns), 89, 98, 128
Silvermere Club, 220
Silver Rest Golf Club (Va.), 47
Simkins, George, 171–75, 176, 213–14. See also *Simkins v. City of Greensboro*; *Wolfe v. North Carolina*
Simkins v. City of Greensboro (1957), 163, 171–74, 185, 200
Simon, Richard, 44
Simpson, Eneil, 41
Simpson, O. J., 321
Slavery, 3, 18, 34, 50, 53, 80, 146, 244, 251
Sledge, Percy, 124
Small, Len, 128
Smith, Emile, 250
Smith, Horton, 120–22, 143, 210
Smith, Hugh, 89, 94, 112
Smith, Thomas, 31
Smith, Tommie, 224
Snead, Sam, 106, 138, 210
Somerset Hills Country Club (N.J.), 38
South Africa, xiii, 204–5, 206, 224–32, 263. *See also* Apartheid; Elder, Lee; Mandela, Nelson; Million Dollar Challenge; Player, Gary; South African Open; South African PGA Championship
South African Open, 228
South African PGA Championship, 228–30
South Carolina, 158, 175, 261. *See also* Charleston, S.C.; South Carolina State College
South Carolina Golf Club (Charleston), 2–3
South Carolina State College, 247
Southeastern Golf Tournament, 124, 125
Southern Christian Leadership Conference (SCLC), 148, 179, 181–86, 190, 192, 197, 198, 201, 249, 251–55, 264,

INDEX (359

268. *See also* King, Martin Luther, Jr.; Lowery, Joseph
Southern Open (UGA), 46, 94, 110, 128, 133, 134, 140, 150
South Park Golf Course (Pittsburgh), 53
Spain, 196, 207
Speedy, Nettie (George), 23–25, 27–28, 41–42, 83, 86, 97
Speedy, Walter, 23–25, 27, 41–42, 86, 88, 97, 101, 105, 135
Spencer, Howard, 12–13
Spiller, Bill, xii, 99, 101, 112–14, 137, 139, 239, 244; and PGA events, 116–23, 143, 208–16
Spring Lake Golf Club (N.J.), 38
St. Andrews (Scotland). *See* Royal and Ancient Golf Club of St. Andrews
Stanford, Max, 188–89, 193–96, 207, 223
Stanford, Max, Jr., 188–89, 193–96
Stanford, Winnie, 188, 194
Stanford University, 239, 252, 261, 263
Starks, Nathaniel, 216
St. Augustine's University (Raleigh, N.C.), 46
St. Croix, U.S. Virgin Islands. *See* Fountain Valley massacre
Stewart, Jimmy, 236
Stills, Adrian, 216
St. Louis, Mo., 26, 85, 98, 104, 123. *See also* Forest Park; Old Warson Country Club
St. Michael's Episcopal Church (Charleston, S.C.), 3
Stout, Elmer, 102–4
St. Paul Open (PGA), 119, 123, 124
Strickland, Cliff, 89, 91
Stroble, Bobby, 216, 241
Student Nonviolent Coordinating Committee (SNCC), 182–83, 192, 198
Student Organization for Black Unity, 225
Sugg, LaRee, 216
Sullivan, Jere L., 30
Sunset Hills Country Club (Ill.), 46, 89, 93, 95, 97, 129

Sweatt v. Painter (1950), 164, 165, 169
Sweeney v. City of Louisville (1951), 169–70
Sweet, Ossian, 27, 52
Swimming, 25, 45, 66, 74, 149, 164, 169–70, 193, 200
Syracuse University, 26–27

Taft, William Howard, 14, 33
Talmadge, Herman, 154, 155
Tam O'Shanter Open, 104–6, 107, 116, 118, 125, 128, 142, 205
Tanzania, 207
Taylor, Clarence, 39
Ted Rhodes Golf Course, 109, 168
Tees, 5–7, 31
Television, 84, 116, 127, 128, 131, 153, 155, 182, 202, 205, 208, 215, 220, 223, 236, 237–38, 242, 244, 252, 255, 258, 261–62, 265–67. *See also Oprah Winfrey Show*; *Shell's Wonderful World of Golf*
Tellier, Louis, 15
Tennessee, 57, 93, 168, 181, 200, 203. *See also* Memphis, Tenn.; Nashville, Tenn.
Tennis, 20, 22, 45, 49, 50, 51, 52, 64, 67, 70, 115, 149, 162, 174, 181, 192, 247. *See also* Ashe, Arthur; Gibson, Althea
Terry, Ron, 216
Texas, 29–30, 54, 64, 72, 75, 108, 117, 118, 142, 165, 221. *See also* Beaumont, Tex.; Corpus Christi, Tex.; Dallas, Tex.; Houston, Tex.; Lions Municipal Golf Course; Prairie View A&M College; San Antonio, Tex.; *Sweatt v. Painter*; Wiley College
Thailand, 206, 263, 267
Thomas, Dave, 220
Thomas, Mark, 33
Thomas, Richard, 90
Thomas, Roscoe, 151, 155
Thompson, Hall, 251–55
Thompson, Marie (Jones), xii, 59, 89, 97–98, 114

Thornton, Eoline (Jackson), 90, 114, 126
Thorpe, Chuck, 216, 241
Thorpe, Jim, 216, 241, 242, 246, 249, 251–52, 257, 266
Tiger Woods Foundation, 260, 261, 266
Till, Emmett, 157
Tillinghast, A. W., 72
Timmerman, George, 158
Toronto, Can., 84–85
Torrey Pines Golf Course (San Diego), 91, 101, 133
Tournament Players Division (PGA). *See* PGA Tour
Townsend, Ron, 255, 260
Travelguide, 148, 150
Trevino, Lee, 230, 232
Trinidad, 190
Tucson Open (PGA), 122
Tupelo, Miss., 9, 201–2
Turner, Nat, 226
Turner, Vernice, 90, 194
Tuskegee Institute, 47, 60, 140, 145, 149, 150, 215
Twain, Mark, 30, 34

UGA Championship. *See* UGA National
UGA National, 85; origins of, 86–87; results of, 89–91
Uganda, 229
UGA Open. *See* UGA National
United Golfers Association (UGA), xi–xii, 322; female players in, xii, 97–99, 105, 114–16, 125–26, 219; origins of, 49, 85–87; male players in, 88–97, 106–14, 149–51, 221, 223, 241–46; and PGA events, 124; supporters of, 127–34; white players in, 135, 137; and gambling, 138–39; and World War II, 142; and Dwight D. Eisenhower, 179–80; decline of, 207–8, 239, 241–42. *See also* Adams, George; Pernell, Porter; Stanford, Max; UGA National; *and individual events and players*
United Nations (UN), 179, 206

United Negro College Fund, 228
United States Golf Association (USGA), 6, 106, 114, 254, 255, 266, 317n69; origins of, 33–36; and World War II, 142–43. *See also* U.S. Amateur; U.S. Amateur Public Links Championship; U.S. Junior Amateur Championship; U.S. Open; U.S. Women's Amateur; U.S. Women's Open
University of Georgia, ix, 158–59, 170
University of Michigan, 145
University of Minnesota, 53
Urban League, 68, 119. *See also* Young, Whitney
U.S. Amateur, 33, 35–36, 117, 239, 251, 266. *See also* United States Golf Association; U.S. Women's Amateur
U.S. Amateur Public Links Championship, 102–4, 208–9. *See also* United States Golf Association
U.S. Census, 257, 267–69
U.S. Junior Amateur Championship, 239–40. *See also* United States Golf Association
U.S. Open, 5, 6, 8, 10, 13, 86, 102, 104, 142, 227, 231, 237, 241, 243; first black players in, 33–39; postwar reintegration of, 124–26. *See also* United States Golf Association; U.S. Women's Open
U.S. Women's Amateur, 126, 217–18. *See also* U.S. Amateur; United States Golf Association
U.S. Women's Open, 115, 126. *See also* United States Golf Association; U.S. Open

Val Verde Resort (Calif.), 47
Van Cortlandt Park (New York, N.Y.), 26, 27, 55
Vardon Trophy (PGA), 243
Varner, Harold, III, 216
Vaughan, Sarah, 55
Venezuela, 207
Vermont, 3, 49

Vernondale Golf Club (Los Angeles), 83, 85, 86, 114
Vesey, Denmark, 3
Virginia, 34, 65, 81, 142, 148, 154, 182, 207, 228, 255. *See also* Norfolk, Va.; Portsmouth, Va.; Richmond, Va.
Virginia-Carolina Open Championship, 72
Virgin Island 5. *See* Fountain Valley massacre
Von Nida, Norman, 96

Waco Turner Open (PGA), 221
Wake Robin Golf Club (Washington, D.C.), 65–68, 99, 129
Walker, James, 91, 216
Walker, Wyatt Tee, 181–82, 184
Wall, Art, Jr., 249
Ward v. City of Miami (1957), 163, 166, 176, 185
Waring, Fred, 117
War of 1812, 2
Warren, Earl, 173
Washington. *See* Seattle, Wash.
Washington, Booker T., 5, 52, 64
Washington, D.C., xi, xii, 5, 20, 34, 38, 60, 86, 90, 177, 196, 197, 204, 208, 233; integrating municipal courses in, 62–68; and the UGA National, 129, 180, 223. *See also* Bethesda, Md.; Howard University; Langston Golf Course; Lincoln Memorial Golf Course; National Capital Country Club; Potomac Park; Wake Robin Golf Club
Washington, Kenny, 129
Washington, Porter, 88, 89, 102, 111–12
Washington, Sarah Spencer, 46
Washington, Walter, 204, 233
Waters, Ethel, 102
Watson, Tom, 242, 250
Wawashkamo Golf Club (Mich.), 34
Wayside Country Club (Chicago), 47–48
Webb, Chick, 55
Weiskopf, Tom, 145

Weissmuller, Johnny, 126, 130
Westchester Classic (PGA), 236
Westchester Hills Golf Club (N.Y.), 160, 161
Western Avenue Golf Course (Los Angeles), 82, 197, 211, 219, 248
Western Golf Association (WGA), 104. *See also* Western Open
Western Open (WGA), 34, 104, 123, 253
Western States Golf Association, 86, 111, 219; and *Tee-Cup*, 134, 136, 139
Westfield Golf Club (N.J.). *See* Shady Rest Country Club
West Virginia, 3, 53, 280n27. *See also* Greenbrier Resort; Oakhurst Links
Wheeler, Howard, xii, 89, 90, 94–96, 102, 104, 105, 108, 109, 110, 114, 116, 126, 128, 137, 139, 142, 145, 194, 242; and PGA events, 118, 208; and U.S. Open, 125.
White, Don, 182–83
White, Journee, 48
White, Walter, 159, 168, 206
Wie, Michelle, 258
Wilberforce University, 145, 146
Wiley College, 54, 112
Wilkins, Roy, 53, 158, 159–60, 181, 195
Williams, Asa, 66
Williams, Ben, 16–17, 31
Williams, Bert, 29
Williams, Eugene, 25
Williams, Fess, 55
Williams, G. Mennen, 128
Williams, Jimmie, 41
Williams, Lucy, xii, 89, 90, 98, 99
Williams, Robert F., 193, 196
Willie, Louis, Jr., 252–53
Wills, Harry, 129
Wilson, Butler, 5
Wilson, Flip, 228
Wilson, Geneva, xii, 59, 89, 98, 105
Wilson, R. B., 36
Wilson, Woodrow, 8, 16–17, 31, 33, 64
Wimbish v. Pinellas County, Florida (1965), 163, 167

Winchell, Walter, 120
Windy City Golf Association, 25, 85, 86
Wisconsin. *See* Casa Loma Country Club; Greater Milwaukee Open; Miller High Life Open
Wolfe v. North Carolina (1960), 163, 172-74, 213
Women, 175, 248, 264-65; in the UGA, xii, 97-99, 105, 114-16, 321; black women in Chicago, 23-25, 42; black women before 1920, 27-28, 321; at black country clubs, 43, 46, 51, 321. *See also* Baker, Ella; Chicago Women's Golf Club; Hathaway, Maggie Mae; Ladies Professional Golf Association; Speedy, Nettie (George); Vernondale Golf Club; Wake Robin Golf Club
Woodard, Tom, 216
Woods, Abraham, 251-55
Woods, Cheyenne, 216
Woods, Earl, 236, 238, 240, 242, 249, 258-59, 260, 262, 263, 264, 266, 267
Woods, Kultida, 267
Woods, Tiger, xii, xiv, 34, 216, 237, 249, 250, 252, 268-69, 322; early life of, 236, 239-46; and the Masters, 238, 241, 242, 246, 249, 251, 255-67, 321
Works Progress Administration (WPA), 60, 65, 73, 171
World Golf Foundation, 257-58
World Golf Ranking, 239, 243
World War I, 64, 143
World War II, 93, 95, 100, 104-6, 109, 115, 129, 141-44, 146, 162, 193
Worsham, Lew, 138
Worthing, Helen Lee, 48
Wright, Bill, 209, 216

Xavier University (New Orleans), 74, 145

Young, Andrew, 159
Young, Lee, 55
Young, Whitney, 119, 195
Young Men's Christian Association (YMCA), 20, 56

Zaharias, Babe Didrikson, 106, 115, 118, 217, 259. *See also* Babe Zaharias Open
Zaire, xiii, 230
Zoeller, Fuzzy, 263-64